Amalya's Beads

DINA WOOD KAGELER

Amalya's Beads

Journeys Along a Philippine River

Dina Wood Kageler

PLEASANT COTTON BOOKS

Amalya's Beads
Journeys Along a Philippine River
© 2023 Dina Wood Kageler
Pleasant Cotton Books
Distributed by Epigraph Books

Fonts used:
Baker Signet, Lora, and
Bodoni Ornaments
◉◉◉

ISBN: 978-1-954744-98-1

Library of Congress Control Number: 2023900305

To
The Volcano School of Arts & Sciences
A HAWAIIAN-FOCUSED PUBLIC CHARTER SCHOOL
IN VOLCANO VILLAGE, ISLAND OF HAWAI'I

Back in 2000-2001, I was one of the founders of the Volcano School of Arts & Sciences, a public charter school in our Hawai'i Island community. In our efforts to create a school with the few resources available to us, I couldn't help but notice parallels with the front-porch school in the remote mountains of Mindanao in the Philippines that my friend Janet Bauer and I started almost thirty years earlier. Both community schools began with not much more than a cardboard box of supplies and keen enthusiasm. When our local charter school in Hawai'i opened, there wasn't a horse biting our toes through the gaps in the walls or a screeching chicken atop the blackboard, but our small school began by embracing our community's families and simply facing the task at *hand. We charter school teachers and students together created our own books and curricula, and we learned from our neighboring scientists and from the forests, from the lava lands and from the ocean around us. We taught and we learned side by side—reading and writing and counting, singing and drawing and dancing. And, most importantly, we listened carefully to one another's stories.*

The Volcano School continues today, educating with aloha many young, creative global citizens, with a special focus on learning from the land and the traditional cultures of our place. To past and present Volcano School teachers, administrators, and support staff who have taken on the daily challenge of doing so much with so little, I dedicate these stories.

Dina Wood Kageler
Volcano Village, Hawai'i Island
Spring 2020

Contents

PART IV   Beyond

Prologue

Mom is here—her first time visiting her new grand-daughter. While we were swinging baby Emma on the back porch, she asked why I adopted instead of having a child of my own. This is a conversation we never had on the phone, and I started telling her about the kids in the Philippines and how I felt there were already so many children in the world who didn't have much of a chance. "Those years really affected you, didn't they?" she asked. I had to admit they had. She said it in a sad sort of way, maybe because she wanted the old me back again, when I was a regular Texas girl, before the Peace Corps changed me.

                —from my Journal, November 1993

☉☉☉

Last night I took down the hand-stitched leather pouch and looked at Amalya's beads for the first time in years. They're old now; it's been nearly half a century since Amalya placed them around my neck alongside that faraway river. In some ways, they are not exceptional, merely tiny plastic specks woven together. When I think of the glamorous baubles at any boutique these days, Amalya's beads might seem ordinary. But the afternoon she gave them to me, they shone brightly, their colors flashed magnificently against the deep browns of her skin and the earth, even gaudy against the gray sky and silver river.

Last night I held Amalya's beads for a while, feeling the knobbiness of the twine that binds them. The beads are still tight, each secure in its place, yet they're fragile; their links could easily be broken by something sharp or forceful. And I began to wonder about the river people and their traditions, once tightly woven and sure in their ways. Are they dispersed now, lost to mobile phones and bulldozers? I've been thinking about my days in the mountains as I reread my fading journals, remembering how young I was and how little I knew of life. I've been reflecting on the role I might have played in influencing the culture of those river people, wondering if we did the right thing offering pencils and reading lessons and stories. Did we open doors that should have stayed closed? Did we help or hinder? Perhaps in the end, we made no difference. The world was already changing, and perhaps we were simply the first ripples of the inundations to come.

Amalya's Beads is a collection of stories of my life in the Philippine lowlands and among the upriver Manobo in the early 1970s. These stories hold a view of history that I like to think is of value to the children and grandchildren of our Manobo neighbors as well as for all of us who respect the knowledge of old ways. And I continue to hope the beads Amalya wove for me will sparkle for many more years, swaying with the breath of each new generation. I hope the old ways of life beside the mountain river, and indigenous knowledge worldwide, will not be forgotten.

Amalya is really good at beadwork. She was on her porch working on a piece, and I went over to watch. She proudly displayed all her jewelry—beaded necklaces and ear pieces, brass bracelets and anklets, and a very old-looking wide bracelet made of a single piece of smoothed and polished bone. She weaves her beads on a hand loom that looks like a small harp with a couple dozen strings—a bowed piece of wood strung with thin twine rubbed with beeswax. One by one, each on the tip of her needle, twenty-five beads are placed between the warp threads of her loom, then she passes her needle through the row, securing them among the warp threads. With her thumbnail, she pushes the beads into place, tightening, adjusting, making sure the row is straight. She pulls the needle string tight, but not too tight, then begins the next row, heading across the warp strings in the opposite direction. She sees the pattern she is creating in her mind's eye—the bright slanting stripes of yellow, white, dark blue, and bright red.

— Journal, April 23, 1972

Amalya's Beads ◉ xiii

PART I

◉

Upriver To Madga

1972

Beginnings

Typhoon. Communications to Mindanao were cut off for a week. No flights in or out, no mail, no telegrams. No electricity in the entire mega-city of Davao. So my Peace Corps host had no idea when (or if) I'd arrive.

Peace Corps Manila sent me here on the first flight after the storm, but of course no one was at the airport to meet me. In the open-air terminal, there was one worker behind the airline counter, and he was packing up to go home after the one flight of the day. I waited a long time until it became unmistakeable that no one was coming to fetch me. I was in a very foreign city with nothing *but my host's name handwritten on a scrap of paper. So I approached the counter and told the man who I am and who I was supposed to meet. He hollered—in the inscrutable foreign language I'm supposed to know—to a coworker in the back luggage area, who hollered back and the counter guy told me—in English, phew!— to wait. Half an hour later, another guy showed up, the boyfriend of Sonia, my hosting volunteer, and offered to take me to her. So I left the airport with this total stranger!*

It turned out okay. The back room runner had scurried over to Sonia's boyfriend's workplace to fetch him. They told us about this phenomenon during training— everyone-is-going-to-know-everything-about-you, so-get-used-to-it. It's obviously true for Sonia.

— Journal, October 26, 1970

◉◉◉

The Republic of the Philippines is an island nation just north of the equator and south of China, near a curving bay of the Pacific where the waters of three great seas merge. There are more than 7,000 islands in the archipelago, most of them rock-and-sand outcroppings that might host an occasional, passing fisherman. Fewer than fifty of the Philippine islands are permanently populated.

Mindanao is the southernmost main island in the archipelago and the second largest, sprawling more than 300 miles at its widest. On a map, Mindanao looks like an elephant dancing on its front toes, with its trunk—the Zamboanga Peninsula—stretching off toward the neighboring wildlands of Borneo and Indonesia.

Mindanao has ancient civilizations layered one atop the other as each new colonizing group pushed former inhabitants further into the densely forested mountains. Archeological finds show that coastal Mindanaoans have been trading internationally for a thousand years. I can attest that they were still trading in 1970. From my second-story bedroom window in Butuan City, I watched enormous mahogany logs floating down the Agusan River bound for Japanese freighters waiting in Butuan Bay. These massive logs came from the dense forests of Mindanao's interior, where there are no cities or towns.

"Aloy, you bad boy! Your mama send you live with dirty Manobo. They eat bad boys like you!" I heard this admonishment in the Bila family home where I lived in Butuan City, when I first arrived in-country to be a teacher. The threat worked. Four-year-old Aloy, who could be obstinate, mended his behavior instantly. So I began to wonder, who are these Manobo people of the interior mountains? Would they really eat Aloy, however tough his recalcitrant pre-school hide might be?

Whenever I asked about the mysterious mountain folk, I generally received a mere sweep of the arm and some disparagement. Those enigmatic lowly folk were considered subhuman makers of beads and baskets who lived in the dense forests. No one seemed to know more than that, nor did they care.

I continued asking around, and my neighbors laughed at my curiosity. They told me all manner of information and misinformation: that the mountain people ate only tiny river fish and grew only potatoes, that they were dark-skinned and very short, that they were light-skinned and tall, that they killed strangers in their territory, that they stole women and children from outlying towns, that they were naked and dirty and stupid, and that they were pagans worshipping the old river gods. I was fascinated.

One day a teacher friend from Butuan City Elementary School told me that a Manobo couple from the mountains was visiting her Protestant church, and she invited me to meet them. That's how the story of *Amalya's Beads* began.

◉◉◉

The nights are getting dark faster, and the darkness is blacker and lasts longer. There's no electricity in this part of the city tonight. It'd be nice to go downtown to the movies, because there's always electricity downtown—well, usually—but I've seen all the movies in Butuan City. I guess I could see them again. Sitting around this dark house, writing letters or playing guitar by the glow of a smoking kerosene lamp, is losing its appeal night after long, dark night, week after week, month after month. I need an adventure.

—Letter home, March 15, 1971

◉◉◉

Going Upriver

I'm sitting at my desk in Butuan City—not even moving—sweat dripping down my back, drenching the waistband of my shorts, a sure sign it's summertime here in the tropics. It's so hot and the sun so glaring that I stay indoors. But I always make exceptions for adventures, like the one last week.

—Letter home, March 1972

⊙⊙⊙

The narrow gangplank had no handrails and rocked side to side with the pulse of the water as vertigo teased me tipsy toward the deep and dirty Agusan River. The skinny man in front, toting an enormous stalk of green bananas, scampered goat-like up the gangplank. If he could do that with a hundred pounds on his shoulder, surely I could cross the chasm toting only my little duffle. I set my course, kept my eyes set on the open deck ahead, and forged forward.

The barge was packed. There were hulking pieces of machinery—a boiler the size of car, gears bigger than wagon wheels, and steel bolts each the size of my forearm. Steam-engine parts were my first thought. Then remembering where I was heading, I figured the parts were for the logging companies—the machinery necessary for moving earth and hauling massive trees.

As if on cue, the passengers cramped beneath the tattered canopy each looked up. White girl. Spectacle. I asked, "Joe and Flor Habana, missionaries?" An older woman pointed toward the bow, to another canopy-covered section. I thanked her and threaded my way between piles of lumpy gunny sacks of food, dry goods, or heaven knows what, stacks of squawking chickens in bamboo cages, and two trussed-up pigs lying on their sides. I set my foot too close to one pig, and it jerked and squealed. I jumped back and made a wider circuit. A man was sprawled across the pathway, sleeping on a pile of gunny sacks with a towel across his face. I avoided stepping over him, as I knew the rules of etiquette— never-ever step over a sleeping or prone person. In the proper way, I set my palms together like a prow of a ship, bent slightly forward at the waist, whispered *tabi usa*, and skirted quickly and humbly around him, continuing to search for Joe and Flor.

I found Flor near the front of the boat. She sat cross-legged on a woven pandanus mat, her back against a pile of gunny sacks and boxes that leaned tall and heavy against the wall of the steering cabin. She cradled baby Lilly Jean in her lap, nursing. "It is good you have found us. Sit with us. Would you like bread?"

I was accustomed to this stereotype. Americans eat bread. Flor had no doubt gotten bread especially for me. But I knew better than to accept it right away. It would signal that I was either starving or greedy. So I deferred. "Thank you, no. I am still full." It was the polite thing to say. "Have you been on the boat long?" From the look of the space around her, she must have been there quite a while. A bedroll. Plastic thermos.

Large cracker tin. Some towels. A small woven pandanus fan that she see-sawed above Lilly Jean, shooing a fly from the baby's face.

"Joe has stayed the night here so that we would have a place to sleep. But Lilly Jean and I arrived only this morning. A lot of people arrived this morning."

"Do you think we will leave soon?" I asked.

She shrugged. "Maybe soon. Joe has gone to check with the captain."

I was no novice to Philippine transportation. "Maybe soon" meant maybe within minutes, when the river barge was fully loaded and couldn't hold a gunny sack more, or maybe we would depart in hours, or perhaps not today at all. Philippine time stretched and oozed and had no form.

Joe returned and sat on the mat beside Flor to report that the captain was not yet on board, so I knew it would be a while before we departed. Although I'd spent some time with Joe and Flor in Butuan City, they were still curious about me, and I was curious about them. They were ethnically Manobo, a minority group from the upriver interior mountains, but just what that meant, I wasn't sure. To me they looked like all other Filipinos, perhaps a bit shorter than most, with perhaps slightly more flattened and broad facial features, but the differences were minor. I saw little overtly distinct about their features, dress, or mannerisms. They seemed relaxed and easy-going. I kept looking for signs, characteristics that would mark them as "Manobo," but I saw nothing special. They just seemed like nice folks.

Flor pushed the conversation forward, and I sensed she was the family leader. "Why did you decide to come to the Philippines?" she asked.

I knew the pattern. Before I could ask my questions, I would answer theirs. I'd done it a thousand times. I had stock answers. It was like a dance, these questions and answers, a sort of get-to-know-you game. And as I answered in the local Visayan language, they were checking my linguistic abilities, to see if I was fluent enough to handle what lay ahead.

"I was finished with school and I wanted to travel, to see different people and places. The Peace Corps asked me to come here and be a teacher. I've been here almost two years now."

"And how do you find the Philippines?" This question was one of my favorites. Sometimes it was asked in English, as Flor did this time. And the answer is supposed to be something about how wonderful the country is. I knew one volunteer—a miserable guy who terminated early—who would answer literally, "Fly west out of Seattle, turn left at Tokyo." Then he would cackle rudely at his own joke, which left his hosts bewildered.

My own Visayan response was polite, if shallow. "It is very beautiful. Always green. There are more fruits here than in my country, and they are always sweet and delicious." I would never say that I thought the country was in big trouble socially, economically, and politically. It was an abyss of greed and ignorance. There were far too many children living in the streets. Filipino men were macho, sex-driven, and obnoxious. The women were far too reticent and accepting of their plight. "And the children of the Philippines are the most beautiful in the world," was what I actually said. So yes, I spoke the truth, just not the whole truth. It was the way to play the game.

Joe and Flor nodded. "And where are you from in America?"

From this question, I knew that Flor had been educated, and she knew that America had states. "Texas."

"Ah, Texas. I see," said Flor. "Are you a cowgirl? Do you have a ranch?" Now I knew that Flor had seen movies.

"No. My family lives in the city. But my uncle has horses, and sometimes I visit him and ride them."

She nodded knowingly. "If you ride a horse, then you are a cowgirl. Tell me, did you ever kill anyone with your six-gun?" Flor had definitely seen westerns! I stifled a guffaw at the absurdity of the thought.

"No. Cowboys with guns are just from the movies, stories about the old days, a long time ago. It's not like that in Texas anymore." But I could see how Flor might think it was. Here we were in Butuan City, where men carried guns every day and drunken shootings were an ordinary occurrence.

"Then what is it like in your place these days?"

Responding to this question is tougher, for what is ordinary in my place—cars, roads, traffic lights, brick buildings, uninterrupted electricity—seemed uncommon and wealthy here. "Ah, it is different there," I started. Looking out across the dock to the tangle of city traffic without order, the squat wood frame buildings, some of them leaning, ready to topple in the next big wind, the boardwalk and stinking open sewer that bubbled like black tar, the pedestrians carrying heavy loads in baskets balanced on heads. How to explain? "My city is different. There are many people, but the streets are wider, and the cars obey the laws with lights that tell them when to stop and when to go. People drive to their work every day and then come home to cook supper for their families. No household helpers. My mother and father work in offices during the day. In the evening, my mother and father work together to cook supper for my family. Then they clean the house and do the laundry at night while the kids do homework and study."

"But is it not true that in America everyone is rich?" There it is, the most common of all stereotypes. Tricky to explain, for in a way, it's true. Even the poorest family I knew in Texas would, by comparison, be rich here. In Texas, even my poorest acquaintances lived in a house with more than one room. They had drinkable running water inside the house, and they probably had a flush toilet. And there was food to eat, several times a day.

"It is different there. Not everyone is rich. It takes a lot of money to live in America. America is expensive. A loaf of bread that costs seventy-five centavos here might cost a dollar in America—which is more than six pesos. So yes, people have more money, but it takes more money to buy food and pay for a house. And in the winter, the weather is very cold, so we must spend money to make our homes warm and buy sweaters and warm clothing. So no, not rich. Not everyone."

"But in America, everyone has a car. Does your family have a car?"

"Yes, we have a car." I didn't say that there were three cars in my family of five people. "But in my place, there are no jeepneys, no passenger tricycles, and only a few buses, so everyone needs a car to get to work or to school. Life is different there."

"And how many children are in your family," Flor asked me.

"I have two brothers. I am the only girl."

"You are the only girl, and your parents allow you to travel alone to the Philippines?" I knew that within this culture, such independence would be unfathomable.

"I graduated from college and wanted to travel. So I joined Peace Corps." Joe and Flor looked at one another, then at me as though I were an alien creature.

"Ah, your family must miss you very much," Flor finally said.

"Yes, they do," I added honestly. That might be the only constant cultural value I'd discovered on my travels—mothers love their children and want to keep them close and safe.

The first hour of waiting passed easily in light conversation as Joe and Flor—and a handful of passengers sitting nearby and who were leaning in—listened to the white girl from America. Lilly Jean slept, then woke to crawl over her mom and play with the lid to the cracker tin, sucking on it and banging it on the mat-covered deck.

When the captain came on board, all eyes followed him, a prince in his kingdom. He was small and wiry, about fifty-years-old I guessed, and he wore oversized khaki pants lashed up with a hemp belt, a kid-sized, too small T-shirt, and a hat like a baseball cap with fuzzy ear flaps tied up.

"Here, eat," said Joe. "We will be leaving soon." Joe passed me a brown wrapper of bakery buns. "Is it true Americans eat only bread? You don't eat rice?" he asked.

Another stereotype. "Sometimes we eat rice, just not every day, not at each meal. Sometimes we eat bread, but not every day, not at each meal. We eat different kinds of foods, like here in the Philippines, but the way we prepare the food is different. Americans eat vegetables. Beans. Cabbage. Tomatoes. Potatoes. We eat eggs and cheeses. Sometimes we eat noodles. Sometimes fish from the ocean. Sometimes fish from the rivers. Sometimes beef. Sometimes pork. And I've been living with a Filipino family for two years, so I have become accustomed to the Filipino way of eating." What I didn't mention was that my family in Texas ate meat at just about every meal, roasted slabs of beef on Sundays, and every day we had hamburgers or hot dogs, southern fried chicken, barbecued beef brisket sandwiches, chicken-fried steak, smothered steak, T-bone steak, bacon, pork chops, bologna, ham, or salami. I knew that in the Philippines, meat was a luxury, where slivers of beef might appear in a fried-rice dish, or small chunks of vinegar-and-salt pig fat might be a side to a mound of white rice.

"And what is the food in the mountains?" I took a turn asking questions.

Joe and Flor glanced at one another. "There is not so much food in the mountains," Flor said. "Sweet potatoes. Sometimes upland rice.

Sometimes sweet corn. Sometimes fish from the river. Sometimes fruit."

"Fruit? I like the fruit of the Philippines. What kind is in the mountains?"

"Sometimes lansones." That was good to hear. I loved lansones, small grape-like fruits with sweet white flesh, a thin leathery skin, and a single almond-sized seed inside, very bitter if accidentally bitten into. "Maybe durian," Flor added. I wasn't crazy about durian. It had a reputation for smelling and tasting like old socks, but I'd found the not-quite-ripe durian wasn't bad. "Sometimes papaya." A perennial favorite of mine. "But there is not as much fruit in the mountains as here in Butuan City. It is very expensive to buy fruit in our town of Sagunto." I was disappointed. I had envisioned mountains trails with hanging fruits, free and abundant for the picking.

"And what about your school? How many students do you have?" I asked.

"Now we have seven children who live at the school with us in Sagunto. Sometimes there are more, then they return to their families in the mountains."

"And what do you teach? Do you use the same school books as here in Butuan City?"

"We have no books. We teach the children to read and write. We use the Bible as our book."

"Oh, that must be hard," is what I said, but I was thinking, well, that's the end of that. I should have expected that theirs would be a church school, which meant the Peace Corps would restrict any association I could have with their school. Peace Corps regulations were clear about that. Volunteers could not advocate a particular religious belief, and teaching from the Bible wouldn't go over well at all. Oh well, at least I'd get a small adventure from this, even if it doesn't work out in the long run.

When the boat's engine started, conversation ceased. The pounding was deafening—and stomach-churning. As the boat began to move, I became nauseated. I leaned against the wooden plank wall and watched the mesmerizing Agusan River roll by—forests in deep shade and small nipa-palm-thatched houses perched in sun on the riverbank. An occasional houseboat was tied to the shore. Naked children splashed in the shallows, women beat laundry against rocks and strung it to dry across low branches of weedy shrubs near the riverbank.

Slowly we moved upriver, pushing into the strong ocean-bound Agusan current and pulling to the side of the river to yield right-of-way to river tugs guiding tons of floating Philippine mahogany to the freighters waiting in Butuan Bay. The wood would go abroad, mostly to Japan. The logs were six or eight or ten feet across, dwarfing the men who stood atop the floating log packs, poking and prodding with long poles to keep the logs lassoed tight. I didn't know trees could be that big.

Babies cried. A woman lying on a mat near me coughed deeply, a spasm racking her body, and she spit a dark glob into the river. Tuberculosis, I figured. One in three people in the Philippines were active carriers. A man walked to the side of the boat and urinated into the river, a high arc of urine up and outward. He's lucky, I thought. Where was I supposed to pee? Bare my butt and squat over the side? I decided not to drink anything till I found a bathroom.

In the late afternoon, we pulled up to a small pier. I had no idea where we were, but I got off to find a comfort room, or more accurately, a reeking hole in the ground surrounded on three sides by plywood walls. I held my breath against the stench.

Back on board, Joe and Flor and I shared an evening meal. From my bag, I produced a warm Pepsi for each person, a hand of bananas, some bread, and a yellow food product that was marketed as cheese. Among us volunteers, this cheese was a joke. It was non-dairy, would stay mold-free indefinitely without refrigeration, and—most telling—even the rats wouldn't eat it. I suspected it was made of wax.

Joe and Flor shared white rice and a cooked fish with me, while Flor fed small pinches to Lilly Jean. I picked lightly at the fish while Flor and Joe relished it. It was Flor who finished it off, sucking the eyeballs from the skull with loud smacks in the Filipino way. As the evening shadows lengthened across the river, I contemplated the Agusan, the people who lived beside its banks, and the bleakness of their lives. The river was utterly filthy, with industrial and human waste. Then the people wash and drink from it too. Do they not notice the sewage and rubbish and poison? Do they feel they have no options? Do they even think about options?

I didn't get it. Why didn't they take some action, do something to protect their health and the lives of their children? Why don't they stand up and holler? How can they live like this? Should I do something? What? How? It made me tired just thinking about it. There was nothing I could do. This is third-world poverty. Did I really think I could solve that problem? How long had I been here, and I still thought I could save the world?

Maybe I've been in this god-forsaken, lousy country too long already, I considered. Maybe it's time to go home. I sat with my back against a pile of poking metal parts, wrapped in my *malong* sleep tube with my wadded-up duffle cushioning my back, watching the night shadows on the river, considering going home, back to America, while the boat's steady throbbing engine pounded like the heartbeat rhythm of the country—uncomfortable, relentless, entirely overwhelming, and truthfully, not much fun to be around.

◎◉◉

Day after day, I keep trying to smile, pretending to be cheerful, when all I really want to do is move on. Day after day, I read the same books, play the same songs on my guitar, and dream the same dreams of more pleasant surroundings. I've tried to reach out and talk with people around me, but somehow the link is missing, there's nothing there. I keep pretending that I'm happy, but I'm not. The days roll past, one after another. I'm stenciled into my life here. Can't get beyond the lines.
—Journal, June 26, 1971

◎◉◉

Hard to realize I've been here more than a year. They say the second year goes faster than the first, but I'm not so sure that's true. Sometimes I think I'll just quit right now. But if I terminate early, I can't travel on my way home. Rules say you have only three days to get home if you terminate early. And, I wouldn't be eligible for any Peace Corps scholarships or grants or other perks if I terminate early. And what if I come home and can't understand English any more – you'll have to talk slowly and use hand gestures.

Well, I'm off to the movies this afternoon with Nan to see Chisum *starring John Wayne, and it's a double feature with a Japanese film, with subtitles, a kung-fu kind of movie, and these are usually very entertaining. But the theater is uncomfortable since you have to keep your feet perched up on the balcony rail to keep the rats from traipsing across your toes, and the rats have been known to bite our toes. Very startling.*

—Letter home, April 13, 1971

Mountain Magic

When I got back to the boat, I saw a cowboy-hatted guy holding a ten-inch baby crocodile. He was obviously very proud of it. From what I could gather, these crocs used to be abundant in the Agusan River, but now they're hard to find. They used to give the boaters and fisher people a hard time, especially the people who live on the banks of the river, and most especially the children of these families. The kids got chomped. Now the crocs are more of a curiosity. I thought this croc was sort of cute, and pathetic. I hope it gets to grow up. But I doubt it, the way this cowboy is handling it.

— Journal, October 28, 1970

◉◉◉

The people on the barge were settling in for the night, spreading mats and blankets, quieting children, making themselves as comfortable as possible despite the sparsity of open deck space and the gut-churning pounding of the engine. Since there was no way to stretch out, Joe lay across his family's mat curled in on himself, catlike. Flor sat cross-legged, leaning against a cardboard box while she nursed Lily Jean. I was sitting on my sleep mat, wedged between a pile of stuffed burlap bags with the metal parts jabbing my back and some bamboo crates that held inscrutables huge and heavy. A tube of cotton fabric was my sleep sack, a woven poncho was my blanket, and my nearly empty duffle served as a pillow. The hypnotic river flowed past, black and silver moonlit luminescence as the boat's engine chugged us slowly up the Agusan.

A young man approached and said in good-try English, "Mum, the captain say you come sleep at cabin. No sleep here."

I answered in Visayan. "That's okay. I'm comfortable here with my friends. I can sleep here on the deck."

The boy repeated in English, "Mum. The captain say you come sleep at cabin. No sleep here."

Flor said, "You go. The captain is inviting you." She no doubt too, realized that she would have space to lie down if I were elsewhere.

I picked up my gear and, following the young man, made my way around bodies and over bags. Inside a stifling cabin, behind the ship's wheel, stood the barefoot captain, shirtless, with his fuzzy hat ear muffs pulled down. The cacophony in the cabin was even louder than on deck.

The captain didn't say a word—and I wouldn't have been able to hear him above the pounding engine noise even if he'd tried to speak. With a flick of his arm and head, he motioned me to a bench the width of a bookshelf on the back of the cabin wall.

"But you?" I shouted and gestured over the noise, "Where will you sleep?" He gestured that he would steer all night, not sleeping, and that I should sleep on the shelf.

I didn't really want to sleep in the loud, airless cabin, but I didn't want to offend the captain, and Flor was probably curled beside Lily Jean across the space where I'd been sitting. So I accepted, setting my mat and duffle on the shelf, and for a while I watched through the wide cabin window as the stars over the river flickered behind thin clouds. Along the riverbanks, the elevated nipa-palm-and-bamboo houses looked like boxy skeletons on spindly legs. The engine was steady, penetrating and hypnotic. I lay back, balancing my body on the narrow plank, allowing myself to sleep, but not to move.

When I awoke, the night was deep, the engine pounding on. I felt something odd within myself, a creeping discomfort, a fear. The captain stood at the wheel, his back to me. But for the two of us, the cabin was empty. So why this feeling? Without moving my body, I looked around.

There was a window above my sleeping shelf, a small opening to the deck behind. And in the window was the face and elbow of a man. He must be perched quite a bit above the deck sitting on some of the machinery. He didn't move. In the darkness I stared at the silhouetted face in the window and could barely discern the features—not youthful, not leering. The face was only a couple of feet above my belly, and I felt as if there were a pulling or pushing on me, yet the face and the arm hadn't moved. The feeling wasn't as real as a physical touch, more an internal rustling, like an emotion stirring in my gut. It was eerie, and frightening. In the moonlight reflected from the river, I could see the white of his eyes, open, staring forward, and I tried to calm my racing heart. He hasn't touched me, I considered. He's just there. The stirring feeling must be my imagination. Maybe it's the fish I had for dinner making me queasy. No, it was more than that. I'd heard stories of mountain magicians, people with special powers who live in the wildlands. With sudden certainty, I knew this was a magic man and he was doing something to me. What should I do? Get up and leave? Ask him to get out of the window? Say something to the captain? None of these seemed easy or appropriate.

So in my mind, I used my own kind of magic. I concocted a cocoon of protection about myself, envisioning it like a sleeping bag, a web of safety. I colored it a glowing pewter, silklike, shimmering, and tightly woven. Inside my web I was strong, solid, and invincible. I held tenaciously to my cocoon of protection, I believed it into reality, and I willed a light sleep.

When I awoke later in the night, the face was gone. And so was the queasy feeling. What kind of place am I going to? I wondered.

⊚⊚⊚

My trip up the Agusan River, first to Sagunto, then on to Madga, was long—almost three days upriver from Butuan City and two days back. On the way upstream, I could see that the recent floods along the Agusan had subsided, but many nipa houses close to the river were still partially underwater and quite damaged—walls gone, roofs cockeyed. Crops were washed away, and some really poor-looking people stood beside the bank waving at us. I think they were stranded or needed help, but our barge didn't stop. The further upstream we went, the less damage we saw. The worst devastation was downstream, where the dirty Agusan River ran deep and wild. Coming back down the river after visiting Sagunto and Madga, I didn't see any crocodiles in the river, just a couple of whirlpools our pilot skillfully steered us around.

—Journal, April 8, 1972

⊚⊚⊚

When I got back to Butuan, I found that someone had broken into our apartment and taken pretty much everything, including most of my clothes and all my books. They even took my hairbrush and underwear. And my precious cassette recorder and music tapes. Well, the recorder was semi-broken anyhow and the tapes were sticky and warpy from the humidity, voices stretched and garbled like they were made of rubber, but still, that music was my lifeline to my own culture, my place, my poetry. Simon and Garfunkel are gone. That bridge over troubled water has collapsed and *washed away. It feels horrible. Like I'm an onion, and layer by layer my entire personhood is being peeled away. My own language, gone. Favorite foods, gone. My own clothes and styles and femininity, gone. Hairstyle, gone. Transportation—my ability to go where I want, when I want—that's gone. Humor, finding people who laugh at the same things I do, that's gone too. Friends, real friends, gone. I'm pretty much down to my own sweat. I still have plenty of that.*

— Letter home, never mailed, March 1972

The People Upriver

It's typhoon season, and the storms have been hitting us hard. The brother of one of my students in Butuan drowned during a recent typhoon. He slipped and fell into a raging drainage ditch and was swept away. Flying coconuts are also killers during extreme winds. They fly off the trees, and if one should hit you, especially in the head, you're a goner.

Elections are another danger. Politicians are murdered over votes. Word is that all the elections are crooked, and most of the votes are bought—for ₱5 (slightly less than $1), or one ganta (maybe a couple of quarts) of rice, per vote. Democracy doesn't seem to work here. People aren't educated enough to use their votes wisely, or independently. It's tough; it's not as if they *can listen to the national news for information or watch the candidates debate on TV. All information is misinformation, rumors and half-truths, or more-than-half untruths. Those who have an education and money can bribe the lawyers and judges, and are not prosecuted no matter what they've done. We volunteers laugh among ourselves when we hear the Philippines touted as "the showcase of Eastern Democracy." But politics and power grabs are city stuff. I think life will be different away from the city, and I want to get out and see other parts, upriver, toward the mountains, as far from these corrupt city politics as I can get.*

— Letter home, November 7, 1970

◉◉◉

"Come, we will take you to our school."

From the pier at the barrio of Sagunto on the outskirts of the little town of La Paz in the province of Agusan del Sur, it was a short walk to Joe and Flor's school, through dusty, rutted roads, past unpainted wooden buildings that resembled the back lot of a Hollywood western set— except that the signboards were in Visayan: a place to eat, a place to buy household goods, a *sari-sari* store with stacked wooden crates of Pepsi and beer and a gigantic arm of ripening bananas hanging from a rafter. There were a few houses of rough-cut slats, simple and unpainted, with wide verandas swept clean and edged with potted greenery. These were the homes of the merchants and the well-to-do. And on the outskirts of the barrio was a small, unpainted church with a hand-lettered yellow sign over the doorway: Free Methodist Church, Light and Life in Jesus Christ. Behind the church was a gray, weathered house, and we entered through the back door. Inside, three young people were cleaning the floors and table. "Meet our Peace Corps volunteer from America," Flor said. I smiled, greeted them in Visayan, and the kids gawked.

"Make yourself at home. Ita, go buy the Americana a Pepsi. Boys, go to the dock and bring up the parcels for the school."

The classroom was in the back of the house. There was a table, a few chairs, and a small blackboard. On the walls were faded cardboard cutouts of Bible characters. There was one door to the outside and one window with a view of a dirt-patch yard surrounded by a bamboo-slat fence.

"What do you think of our school?" Flor asked me.

Bleak, I thought. "Nice," I said. "It is good that the Manobo children are able to come here to learn to read."

"What do you know about the Manobo people?" Flor asked me.

"Only a little. The only Manobo I know are you and Joe. I asked questions in Butuan, but no one told me much of anything. I'm here because I'd like to know more."

Flor nodded and led me to the kitchen, where we sat at a table covered with a red plaid oilcloth. Ita shyly offered me a bottle of warm Pepsi. I thanked her and she ducked away, grinning.

"There are many Manobo people in the mountains, people who never come into town," Flor said. "It is a hard life now for the Manobo, because the old ways are changing. The logging companies have been taking the trees from the old forests and those are the places the Manobo live. Sometimes the families send their children here to study with us, so they can learn to read and write. Some families believe that if their children are educated, the Manobo people will be able to talk with the logging companies and maybe there will be no fighting between the loggers and the Manobo."

"Do the Manobo and the loggers fight?"

"Sometimes yes, and people are killed, both the Manobo and the loggers. Sometimes the Manobo houses are burned. Sometimes their crops are ruined, and the Manobo people go hungry. They fight because the loggers are taking the forests. But the law agrees with the loggers, and the Manobo are usually forced to leave their lands and go further into the mountains. These days, there is hardly any place left to go. The loggers are cutting trees from even remote forests.

"But it is hard for families to send their children to school here in Sagunto," Flor continued. "Most Manobo people have no money, and the children are needed at home to help with the work. They have been asking Joe and me to bring our school to the mountains, but we have our home and family and church here in Sagunto, and we cannot go. We have been searching for a teacher who could go to the Manobo and teach them to read and write. When we were in Butuan, we asked at the Division of Education but were told that no teacher would come into our mountains. We were just about to give up when we met you. That is why we are asking you if you will travel with us up the river to meet the Manobo and if you will teach the mountain people," she said.

The thought of seeing the mountain folk appealed to me, and I would soon have an opportunity to select a final summer project for myself, but the idea of associating with a Christian school went against Peace Corps policy and my own instincts.

"Flor, I am a Peace Corps volunteer, not a missionary. The Peace Corps says I can teach school, but I cannot teach the Bible. I cannot be like a church or teach about God."

"That's okay. You can teach whatever way you like. You do not need to use the Bible. You can use textbooks from Butuan School or whatever you like. Tomorrow let us take you into the mountains to see the village at Madga. You will meet the Manobo people. Then you can think about it."

It was a long morning's boat ride in a shallow canoe carved out of a single log, a *banka*, with an outboard motor. From Sagunto, our boat went up a murky river, then up streams until the water grew shallow and was so clear I could see the bottom sand and river rock. In some places, the river was just inches deep, then around a bend, the riverbed might tilt away to a depth or ten or fifteen feet. I was mesmerized by the clearness of the water and the earthy reds, browns, and golds of the smooth stones below. At noon, we stopped at a bend in the river and sat together on an outcrop spit of rocks. The forest at our backs was thick, towers of green swaying with the breath of the river. It was quiet except for the chuckle of the stream over the rocks. Joe, Flor, and I shared cold rice, steamed fish left over from last night's dinner, and bananas.

"You know, the Manobo at Madga may be very surprised to see you," Flor said. I sensed she was warning me about something.

"Because I am an American?"

"Yes. The last time an American was in these mountains was in 1956. A missionary man named Grosbeck came here. He stayed only one day. Most people in the mountains have never seen a white person, and none have seen a white woman. The people may be curious or shy when they see you."

Ee gads, I thought. What am I getting into? I hope they don't stone me for being a freak of nature. I nodded. I usually did stand out in a crowd.

"Do you know the word *datu*?" Joe asked me.

"No."

"The leader. The one who makes decisions for the people. He settles the disputes and divides the food, decides when to plant and when to harvest. The people follow him. The leader in Madga is Datu Tagleong."

"Datu Tagleong," I nodded, repeating the name. I wondered how I might deal with such an authoritarian figure.

"What if the people don't want to follow the datu? What if he is not a good datu?" I asked.

"Then the families move to the place of another datu," Joe explained.

"In the old days, there were more Manobo people living in the mountains and the power of the datu was greater. But when the Japanese and Filipino soldiers came into the mountains, there was killing." He was talking about World War II. "Even Datu Tagleong killed many men before he was forced to run from the soldiers. Then amnesty was declared for all the Manobo warriors. Since that time Tagleong and the people have lived peacefully," Joe explained.

"How many people are with Datu Tagleong?" I asked.

"Maybe thirty families," Joe said. "But some live far away, a day's walk through the mountains. Only a few live at Madga. You will see."

We continued upriver. The river was becoming increasingly shallow. At what looked like just another gooseneck bend, the water was so shallow I could have reached out and touched the river stones below. Joe pulled the banka to shore and stepped out. "It is a short walk from here," he said. "Come."

Before I was even out of the boat, several curious faces appeared from the tall grass at the shoreline. By the time we had walked up the steep mud bank toward a group of houses, a half dozen adults and a dozen children had materialized. Joe and Flor hailed them and began a rapid dialogue in a language I didn't understand.

Everyone sat or squatted in the shade of the longest house in the clearing as inscrutable discussions ensued. The Manobo language was not like Visayan. Everyone was watching me closely, and I knew they were talking about me. I smiled at the children who hadn't taken their eyes off of me. I looked around the village.

There were three houses. The largest was about five feet off the ground, built on poles. A single notched pole led up to the porch. I was glad I didn't have to climb it; I wasn't sure I could. It looked tricky, unstable. The biggest house was built with rough-cut wood and had a nipa-palm roof. The other two were much smaller, about ten feet square, had bamboo slat walls and nipa palm roofs and were also perched on poles. Under one house were chickens, and in the shade of the big house a black pig lay on its side grunting.

The little children wore nothing; two small toddling girls and a preschool-size boy each had distended round bellies. Either they're really full from a good-sized meal, or more likely, those kids have worms, I thought. Under the nose of one toddler was an enormous glob of mucous that swayed lightly with each breath.

The older girls wore the most dirty, ragged, and tattered dresses I'd ever seen. Sleeveless, hemless, zipperless, buttonless rags, the patterned fabric only ghostly visible through layers of grime. The older boys wore shirts and shorts, equally tattered.

One adult woman was very pregnant and bare-breasted. She wore only a loosely wrapped piece of faded fabric. She had long black hair tied up on her head and she carried a red-brown glob of something between her lips. It had stained her lips and teeth an unnatural shade of scarlet. A fat woman wore a tight-fitting, straight-cut dress and her hair was cut short, almost stylish, but wild, standing out from her head like a thick bush. She too carried a reddish wad between her lips.

The skinny Manobo man doing most of the talking wore loose shorts and carried a sheathed *bolo* machete at his waist. He had a bright-red bandana tied on his head and I figured he must be Tagleong, the datu.

Peoples' feet were shoeless and extraordinarily wide. I studied Datu's feet, six inches across I guessed, with toes wide apart, long and prehensile-looking. Amazing feet below fantastically muscled calves. This guy does a lot of walking, I thought. Barefoot.

I couldn't identify the smell in the village. Sweetish. Sourish. Unpleasantly pleasant. A baby cried from inside the big house and the fat woman hurried up the notched pole ladder to investigate.

Finally Joe spoke to me in Visayan. "This is Datu Tagleong. He is asking if you will come to teach school here in their village." I had the impression that wasn't all that Tagleong had been saying. It was probably more like: What the hell is *that*? We ask for a teacher and you bring us a white girl!

I intuited that it was my turn to speak, to let them know I spoke Visayan. My throat was in knots, but I said, "Thank you, but I am not sure yet if my Peace Corps supervisors will allow me to live here."

That brought another round of conversation, also not in Visayan, with much gesturing and waving. Datu stopped his talk several times to spit a gorpy red juice on the ground. I felt there was a negotiation underway, and Joe was my advocate.

"Okay," Joe said finally, "Datu Tagleong says that he will build you a house, there." He pointed to a patch of low weeds across a dirt path, "And that you can have the school here, on the front porch of his house. He wants to know when you can begin."

"Thank you. But I will need to ask my supervisors first. Maybe they will allow me to teach here, but maybe they will say no. This is very far from the place where I live in Butuan City. The mountains are beautiful, but I am not certain that I will be allowed to stay."

That brought another round of talk, spitting, gesturing, and side glances at me. While they talked, Flor carried a bag of sea salt to the wild-haired fat woman, who was sitting on the porch nursing a baby. The woman was obviously pleased with the gift, and the two women talked rapidly the language I didn't understand.

A trail of grinning children followed us back to the boat, and two of the bigger boys helped push the banka from the rocky shoreline into the central flowing channel. With waving arms, the children said goodbye, and Joe pointed the banka downstream toward Sagunto. Early the next day, I boarded a passenger boat headed back to Butuan.

I had plenty to think about during the short trip downriver. I liked Joe and Flor and the Manobo people. I felt safe there. The people seemed bright and remained anchored in their traditional language and ways. I wanted to stay for a while in the village at Madga, just to see what life was like. It seemed possible. It was mid-March. Public school would soon dismiss for the May-through-July break. It was time for me to select my final summer project to complete my second year as a volunteer. I could request this assignment, a three-month tour in the mountains.

Yet there would be problems. I'd had nearly two years to learn Visayan, but the Monobo language was entirely different. Flor had assured me that the Manobo people spoke Visayan as their second language, and that a school taught in Visayan would be fine. But I didn't get that feeling when I was there. Language almost certainly would be a problem.

What about logistical support—supplies, communication and transportation? Getting to and from Madga would be a trick. I didn't want to rely on Joe and Flor, as they clearly had their own family, school, and church priorities. Who could I count on to help? And what if I needed medical assistance? What if I got seriously sick or injured and needed to get out?

And finally, what would the Peace Corps say if they found out that the place was so remote? Perhaps, if I could phrase my letter in a way to make it sound less isolated, the assignment could be acceptable.

This might work, I thought, if someone were to accompany me. A companion. Another volunteer. I knew just the person, a friend from my Peace Corps training group who was working up north on the island of Luzon. Her name was Janet Bauer, and she was interested in anthropology. It was a long-shot, but this would certainly be an adventurous finale to my Peace Corps years. I began composing letters to Janet and to the Peace Corps directors in Manila even before we reached Butuan City.

As it happened, Peace Corps Philippines was shifting staff. Both the country director and my Mindanao regional representative were departing, and their replacements had not yet arrived. My request arrived in Manila and was approved by a temporary staffer who had little knowledge or experience of the wilds of Mindanao. All I knew at the time was that my final summer assignment had been approved and I was headed for adventure.

I have several tasks to finish up here in Butuan before I leave for the mountains. The floating library I've put together to "float" up the Agusan River to the little barrio schools—sort of like a bookmobile, only it goes around by boat—well, it's not really floating yet. I keep asking the shop teacher to finish up the box—just a crate, like a trunk. He says he's about finished; I have the books to put inside it. The books I was able to get aren't that good, most of them are old textbooks (math and science), cast-offs from America that were cast off again from other schools. I did find a few English picture books and the younger kids will enjoy the pictures, even if they can't read the words yet. I'll take the floating library to a barrio school next week, then with its floating schedule, it can make the rounds through the upriver schools in this district. I'm hoping it will continue to float after I leave.

— Letter home, March 6, 1972

◉◉◉

I don't know what you did to rear a kid with such itchy feet, but you certainly did a good job of it. The thought of being tied down to a daily office job sends shivers of revulsion up my spine. I feel myself decaying. On second thought, I think I know what it was—in college, when I was working nights at Montgomery Ward in the credit department watching people go deeper and deeper into debt buying junk they didn't need. Yup, that's what did it.

— Letter home, August 9, 1971

The Wild Woman in Gold

We've been welcomed to Madga, but without the usual effusive Filipino fanfare of parties and gifts. People of Madga are friendly, but not pushy or gawking. Little kids are curious and their deep, dark, beautiful eyes seem to take in every tiny detail about us. They're especially curious about the things we brought with us to start the school.

I'm impressed with Datu Tagleong. This morning he adopted Janet and me as his daughters, saying he would protect us even with his life. He would even kill to protect us, he said, and I believe him. I'm sure it won't come to that, but I feel really safe with him and these people, much safer than in my apartment in Butuan City! Right now, in the steaming heat of mid-morning, two men *are walling our outhouse and another man is building an outdoor cooking platform onto the porch of our one-room bamboo and nipa-palm house. Joe Habana is still here with us, supervising the construction and getting us settled in.*

Mrs. Datu Tagleong—her name is Ricarda—has been supplying us with food. Last night they killed a chicken, and this morning she brought over hot sweet purple kamote sweet potato. We felt guilty taking it, because we know we are taking their food. They say the rains and flood took out crops a couple of weeks ago, and they are having hard times now. Last night, we shared what remained of our fresh fruit—mangoes and bananas—but I feel like we can't be giving away our canned food, as we brought upriver just enough for us, not enough for the whole village.

— Journal, April 8, 1972

◉◉◉

It was our third day in Madga, and Janet and I were settling in. Our neighbors were building us the only outhouse in the village. For two days, Joe Habana supervised, showing our Manobo neighbors how deep the pit should be, how to mount the squatting frame over the hole, how the bamboo slat walls surrounding the hole should reach all the way down to the ground.

One man in the hole used a pointed stick to loosen the sandy dirt and then scooped it into a basket, while a second man hoisted the heavy basket and tossed the soil to the side. Over and over they managed this, hour after hour, all day long, sweating in the sun, while I watched feeling guilty for making them work so hard, yet grateful we wouldn't have to go to the river's edge to squat in the shallows, in the open, like everyone else.

The hardest part was when kids, who stood barely to my waist, walked up from the river toting baskets filled with heavy river rocks on their heads to line the bottom of the outhouse hole and to spread around the lip of the pit. Little kids with glistening sweaty faces smiled shyly at me as they passed. How could I ever repay them for their effort?

On the second day, the men used bolo machetes to hack the saplings and strip off the outer bark to build a wooden frame around the hole. And then, for the last step—making the walls and roof—they split bamboo into strips, making "planks" that they lashed horizontally onto the sapling frame. The entire outhouse was built without a nail—just little trees, rattan lashings, and sliced bamboo, with a nipa coconut-frond roof—wide palm leaves, folded and overlapping, like fish scales.

On day three, I tried the new outhouse. I wasn't accustomed to squatting on my heels while doing my business and when I exited the outhouse, I was slow, shaking loose the muscles in my legs as I walked back to our little bamboo house.

It was not yet seven in the morning, and already hot outside. Little puffs of dust floated from each step I made along the dirt path and blushed my ankles reddish-brown. I stood a moment at the base of the notched pole that leaned against our elevated front porch. Climbing up the pole was a trick. I dug the toe of my rubber slipper into the lowest notch, but the notches weren't deep enough to hold my foot. Only my toes fit in the notches. I tipped forward, off-balance, and clambered ungracefully, using both my hands to hoist myself onto the shade of our front porch. My last heavy heave jarred our little nipa house.

Janet stuck her head out from inside the house. "We need water for breakfast," she said, still folding up the sleeping mat and mosquito net. "You want to get it?"

"Sure, but getting up and down this pole is nearly impossible. There's got to be a better way—a real ladder with rungs. Think we could show them how to make one?"

"Maybe. But everyone else seems to manage with a pole. If we ask them to make us a ladder, it will be another thing that makes us look dumb. Maybe we can make it work. Everyone else does it, right?"

"Right," I said, wondering if Janet was electing to build the fire and start breakfast so she wouldn't have to climb up and down the pole. I took the bucket and backed myself down the pole, still trying to get a foothold in the shallow notches. I made my way down to the Madga and across river rocks to the center channel where the water ran knee-deep and was the cleanest. I dipped the plastic pail down and lifted it up full, then poured a third of it back to lighten my load and reduce stress on the handle. Then I headed back across the slippery rocks and up the steep muddy bank toting about three gallons of river water.

Janet had the fire going and I lifted the bucket up to my chest as she leaned over and hoisted it up. Then I climbed back up the pole, hand over hand, clumsy, graceless. She set a pot of water on the metal fire ring. The water would need to boil a full twenty minutes before we could make oatmeal and tea from it. She stoked the fire, then went inside to brush her hair and put on a clean shirt. I kept the fire going and began looking through the teaching supplies we'd brought upriver. I was getting nervous. School would start on Monday and I had no lessons planned. I didn't know how to begin. How do you teach someone to read and write?

A single cardboard box held our school supplies. Coca-Cola Company had donated lined composition books and bright red pencils. I had some cardboard, colored chalk, a few colored pencils, half a ream of blank office paper, and a packet of carbon paper that I'd borrowed—okay, stolen—from the Davao City Peace Corps office. Silco Logging Company loaned us a small blackboard. We had a few Dr. Seuss books in English, donated by the United States Information Service office in Davao City. We had a kid-sized pair of scissors and a small box of crayons. We had a Caltex Petroleum Company map of the islands, showing the roads on all the main islands. There were some picture postcards of Philippine landmarks that I'd been using for bookmarks, and a toy truck pencil sharpener. Was this enough to start a school?

"Looks like company's coming," Janet said, nodding in the direction of the path. Three little girls were inching their way toward our porch, punching one another lightly, each pushing the other forward first.

"Here we go. Put on your best smile," I told Janet. "We don't want to be intimidating."

"Good morning," I said leaning over the porch. "Come up and sit with us."

The trio climbed up the notched pole agilely and plunked themselves down beside my feet. They didn't say a word, and I continued sorting through the box. The girls leaned forward, curious about the box and someone's long black hair brushed my leg. Then one little girl leaned into another and whispered something quick. The second girl giggled, while the third reached a tentative finger toward a book, then jerked her hand back with a quick smile at her friends.

They were definitely cute. I produced a 3-D postcard, a scene of mountains and rice fields and water buffalo.

"Look, a picture of another place in the Philippines," I said. The girls giggled in delight and passed it from one dirty little hand to another. The first little girl jumped off the porch and raced to the house next door, then reappeared a few minutes later leading her mother, our pregnant neighbor.

Janet and I were working on names. "You are Darna, and you are Norma." We had gotten that far. "And this one?" we asked of the returning first girl. "Dita. She is Dita." It was Darna, the largest of the three who answered with a smile.

"Okay. Darna, Norma, and Dita, right?" All three nodded. I felt like we were making progress. "And you are Dita's mother?" I asked the pregnant woman. She had a reddish wad of soggy leaves between her lips and was staring intently at the postcard. She didn't answer.

"That's your mom, Dita?" Janet said.

"Yes, Mum."

"What's her name."

Dita touched her mother's arm and there was a rapid conversation between the two in Manobo. Amazing, how that woman can talk with that wad between her lips, I thought. Like a ventriloquist, she talks without moving her lips. Then Dita said to us in Visayan, "My mother is Amalya." Or at least, that's what it sounded like. I nodded, "Good morning, Amalya." Amalya smiled back at me through the wad.

Janet got out the toy-truck pencil sharpener and began to twist a red Coca-Cola pencil beneath the little blade. By the time she'd finished, the crowd at our porch had grown to nearly a dozen kids and half that many adults. As each newcomer climbed up the pole onto our porch, I watched the feet. Somehow each large and small person climbed that pole gently and gracefully. How did they do it? Why couldn't I manage? The little truck was being passed from hand to hand as though it were a rare treasure. We sharpened all the pencils we had, and the kids laughed as wood shavings rolled out the truck engine.

Darna, Norma, and Dita were sitting close, and Norma reached out to touch my arm, a gentle stroke. Then she turned to Darna and whispered, "Hair."

"Umm," I said. "Americanas have much hair, even on our arms." The little girls giggled and ducked their heads.

Janet scooted on to the narrow porch bench beside me.

"Feels kind of weird, huh," I said. "I mean, all this attention."

"Yeah. We need something more interesting and educational to show them," she said.

"Other than our bodies, you mean?"

"Here," Janet said, reaching into her journal to retrieve a snapshot of herself with her former host family in Cavite on the northern island of Luzon. She passed it around the crowd, explaining in Visayan how the picture was taken with a camera. Then she showed them her camera, a box that takes in light and gives photographs. I doubted that that concept sounded believable or was understood, but the audience nodded politely while ogling the snapshot.

Picking up my guitar I began to strum. It was something familiar to do, something that might be considered friendly. I kept it low and hummed a tune.

The porch shook as someone new arrived. It was Ricarda, wife of Datu Tagleong.

"*Maayo*," Ricarda called in the Visayan way of greeting as she climbed our notched pole. I studied her feet closely and—I thought I saw something about the way her foot fit into the notch, but the moment passed so quickly, I couldn't quite get my mind around what it was.

"I am bringing someone to meet you," Ricarda said gesturing to an old woman nearing our porch.

"She has hiked over the mountain to see you," Ricarda explained. I smiled and extended the traditional greeting. "Come up, sit down." I watched the newcomer's feet—the way she climbed, slowly, in an old-lady way, and that's when I spotted it. The key was stepping up the pole sideways, with the weight on the outer edge of the foot at the base of the little toe, and the next step on the outer edge of the foot at the base of the big toe. Success was found in an upright, balanced sideways ascent, not a front forward assault.

Ricarda shooed the children aside to make room for the newcomer. The woman wore a ragged and dirty, loose cotton dress, probably once gold in color, now merely muddy and muted hues of gray. From her shoulder hung a tightly woven basket, waterproofed with black pitch. The woman extended her left hand in a handshake gesture. I extended my left hand and lightly clasped her fingers, gnarly thick and stained red-brown with betel nut and dirt. Hands that work hard, I thought. Hands of character. Hands that match her bare feet, dark and tough and worn and strong.

A baby cried across the path and Ricarda turned to leave. The woman in gold squatted on her haunches near my feet. I wasn't sure what to do or say. "You walked from the mountains?" I offered as an opener.

It was obvious she didn't understand and probably spoke only Manobo, not Visayan. She picked up the toy truck pencil sharpener, then the snapshot, then a book, touching each item shyly, as though unsure what it was. I wanted to explain but didn't know the words. I strummed my guitar. What was I supposed to say? How should I be? What did she want? Everyone else drifted home but she stayed, watching Janet and me. What's going on?

I hummed and picked the guitar. Freight train, freight train, going so fast. I felt I might have been on a whizzing freight train of my own, destined for points unknown.

Like Amalya, the old woman carried a wad of tobacco between her red-stained lips, and she seemed to be scrutinizing every detail of my feet and legs, leaning in to gently touch my ankle and calf, as if she'd never seen a leg before, at least not one like mine. I sat still, letting her examine me, like a new species of fruit fly beneath a microscope.

When I finished humming and set aside the guitar, the old woman stood up and brought her face close to mine, our noses barely inches apart. She stared deeply into my face, as though she were looking not at me but through me. I could smell her sweat and pungent tobacco breath. I looked back at her softly wrinkled skin, dark hair falling in sweaty wisps, deep black eyes that were crying, lids brimming with tears. With the back of her gnarly hand, she wiped the tears from her cheek.

I was stunned. I had no idea what I might have done. I smiled, a dopey forced smile, but could think of nothing else to do. She said nothing, stayed just a bit longer, then was gone, walking sideways down the notched pole on the outer edges of each foot, leaving me enlightened on the secrets of negotiating the notched pole, but totally confused about her visit. Who was she? Why had she walked over the mountain to see us? What was she thinking? Why was she crying? Had I done something wrong? Or right? Were those really tears? Maybe she had pink eye. Would I ever understand anything about this new world into which I had landed? Could I really negotiate the notched pole now?

I tried the pole, leaning my weight in, balancing down the pole with sideways turned feet. I nearly laughed out loud at the simplicity of it, at how silly I must have looked the past three days. I walked back to the river for more water, then toted it smoothly up the notched pole, the perfect inclined plane.

Later, when Ricarda came back for a visit—or to see what we were doing, it was hard to tell the difference—I asked about our visitor.

"Oh, she is a wild woman," Ricarda told me.

"Wild?" I asked

"From the mountains. Far away. She knows nothing. Crazy." Ricarda waved her arm, gesturing to the dark tangle of forest on the mountainside to the west, dismissing the thought of the wild woman in gold. It was the last I ever learned of her.

◉◉◉

Next door is Amelia, or Amalya —or maybe they are saying ah-Malya; it's hard to tell, the way the syllables slur and slap together as they speak, especially with wads of red-brown tobacco balled between their lips. Amalya and her husband Suat—and their several kids whose names I don't quite have yet—are our nearest neighbors. And Amalya is pregnant. Very.

I can't believe so many people apparently do nothing all day. Maybe I don't see what they're doing. But it seems, right now, that everyone is sitting on Datu Tagleong's long porch at his house across the dirt path. Not sure, but I think they're talking about us. They look over this way, keeping an eye on us, like they don't want to miss any-thing. The moms are grooming their kids' hair, looking for lice and popping the nits between their thumbnails. It seems like family together time. And everyone is talking casually, comfortably, with some easy laughter.

—Journal, April 9, 1972

◉◉◉

A Teacher, Who Me?

My hips are bruised from sleeping on a mat on the floor. I'm too sore to walk or bend. I guess I'll get used to sleeping on a mat on the bamboo slats, and I'm grateful for the tiny bit of flex the bamboo has, which isn't much.

The village kids are being extremely helpful, fetching us buckets of water, and this morning they put rocks around the perimeter of our "yard"—which is just some dirt. They even swept the yard—they use a bundle of long straight twigs to scratch at the open dirt. It does make the place look neater, with the little lines in the dust, but really, it seems futile to me. Something green and growing in the dusty yard might be nice. But there is plenty of jungle green in the surrounding forests. I suppose a piece of scratched-clear dirt is good too; it's calming

to my mind. Besides, the open dirt yard provides fewer
places for snakes or rats or centipedes to hide.

—I just learned that their "broom" is made from the
dried center stem of the coconut palm frond. Those trees
are certainly useful for a lot of things—baskets, hats,
ropes, medicine, skin lotion, floor polishing brush, so
many kinds of food and drink, toys, charcoal, toothpicks,
musical instruments, roof, fermented alcoholic bever-
age—and, of course, the broom! And those are just the
uses that pop instantly to mind!

— Journal, April 9, 1972

◉◎◉

The dugout banka pulled away from shore, and Janet and I stood on the shore rocks waving goodbye. The little boat slowly followed the curve of the Madga River southeast and disappeared beneath the overhanging greenery along the banks. With Joe Habana went our last link to the outside world.

"And so, it begins," I said, announcing the commencement of a big adventure. I was excited, scared, and very glad I wasn't alone.

"Uh huh," Janet replied. She looked like a princess standing on the smooth river stones, gazing southward. A princess in khaki shorts, a T-shirt, and blue rubber slippers, regal with the countenance of a proper Midwesterner. She was willowy, and her perfectly postured body reflected in the clear shallows. Her brown hair was pulled back in a long, wavy ponytail well past her shoulder blades. It lifted in the morning breeze when she turned to grin at me with her perfect teeth. "What shall we do first?" she asked. The princess was my co-adventurer, companion, and friend. She was as excited as I was.

"Let's unpack the school box and begin registration."

"How many kids do you think we'll have?"

"Don't know, but there seem to be enough of them around."

A line of ragtag youngsters followed us up the riverbank trail to the shade of our porch. I pulled out the school supply box, my guitar, and the little chalkboard and handed them to the kids. We marched across the dirt path to Datu's house, and one more naked little boy joined the parade, dancing around us as we walked.

We'd been in the Madga village for three days, settling in, while Joe Habana oversaw the completion of our bamboo house on stilts. The village kids were starting to look familiar, but I still had trouble attaching their unfamiliar names to their all-too-similar faces.

A big girl took a piece of rebar and flailed it on a piece of what looked like part of the chassis of a logging truck. The clanging reverberated through the village, across the river, and into the hills, and soon more kids appeared, their legs glistening from crossing the river.

Janet and I sat on the long, rough wooden bench on Datu's front porch, notebooks in hand, ready to record the names and ages of the kids that appeared for school.

"What's your name?" I asked in Visayan. And although it wasn't the first language of most of these kids, they were good in Visayan. It was a second language to almost everyone, a common middle ground for communication.

Well, that's not quite true. Janet had been living nearly two years in the northern part of the Philippines, on the island of Luzon. She spoke Tagalog, another language of the archipelago. But since she had heard about this opportunity to work with mountain people of Mindanao, she had been studying Visayan, the general language of the South. And unlike me—who had slogged through language studies and learned excruciatingly slowly—Janet was a linguistic wizard. Her Visayan was already nearly as good as mine, and she'd only been in the southern Philippines a few weeks.

"Darna," said a middle-sized girl with fluffy dark hair and calm eyes.

"How old are you, Darna?"

She grinned and ducked her head. I asked again, "How many years do you have?" Silence. "When were you born?"

"Yes."

I looked at Janet, who was recording beside me, and in English I asked, "Am I saying that right?"

She shrugged. "You're the expert."

"Okay," I smiled back at the little girl. "Who is your mother?"

"Ricarda."

"Well that makes it easy," I told Janet. Ricarda was the wife of Datu Tagleong, and this was their front porch. Ricarda was inside, cleaning her collection of the long pliable leaves of the pandanus tree, readying them for weaving. "Go see if you can find out how old she is."

I recorded the names of more kids: Serhio, Poring, Dita, Norma.

"How old are you?" I asked each one of them.

And they just grinned and nodded, "Yes," watching me write in my book, and then going over to look at the Caltex Petroleum Company road map of the islands that we'd mounted on a piece of cardboard and hung by a long shoestring hooked over the wall.

More kids appeared: Junior, Tessie, Aida, Saldi, Norma.

"Two Normas," I said. "So you can be Big Norma. Is that all right with you?" Big Norma smiled.

"I am thirteen," Big Norma said.

"Great!"

"And I went to school before."

"You did? Where?"

"Malaybalay. Before, I lived near Malaybalay. In the time before I was married to Ben."

"Married? You are married?"

"Uh huh. That is our house, there," and she pointed to the third bamboo stilt house on this side of the river. "Is it okay if I come to school here?"

"Yes, of course. You can help us teach the little ones." Big Norma grinned again.

"But Mum," Norma told me. "The others will not know their age. I know because I was in school before."

"I see." I figured Big Norma was telling me that she knew how to count.

Janet returned with Ricarda.

"Ricarda," I asked. "It is hard for the kids to tell us their age. Can you help?"

"Age?" she asked. "You want to know how many years each has?"

"Well, yes."

Ricarda laughed, a chuckle that jiggled her large belly. "No one knows. Children are just born. No one counts the years. They are small and they grow. Then they are old enough to marry. It is enough."

"Of course, enough." I was suddenly very embarrassed. I was asking a culturally insensitive and irrelevant question. Dumb Americana. No wonder I was getting no answers.

We condensed the age category to two groups, Big Kids and Little Kids.

"You want to take the Bigs or the Littles?" I asked Janet.

"Maybe I should take the Littles," she said. "They are just learning Visayan, like me, so we'll be at about the same level. Anyway, they're cute."

"All right. And I'll take the Bigs." Janet had seven Littles in her group. I had nine Bigs. We filled up Datu's porch on that first day of school.

As we cooked supper that evening, Janet and I had a serious conversation about school.

"We really should teach them something. Reading. Writing. Arithmetic. Those kinds of things," she said.

"Sure. They seem bright enough. Eager to learn and all."

"Have you ever taught anyone to read before? From scratch I mean?"

"Well, no. Have you?"

Janet shook her head. Silence.

"But we both learned to read once. And Visayan is easier than English. More straightforward. We'll teach it phonetically," I said.

"Maybe your Bigs can learn it. But I'm not sure about the Littles. We might not get past which end of a pencil to use."

"It doesn't really matter really." I suggested. "Just teach them anything. Shapes. Colors. Stories. Songs."

"Uh-huh. Maybe so. But I think we ought to offer them more. Something real. They're looking to us as if we're real teachers."

Until now, I'd gotten by pretending to be a teacher in the lowland schools in the district that fronted the Agusan River. For nearly two years, I'd been helping teachers improve the way they taught English as a second language. I'd never been responsible for a class. Now we were responsible for real kids, and their families were looking to us.

"So we will keep pretending," I said. "Maybe by pretending, we'll actually teach something."

"Maybe," said Janet.

"Anyhow, we'll learn a lot," I suggested.

"Uh-huh," she said. "I just hope we can teach them something useful to their lives."

I hoped so too. At this point, it didn't seem likely.

◉◉◉

Today I had my second lesson in the Manobo language. Sadly, I struggle simply to hear any distinction between syllables. Maybe if I saw it written, I could differentiate between the words. But it's not a written language and what I am hearing sounds to me like a stream of pebbles jumbling and tumbling down a hill.

This afternoon as I sat playing my guitar, suddenly our porch was crowded with people who came to sit and listen. Mostly women and children sitting close to each other, all watching me intently. They seemed to really like the music, although I doubt they understood the words. I sang the songs I knew—like "Freight Train," "Where Have All the Flowers Gone," "House of the Rising Sun," "Alice's Restaurant," "Puff the Magic Dragon," and "The Marvelous Toy," the song with sound effects in it. They loved that part, and I got everyone to make the sounds. It was very funny and everyone was laughing. And I picked a little bluegrass, "Wildwood Flower," the way I used to play with my college bluegrass friends, but I missed having the banjo player. I also sang a bunch of Visayan folk songs that I learned in Peace Corps training: "Si Pilimon," "Alibangbang Bukid," "Inday Baili Ta," and "Sa Lungsud Sa Buenabista." It wasn't much really, just a few songs, but music seems to build an easy bridge between us.

— Journal, April 9, 1972

◉◉◉

Medicine

Being doctora is outside my area of knowledge. I know a little about keeping a wound clean while it heals, but really, I know nothing about medicine. Yet with the needs I see around Madga every day, I know that I have to do what I can to give help when they ask, and hope I'm not hurting anyone. We didn't cover this in Peace Corps training.

— Journal, April 11, 1972

⊙⊙⊙

It didn't take long for me to understand what our Madga neighbors wanted from us. First they wanted reading lessons. Equally important was our Peace Corps medical kit.

In the 1960s, medical kits had been standard issue to each Peace Corps volunteer, but with budget cuts by the time I arrived in the 1970s, there was only one kit issued per assignment area. In my Butuan City assignment, I was keeper of the kit because I was located most centrally for the eight volunteers in the district. Two years later when I moved to Madga, the Butuan-area volunteers were reaching the end of their terms so I brought the medical kit with me upriver. It contained bandages, soap, disinfectant, antibiotics, cold medicine, fluoride drops, iodine water-purification tablets, antacids, a snake-bite kit, adhesive tape, rubbing alcohol, cough medicine, first-aid cream, and a booklet on common tropical parasites and diseases. With these and a few other items like tweezers and a compression wrap bandage, Janet and I—reluctantly—became the village doctoras.

It would have been hard to find anyone more squeamish about blood than I was. The time Suat came walking into the village with a huge bolo gash across his shin, I thought I would faint. He came up to our porch, blood trailing down his shin and over his foot. He'd walked across the mountains with the gash packed with some gooey substance and lashed up with leaves and vines.

"What's that?" I asked as I washed his leg with disinfectant.

"Medicine from the forest," he said.

"What kind?"

"From the spiders."

Spiders' webs. I was interested. "Any kind of spider, or just certain spiders?" Suat told me how he had located the spider web in an old tree. He told me that the sticky web helped hold a wound together and stop the bleeding. I was skeptical. I thought he needed stitches. Yet between the spiders' webs, our cleaning, and a fresh bandage every day, the gash left a scar but healed clean. I acknowledged that maybe the webs had worked.

Another day Laurentina walked across the river bringing us her little boy with a burned foot. It looked like infection was setting in. I didn't know what to do, but I washed his foot with disinfectant soap and put on a topical disinfectant. I know that red stuff hurt, and the baby screamed while his mom kept stuffing her breast into his mouth to calm him. I felt like a torturer. But when I put on first-aid ointment, it cooled his foot down and he stopped screaming. Then the bandage. But I knew the bandage wouldn't stay on the foot of a toddler for long. I told her to keep him off his foot, and to return every day for a clean bandage.

An old man came to us reporting blood in his stools. That one had me puzzled, and I told him he should see a real doctor downriver at the logging camp, but I knew he wouldn't go.

The worst wound I saw during my first weeks in Madga was a mute man with his arm in a homemade sling of torn rags. This was Donkilyo, one of Datu's grown sons. He didn't speak, but Donklyo brought his brother as an interpreter. Together they had a kind of sign language. I learned that Donkilyo had had an accident weeks earlier and he showed me his left hand, swollen and greenish, with the middle finger oddly angled. I was sure his finger was broken. I knew I couldn't do anything about this either, and I told him he was definitely going downriver to the Silco Camp doctor with us the following week. He did. He got a splint and medicine and eventually recovered the use of his hand.

Boils, cuts, infected insect bites, and burns. These were the most common problems. And I got better at cleaning wounds. I learned not to puke when maggots came crawling out of a smelly, oozing infection on the side of a baby's head. I learned that red-black blood meant coagulation and was not a bad thing to see in a deep cut, and that a wound with bright, red, free-flowing blood needed to be held tightly until the flow slowed. I learned that flies were attracted to open wounds and that bandages had to be anchored on all edges to keep the flies out, but that wounds also needed air and space inside the bandage so the skin could dry out and heal. I learned that we could never get enough bandages to fill our needs, and at one point we resorted to tearing strips from an old undershirt. I learned that cotton cloth was too heavy; it held moisture in and promoted infection. I learned that these people needed more medical help than I could give.

Meanwhile, the people of Madga were giving us so much. They brought food every day, sharing whatever was in season—fresh hot purple sweet potato or roasted corn or plates of steaming upland rice or the occasional melon, cucumber, eggplant, papaya, sugarcane, lansones, durian, or passion fruit. When we made trips downriver to Davao City, we'd return to find repairs on our home—a broken bamboo wall replaced, the roof patched, the yard weeded and broomed clean.

And there was the time I was walking across our porch and the bamboo flooring splintered and collapsed beneath my weight. My leg was wedged in up to my thigh, and I hollered—loud. Datu Tagleong came over, helped me get out of the floor relatively unscathed, then lashed in more bamboo slats to repair the hole.

So we tried to give back to our neighbors. We taught them in school. We tried to help with first-aid. And we shared food.

On a Saturday morning in May 1972, Janet and I were making a batch of griddle cakes to share with our neighbors when Laurentina showed up again with her toddler. This time he had a huge boil on his thigh, and his leg was covered with orange goo and wrapped with a wide shiny green leaf. I inquired and learned it was a papaya poultice, which might be fine medicine, I thought, once having had myself a pore-cleansing papaya facial. The skin of the baby's leg was not broken, but there was an obvious internal infection covering much of his upper thigh. Was it related to his burned foot weeks earlier? The boy could hardly hobble, and he whimpered when she put him down. From what little I knew, I thought an antibiotic might help. But what dosage for a little kid? I decided to guess.

"Okay. If two tablets a day is dosage for an adult, how about a third of a tablet—half of that third in the morning, and the other half in the evening? What do you think?" I asked Janet as she cooked.

"He's a pretty big kid as they go, so I guess so," she said, mixing the ingredients to make pancakes.

I got out a razor blade and sliced the tablet, twisted each section in a scrap of paper and told Laurentina to give the medicine to her son with some food that morning and again in the evening, and to bring him back the next day.

With flour, water, and a little bit of salt, Janet cooked up Saturday-morning pancakes and sprinkled them with sugar. We took a bunch of warm cakes across the path to Ben and Norma's, then to Suat and Amalya's house. Inside, the kids whooped with joy.

"I guess we do our best, but what they need is a real doctor. And real teachers," I said. "And a nutritionist wouldn't hurt either."

"Uh-huh. But they've got us. We'll just give them bandages. And pencils. And pancakes. Here's the plate for Datu's house. Let's deliver."

I couldn't help but worry. Was I wrong? Was I poisoning that child? Or maybe the antibiotic dosage was too low to make a difference.

Laruentina came back the next day, and the next, each time she appeared with the toddler, she reported that he had taken the medicine, and he continued to have a papaya poultice on his leg. And each time I saw him, the infection looked no worse. Within a week, there seemed to be an improvement, a lessening of the painful, tight, pale skin. Slowly the boy got better, but there was no assurance that our medicine had helped. He might have gotten better in spite of it. Maybe it was the poultice.

One morning I realized that I hadn't seen the boy in a while. I took his absence as a good sign. And since it was another Saturday morning, we sprinkled our griddle cakes and made the neighborhood rounds. Sharing sweet cakes was so easy—no mystery, no guesswork, no lingering questions about dosage or appropriateness. Poultices of smashed papaya and spider webs were safe mountain medicine. I wasn't sure about our Western medicine.

◉◉◉

I really like life here in Madga. But I have brought along my own cultural inhibitions. For example, everyone else runs around naked, or almost naked, and bathes in the river, while I continue to carry heavy buckets of water from the river to our outhouse so I can dip and pour water for a private bath. Why can't I just swim naked in the river like everyone else? But I am so American, I can't, at least not yet. It's also funny how quickly my perceptions have changed. At first the peoples' dress—or lack of it!—embarrassed me. I would look at somebody and see weirdness and rough manners—dirt, rags, spitting, shouting—and I was sort of scared of people. Now I see them as friends. I know their individual personalities,

and it takes away the strangeness. Maybe they feel the
same way about us.

— Letter home, April 29, 1972

◉◉◉

Coming down out of the mountains this time was a
real experience. We left our little nipa house at 4:30
a.m. on Saturday and started downriver in the predawn
moonlight. The river was low so the boat ride down the
Madga and Adgawan to Silco Camp took seven hours; at
times we had to get out and pull the boat over rocks. At
Silco Camp we found that Dr Troucio was getting ready
to take his jeep into Davao City. So after a quick shower
in the camp guesthouse, Janet and I took off with him for
Davao—a four-hour jeep ride, super dusty and lurchingly
bumpy. The jeep had only two seats, one for the driver,
so Janet and I shared the passenger seat. The Jeep didn't
have doors, and I had to keep half a butt cheek on the seat
and half my body out the doorway, hanging on tight and
riding it out. In Davao, we went straight to our regional
rep's house to get paperwork to request an extension on
our term. Phil and Lynn Lilienthal are our Peace Corps
administrative support here in Mindanao, so of course
they were happy to see us and they fed us grandly. After
two or three hours of catching up with them, getting news
of Peace Corps and the world, I caught a midnight bus to
Butuan City to get some supplies I had in storage there.
The bus was full of crying kids, and even the chickens and
pigs were screaming. It was incredibly crowded. I was
jammed up tight against the person next to me, but at
least I was sitting. A woman was standing, but leaning
in, practically sitting on my lap, and I let her lean heavily
on me, because I know how incredibly hard it is to stand
up for eight hours, especially along that washboard road.
I was hassled by a dirty old man the whole trip. Behind

me sat a friendly, pregnant woman, and she kept leaning forward to rub my shoulder or neck. I know why, and it wasn't in a rude way; she just wants her baby to be born with light skin, so she touched me, or rubbed my skin, hoping to bring "good" skin to her baby. I cut my foot on a piece of metal under the seat in front of me, bandaged it with my handkerchief, and tried to keep my weight off it. My luggage wouldn't fit inside the bus, so they put it on top. I had to climb on the roof of the bus to lash it down, causing all sorts of catcalls and jeers from the crowd of gawking, gaping dirty old men. The bus broke down only once, but it caught on fire and caused a panic and stampede over luggage and people as everyone rushed for the door. I just sat there, figuring I'd go out the window if I had to—better to fall six feet down than be stampeded. The fire was in the wiring around the driver's seat. They got the fire out, and we were back on our way, arriving in Butuan about 9 a.m., after almost 30 hours of travel.

— Letter home, June 22, 1972

◉◉◉

The medical aspect of our mountain adventure has been the most sobering part of the experience. It shows me the contrast between the new and old worlds. Do I prefer the unsophisticated, primitive life in a community that comes with injuries, disease, and malnourished children—and yet has compassion and equity and inclusion for all? Or do I prefer a modern, Westernized life with good nutrition, hospitals, and life-saving drugs, yet cultural complexities that send us spiraling in circles, ostracizing and isolating one another based on socioeconomic status or ethnicity, while we pollute our planet and threaten our own species' survival. Which world do I want to inhabit? I don't know the answer.

—Letter home, July 1, 1972

Curtain Across the Moon

Thinking about yesterday's departure from Dallas, I'm sad. I hated leaving my family, turning away and walking down the jetway and onto the plane. Sitting there for takeoff, I felt choked off, like a steer being squeezed and pushed toward the dip bath. There was a pressure I could hardly stand, a heaviness that was collapsing me. I'm only comforted by knowing that at any time I can turn around and go back home. I'm not sure I can do this.
—Journal, June 29, 1970

◉◉◉

Night came early to Madga. As the sun edged over the western mountains, I started preparing for dark. Supper finished, dishes rinsed and stacked. Time to light the tin-can kerosene lamp and spread the mosquito net, hooking it from the rafters and tucking each edge completely under the sleeping mat. If even an inch escaped, night-raiding, blood-sucking mosquitos and small, crawling vampire-creatures that feasted on body fluids would find the gap and pounce.

The hours of darkness were for writing and reading. Alone time—or as alone as it got because Janet was there, sharing the sleeping mat under the net. We'd worked it out and knew how to be comfortably alone together.

One night, I sat cross-legged beneath the *mosquitero*, my journal on my lap while the kerosene lamp flickered yellow shadows across the page. I was writing about how confused I felt, how incompetent I'd become, and how beautiful the kids were. Then my mind wandered to the comforts of home, my loneliness for family, and my craving for American food. How did I get here? It's too far away, I wrote, and too crazy to have been concocted in any coherent plan. I'd merely stepped out onto life's riverbank and started sliding—no control, just freefall—and here I am. The wild wind of destiny at my back must have propelled me to take that first step onto the slippery slope.

I remembered how it had been. It was late and my Texas household slept. The dry winter Texas air was thin as cellophane and wrapped my family in a silence easily torn by footsteps on the hall carpet or the yipping of the dog next door. When I listened closely, I could hear my father snoring gently in the bedroom across the hall.

These were moments when I broke the rules. I pulled open the curtains, lay on my back across my bed, and stared out at the night sky. Our household rule forbade opening the curtains after dark, lest some unseemly character peer in. But the only nighttime intruder I'd ever encountered in our fenced, suburban yard was a curious, beady-eyed possum. That winter night, the sky beckoned as the nearly full moon hung above the telephone wires. I watched it slowly set, first touching the upper wire, then the lower.

Could this really be the same moon that's shining—at this very moment—over Denver and Santa Fe? Would the moon be nearly full there as here in Fort Worth? What about New York? Or Los Angeles? Does this same moon, still nearly full, shine on Paris and Bombay? Is it shimmering tonight on the Amazon and the Ganges?

Perhaps, I considered, Paris and Bombay aren't real. Perhaps they're illusions, tricks conjured on those of us who don't know any better. Maybe those photographs in *Life* magazine are a hoax, actors on a Hollywood set. Maybe the world really does end just north of the Red River and south of the Rio Grande.

I got dizzy staring at the sky and crawled beneath the blankets. But I kept the curtains open, watching the moon, wondering, feeling a whisper not quite audible.

When a US Peace Corps recruiter came to my college campus, I interviewed him for our student newspaper. What was it really like, I asked, living in Africa? He told me it was wonderful and it was awful, but well worth it. Try it, he said. Here is the application. See for yourself.

I carried it around for days. It was long, a booklet actually, and would take effort to fill out. Then what? Was I brave enough to leave my family, my friends, and my new teaching career? I was twenty-one years old. In two months I'd be a college graduate, a certified teacher, and I was already getting calls from local public high schools that wanted to interview me for positions in their English and Journalism departments.

And then—one day—I simply knew I was leaving. I realized I would expire of boredom if I didn't get out of Texas, at least for a while, at least long enough to see what the moon was like somewhere else in the world.

I mailed the application to Washington, DC on May 1, 1970. I was still trying to figure out how to tell my parents that I had applied to the Peace Corps when the notice of acceptance came. Would I accept a teaching job in the Philippines?

I went to the campus library. I couldn't spell Philippines without looking at the Peace Corps letter, and I didn't know where to look for it in the *World Atlas* without checking the index. Finally I located it, a string of islands not far from Japan, China, and Indonesia. They called the area Southeast Asia. It was far away from Texas. It would do.

In late May, I graduated. In early June, I was maid of honor for my best friend's wedding in Fort Worth. We hugged goodbye. She thought she was the one leaving me, but I knew better. I knew that I was the one leaving all of Texas behind. Not forever, of course, but for a while, until I'd sorted out the moon thing. "See you soon," she said, meaning after the honeymoon. "Uh-huh," I said, between tears, "soon." Two weeks later, I was on a plane, frightened and overdressed, heading to Philadelphia for Peace Corps staging.

$$\odot \odot \odot$$

It's my first day away from home. Ever. I lived at home during college. I never even went away to summer camp. Today I got on a plane and left my family. And I've been thrown in with a hundred young people who have the same questions and ideas as I do, and I feel almost unafraid, and un-lost. Almost. Okay, I'm terrified.
                                                    —Journal, June 29, 1970

$$\odot \odot \odot$$

Staging

Later today I'll meet with the psychologist for a personal interview. We have to pass some sort of evaluation to go on from staging into training. I don't know the criteria for passing the test. I hope they aren't going to de-select me on the basis of being so scared I can hardly speak. Yet I look around me and see some really crazy-looking kids here for staging. Especially the draft-dodger boys who want to join the Peace Corps so they don't have to go to Vietnam. Some of them, loud and long-haired and scruffy, scare me more than the psych exam.

— Journal, June 29, 1970

⊙⊚⊙

I was irrevocably on my way into the abyss, *sans* friends, family, or even a roadmap. Just an airline ticket, an official letter of welcome, and the address of a hotel in downtown Philadelphia. I wore my best pink polyester pantsuit and a hair piece—my "fall," a hank of blondish hair matching my own, that gave my own hair extra body and lift. I'd worn it every day of my senior year in college, every day of student teaching, every Sunday to church. I styled it in a flip, pinned it on, and it intermingled with my own teased and sprayed hair. I toted a shoulder strap purse and a briefcase-style zippered carry-on, stuffed with cosmetics and a sweater. And in another zippered fabric case slung across my shoulder was my old Yamaha guitar. In the check-in luggage bin below rode my big Samsonite suitcase with jeans and T-shirts, school dresses, heels, sandals, books, pens, jewelry, and my electric rollers. I didn't know it then, but I would soon jettison the rollers, the hairpiece, and the heels, while those T-shirts—newly purchased in the men's department at Sears—would serve me for three years before I passed them along to the Manobo. I didn't know it then, but in the months to come I would wish I'd packed a pocket knife, nail clippers, canteen, compass, scissors, flashlight, lacing canvas shoes, a folding umbrella, sun hat, hand lens, and quality sunglasses. But I'd been raised a suburban girl of fashion, and I knew nothing of rustic living. Yet I was also the girl who rebelled when my parents tried to send me to "finishing school" to be polished with the social graces to attract a suitable mate.

"I'm already finished," I'd whined. "I want college." They acquiesced, allowing me to attend a local college that specialized in producing teachers—a respectable career choice in their eyes.

I watched the stewardess carefully, how she moved with grace and politely served and chatted with male passengers while maintaining a constant smile. That was another path I hadn't taken. Only a few months earlier, my sorority sisters and I were being recruited by the airlines to train as stewardesses. We were told we had the appropriate look. When the airline officials in Dallas measured and weighed each of us, I came in only slightly below the upper weight limit. The physical beauty criteria were discouragingly strict, and I knew they would ground me if I gained even a little weight. Anyway, I disliked the thought of being perpetually nice to cigarette-smoking businessmen, which seemed to be much of what the job entailed. I had realized I needed a different sort of life adventure.

I had a window seat, and as we approached Philadelphia International Airport, I looked out at hulking ships, an aircraft carrier, and submarines in the harbor, and these things translated to me as thrilling adventure. I had briefly considered joining the military as an exit strategy, but with friends from high school and church returning from Vietnam in body bags, I'd decided against it.

After claiming my baggage, I realized I had more than I could carry. I noticed a young man holding a copy of the same letter that I had. He also carried a guitar. I asked and confirmed that he was Peace Corps and heading for the same hotel I was. We pooled resources, shared a taxi, and made our way downtown to a hotel lobby teeming with young people. There were nearly 200 of us, a new batch of volunteers, some heading for South or Central America, some for Asia and the Pacific. They sorted us out, assigned us shared rooms, and handed us orientation schedules. I'd cleared the first hurdle.

That evening, I stared out my ninth-floor window at the strangeness below. Houses like matchboxes up on end. Trollies. Pretzel vendors. Newsboys hollering the headlines. A fenced, green city park and kids dodging traffic to play ball in the street. When it came time to get ready for bed, my roommate Cassy sat reading in bed and chatting with me. She was from upstate New York, cheerful, and very excited. I told her I was scared.

"Of what?" she piped. "This is great fun!" Her confidence cheered me on.

When I took off my hairpiece, apparently lifting off half my scalp, her eyes got big and round. "Are you kidding? You wear that all the time? Why? You already have hair."

I'd never thought about it. That night I didn't curl my fall, and when I went to the first orientation class the next morning, it slept in like a sleek rat in a side pocket of my suitcase.

⊚⊚⊚

They tell us our group is going to train in Saxtons River, Vermont. Three months in rural Vermont in the summer! They say Saxtons River is really beautiful, with a mountain stream running through town. We'll be staying at a boys' boarding school that's unoccupied in summer. And they say Peace Corps training is tough, especially the language training. I'm hoping two years of college Spanish will help, but I'm (still!) scared. I'm just keeping quiet, listening, and trying to smile.

— Journal, June 30, 1970

◉◉◉

Now I'm a Peace Corps Volunteer. We all stood together, taking the oath. I expected something a bit more glamorous, but they handed us little slips of paper, we raised our right hands, and read it aloud. I can hardly remember what I promised, but it had something to do with upholding the Constitution of the United States, whatever that means. What would it take to NOT uphold the constitution of the US? Anyhow, the main thing is I made it through training!

— Journal September 25, 1970

◉◉◉

In a matter of hours, we leave America. I can't grasp the reality of it. I'm numb. I feel like I'm spinning in space, rudderless, with a creepy hollowness in my gut. We trainees who have become so tightly bonded over three months of rigorous, brain-numbing, nonstop training, will now be parting ways, heading for different areas of the Philippines. It's the separating, the loss of my support-ive group of friends, we who have struggled side-by-side these past months, this loss of my pals is the saddest part.

— Journal September 26, 1970

◉◉◉

Piecing it Together

When I came back upriver from the supply run to Davao, I brought a sack of old clothes I'd had in storage, and passed them along to Ricarda to give away. Today I see a couple of my old skirts and T-shirts on others. I thought these old clothes were in pretty bad shape, but here they look clean and new. Among them was a red fabric tie belt that I've already seen on two guys. One of them, Polynio, wore it yesterday as a headband. Donkilyo is wearing it now as a necktie. Donkilyo is the broken-handed mute who, unlike anyone else in these mountains, always wears long pants and a suit jacket —with no shirt. With the red belt around his bare neck, and his wild hair, he looks like a parody of a businessman. I wonder if this "business" look is intentional. Probably not, because it *seems that he—like everyone here—has only one set of clothes. The rule seems to be you find something that fits and wear it till it falls off. Even if you're a growing kid or a pregnant woman, as your size expands, seams burst, and buttons pop, you just keep wearing the same outfit, ripped open at the sleeves, neck, chest, side, and back.*

People seem proud and happy wearing my hand-me-downs. I don't think they know where they came from, but they can probably guess. No one mentions the new clothes or says anything like "thanks," or even mentions it, because sharing whatever you have is merely normal behavior here, as ordinary as breath.

—Journal, April 23, 1972

◉◉◉

The pieces were starting to fall into place for Janet and me, in part because we'd been asking so many questions. Maybe our neighbors were laughing at our nosiness, but they also tried their best to answer us—although sometimes their answers confused us further.

"So the wives keep their own names, but the kids take the last name of the father, right?" Janet asked.

"Seems so. So Tagleong's last name is Kogit. Is that with a K? Or would it be Coguit? Is it 'g-i-t'? Or 'g-e-t'?" "Or "g-u-i-t"?

"Maybe it's never been written, so you get to decide. What do you think?" Janet asked.

"I'm gonna write it with a K. That seems most likely, since Visayan has no C. Although it sorta sounds like they're saying Colgate, like the toothpaste," I laughed. "But it's probably a 'g-i-t.' Anyhow, it's only for my journal. Okay, so Tagleong Kogit (Coguit? Cogit?) has had three wives. Is that what you understand too?"

Ricarda came over to borrow some salt, and Janet and I began talking with her. I used the term that translates literally as *borrow*, but seemed to imply no intent of return. Yet sharing fully was intrinsic to their culture. I twisted some of our rock salt into a piece of paper and handed it to Ricarda.

"Uh huh," said Janet, as we debriefed about Datu Tagleong's family tree. "The first two wives died, and their kids stay a part of Tagleong's big family. Eddy might be the oldest." Eddy and his wife Alang were parents of infant Zoon; they lived across the river.

"Then there is Donkilyo." He was the mute hunter who apparently could hear but not speak. "And Saldi," I said. Saldi might have been two or three years younger than me, possibly still a teenager. "Okay, so those three boys, Eddy, Donkilyo and Saldi are from Wife Number One. Right?" I asked Janet.

"Maybe. Let's go on," she said.

"Wife Number Two. There is Tassio, and the twins Tessie and Aida, and another girl studying with Joe and Flor in Sagunto. Sound right?" I asked.

"I think that's what Ricarda said. Then there are Ricarda's kids, some from her first husband who died. Like Darna." Darna was the little mother in Datu's house. She sang the little ones to sleep at night. Darna, maybe eight or nine years old, was in my class of Bigs, quietly competent with wide, dark, wise eyes. Darna was Ricarda's daughter, but not Tagleong's.

Then there are the kids that Datu and Richarda have together. "Who's the oldest? Little Aning?" She was about five, and was in Janet's class of Littles.

"Next is Lando, you think?" He was about four. Always naked, always curious, always moving. "And then there's Tata. Her real name is what?"

"Merl, I think." said Janet. Tata was about two. She was somewhat crippled. She limped, and became my favorite Madga kid.

"And then there is baby Lakak. Other name Imelda, right?" I asked. She was an infant, not yet walking on her own.

"You're asking me? I'm not sure," she said. I wrote these relationships in my journal surrounded by question marks.

There were more entries, more question marks. Datu Tagleong and Suat are brothers? Joe Habana is the brother of Ricarda? Maria is the mother of both Amalya and beautiful Penang, one of my Bigs? "Amalya and Penang do look alike. Maybe that's right," I said.

Months later, in September, Ricarda was perched on our porch again. She proudly told us she was pregnant, for the tenth time she said, explaining that here in Madga they don't have the things to keep down the number of pregnancies. She said that Flor gets injections from the doctor so she won't have another baby.

"But we have the same kind of blood," Ricarda said about Datu. "So we make babies quickly." She laughed and said that since Janet and I had stopped teaching evening classes to the adults of Madga, there was no family planning. "More babies now," she laughed.

I started doing the math.

"What year were you married?"

"1968." Four years ago. And four babies born to her and Datu? More question marks for the journal. In the end there were more question marks than established facts.

As I grew more and more confused, flustered by the tangled lineages, I realized that sorting out the family trees of our Madga neighbors might not matter so much, and I gave up trying. Janet kept at it. The genealogical diagram that expanded across her journal pages sprawled with arms and links and generations. I thought she was slightly obsessed, and more than slightly brilliant.

⊙⊚⊙

Penang is a beautiful girl, a young woman actually, I'd guess thirteen or fourteen years old. She has glowing skin and big, bright, dark eyes that spark with happiness and enthusiasm and health. But her smile is the nicest thing. You can glance at her and she'll beam back a warm, dimpled smile. She's a younger sister of Amalya, a daughter of Maria. Penang is a large, big-boned girl, like Maria, and is larger than Amalya. Pablito is their younger brother, and he's not too bright in school, not like Penang, and he is somewhat crippled. One of his legs is shorter than the other and it seems like it isn't growing. He still runs and plays as usual, but in a lopsided way. Pinang—whose other name is, I think, Josephina—is really bright, but she will be getting married soon as she is "dalaga na," meaning she has had her first period and is ready for a husband. They say, however, there are no boys here of marriageable age who are interested in getting married. I wonder how much of a choice Penang will have in this.

— Journal, September 26, 1972

◉◉◉

The Blind Man Ceremony

Janet and I spent a week away from Madga. We didn't intend to be gone that long. We left for Davao on Friday morning, telling the kids we'd be back for school the following Tuesday. On the way out, it went smoothly and we were in Davao by Saturday afternoon, early enough to do some shopping. But on the way back, first we were delayed leaving Davao, then we ended up waiting two days at Silco Camp for a banka that could bring us upriver to Madga. Then, when our banka got about halfway upriver, it started raining so hard that we had to pull over because the boat was filling up with rain and we couldn't bail fast enough. We pulled the banka to the side of the river, and Trining and TingTing went into the forest and cut some giant roundish leaves, big as umbrellas, and we put several *atop our cargo and we each held one above our heads. It was raining so hard and pounding so loud that we couldn't even hear each other shout, and I was worried about our supplies getting drenched, especially the magazines and paper. But the leafy umbrellas worked astonishingly well.*

Later, in the evening when it was getting too dark to travel on the river and there was no moonlight, Trining and TingTing made a lean-to shelter from sticks and big leaves, and we spent the night there, pretty miserable I might add. It was too wet to get a fire going, so we shared some cold rice and canned mackerel. Early the next morning, we came on up to Madga. Phew! I thought we'd never get back, and I was glad to see our little house and put on some clean, dry clothes. Now back in Madga, the world has once again shrunk. Here, the world is just us and the people and houses at this bend in the river.

Several new faces have arrived, including a blind man and his family. Last night we began to hear chanting and it went on and on and on. There were high-pitched shrieks and horrible-sounding groans that repeated and repeated. It must have been a ceremony of some kind, having to do with the strangers—hard to say what, but really weird. As usual, I don't know what's going on around me.
— Journal, April 23, 1972

⊙⊙⊙

The blind man walked in with his family from the eastern river crossing, a small bundle tied on his back, a walking stick in one hand, his other hand resting on a companion's arm. He wore tattered shorts and had a kerchief around his head that barely contained his long, wild hair. His face was old, wrinkled, and his nearly black eyelids covered the craters in his skull where eyes should be. His whole countenance was shrunken and rigid. He didn't move with the fluidity and grace of the Manobo people, but with a ramrod stiffness that led me to think he'd been blind much of his life.

His wife was small and thin, not old but bent in the shoulders. She wore Manobo beads around her calves, around her neck, ear to ear under her chin, and around her wrists, in the traditional Manobo way. She carried a baby in a sling over her shoulder. Two shy, preteen girls were with them. The girls stayed close to their family, perhaps frightened of us white women. The blind man always had a hand resting on the arm or shoulder of one of his family members.

I was surprised he didn't head directly for Datu's house, but rather to Suat and Amalya's, and they stayed there for days. His girls helped with chores, and after a while they became brave enough to smile at me when I greeted them. They didn't come with Amalya's kids to our school, but spent their days at the river or in the forest.

On the bright full-moon night in April 1972, a ceremony began well after dark. First we heard loud chanting. I went out on our porch to see what was going on, and I saw the blind man standing stiffly in front of a candle atop a mat in the house of Suat and Amalya, chanting in a monotone that increased in volume. Then another voice began, a male voice, perhaps Suat's. I decided it must be a religious ceremony. The monotone chanting went on and on, then stopped abruptly. The man moved and I could no longer see him, but I could see his wife stretched out on the floor, then sitting up to comb her long hair. Then the voice started again, this time faster, a gargling sound, not at all like the common Manobo language. It ended, then there were other monotone male voices, then a groan and a shriek, and the baby inside the house cried. Then people were on the porch, watching me.

I wrote:

The candle is blown out and one of his girls comes to sit on their porch. I think it's over.

It isn't.

Now there's more chanting, louder. Shouts. Even louder chanting.

Now his two daughters are on my porch. They watch me write. They are smiling. I assume the occasion isn't a bad one.

Then the tone of the chanting changes. It's lighter, perhaps a happiness chant. And the blind man comes out to sit on Suat's porch for a while. I watch him gently pick up the Manobo necklace and bells that he had out on a handkerchief and put them back into a bag.

His girls leave my porch and return to Suat's. I think they'd been sent over to see what we were doing. The chanting resumes inside, and the poor guy's throat must be hurting. It's been going on for so long.

Stops.

Starts again. Another verse? Another part of the story? More of the ceremony? Who knows!

The blind man's wife goes back into Suat's house. It's dark inside there now. I can barely see, but people seem to be lying down. And the chanting continues for at least half an hour. Janet thinks it will go on all night. The blind man must have incredible endurance to keep up the loud vocals. He stops once in a while for ten or fifteen seconds, then starts up again, on and on and on.

What is all this? Does it have to do with Amalya being prodigiously pregnant? I'll probably never know. No one speaks to us about these kinds of things. It's like a frog living inside a shoebox with holes punched for light and air, but the poor little frog inside has no idea where he is or what he's seeing through those holes. I'm the frog.

◉◉◉

Before leaving Madga with his family, the blind man came to visit with us. He stayed and talked until after midnight. Maybe if you're blind, it doesn't matter what time of day it is. Anyhow, he talked and talked, through an interpreter, Manobo to Visayan and then Visayan back to Manobo. He says that Janet and I need men to keep us warm at night. He also wants to know what it's like to ride in an airplane—is it hot, or cold, and aren't we frightened to be so high in the air? Somehow this blind mountain man knows about airplanes. His daughters came over and sat in on the conversations. They are uncommonly beautiful children. We tried to ask about the ceremony, but got nowhere, merely vague, not-making-sense responses, which is the culturally polite way of saying that he wouldn't say, and we shouldn't ask. The frog peers out of the shoebox, to no avail.
— Journal, April 29, 1972

We Tried That

The stinging red ants are terrible right now, but the flies are worse. They crawl on wet, sweaty skin, and they love wounds. The other people here don't seem to mind that their wounds are constantly tickled by flies, but I hate it. I have open sores on my legs from unhealed insect bites, and the flies are all over me. They even push bandages with their surprisingly strong little bodies to get beneath and suck at the oozy wounds! Beyond irritating. Disgusting and unhygienic.

There was a noisy tree frog in our house last night, and the scratching and croaking noises frightened me till we found the source and identified it. We managed to catch it and throw it out the door. I hope the stupid chickens *get it. A chicken has been coming inside and roosting on our wall, and it poops inside our house. Although we did enjoy the egg it left. We didn't tell anyone that it laid the egg, or we might have had to give the egg back. Janet cooked it and after we ate it this morning, we buried the shell. If we're gonna get the poop splattered on our duffles, we might as well get the egg.*

—Journal, April 23, 1972

◉◉◉

In Madga, the cackling and crowing of chickens came before, during, and after first light. I pulled the sheet and cotton blanket over my head. The bamboo slat floor felt uncannily comfortable, and in a dream I drifted someplace sweet, where food was plentiful and I was comfortable inside myself. Then a rooster crowed four feet beneath my head.

I clung to the dream, not giving up sleep, but counting, patiently, each annoying crow. After four loud and long screeches, the rooster rested. I hoped he had gone. He hadn't. At seven screeches, I knew my sweet dream was gone for good. At ten calls, I thought of throwing something large and heavy at him. At thirteen, I emerged from the mosquito net and stepped out onto the front porch. The rooster, still crowing, stretched his neck, flapped heavy wings, and sauntered from under my bamboo floor, strutting to Amalya and Suat's house across the path, still crowing.

"Stupid chickens, I hate them," I said, pouring a slosh of yesterday's boiled water into my enameled tin mug. I brushed my teeth and watched the low-angled sun strike the billowy western clouds, then I spit the water and toothpaste from the porch where it splayed onto the customary spot, now a white patch in the red-brown dust. I made my way down the pole ladder to the outhouse.

By the time I finished changing into school clothes, Janet had started the morning fire and the two of us had a cold rice and hot tea breakfast. We shared the teabag, alternating mornings who got it to use it first. Each small bag was a treasure brought lovingly up the river.

Our breakfast was brief and silent. These days, after several months upriver, Janet and I talked little. We both knew the routine, what it took to keep our little house going, who did what and when, and so conversations were brief. No anger or hostility, only silence, a cold, empty, painless silence. I watched her during breakfast. There was grace in her every move, the way she stirred her tea and placed the bag just-so, then tasted her rice delicately. She could have been having high tea with the Queen of England rather than sharing a twice-used teabag on a hard bamboo floor in a dusty, little river village two or three days' boatride from civilization.

Then I looked down at myself. The waistband of my cutoff jeans didn't lie. I was getting fatter. The less I ate, the fatter I got. My T-shirts were starting to bind my shoulders. Even my bra was getting tight. And my legs—oh gosh—looked like turkey drumsticks. Not only fat, but the skin was like a minefield littered with craters of insect bites, ulcers and lesions. I counted seventeen on my left leg, and nine on my right, as I took my turn with the teabag and slapped a mosquito sucking on my shoulder. I picked it off my skin and examined its flattened body. It had tiny black and white stripes on its abdomen. I pressed it into the pages of my journal and wrote, "This had breakfast of ME as I had breakfast of tea and rice."

Our neighbors were doing their morning chores. Dita was on her way to the river. She was a waif of a child, only twice the size of the bucket she toted, but I knew she would make it back up the slippery embankment with water for her family. That girl, like all the Madga kids, was a tough little cookie.

From Datu's house across the path came the wail of a crying baby, and I could hear Darna singing to hush her sister. I watched Ricarda standing in her open kitchen rattling tin dishes as she prepared the morning meal.

After we rinsed our breakfast dishes with boiled river water, Janet and I were ready for school. It was a little after seven.

"You ready?" she asked.

"Guess so," I said. "You can ring it today."

Ringing the school bell was one of the small highlights of our life in Madga. The bell was a piece of heavy metal that in a previous incarnation had been part of a logging truck. It now hung suspended from the floor beam of our house. Janet lifted a two-foot piece of rebar and began beating the metal. When the clanging stopped, after about fifteen seconds, echoes reverberated from the hills.

The kids began congregating immediately. From the three houses on our side of the river came the earlybirds—Big Norma, Darna, Aning, Dita, Poring, and Serhio.

Serhio's appearance gave me a jolt. "Where is your hair?" I asked.

"No more," he responded, rubbing his shaved head with a hand and grinning. "It itched."

Janet and I looked at each other and laughed. "That's one way to get rid of lice."

From across the river more students came until Datu's front porch bench was filled with small bodies squirming and laughing.

In the early days of our school, we began each morning with exercises, lining the kids up in the open dirt yard in front of Datu's house. The line was a new concept I'd offhandedly explained, "Like a fence, one after another," until I realized these kids had no clue what a fence is. Finally, I placed them in line, one by one, telling them to stand still. "This is a line," I declared, "like ants walking."

Janet and I had led jumping jacks and the students had dutifully followed, leaping and flailing and laughing. Then we led stretches and bends, and the kids followed, some playfully kicking out at one another.

"What are we doing this for?" Janet asked me one day. "By the time these kids get to class, they've chopped wood, hauled water, hiked a mile, and crossed a river. Why do they need jumping jacks?"

"True. But they do seem to enjoy them," I'd said.

"Probably because you and I look so ridiculous doing them," she'd replied.

That's when we stopped the morning exercises. These days the first morning activity was washing up. We took the class down to the river and passed around a tiny bar of Ivory soap that we'd brought up from the lowlands. Everyone washed and splashed, laughing and playing.

This activity too, had begun at the instigation of us Americanas. "Look at this paper," I pointed out to a student in class one day. "It's very dirty, like it walked across the river through the mud." The student only smiled, unabashed. Of course, I thought, mud and dirt are part of daily life. White paper and cleanliness are not.

"Dirt can make you sick," I tried to explain. That brought only questioning stares.

"There are little things in the dirt." I knew no word for germs. How to explain it. "Little animals, not animals, but like animals. You can't see them, but they can get inside your body and make you sick. You need to clean your hands, especially when you eat food."

The kids looked perplexed, especially at the part about the invisible small animals in the dirt.

Yet everyone was happy to accept the ritual of the morning wash. They liked the smell of the soap and the slippery feel of it swiping across hands. Other lessons in personal hygiene followed. It was no secret that we Americanas had strange rituals.

"Mum, what are you doing?" students asked as we brushed our teeth. "Why do you spit the white?"

"Cleaning teeth," I said.

"Why?"

"So that our teeth don't hurt when we get old."

"Why?"

"Cleaning teeth helps them be strong. The white stuff helps keep our teeth clean and strong."

"Does it hurt?"

"No pain."

"Is it delicious?"

"Here, taste it," I said, offering a small smear on tiny fingers.

They tasted, then turned up their noses. Then they laughed and ran away.

On our next supply run to Davao City, Janet and I visited a branch office of the Colgate-Palmolive Company. We met with a company manager, explained our school project, and left with a donation of two dozen toothbrushes and small tubes of toothpaste.

For a little while, the morning wash at the river exploded with the enthusiastic cheers of happy brushers. As the days passed, I noticed some kids were only pretending to brush and others were avoiding the toothpaste. One or two kids were even showing up for school late, deliberately it seemed, to avoid the morning brush.

We discontinued the morning tooth brushing. "Oh well, we tried that."

Another thing we tried in our early days at Madga were evening classes for adults. At first the classes were well attended and the bench was crowded with adults who came to see what this new school was all about. But it wasn't long before we realized that it was the kids who wanted the evening classes. The adults had a hard time manipulating the pencils and were very challenged trying to remember the sounds and shapes of letters. The adults liked our picture stories, and it became obvious they'd come to be entertained and were not really interested in learning to read or write. The kids would sit beside their parents, showing them the way to shape the letters, while the adults grinned proudly. After a while, adult attendance fell off, and we were left with only the kids.

So we discontinued the evening classes. "Oh well," Janet and I finally concluded, "we tried that." Those words became our mantra as we tried out ideas that seemed worthy, but didn't actually work. Team sports. Starting school precisely at 7 a.m. Planting a garden. Learning the Manobo language by listening to the kids chatter. Spraying our house with insecticide to get rid of fleas and flies and centipedes. Burning our rubbish. Setting the tusked jawbone of a pig in our rafters to keep the chickens from roosting inside our house.

"Oh well, we tried that."

That last one was, at best, a long shot.

⊙⊙⊙

Another form of civilization appeared today, this time, unwelcome. From the north side of the river came lowland forestry guys from Dongalyo Logging, the neighboring logging concession, the ones who legally hold the government rights to cut the forest on the north side of the Madga. Maybe these loggers heard about us Americanas being here, because they came strutting into Madga with the same old lowland male chauvinist questions: Do you have a Filipino boyfriend? (and then they'd volunteer for the job!) Do you eat rice? How do you find our country? And, with great incredulity, "Why are you living here?" Then they informed us that the people of Madga are very stupid and dirty and, "You'd better come downriver with us." This is the consciousness of the regular lowland Philippines, and how I hate it!

One of these forester guys said he was a palm reader. I think it was a ploy to touch my hand, but I went along. He said that I, not Janet, will be married within two years. Yuk! Not gonna happen! Fate worse than death! I certainly hope he's better at forestry than at palm reading.

— Journal, April 12, 1972

⊙⊙⊙

This time when we got back to Madga from Davao, there was a front door on our house! No longer would we have to hang a blanket for the illusion of privacy. And the sagging bamboo wall was fixed too. The bamboo slats of the new door are nicely lashed together, but there are no hinges, so we have to physically lift the door up and move it aside to pass in or out. So we gave Donkilyo an old leather pouch (that formerly held my hair brush and pins) and he will cut it up to make some "hinges," tying leather strips between the door and the door frame, and the new door will be able to swing open and closed. First class! Uptown! Wow!

When we asked Donkilyo about the jawbone—complete with massive tusks—that's hanging from one of the rafters, we were told that he had killed the boar. I got the feeling that we are living in Donkilyo's house, that he is letting us stay here as long as we're in Madga. He's staying at Datu's house. No one told us this is his house; I just feel it.

— Journal, April 23, 1972

⊙⊙⊙

Two Pigs and a Deer

Breakfast was a shared bag of black tea, half a cookie each—now the cookies are all gone— and one-and-a-half Skyflake crackers each. And now the crackers are all gone, too. I think of it as a "continental breakfast."

Lunch was some leftover, cold kamote and two dill pickle chunks. I'm thinking of it as "potato salad."

Supper was some cornmeal—boiled to a mash—and a curry sauce made by Janet. Then our neighbors brought us fresh, hot kamote which we sliced and sizzled in some oil. I think of it as "Bombay grits and hash browns."

As I write this, the rude loggers from Dongalyo have crossed the river and are back in Madga. They borrowed my guitar earlier, and are now standing outside our little house, serenading us. It's a harana—a custom borrowed *from the Spanish, where the sweetheart sings to his beloved outside her window. She's supposed to gaze lovingly down on him, and maybe toss him some token—a flower, a scented handkerchief. It's dark here, and I'm not going outside. The loggers are roaring drunk; this is so disgusting. It might be funny, except it isn't. I'm turning on the radio, even if it's only static. Maybe they'll get the message. I want them to go away!*

— *Journal, September 19, 1972*

◎◎◎

Donkilyo and Serhio brought over meat as the afternoon shadows lengthened and the day cooled. They appeared on our porch, Donkilyo carrying his spear in one hand, and Serhio offering us a foot-long rattan thong skewering a dozen hunks of red *baboy*, fresh pork. It was our portion from Datu, who can butcher a pig with his machete in minutes, reducing a carcass into chunks of meat for every family.

"The hunters caught two pigs," Serhio said.

"Two?" My eyes were wide, my grin wider.

Donkilyo nodded shyly, obviously pleased with himself. There was nothing wrong with Donkilyo's hearing or understanding. He simply didn't talk. Ever. Maybe there was a physical reason for his lack of speech. Or perhaps he had a psychological block. Either way, Donkilyo gestured and grunted. He communicated in his own way, and we, like everyone else in the village, accepted it.

"Donkilyo, that's wonderful!" I told him. "You're a fine hunter! Thank you, thank you—a very big thank you." I didn't have to feign enthusiasm, since we'd been without fresh meat for days. The hunters went out day after day, returning empty-handed. Janet and I managed by slowly doling out the last bits of lowland food supplies, along with kamote purple sweet potatoes from our neighbors. These same neighbors were hungrier and had even less than we did, uncomplainingly eating kamote leaves and a few small tubers. And now there would be fresh meat, protein for everyone. Two pigs in one day! It was remarkable.

I poured a bit of Baguio oil from the tin into a lidded pot, added a generous splash of boiled drinking water, put the meat in the pot, sprinkled it with salt, and put the lid on to keep the flies off while we got the fire going.

Janet was under the house chopping kindling when Suat appeared at our porch. He held out a short rattan thong.

"Deer," he said.

"You got a deer today?" I was amazed.

"Yes. Datu and Donkilyo got pigs, Tirso and I got a deer. It was a lucky day for hunting."

I'd never heard of such phenomenal luck. "Madga hunters are the best!" I said. We would have enough meat for two meals.

"But Mum, there is one thing," Suat instructed. "Do not cook the pig and the deer in the same pot."

"Huh?"

"The pig and the deer cannot be cooked in the same pot."

"But we have only one pot." I thought I wasn't understanding this correctly. "We should not cook them together?" I was seeking clarity.

"Yes, do not cook them together."

"But why?" I was baffled.

"The scent. The dogs will be confused next time and will not be able to hunt well. The smells of the meat cannot be together."

"Oh. I see." I didn't see, but at least I decided I had the message straight. Cook the two meats separately to avoid confusing the hunting dogs. "I understand, Suat. Thank you."

"Venison too, from Suat," I told Janet as she mounted the pole with an armload of kindling. She laid it on the stove platform with a splash of kerosene.

"Amazing! Famine to feast in twenty minutes. Toss it in and we'll get it cooking. Maybe add some kamote, maybe make a white sauce. Make a great stew. What do you think?"

"Um. Well, we can't cook the pork and venison together."

"What are you talking about?" She was bending over, blowing on the kindling, trying to make the fire catch.

"Suat said we can't cook the different meats together, that it will throw the hunting dogs off the scent." I felt ridiculous saying it, and Janet looked at me as though I was making it up.

"We can't possibly cook all the pork, then start all over again with the deer. Are you crazy? We'll be here all night. Besides, we don't have enough firewood for two cookings."

"But Suat asked us; he told us. We just can't."

"Are you sure you heard him right?" I knew my language skills were sometimes shaky. And Janet knew it too.

"Yes. I asked twice. That's really what he said."

"Well great. You be the one to go out and get more firewood. After dark. You be the one to stay up half the night getting the second pot of meat cooked. Not me. I'm cooking this meat, eating it, and that's all there is to it. You're not going to believe that about the dogs messing up with the scent, are you?"

"Well. Not really *believe* it. Just do it because he asked."

It was almost dark, and the fire was going strong. Janet picked up the pot of pork and opened the lid toward me. "Okay. Cook the venison now, with the pork, or don't. Your choice."

I hesitated. I wanted to do as Suat had asked. But mostly I wanted to eat, do my lessons for tomorrow, and then sleep. I was tired. I was hungry at a level far beyond merely having an empty stomach. My entire body craved meat, and craved it *now*.

With a glance I checked Suat's house. The family was inside, I could hear them talking. He would never know. With my back to his house so that they couldn't see even if they were to look, I placed the venison chunks into the pot where they sank with small plops.

Janet made white sauce. The stew was beyond delicious, filling my body and soul in a way that no mere sweet potato ever could.

Later Janet said comfortingly, "I think the sauce covered the scent of the meats. The hunting dogs won't be confused."

"I hope you're right." I whispered. That night, for the first time in weeks, I went to bed grateful and full. And uncomfortably guilty.

◉◉◉

They've told us that sometimes they bury the pig meat for a while, till it starts to rot, then they dig it up and cook it. They say it tastes really good that way, lip-smacking good by the way it was described to me. Or maybe they are kidding me. Can't tell, but so far, we only gotten fresh meat from our neighbors. Fine with me.

— Journal, September 3, 1972

☉☉☉

In cleaning out my duffle searching for my missing nail scissors, I came across a stick of chewing gum from our last trip to Davao. I didn't even share it with Janet—I chewed the whole thing myself! Delicious!!!

—Journal, September 11, 1972

☉☉☉

Right now, I'm sitting in the dark, beside the tin-can kerosene lantern and listening to Voice of America from Washington, D.C, transmitted to us from Hong Kong. Last time we went downriver, we returned with a wire that we attached from the north-ish side of our house to the radio's rabbit-ear antenna, and the reception is now slightly stronger. It's still iffy; the sound fades in and out; and some nights are clearer than others; but when we do catch a signal, like tonight, we get to hear news of the world. Uganda and Tanzania are fighting. Vietnam is releasing three American prisoners of war. There is a US presidential election coming, and McGovern is not doing well in the polls. I don't like Nixon, but it looks like he might win. This is the first presidential election since I turned twenty-one, old enough to vote. But I don't get to vote, being here. I have no idea how to vote absentee, and besides, from here, voting seems impossible. It will be four more years till I can cast a ballot for president. I'll be twenty-eight! What will the world be like in 1976? Will I still be constantly hungry?

— Journal, September 18, 1972

Reading Lessons

The beauty of teaching these people is incredible. The kids are wonderful, astounding, as they take a pencil for the first time and we work on numerals: 1, 2, 3—learning to associate the concept of quantity with the shape of each numeral. They understand counting, but they never associated counting with the shape of a pencil mark. We play counting and numeral-writing games with little river stones. These kids are very smart and quick learners.

In our adult night class, a beautiful toothless grandmother just wrote for the first time—first a page of a's. She had a tough time, reversing the shape till finally she got it. Then we tried e's, which was just as hard for her. We worked on it for an hour, truly testing my patience.

But the joy and pride in her eyes was well worth it—she was writing!

                                    — Letter home, April 11, 1972

◉◉◉

I'd learned that the ancient peoples of the Philippines relied on oral tradition to record folklore and folk history. In the thirteenth century, writing systems derived from the Indian-influenced cultures of Indonesia and Malaysia came to the islands and by the sixteenth century, Christian missionaries from Spain introduced the Latin alphabet into the lowland cultures. Yet among the minorities of the interior mountains, histories and stories remained oral.

Reading lessons in the Visayan language were the main subject in our school. In my class of Bigs, I started with the vowels—a ,e, i, o, and u. In a land heavily influenced by 400 years of Spanish rule, the Visayan language uses the same Latin alphabet as Spanish. And, unlike the convoluted rules of English spelling, Visayan lacks the challenge of long and short vowel variations. I approached my classes by introducing one letter at a time. Then the class discussed the sound it made, took turns writing it on the blackboard, and practiced writing the letter in their notebooks. Together we created a poster with a picture of an object that started with the sound of that letter.

a is for *agianan*, a path through the forest. And I sketched a forest path.

i is for *isda*, the fish in the river, and I sketched a little river fish.

u is for *umayan*, the river downstream from us, and I drew a river.

When we got to the letter o, we were stumped. No one could think of any object that started with the sound of o.

I had to think fast. Taking a cue from the shape of the letter itself, I drew a picture of a face, with eyes crossed as it stared at the tip of its nose. Upon the nose sat a big fat black fly. And the lips of the face in the drawing were circled in a perfect wide-with-surprise O.

"O," I said. "Oh, ho, hooooo," and the kids hooted with laughter. I wasn't totally sure that "Oh!" would be the expletive of choice in their culture, but it was close enough to work—a sound association they remembered.

When they had the vowel sounds and the lower case vowel letters learned, I introduced "the tall partner," uppercase letters. Then we moved on to the consonants. There are fewer letters in the Visayan alphabet than in English, and the sound of each letter is distinct and unchanging.

One day, we were working on punctuation and capitalization when Serhio brought me his notebook to check. He had written: *Maglakaw si Serhio sa suba. Mukuha siya ang mga isda. Malipayong ang inahan niya.* Serhio walks to the river. He catches some fish. His mother is happy.

Serhio had managed to sound out the words, remembered to capitalize the first letter of each sentence and his own name. He had punctuated correctly. He had even drawn a picture of himself at the river. I looked up into his smiling face. "Very good, Serhio!"

In that moment it struck me. He could read! He could write! These kids, I realized, are incredibly bright and eager to learn. Even with my unsophisticated lessons, they have learned more than I ever thought they would. It had taken less than six months for my Bigs to learn to read and write.

I had to laugh when the Bigs created a game, "Flying to Manila." The idea grew out of my efforts to help them grasp a world view beyond their own village, beyond Silco camp. They needed to know about the world. They'd seen our maps and were beginning to understand the geography of their archipelago and the location of other islands. We spoke of Manila, the capital city of their country. We spoke of the vast and deep ocean. We spoke about airplanes and big ships. They'd seen photos in our magazines, and they'd seen words written with letters they could read.

"I'm flying to Manila in an airplane, and I take…" We would fill in the blank with all sort of ideas, writing words on the blackboard, sounding out the syllables, using our alphabet sounds. We might take simple items like a dress or a stick from the forest or a pig. Or we might take along more esoteric items like the smell of betel nut or the taste of fresh kamote.

One day after we'd been playing this game for a while, one boy noticed an airplane overhead. This was not a common sight; that part of Mindanao was not highly trafficked air space. It might have been a private plane, because it was flying fairly low, out of the southwest, heading north-ish, toward Butuan City, toward Manila.

The kids watched the plane, then independently, without my help, they began the game. "I'm flying to Manila in an airplane, and I take..." A chicken. A blanket. My baby brother. A rock. And on it went. We rapidly wrote words on the blackboard. What's the first letter of rock? What's the next sound? They sounded out "b-a-t-o (rock)" and spelled it correctly. We laughed at how full and heavy our imaginary airplane was becoming, so we took some items that we could take in our thoughts, in our memories—a cloud from the mountain, the smell of rain, the sound of a bird. I was so proud of them. Their world view was expanding—both in the physical sense, and in their imaginations. No one could have been more surprised than I was. Perhaps we had created a real school after all.

⊙⊚⊙

We really don't have much in the way of supplies to start a school. Fortunately, we have a little chalkboard and some chalk. And some paper, mimeographed on only one side, so we can use the other side. We have a pair of little scissors, and some carbon paper, so I can make worksheets, two or three carbon copies at a time. And we have the Coca-Cola pencils and the toy-truck sharpener. And the wonderful Coca-Cola composition books. That's it. Can we teach a whole community to read and write with just these things? I think we can. These people are so eager and bright, I think we could teach them with just a pointed stick scratching in the dirt. Really.

— Journal, April 12, 1972

⊙⊚⊙

I did a whole morning of school with no lesson plans. It was tough. It's so much easier when I make work- sheets and story sheets every day; it helps keep things rolling along. Copying straight from the board is too time-consuming for them. Plus, the chalkboard is so small, I can get only one small sentence on it at a time.

What an interesting study it would be to look at art made by kids who are having pencils/crayons for the first time. My kids draw houses on stilts. River. Pig. And their families.

— Journal, September 15, 1972

◉◉◉

Dr Pepper

The Bigs have been asking to borrow my playing cards. I don't know how they even knew I had cards; I haven't had them out. They must have gone through my duffle while we were downriver. And although that might seem like an invasion of privacy, I can't blame them for being curious about us. Besides, there is no concept of privacy here, except that which we Amerikanas imagine for ourselves. When I was in Butuan, I was so lonely I played a lot of solitaire, but not anymore—there's too much to do here in Madga. So now I let the kids use the cards, and the cards are getting bent and dirty. I can't tell what game they're playing right now. Maybe Trining taught them poker, or maybe it's something they *made up. They also play Go Fish; I showed them how yesterday. Playing cards helps them recognize number shapes, adding, sequencing, and matching sets. It's math. Although I doubt if any educator— at least where I come from— would agree with that; yet it seems to be true.*

— Journal, October 1, 1972

◉◉◉

"Good grief, what is *that*?" Janet asked, peering into my open duffle on the bamboo slat floor.

"A Dr Pepper," I said.

"Where in the world did it come from?"

It was a crazy story. I exhaled, took a calming breath, and started at the beginning. In college, I would drink a Dr Pepper for breakfast, another with lunch, and a couple more in the afternoon as I worked on deadlines in the journalism office. If a friend headed across to the Student Union Building, I'd give her a quarter and ask her to "bring me a coke"—in the generic sense. Everyone knew that the only soda to bring was a Dr Pepper. We were, after all, in Texas—Dr Pepper-land. As far as I knew, the whole world was the same.

When I got to the Philippines, it was cold turkey for me. There were Pepsis and Cokes, but no Dr Pepper. How I craved one.

"It's the caffeine," a friend had told me. "Try coffee or Coke."

Cokes tasted to me like sugar syrup, and Pepsis were no better. Coffee in the Philippines was a bitter, tepid concoction, and if I added sugar, I'd get the pervasive tiny swimming ants that inhabited every sugar container. I longed for a simple, cold Dr Pepper, frosty with crushed ice in a waxed-paper cup, with a straw.

One day I visited Clark Air Base, a slice of America in the northern Philippines, and lo and behold, I saw vending machines with cans of chilled Dr Pepper. The soda was also served over ice in the lounge, and six-packs were available from the commissary. Like a camel trying to stock up for a trek, I guzzled a six-pack in two days and when I left Clark Air Base, I had a can stashed among my clothes, inside a sock, tucked in my underwear pouch. It was a jewel, my treasure, insurance against hard times. And when I packed for Madga more than a year later, the sock-shrouded beverage went with me, still nestled among my underwear.

"And you still have it?" Janet asked, astonished. "Why don't you just drink it and get it over with?"

"Someday, when I'm ready." Part of me believed I would drink that last Dr Pepper, but another part knew I really wouldn't. I'd had it more than two years by then. I still longed for a cold one, but as long as I had this can by my side, I knew I could wait a little bit longer.

Janet laughed. "You're crazy, you know. You're as bad as Lita in Cavite."

"What do you mean?"

"The family I lived with, you're just like them."

"Not either."

"Yes, you are. Think about it."

I had visited Janet up north in her host's house, where the central display in the living room was a shrine of American-made products—condensed Pet milk, Hormel Spam, Chicken of the Sea tuna, Del Monte tomatoes, and Green Giant sweet corn. When I asked about the display, Janet told me that Lita's husband was in the US Navy and was able to send these goods to her.

"You eat this way all the time?" I asked.

Janet glared. "Nobody touches this stuff. It's strictly for show, for status. We eat fish and rice, like everybody else."

"You mean you have a half a dozen cans of Spam just sitting there, and no one eats them?"

"Right. Don't even mention the idea of eating them, or Lita will feel she has to open a can for you. And there's no telling how many years they've been here."

"I'm not hoarding Dr Pepper to show off to my neighbors," I told Janet that day in Madga.

"But hoarding it just the same. I don't see you popping the top for a sip of Dr Pepper." She was still laughing at me.

"I just like having it, that's all." I couldn't explain further and let the matter rest.

Many weeks later, Janet noticed a wet spot under my duffle. "Something's leaking," she informed me one afternoon.

I opened my bag knowing what I'd find. The clothes were damp and a soft fizzing came from my underwear. A tiny fountain had spouted from the side of my beloved Dr Pepper, a pinprick in the aluminum hissed a sustained whisper of slow decompression.

I picked up the can and carried it to the front porch.

"It's your Dr Pepper, isn't it?" Janet said. I couldn't tell if she was laughing at me.

"Uh-huh." I said. "I'll take care of it." I took the machete from the hook by the door and started down the bamboo pole.

"See, you should have drunk it a long time ago. Now all you have to show for it is a duffle bag of soggy clothes." She didn't have to say it. I was already calculating the hours it would take me to wash the stickiness out of my clothes.

I walked behind our house and scraped a shallow hole with the machete and bamboo scoop. On the ground beside me the can hissed, froth pooling in a puddle at its base. By the time the hole was ready, the hissing had stopped. There was a bit more liquid in the can and I shook it. Then I stuck my tongue to the hole and tasted it. There was a familiar and friendly tingle on my tongue, like a long-lost pal. A cup of ice might have helped, or maybe it was just too old. Either way, it wasn't nearly as tasty as I'd remembered.

I tried to bury the can, scraping dry, brown earth across the red and black logo. Janet watched me climb back up the pole and gather my clothes. I took the bucket and laundry soap and headed for the river.

She caught up with me there, her own laundry on her shoulder. We washed our clothes, side by side at the river. After a few minutes she said quietly, "I know. There are things I miss about home too."

Three days later, I spotted Serhio in the shade of his house playing with a new homemade toy logging truck. There were six wheels of roughly carved wood, and three axles made of split bamboo. The cab and bed of the truck were a flattish chunk of wood that had been hacked and smoothed with a machete. Spanning the truck's rear body was an aluminum can that had been split open, flattened, reshaped to arc atop the wooden bed, and then fastened to the wood with bamboo slivers through the aluminum, like staples. And across the aluminum body was the familiar Dr Pepper logo. Serhio pulled the truck along with a length of rattan as it rolled across the dirt.

"Hey, Serhio," I hollered down from my porch. "That is a nice truck. Did you make it?"

Serhio looked up with a huge smile and obvious pride, "Yes."

It wasn't exactly the end I'd envisioned for my beloved Dr Pepper, but it seemed, after all, a fine fate.

☉◉☉

A few weeks ago I visited Janet in her assignment in Cavite, and thought her house felt a lot like America; there was even a television! And it was connected to electricity! And it received programs! So I was sitting on the sofa watching a Tagalog drama (like an overly-dramatic soap opera), and after a while, felt an odd creepy awareness at the back of my neck. I turned, and just about jumped out of my skin. There, behind me, outside the louvered windows, were about fifteen people, all standing silently, watching the TV over my shoulder. No, this definitely isn't America!

—Letter home, December 18, 1972

☉◉☉

It's a lazy Saturday morning in Madga, and I'm here in our little house beside the river. The kids came over and wanted to have school today, so we played ball for a while and then handed out pencils and crayons for free-time art. Right now there are a lot of people on our porch, drawing and coloring, and watching me write. Almost every evening lately, just before dark, we've handed out crayons and pencils to whoever comes over and it's fun for everyone—the mamas and daddies and kids, all drawing and coloring together.

—Letter home, April 29, 1972

It's dark in the mountains tonight. There's no moon, and we're picking up Louis Armstrong and Duke Ellington on the Voice of America radio station, the old kind of bluesy-jazzy music, drifting in and out of the static. It sounds like the soundtrack of a cartoon. I close my eyes and transport myself fifteen years back, sitting cross-legged on the living room floor, watching Saturday morning cartoons, while Mamaw is in the kitchen making me a tuna sandwich with homemade french fries cut thick and fried crisp the way I like them. And there's clear water in an old pancake syrup bottle, kept cold in the icebox just for me. Or, if I get really lucky, I'll split a bottle of Dr Pepper with my big brother. With that sweet, simple vision of home, I'll blow out the lantern, tuck in the mosquito net, and hope for good dreams tonight.

— Journal, September 18, 1972

Mad at it All

There was nothing for breakfast today except the last of the instant coffee. Lunch was better. They brought us some kamote, and we had canned fish with it. For supper, we had fresh rice, harvested today, and the rest of the canned fish, this time covered with a garlic white sauce that Janet made. Not that good, but not bad either. Fresh rice is certainly the best part.

We had no afternoon class. Only Penang and Darna showed up, so I read them a story and let them draw and look at magazines and we talked about the pictures. We ended early so I could go to the river and wash my hair. I don't think I have lice, because after I washed my hair the itching stopped. Phew! I have to be careful not to get my head too close to the kids when we're in class or when

I hug the Littles. Being this careful makes me feel kind of heartless, but I really don't want to get lice. Everyone seems to have them except Janet and me. It's a sort-of bonding experience for everyone else, I think. They sit on their porches, picking and popping nits from each other's heads. I've even seen a circle of six or seven people each picking from the person in front of them. It's sad that I need to be so concerned about physical contact with my kids.

— Journal, September 20, 1972

◉◉◉

I'm mad at it all. It's just too much. All of it.
The screaming, hollering, noisy kids outside our door, in our yard.
Never silent. Never peaceful.
I'm never alone.

Those obnoxious logging guys from Dongalyo logging camp
on the north side of the river,
trouping into Madga and sitting in my class
and mocking me while I'm trying to teach.
They think they're being cute and clever.
Just rude!

And the squawking chickens flying through the school room.
The rooster constantly screeching in my ear while I'm teaching.
Really, does the chicken have to be lashed
by his scrawny ankle to the porch rail where I happen to teach?
Does the creature have to roost atop my chalkboard?
Does the overly pampered, preening miscreant have to
screech and scream and squawk unceasingly, at absolutely nothing?

And the hunting dog howling and yapping
from inside Datu's house as I'm teaching.
I'm trying to say something here,
something that might be relevant

for a survivable future for these children.
But no, I just have to shut up
and wait out the ever-wailing, crowing, howling animals,
and that includes the wretched
toddling, crawling, crying, pooping babies.

The horse bites my toes through the floor or walls
while I teach. It hurts!
Or biting the little kids.
We'll be writing, and someone will suddenly cry out in pain.
What a nasty nag!

Our precious pencils and crayons,
constantly falling through the slats.
I send kids scrabbling in the dirt beneath the house.
Be quick, before the pig eats them!

Kids who won't learn. Resistant. Bored.
It's not working.
I'm not teaching right.
Failure.
It's like somebody says,
"Here's a pencil and twenty pages in a Coca-Cola composition book.
Now teach these kids to read and write.
And while you're at it, teach them about the world,
and make every lesson interesting, fun, and relevant to their lives,
while you yourself slowly starve."
It's impossible.

The evening class for adults
that only kids come to
for a double dose of school.
Another failure.

People asking to borrow my guitar
or asking for food

or our radio.
Wanting clothes.
Begging for soap.
Or salt.
People perching on our porch just to watch us.
Watch me do what? Breathe?

Kids eternally borrowing the balls
and rolling them off our nipa roof,
breaking the fronds,
and the rain blows in through the roof
dousing us in the night,
jolting me awake.

The pig scratching against the house posts
in the deepest part of the blackest night,
shaking me awake and
scaring the living daylights out of me.

Food—kamote, kamote, kamote
Please, no more kamote!
We boil it, fry it, sauté it,
put white sauce on it,
scramble it with canned fish or peanut butter.
And it's still sweet potato.
Every night I dream of food.
Real food. Texas food.
Gimme flesh from dead animals
—juicy, thick, roasted, charred, and gnawable.
I wanna rip it with my teeth and feel it
fall into the hollow vortex of my aching gut.

One more *samad* and I'll scream.
We're almost out of Band-Aids.
We used eighteen today!
The tiniest little cut or scratch comes to us.

How do I tell the little kids to go away,
that their measly wounds don't merit a Band-Aid.
Come back when you're *really* hurt.
Is that what I should say?

The flies! The ants! The tiny biting bugs!
How can there be so many!
My body their buffet.
Insidious, biting, crawling,
flying, fiendish creatures
of sneaking, sucking stealth.

Consider the mosquitoes—
The big ones are so slow and whiney
I can swat and smear
their blasted bodies across my arms, shoulders, legs, and face
leaving bloody trails,
like scarlet comets crashed against my skin.
But the little ones, they're secret and silent,
nearly invisible. And they pack a punch
with their blood-sucking needle noses.
Day and night, night and day, always,
these monstrous, malicious mosquitoes.

The unsupervised toddler drags
Datu's dog's newborn pups by the neck.
Strangling them.
It's so sad.
Even if I hate
that mangy, skinny, barking, hostile hunting dog,
the puppies don't deserve death by toddler.

Toting all our water from the river,
finding firewood and chopping it, it's all hard work,
and we still have all that water to boil,
twenty minutes per pot, two pots a day.

It's a lot of wood,
a lot of breath, bending over the stove
and blowing and blowing and blowing
to keep the fire going and going and going.

We're like a carnival grab bag.
Come, take what you want.
Sucker Americanas, right here.
Ask for food, the Americanas will give.
Ask for clothes, they've got plenty.
Need medicine? Soap? Salt? Come on over!

We're almost out of food.
Too many people "borrow" food.
As if they could replace it; they can't.
As if we had plenty; we don't.
As if I could say no; I won't.

People borrow my guitar, and take it across the river.
One time it came back wet.

It's hard to keep my temper in check.
Hard to muster a smile.
And, I'm constantly, *constantly* hungry.
especially after I eat kamote.

To get away, Janet and I walked across the river
and up to Eddy and Alang's house.
Ugh! An awful stench, their baby has diarrhea.
We talked to them in the yard.

Walking back home, Janet went ahead.
I stood in the middle of the river.
It's quiet there, in the chuckling water.
Cool. Calming. Washing away some anger.

How long can a person stand alone
knee-deep in the middle of the Madga
before her toes wrinkle and shrivel?
Before they think she's crazy?
Before she *is* crazy?
Before she tumbles face down
into the mesmerizing, shimmering water
and simply floats away downriver?

◉◉◉

I'm hating school. I need to do lesson plans and have zero enthusiasm. I should write a bunch of little stories on different reading levels and let the kids read their way through them, working up their skills; but I'm having a hard time creating one interesting story a day for my Bigs, then making all those carbon copies. It's so time-consuming. But they do love it, especially when I write about the kids themselves, naming them in the story, simple stuff like gathering wood or washing the kamote for supper—or the story about Serhio and the squirt gun that we brought him from Davao. Another story was about Janet's lost shorts that went for a three-week swim down the river. They really laughed at that one. But it's a lot of work. Really.

— Journal, September 18, 1972

◉◉◉

It's never been easy, from the get-go. I sometimes wonder, was it one enormous mistake to come to this stupid country?

— Journal, March 1971

◉◉◉

PART II

◉

Butuan City

1970-1971

First Shower

It's not just the rain. It feels like a big, heavy, gray, wooly blanket smothering everything, making it hard to breathe, as if each breath is taken underwater, as if there isn't enough oxygen in the atmosphere. Everything is wet, heavy, bleak. It's impossible to find an envelope that isn't pre-sealed by humidity, so I have to rip it open to get a letter inside to send. Or one where the glue hasn't been nibbled by cockroaches or some other creature, leaving the edge of the flap oddly serrated. Every new envelope looks ratty before it's even used. I wrote home, asking my folks to send me some plastic bags so I could protect some things from the dampness; there are no plastic bags to be found in this country. My family hasn't responded.

—Journal, March 8, 1971

◉◉◉

I started to pour myself a drink of water from a big pitcher that was in the refrigerator, and there was a giant mosquito larva languidly swimming around in it. Yuk! I showed it to Cyd, and she just took the larva out, and put the container back into the refrigerator to cool, and we will have this "refreshing" water with our evening meal!
—Letter home, May 8, 1971

◉◉◉

They'd told us in Peace Corps training during the summer of 1970 that it would take three months to adjust to living in-country, and that during those first weeks we would need courage, patience, and all the humor we could muster. At first, they'd said, you'll feel as if you aren't prepared at all. There will be times when you just have to laugh—if you can. But if you can tough out the early days, it will get better, they said. Really it will, they said. I couldn't image what they were talking about. Nothing seemed more interesting to me than the opportunity to teach in a foreign land. Then I arrived at my first permanent assignment in Butuan City.

It took me a long time even to figure out who lived in the home of my host family. There was a framed black-and-white family photo in the parlor with a dozen kid faces, all strikingly similar, set in various sizes. And there was a cast of other characters constantly in residence, extended family or house helpers or boarders or frequent visitors.

Yet in that home, at last I had a room to myself. It was a small room on the second floor, perhaps six by twelve feet, not that much bigger than a closet, barely enough space for a cot, a dresser, a little desk and chair, with a wooden-louvered window overlooking Gomez Street, where pedestrians strolled, kids played, and jeepneys putt-putted.

It was hot. I'd known heat—the July-August Texas heat that would literally cook the soles off your shoes if you left them on the driveway under the scorching sun. The kind of heat that prickled your bare skin like so many thermonuclear needles. The kind that drove you to drink gallons of Mother's sweet, cold, summer tea—half sugar and half caffeine.

But the Philippine heat was so wet and heavy, it felt like a buffalo on my chest and soggy feathers stuffed in my windpipe. This heat would sneak up and leave me delirious, needing to sit just to draw in the next lung full of gooey-thick oxygen. And this was just the first day in my new home in Butuan City. I needed a shower.

Ced was my caretaker. She was the family cook and nursemaid to the youngest child, and now she had me to look after too. "You must hurry," she was hissing at me. "Soon it will be dark."

"But we have lights, don't we?"

"No electric tonight. But yes, a lamp. But you must shower before dark."

"Why?"

"Before the winds blow from the Agusan. Or you will become sick."

"I'll get sick, because of the wind?" Was I understanding her correctly?

"Yes. River wind. Hurry."

I was trying not to appear confused about every little thing, so I took my towel and soaps and headed downstairs toward the cement stall next to the kitchen. It was a three-foot-square cubicle with a plywood door held shut with a hook and eye.

Problem One. Where to undress. Outside the stall was not reasonable, as I would be standing in the kitchen. Inside the stall was sort-of reasonable, but there was hardly room to get out of my clothes. I should have undressed before coming downstairs. I need a robe I can slip off inside the stall, then snake my hand outside to hang it on the nail on the doorframe.

Problem Two. No light inside the shower cubicle. Ced handed me a kerosene lamp. There was a small perch for it beside the spigot, and it took a minute for my eyes to adjust to the dim glow.

Yikes! Problem Three. The water was cold. There was no hot water, not even tepid. Just a single on off spigot with cold water rushing down, splashing on the floor and up onto my legs. I jumped back. No way would I wash my hair this evening. I'd barely even get my belly wet. Just strategic places. Lather, soap, and rinse with a wet hand, without direct contact with the icy flow.

Over my right shoulder I felt a tickle and looked up. My stomach lurched at Problem Four. Just above my head hung a saucer-sized black spider. Eight legs splayed on a glistening web, and the flickering lamplight giganticized him further, his multiple eyes glistening in the lamplight—glowering, glaring, clearly contemplating a pounce. I stared back, thinking I could keep him in place with mind-control.

It was a quick shower. I wrapped in my towel and exited, sprinting up the stairs to my room. Ced followed me, speaking half English-half Visayan. "Was your shower good?"

"Oh Ced. There is a big. A very big." What was the word for spider? I held my hands out, round, like a plate. "Black," I said, "animal."

"Oh yes," Ced nodded. "He lives in the shower. He eats mosquitoes. Do you have a spider in your bath in America?"

I thought about my bath back home—the sparkling clean tub, sinking to my ears in steamy hot water. The fuzzy, toe-tickling lime green bathmat that matched the tiles. Soft, clean, plush bath towels, warm from the dryer, smelling of scented fabric softener. The carpeted dressing room and vanity to the side, with double marble sinks and a full wall mirror. Indirect lighting. Climate control. Privacy. And emerging from the tub there, my skin would be as fragrant and warm and soft as a newborn's. "No, Ced. We don't have a spider."

"You need a spider. It is our friend."

Ah. A friend. We'd learned in Peace Corps training that it is often a challenge to find friends in a new culture. And here was one—a straddle-legged arachnid, a shower buddy.

In the weeks ahead, I learned that he never moved. A year later, when it came time for me to leave the Bila family house, he remained, hanging in the shower stall, being a helper to the entire household. And just before I moved away, during my last noontime cold shower there, I thanked him for his dependable work and said goodbye.

◉◉◉

The thing is, you have to bargain for everything you buy. You ask the price of a piece of material and they say 21 pesos. You say "Mahal kaayo" (very expensive) and offer 10 pesos. They say that would be a loss for them and that, because it is you, they'll give you a special price of 18 pesos. And you bargain back and forth until you arrive at some kind of consensus. It's like a game. Best if you do this haggling in the dialect because all the shop people smile when you use the language and just for trying, you get a better price.

Actually things are pretty cheap here, if you consider the equivalent in American dollars. But it's silly to consider the American equivalent because we only use pesos, and our Peace Corps allowance is just ₱450 a month, less than $80 American. It doesn't go very far when I'm paying rent, buying food, and trying to save for traveling in-country. New (wimpy!) sandals were ₱10, and junk sunglasses were ₱20. Deodorant is from 6 to 12 pesos, depending on the brand—there is no Ban Roll-On, only gunky cream Mum and Arid that you have to stick your fingers into, and I'm not convinced they work. Perfume is crazy expensive, an extravagant ₱40 or ₱50, so it's only natural aroma for me. I would just sweat perfume off anyhow. I'm constantly dripping wet. I've quit wearing the makeup I brought, because it slides and runs off in little rivers of mud.

—Letter home, October 9, 1970

◉◉◉

It's getting near dark, and there are no lights again tonight in this part of Butuan City. Rolling blackouts, they call it. The local generator has enough power for only part of the city, so we take turns. We get power once or twice a week. It comes and goes without any known schedule. Even the hospital has only occasional power. I guess we're lucky, because if we didn't have politicians and rich families living in this part of town, we probably wouldn't get electricity as often as we do.

— Journal, January 20, 1971

Disappointment Reefer

Mrs. Bila, my "mother," is very nice. She's a home economics teacher at the school where I'm teaching. Mr. Dadong Bila, my "father," is a politician and a banker. I have a feeling this isn't a typical family but a pretty affluent one. I wish I'd been assigned in a barrio, rather than in the heart of downtown Butuan City. I hope I'll like it, but this is not really what I wanted. I don't want to live in a little America.

The hardest adjustment is when the family talks in Visayan. The words fly past me, all jammed up, leaning into one another, slurring, and tangled. Even though I've tried so hard to learn, it's complete mush and I can hardly understand a single word of the cotton-picking language!
— *Journal, October 26, 1970*

⊙⊚⊙

I saw a weird thing yesterday. Mrs. Bila had a black smudge on her forehead, sort of an X, or a cross, like a big charcoal smear. I'm sure it has religious significance, but I don't know what. Maybe it goes along with all the Hail Marys I've been hearing around the house lately, hundreds of them. The whole family gathers every evening, everyone's on their knees at the family altar, and they pray together. I've seen this every day since I arrived, but usually the prayers aren't so long. These days the prayers are looooong. I wait for them to end so I can get back into my bedroom, as the family altar is right next to my bedroom door.

— Journal, February 24, 1971

⊙⊚⊙

I'd been at my Butuan City assignment less than a month and was "adjusting." On the surface, the life I was dropped into at the Bila home was remarkably similar to that of a Western family. The house was made of cement and wood. There was a telephone on the credenza in the dining room and an electric light on the ceiling of each room. The family slept in beds— although those were platforms covered with thin cotton mattresses. And they ate together at a dining room table using a fork and spoon in an almost normal manner. The kids went to school, the adults went to work, and the house helpers stayed home to take care of the chores and cleaning. Everyone spoke at least a little English, or a half-half mix of English and Visayan, although conversations among themselves were entirely in Visayan.

It took me a while to realize that beneath the surface, the culture is significantly different. The cement and wood house sat near a river teaming with filth and an occasional crocodile. There was a telephone in the house, but it was connected only to fourteen other telephones in the city so that the city leaders could talk among themselves—it was not connected to the outer world at all. And the household electricity was available only every third or fourth night on the city's rolling-blackout schedule.

At seven o'clock in the evening, just at dark, Ced rang the dinner bell. "Come and eat," she shouted up the stairwell in Visayan. I set aside my journal and stepped outside my tiny room shutting the door securely behind me. I'd chosen to sleep without *mosquitero* netting; the cocoon made me claustrophobic. So it was imperative I keep the door to my room closed after dusk, when the nightsuckers came out. If I left it open even a crack, they would feast on me all night long.

I went downstairs through the darkening stairwell toward the glow of the Coleman lantern that sat atop the credenza in the dining area, and I took my place in the seat of honor, next to Mr. Dadong Bila, the family patriarch, as he sat regally at the head of the long, mahogany table.

The Bila children drifted in, each approaching Mr. Bila who extended the back of his hand toward each in turn. The children, one by one, pressed the back of his palm to their foreheads, bowed slightly, and murmured, "Good evening, Papa."

He grunted acknowledgment, and each child took a place at the table. The older children sat closest to him, the younger ones farther away. Further still, at the opposite end of the table, sat the Bila boarders. It took me a few weeks to realize that by all rights, I too should be at the far end of the table, a mere boarder. But I was the Americana, the honored guest, and there was no question of changing my seating.

Mrs. Bila, sitting across from me, offered the dinner blessing. Head bowed, hands clasped tightly at her chest, she thanked God for the food and for the health and unity of the family. And much to my embarrassment, she thanked the lord for the Americana guest.

Then Ced brought in the platters of steaming food, and I took a fork and spoon from the glass of water that sat in the center of the table. The utensils soaked in water all day, keeping the bugs at bay, for most ants would not swim the moat to get to the utensils.

It wasn't that there was no food to eat in our house, for certainly there was always plenty of white rice. Bought by the fifty-pound bag, it sat in a huge metal rat-proof drum in the kitchen, waiting for Ced to take out the ten or so cupfuls that would be cooked in a big cast iron pot over a fire in the outside kitchen, and then served steaming at every meal.

And there were vegetables. I recognized the carrots, onions, and peas, but couldn't name the mealy textured veggies—perhaps squashes, diced thin and sautéed in palm oil, piled high atop a bed of noodles and served on a platter, to be eaten alongside the white rice.

And there was fish. Three or four trout-sized fish, fried crispy or steamed, white myopic eyeballs staring blindly, myriad tiny bones poking through slimy black fish skin, daring me to try to get any protein without getting poked in the roof of my mouth.

And there were bananas for dessert, always bananas, to be eaten with a fork with little sections speared off and placed delicately in the mouth, never to be eaten in teeth-to-fruit chomping bites. Polite girls never chomped into a banana I learned, although no one ever told me precisely why. It took me a while to understand the phallic connotations.

And at every meal there was water to quench our thirst, always drunk after, never with, a meal. Cool rainwater, caught off the tin roof of the house during rainy season and stored in big elevated metal tanks out back. The water and banana bites were delicious. The rest of the food I tried to like, but didn't.

I took to hiding bread and peanut butter in my room, and after dinner I'd make myself a sandwich. Until the day I received a health-hazard notice from Peace Corps Manila: it had recently come to the attention of the authorities that much of the peanut butter manufactured and marketed in the Philippines was contaminated with peanut mold, a known carcinogen. So I stopped eating peanut butter sandwiches.

One day as my stomach rumbled and smells of oily vegetables and frying fish rolled from the kitchen, I decided to take matters into my own hands. I would fix my own supper. I'd just march into the kitchen—the domain of Ced—and casually ask if I could cook something for myself. I would look in the refrigerator and find something to inspire a meal. A pickle sandwich? Fried potatoes and ketchup? Scrambled eggs? A glass of milk?

Ced was standing at the "indoor stove," a two-burner Coleman camp stove, frying fish in an enormous wok. "What you like?" she asked me, wondering what I was doing in the kitchen.

"I'd like to look ... in the refrigerator," I said. Ced nodded and turned back to her hot wok. I sidled up to the big white door and opened it. It was at that moment that reality shifted for me. I had approached the refrigerator thinking of my own world in Texas, but in that moment I knew with bone-deep certainty that I was in another world, a universe quite different from my own. For there where the pickles and relish should be, where the mustard and ketchup and sodas and milk and orange juice and the Tupperware of leftover fried chicken, tuna casserole, and Jello should reside, there lining the door and perching on the interior shelves there was—nothing. Blank. Cold air. No food. Not a crumb. Not a pickle. Not a shred of lettuce or a trace of egg. No salad dressing, salsa, or cheese. No Worcestershire, mayonnaise, or barbecue sauce. Just a cold hollow emptiness like the emptiness of my stomach and my spirit. Oh well, not quite empty. For there on the bottom shelf sat a pitcher of cooling rainwater. It would wash away the grease on my tongue after another dinner of white rice and eyeball fish.

I closed the refrigerator door and retreated from the kitchen to the privacy of my own room, my desk, my journal. I put my head on my desk, on top of my journal, and cried, small tears and jerking breaths until whispering and rustling behind me made me turn. The lamplight barely reached to that high corner of my room, but I could sense the shadows of small faces. The girls in the bedroom next door were on the top bunk bed, watching me from a space above the wall, below the ceiling.

I blew my nose, hummed along with the Jackson Five on my cassette recorder and pretended that I had just been resting for a moment. Not crying. Never crying. I picked up my pen and wrote about the cold showers and the bathroom toilet that didn't flush, the greasy fried food at every meal. And the empty refrigerator.

I knew I could never cry again, not even in the "privacy" of my own room.

◉◉◉

Before I forget—the first time I went to visit Nan at her host home on the other side of the Agusan, she wasn't home. So I wrote her a note and gave it to the cook at her house. Later, Nan told me that the cook told her that a "very, very old lady" had left a note. The cook was the first person I've found who didn't understand that I was a light-haired young person, not a gray-haired old person. Funny, and refreshing.

— Journal, November 14, 1970

◉◉◉

It was Berting's birthday, the Brooklyn boy volunteer who is assigned about half an hour out of town. A few of us volunteers gathered to take him to dinner in Butuan City, but the places were all closed, so he ended up with a half dozen mangoes and he went back home, declaring this to be the worst birthday he'd ever had. He called it "the most pathetic." The following weekend I tried to make him a cake. I used the cookbook from the Peace Corps book locker and I could get most of the ingredients, or reasonable substitutes. For an "oven," I had to use the little Coleman hot box on top of a gas burner, but the glass in front was broken, so some of the heat escaped. Well, the cake came out about a half-inch tall on one end, and four inches on the other. So of course, the icing kept rolling to the low end. And by the time the icing had rolled down such a steep hill, it had gained momentum and kept going, right onto the plate and beyond. I couldn't keep that icing on the cake! Well, the icing was supposed to be refrigerated before spreading, but there was no electricity that day, so no refrigeration either. We gave it to Berting anyhow, and he laughed. But you know what, it tasted great, and sweet in the American way. We all wanted a glass of cold milk to go with it, but then, we try not to think of impossible things like that.

— Letter home, July 9, 1971

I was eating a banana and inside was a worm, fat and wiggling. That, however, was not as revolting as finding a cigarette butt in my bottle of Coke. It came with the Coke; the cap was sealed and I'd just opened it. Entirely and utterly disgusting!

—Journal, December 10, 1970

◉◉◉

There was an old man selling oranges outside the school gate. He called me over and insisted on giving me several oranges. Well, I call them "oranges" although they were huge, green, and lumpy-skinned, as if covered by thick green warts. But, he opened one, had me try it, and it was the most delicious sweet fruit I ever tasted.

My teacher friend told me that his gift of the Chinese oranges was thanking me for American help during World War II. Apparently, American military saved his family. He remembers. And he passed his thanks on to me, a proxy who knows little of the war.

— Journal, November 1970

◉◉◉

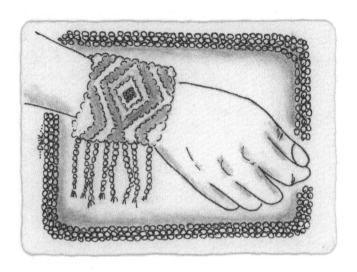

The Sultan

First was the guy with the flash camera who just couldn't stay out of my face. He must have taken a hundred photos of me. It must be my blonde hair, because he wasn't nearly so eager to get Kathy's picture. She's tall and skinny, shortish brownish hair, glasses, very funny, with great stories to tell because she's older and used to be a Catholic nun, but she is perhaps not as "photogenic" as I seem to be here. Way too many men wanted to dance with me. Slow dancing was awful, lots of pawing. And the men are so small, I felt like a giant. I could have crushed them. I felt like I was dancing with bamboo shoots. I hated it.

But one thing about the evening was interesting. William was wearing a beautiful bead bracelet, woven *beads, not strung. And I asked him about it. He said he got it from the mountain people—dirty, uneducated people of the interior, where the loggers are getting the big logs of Philippine mahogany that they harvest and float downriver to the ships waiting in Butuan Bay. My interest is sparked, who are these people?*

Then came the topper of the evening!

— *Journal November 14, 1970*

◎◎◎

I had a lot of alone time in Butuan City. After the school day ended, I'd try to beat the heat by resting before the evening meal. After dinner, I would retire to my room with a small kerosene lamp. The little lamp didn't give much light, and when I turned the wick up, it'd smoke, leaving trails of black soot under my nose or creating blobs of black gunk in my sneezy mucous. I set the lamp close to my book, to get the angle of the light right with enough glow to distinguish words on the page without turning it too high and creating smoke.

Evenings were the time I could listen to music from my cassette recorder, precious music cassettes from home: Crosby, Stills, Nash & Young. Peter, Paul and Mary. Three Dog Night. Carol King. The Carpenters. Cat Stevens. Joan Baez. Jackson Five. Phil Ochs. When my cassette batteries were dead, I'd play solitaire, or lie across my thin cotton mattress listening to puttering jeepneys and cricking night bugs. In the shadowy light of the kerosene lamp, I'd watch the geckos, small ninja house-lizards that scampered up the walls or across the ceiling in rapid spurts of energy. Their suction-cup feet held them upside down as they defied gravity and provided entertainment, snatching mosquitoes or mating. I'd put myself to sleep counting and cataloging their chirps. Later on, I figured out that those pinky-nail-sized eggs, the ones that I found in my pencil box, were theirs. I was careful not to disturb the eggs. I liked geckos.

Breaking the tedium of dark nights in my room came the invitation to go dancing with fellow volunteers Kathy, Joel, and Berting, along with their friends Max and William, sons of a local logging manager. They came to my house in the company's open-sided jeep and we six squeezed in, with me clambering in last so I hung on, only half my butt fully on the seat, while we took off, night wind in my face, over the bumps and dips of the unpaved road leading out of town. I loved it, hanging out of the jeep as the dark wind whipped my hair—the adventure, the moon, the company of peers.

The Sultan Hotel was a low-lying, cement-block building, bright with electric lights from a loud growling generator. William and Max approached the desk and each passed across money, and a handgun from holsters beneath their shirts.

"Really, they're wearing guns?" I whispered to Berting.

"Guess so. Just in case."

"In case of what?" I wanted to know. Berting shrugged.

Inside the crowded hall, the music blared. We made our way to a reserved table at the foot of the stage, passing among tables of men and beautiful, laughing young women. I hadn't been in the country long, but I knew that Filipina girls were generally shy. Demure. Very proper in their behavior. The two young women at the table beside us were sitting on the laps of their boyfriends and sipped from champagne glasses held high. It was refreshing to me to see young women so free. I admired them, beautifully dressed, perfect makeup and long shining black hair.

The boys were ordering San Miguel beer, while Kathy and I got Pepsi. In this country men were expected to drink beer, lots of it. Women weren't, and I was glad for that. William also ordered something special.

"You'll like it," he was saying. "Very delicious. A good accompaniment to beer and dancing. A delicacy here in the Philippines."

My imagination conjured a steaming dish of nachos, corn chips piled with melted cheese and refried beans, with ground beef and guacamole and sour cream. An enormous platter, enough to satiate the six of us. I was, as ever, hungry.

When it arrived, I smiled, not in satisfaction, but at my own unrealistic expectations. We were delivered two saucers of cashew nuts, twenty nuts per saucer. Yet William had been right, they were delicious— warm and sweet—and I got four or five before the saucers were empty.

I remembered how Daddy would bring home sacks of cashews, five pounds at a time, and we kids would gobble handfuls, devouring an entire bag in one evening.

That evening at the Sultan Hotel I first heard of the mountain people of Mindanao. William was wearing a beaded bracelet and I asked him about it. "From the people of the mountains," he told me. "They make these. And they trade them. I traded a hat for this one."

"Who are these people?" I asked.

"They are called Manobo. Mountain people. Dirty. Stupid. But their beads are nice, don't you think?" He took off his bracelet and let me examine it closely. It was about two inches wide, woven of red, black, and yellow tiny plastic beads in a chevron pattern and clasped with a waxed thread hooped over a small wooden bead. He told me to take the bracelet, it was mine. That too, was the Filipino way. If something is admired, it is given to the admirer. But I declined. "Oh no, it fits your arm nicely, and reminds you of your work in the mountains. But thanks for showing it to me." William had done more than show me his bracelet. That evening he sparked my curiosity.

A little while later, Kathy and I excused ourselves to the ladies' room. It was crowded with the Filipina girls. One girl was crying and being comforted by a friend. While I waited for a stall, I tried to listen. I heard only one recognizable word, "Hard," as in challenging or difficult. I'd seen a lot of restroom tears in my years among my sorority sisters, tears usually caused by boyfriend dramas. I watched the Filipinas watching me, the white Americana. Was that curiosity I saw in their look, or envy, or sadness? I smiled, said good evening in Visayan as I washed my hands and exited, envying them their easy, dark beauty.

When the floorshow started, I was ready for a diversion from the guy talk at my table, jobs, travel, trucks, motorcycles, and girls. She walked out onto the stage, in the spotlight, glowing gossamer silk and beads and feathers. I thought she would sing. She began by walking, strutting, one side of the stage to the other, her silk gown and feathers trailing, smiling, sure of each step, gazing straight into the crowd with a look that both enticed and dared.

She took off that flowing gown. And she took off another layer of silk. And another. And the music got louder. Somewhere along the way I realized what I was seeing. I'd heard of strippers, stories from college fraternity boys who had visited New Orleans. And I guessed what was coming. I looked to the exits, but the room was entirely clogged with shouting hooting men. To exit, I would have to push through them. I froze where I was and watched.

It took minutes for her to disrobe, down to panties and bare breasts — almost bare breasts, because at the end of each nipple was a tassel, which she, amazingly, got twirling in opposite directions. I'd never seen anything like this. How does she *do* that? And the shouting of the men got louder, until the final crescendo, when she reached down and snatched away her panties, at the exact moment the spotlight went black. The hooting and cheering went on, until the lights came back on and she was gone. I couldn't look at the boys at my table again, and soon after, we left for home.

The next day at my house, Ced asked me, "How did you like the Sultan Hotel?" I tried to think of a polite answer. "Interesting. Different from going dancing in my place."

"The Sultan, it is a place for the women," Ced said. I still didn't understand.

It was Thanksgiving weekend in America when a body was found beside the Agusan River. A dead girl, about twenty years old they said. There were rumors, whispers. "From the Sultan," they said. "She was no one." "Pregnant." "The will of God."

There were stories told of girls, bought or kidnapped, shuttled from one city to another, from one hotel to the next. They might not even know what city they were in, I was told. Girls who were dressed and groomed and kept. Kept for the men who paid. And then they were discarded.

I remembered the crying girl in the Sultan restroom. Had she been the one found beside the river? And I had done nothing to help. I began to understand, and was ashamed of my ignorance.

All seven of us Butuan-area volunteers, along with all the other Americans in the Butuan City area, were invited to the Stonesmith house for Thanksgiving dinner. Alan was so embarrassing and rude, putting his feet up on the furniture, and he kept laughing during the prayer. Well, the prayer was long and convoluted, but after all, these people are missionaries and their prayers are like that. Alan is Jewish and he was goofing on them. But his religion is no excuse. Nan is Jewish too, and so is Joel, and both of them were completely polite and funny and entertaining the whole evening. We sat at a long table, and I was across from the well-dressed Mormon boys, my age, but weird. They don't talk or laugh, make eye contact, or even smile much. It was like trying to make conversation with mud. But the food was great, especially the mashed potatoes. And when it came to dessert, Mrs. Stonesmith said she had wanted to make an apple pie, but there aren't any apples in the Philippines, so she made a rhubarb pie and spiced it like apple, and it was delicious. Mr. Stonesmith pulled out some photographs, showing us places they'd been. And he showed me a photo of a friend of theirs, another missionary, and had me guess his age. I couldn't tell. Older than me, but who knows. Thirty maybe, I said. Ha! he said. He's sixty! I think he meant to demonstrate how good the missionary life is, but to me it just proved that I can't tell a person's age by looking at a photo. But I think rude ole Alan blew it for us volunteers, and we won't be invited back to the Stonesmiths. I was really ashamed of his disrespect and it's too bad, because they are nice people and the food was great.

— Journal, November 25, 1970

◉◉◉

I went to the movies with some Filipino boys and girls, college students about my age. And it was mentioned by *another volunteer that I like to keep a journal. One of the Filipino boys asked if I'm a spy. No, I said, I like to write things down so I don't forget. He said he really thought I was a spy for the CIA. I had to ask what the CIA was; I'd never heard of it. Everyone laughed, and I began to realize there are some big gaps in my education. My parents never let me go to many movies, so how would I know about international government spies? My companions couldn't believe I've never even seen a James Bond movie. After that, I think that Filipino boy thought I was too stupidly naive to be a spy.*

—Journal, December 1970

Aloy's Nap

No one else has his or her own room in this house. The kids all bunk together, either in the girls' room or the boys' room, and Mr. and Mrs. Bila have their own bedroom. I haven't figured out yet where the helpers sleep. They're always working, so it seems like they don't sleep. The walls of my room are bare; I want to put up posters or something. Well actually, they're not quite bare. There's a crucifix on one wall. It's painful to look at. Jesus is all tortured and skinny, and the crucifix is a weird golden color that glows in the dark. Spooky. Not at all comforting. I feel it would be rude to take it down and put it in a drawer, so I just try not to look at it.

I mostly like the kids in my host family, but there are so many I'm only beginning to tell them apart. I can *identify Ruth, who's about 13 and might make a good language informant for me, someone I can practice my Visayan with. And GingGing is about 10, has short hair, and was introduced to me as a tomboy. She seems rough-and-tumble in this land of girly-girls. I like her. And I definitely know the little boy Aloy, about 4. He's thin, moves like a mosquito, and seems whiney and grumpy and spoiled. I avoid him completely.*

— Journal, October 29, 1970

◉◉◉

Aloy was a wild child. If Aloy didn't get his way, he'd scream, rave, and tantrum. When my host family took me to their peanut farm in the country, Aloy went wild, shouting and tearing about the field, ripping peanut plants from the ground and tossing them into the air or batting them into oblivion with a stick. This was somebody's crop, but no one said anything. That behavior was bad enough, but then he pulled down his shorts and urinated on Nonoy's leg. Nonoy was the teenage household helper who had come along to help take care of Aloy, and Nonoy seemed powerless to object. He merely stood in shocked silence while Aloy's urine ran down his ankle and pooled in the heel of his rubber slipper. Aloy danced about, unfazed and giggling.

One afternoon in Butuan City, Aloy was unusually cranky. "Come Aloy, we will sleep," Ced said to him at naptime.

"No!" Emphatic. Certain. No room for bargaining.

"Come Aloy, we will sing a song together," Ced said, scooping his wiry naked body in a hug and carrying him upstairs. Aloy shouted and kicked at the air, flailing against Ced.

From my own room, with the door open to catch a hint of the noon breeze, I could see what happened next. Ced lay beside Aloy on the narrow cot, talking gently to him in soothing tones, tickling his brown bare belly and rubbing his body with her fingers.

Aloy continued to whine and wail and kick.

Then Ced bent over Aloy and put her mouth over his penis with a playful smacking sound. That got Aloy's attention and he became silent.

Again she bent to him and playfully sucked his penis, pulling it long with her lips, ticking the tip with her tongue. Aloy giggled and relaxed.

Again and again they played this game. His mood softened. Finally, he slept.

I stopped writing at my desk and sat, silently, aghast at what I had witnessed. My own cultural taboos had been violated. Should I report Ced to Aloy's mother? Should I lecture Ced on child psychology and emotional development? Should I speak out to someone to try to save this child from sexual abuse?

I indignantly wrote the event in my journal and then had a long think. Could it possibly be that my own instincts were culturally implanted and not universal? Was it possible that my own values, in this time, in this place, were misplaced? Could it be that the wall of my own cultural biases was cracking and the discomfort I was feeling came from a new way of seeing the world?

That evening I lay in the dark, disturbed and still pondering what I should do about what I'd seen. Nothing, I decided. I hadn't raised twelve kids. After all, with Ced's perhaps unconventional, but apparently pleasant coaxing that afternoon, Aloy did finally take his nap.

I wouldn't argue with success.

◉◉◉

I came to this country thinking I would find universal values, attitudes, and ideals that all people would hold in common across cultural chasms.

I expected logic to be universal. Wrong!

Valuing a work ethic is certainly not a universal value.

Personal achievement and working toward advancement isn't a universal value.

Trying to understand another point of view isn't a universal value.

I think that the only certain universal value I've found so far is mother love. All mothers love their children—although the way that love is expressed is certainly different among cultures.

Resistance to change, well, that one might also be universal.

And perhaps universal too is the need for some daily drama in life, although the scale of need here is way past any norm that I've ever seen. People here seem very content to believe whatever cockamamie hogwash they are told. I think they need television and real evening news reports—an Asian-style Huntley-Brinkley Report of actual, factual news might work—to take their minds off their constant concoctions of outlandish gossip!

—Journal, February 24, 1971

◉◉◉

I'm sending you these three magazine-style songbooks that would be illegal to print in America because of copyright laws. But the laws don't apply here, so these books can be published with dozens of popular American song lyrics and chord arrangements. Sometimes the songs are given in oddball keys with difficult chords. Try transposing. Just remember to keep the chords relative, parallel to each other, from the old key to the new key. It's logical, really.

And keep playing around with fingerings. You'll learn a lot if you try out the Filipino fingerings that are in the chord charts in the book. Use both American standard fingerings, and Filipino fingerings, and find what's easier for you. Finally, be aware of the "green" stuff in the book. Filipinos are fantastically fond of "dirty" jokes and there are a lot of shady lyrics in the songs in these books. However, also realize that what is considered to be "dirty" in American culture is not necessarily smutty in this culture. Smut is a relative value in a culture. If there *is one thing I've learned over here, it's that American culture is really sensitive and judgmental about things having a sexual component, while other cultures just accept these things as part of life and move on.*

— Letter to my brother, June 7, 1973

⊙⊙⊙

Before I left America, I thought that every country in the world had its own everything. Its own published books and magazines in its own languages. Its own manufactured goods, from breakfast cereal to photographic film to steam engines. I had no idea that so much of the world leans on the English language and looks to America for goods. And actually, most "things" just don't exist in many places, at least many goods don't exist here in Butuan City. Boxed breakfast cereal and a carton of homogenized milk—HA! (And anyhow, rats would rip open the boxes, and without continuous electricity and refrigeration, the milk would sour. The support system for many goods simply doesn't exist.)

—Letter home, January 22, 1971

⊙⊙⊙

When I tell people I'm from Texas, they assume I know about raising fighting chickens. I didn't know Texas was famous for fighting chickens. Famous for horses, cowboys, cattle and oil, yes—but for fighting chickens? I went to a cockfight here once, found it crowded, confusing and cruel. Too much bleeding, squawking and shouting, and far too many flying feathers. They put little swords on the heels of the chickens so the fight is usually fatal to the loser. I don't want to go again.

—Journal, July 1972

Butuan Mail Day

Another day. Another 75¢ of earned income.

The mail situation is aggravating. I got two letters since Christmas, from friends, but none from my family since way before Thanksgiving. I've written everybody in my address book and everyone owes me a letter. And nothing is coming through. Or worse, no one is writing.

—Journal, February 2, 1971

☉☉☉

MEMO
To: Country Director Philippines
From: Peace Corps/Washington
Subject: Parent Inquiries from Mindanao

Date: December 11, 1970

We have been receiving an excessive number of phone calls regarding PCVs in the Mindanao area who have written home and told their parents that the mail is not getting through. The parents mention depression on the part of the Volunteers as well as their own frustration that the Volunteers might think the families are not writing.

We would suggest that the recommendation be made to Mindanao Volunteers to try and not alarm their parents if at all possible, that mail can be slow to arrive but will be received in due time. We would also recommend the possibility of addressing Volunteers care of the American Embassy and pouching the letters to the Mindanao regional Peace Corps offices. Most of the complaints are coming from the parents of new Volunteers and possibly things will improve. However, this is a serious problem at the current time.

We only ask that both Mindanao Regional Reps look into the problem that they are no doubt aware of. Any advice that you can give us here in Washington would be appreciated. Thanks greatly.

— Mimeographed memo tucked in my Journal

⊙⊙⊙

I was the mail collector for the seven Butuan City area volunteers, since I could most easily access the city's central post office, a fifteen-minute walk from my house. It was, however, not an easy walk. It was, in fact, a gauntlet of torture.

"Wow, sex-eeee" the catcalls came. "Hey ba-beee, you like banana?" I kept my head down, walked fast past the shops and market and wondered, yet again, what I was doing to provoke such rude and hurtful shouts. I dressed modestly, my skirts much longer than was fashionable. I wore no makeup, pulled my hair back in an austere clump at my neck.

And I certainly wasn't pretty. In fact, I was getting uglier. Zits that came from deep in my skin and stayed as hard cysts for weeks. And I was fat—and getting fatter.

Despite the shouts of rude men, the lure of receiving mail from home drew me to the downtown Butuan City post office twice a week, after each time the plane from Manila landed.

The first time I went to the Butuan City post office, I learned about Philippine crowds. There were no lines, only pushing at the window. I too had to push my way in. People were close, too close, touching, jostling. When I finally got to the window, the clerk sold me stamps and sent me around back to pick up first-class postage.

I took my 75-centavos stamps and backed out of the crowd. The stamps had the image of President Ferdinand and First Lady Imelda Marcos working in the rice fields, an image that made us volunteers guffaw at its absurdity—as if Ferdinand and Imelda would get near a muddy rice field! At first I had interpreted the image on the stamps as satirical humor disguised as patriotism, but then decided that I was giving too much credit to the Marcos pundits. The President and First Lady were, after all, generally popular across the country. Nonetheless, the health hazard presented by the postage stamps of the Philippines were no laughing matter. Never lick a stamp, we'd been cautioned in training. There have been roaches, or worse, crawling on them. The Butuan City post office kept a Pepsi bottle filled with water on a side shelf in the lobby. I could see the filth inside the bottle. Murky, nearly black, dense scummy water, certainly teeming with god-only-knows-what vermin. How should I adhere the stamp to the envelope—lick the filthy back of the stamp or use the scummy water? Either option was a health hazard. Realizing I would only receive mail if I sent mail, I touched a finger to the scum-water and wet the back of the stamp and affixed it to my envelope—and made a mental note not to touch my finger to my face until I could wash my hands, with soap.

I learned to walk around the back of the post office, past piles of stacked, stuffed gray mailbags piled nearly to the ceiling and jumbled like the talus slopes of extinct volcanoes. Across the low piles, I'd see sleeping postal workers sprawled as they dozed with empty mail bags across their faces. I wondered about the mail in those sloping mountains of stuffed pillowing bags. Is this where all my letters from home were?

The first-class mail room was a cubicle on the side of the central post office. It had a lockable door. I knocked. And the game began.

"Ah, our Volunteer Peace Corpse." He always said it like that, as if I were voluntarily dead and peacefully laid to rest. "Come in, come in. How are you today? Join me, I was just about to have snacks." Mr. First Class reminded me of a toad, round and slimy and uncomfortably eager.

"Thank you, no. I must hurry. Any mail for Peace Corps?"

"Peace Corpse, let me see. Won't you sit down?"

I stood. "Just mail, please. I must hurry."

He was shuffling languidly through cubbyholes of letters and stacks of tumbling mail on his desk. "Tell me, do you like the food of the Philippines."

It was one of his standard questions. "Some."

"Tell me, have you tried the Philippine fried banana?" Here it was, the trick question. Any reference to a banana was phallic, I knew that. I knew that he knew that. He knew that I knew.

'Sometimes." Why couldn't I think of quick clever answers that would set him back. Why am I so dumb?

"And swimming, do you enjoy our Philippine beaches?"

"Sometimes."

"Ah, I am inviting you for night swimming. When the water is cool and refreshing. Would you like that, we could go night swimming together. I can bring the Philippine specialty for you to try, fried banana. Yes?" Night swimming, the most illicit of activities for nice girls. Bananas, phallic. I was naive, but not stupid. His hand rested on a packet of mail. Beside his thumb I could see a US postage stamp. Would he give it to me? What if I rudely told him no, what if I said what I was really thinking? I knew what would happen. Sorry, no mail today, he would say, and we'd have to play the whole game over again next time.

"Thank you for your invitation, but no. I do not enjoy the ocean at night." I hated myself for being so syrupy. I hated this man. I hated this game.

"Ah yes, then perhaps next time, we can go to the beach some other time," he said. "You would accompany me some time, yes?"

"Perhaps," I said. Absolutely never—way past the day when hell freezes over, as my grandmother would say. I thought it but didn't say it, and he handed me the bundle of letters. Did I imagine it, or did he hold onto the packet a bit too long, as if a lingering touch to the letters were a touch to my hand. The letter on top was addressed to Bob Johnson. Bob, known to us as Berting, was assigned a half-hour out of the city and would come to town over the weekend to pick up his mail.

I had the precious letters and I hurried away. Back through the gauntlet of catcalls, "*saging ni Pasing, o-o-o*" came the chant, a sing-song call, loosely translatable as Pasing's banana/penis, followed by howls of laughter. "A-mer-i-can-wo-man" sang another. "Hey eggs!" "Wow! Sex-eee!" "Bay-bee."

I tried to block it, chalk it up to cultural differences, an entire society of men who never matured past seventh-grade, body-parts humor. But still, it hurt. It hurt even more when I realized that among that bundled packet of letters for Butuan Peace Corps Volunteers, there were, once again, none for me.

◎◎◎

So I was over at Nan's place, delivering her mail. She got two letters from her mom this week. She read them out loud to me, because I asked her to, because I wanted to pretend they were from my mother. This is weird and sick, I know it. I can't help it. Why don't they write to me?
—Journal, February 7, 1972

◎◎◎

I thought she was kidding me with the talk about Dobi—as in Dobie Gillis, the American TV show. "No," she said, "Dobi Beams, the American movie star." My teacher friend could only barely whisper the scandalous story to me, but I think secretly she found it funny, in a pathetic sort of way. It seems that President Ferdinand Marcos had a scorching secret love affair with Dobi and there were tape recordings under their bed. Seems that somehow those recordings made it out to the public. Lurid pillow talk. And there was Ferdinand crooning Ilocano love songs to his lady, "like a squawking lovesick bird." Imelda, my friend told me, was livid, probably not so much because her husband had the affair (Imelda, after all, understands the norms of this macho-male culture), but more likely her anger was at having the affair made so public in such detail."

Ah, another moment in Philippines' politics.

Later I learned her name is Dovie Beams. It's that B-for-V sound thing again, confusing me, when all my information comes from stories spoken in heavily accented English-Visayan-mix-mix talk.

—Journal, March 20, 1972

⊙⊙⊙

So I occasionally see Visayan as a written language, maybe in a local comic book, but the spellings are crazy. During language training days, I learned to read Cebuano-Visayan (a little, because 98% of our language lessons were oral), but when I see these printed items, the spellings seem very different. I can usually sound it out, because the words are phonetically written, but the inconsistencies slow me down. Perhaps because the spoken language varies too—the slurring and shortcuts and slang—and even the grammar sometimes—vary area to area. It seems the written language isn't consistent, and neither is the spoken.

—Journal, January 1972

⊙⊙⊙

Noli

Belen, the lavandera in our house, came to me this morning, very upset, crying. She showed me my best (only!) pair of good pants, the dark blue polyester ones that you and I bought at Sears just before I left. Well, Belen had never seen polyester, so after washing them in the big outdoor cement tub area behind the house, she had let them dry on the line, then tried to iron them with a very hot charcoal-burning flatiron. My pants melted. There is a big melted-plastic imprint of the iron on the right leg.

— Letter home, November 10, 1970

☉☉☉

There is some sort of relative who comes around the house and he wears eye shadow! Not just a hint of color but blasting turquoise above his eyes. This seems unusual. Yet no one seems to notice much, or care.

— Journal, November 14, 1970

◎◎◎

Baby Cesar was a cousin to the many kids in the Bila household and a frequent visitor to my host family in Butuan City. A babe in arms, not yet walking on his own, he was incredibly cute—round and chubby with a loud cackling laugh. On those days when he wore a diaper, I'd put him on my hip and dance around the living room, just to hear him laugh.

When we stopped dancing and I turned my face toward him to ask if he was having fun or wanted more dancing, Cesar would point his baby finger and poke at my eye. I knew he had noticed, and everyone enthusiastically supported his cleverness. He had spotted my blue eyes: weird, different, American. I had to turn my head or catch his finger as the small hand jerked straight for my face. If I hadn't protected myself, it seemed the little guy might have dug my eyeball from its socket to get a closer examination of the blue-color phenomena. "Blue eyes, blue eyes," someone would invariably chant, playfully encouraging the baby to poke and point.

"Blue eyes," Little Cesar would mimic, and thus I had my nickname.

Cesar's caretaker was a teenager, and an unusual young man. The first time I met him he was wearing bright turquoise eye shadow, and I thought he must have just come from a theatrical production and hadn't had a chance to wash off the stage makeup. Next time I saw him, he wore bright eye shadow again, with dramatic eyelashes and a feather boa that he flipped and fanned and twirled as he spoke.

Noli was conscientious as caretaker of baby Cesar, holding the baby's hand as he learned to walk, feeding him baby-sized bits of this and that throughout the day, talking to him with stories and questions and smiles and tickles. Cesar loved Noli, and it was clear the feeling was mutual. It was slow to dawn on me that he was a young man becoming openly what was called in Visayan "*bayut,*" a male identifying as female.

Through the months, I watched Cesar grow and Noli slowly strengthen her gender identification. Noli's journey was new to me—the girl from Texas where hints of non-traditional sexual identity were opposed, hidden, denied, demeaned, shamed, and squashed.

It wasn't that Noli was beginning to look more and more female that impressed me most, but it was the elegance and beauty of what she was becoming. Noli wore well-tailored clothes, immaculately pressed, and somehow managed to remain wrinkle free even in this land of sweat and steam. And most astounding to me was the open acceptance of the family for Noli's nonconforming gender-identity expression. In Visayan, there are no linguistic gender-specific pronouns, so there was no defining moment when conversation about Noli shifted from male to female. But a shift did happen, slowly in my own English-thinking mind, and I unconsciously began thinking of Noli using pronouns "she" and "her." She was Noli, Cesar's keeper, the teller of funny stories, the epitome of feminine flair and mannerisms.

By the time I left the Bila household, Noli's transition was pretty much complete. There were no visible traces of the teenage boy. She looked entirely female, and elegantly so, dressing in expensive shoes and flowing dresses, wearing her hair long and styled, her nails shaped and polished. And in the end, I envied her grace, beauty, and humor—and her devotion to toddling Baby Cesar.

◉◉◉

Some things around me seem so normal, so similar to home, yet so many other things are entirely different. How can Noli be both boy and girl at the same time? He was a boy, now is a girl, the way he talks, the things that concern him, the circle of female friends around him. He is female, really, and everybody is fine with it. I don't get it, how can such a transition be so easy?

There's a lot, under the surface, I don't understand.

— Journal, summer 1971

◉◉◉

A Nation of Children

I was at the Butuan City cemetery for All Souls Day, a community time for cleaning up the cemetery and socializing, and a beautiful Filipina told me her story. She was there to care for the elaborate grave of her husband who was murdered a year ago. He was a politician, running for office, gunned down in his driveway when he stepped outside their home. No one was ever caught for the murder. His widow just shrugged with sadness. It was a glimpse into the world of those affected by the unsavory politics that seem to fuel this nation. I was amazed at her acceptance of injustice, and at how beautiful she was.

— November 1, 1970

People here tolerate a phenomenal level of injustice. Corrupt public officials rifle public treasuries. For enough money, anyone can buy themselves a public office, or get a driver's license (I've heard it's a ₱10 bribe) or a Certified Public Accountant Certificate (for a whopping ₱5,000 bribe). When a crime is committed, police look the other way, depending on who committed the crime and whether a bribe has been given. Votes are bought on streets, even outside the polling places on election day (they say a vote can be bought for a ganta *of rice).*

And it's all accepted as "the will of God." It makes me crazy. I could scream at all the wrongheaded insanities of the culture, but in the end, if I speak up, I'm the one looking like a nutcase. It's exhausting. To save myself, I have to relax. Merely observe the injustices. Write in my journal about them. I seriously doubt my ability to influence any change in the core corruptions of this culture.

— Journal, March 5, 1971

◉◉◉

In the early 1970s, the cities of Mindanao were awash in children. They were everywhere, spilling from houses, sleeping in storefronts, begging on the streets, peddling rice cakes or fried bananas, and pouring from schools like red ants in the West Texas sands.

Butuan Central Elementary ran two sets of classes—the first from seven in the morning until noon. Then the teachers and students changed and second shift ran until five in the afternoon. Classrooms held forty, fifty, or even sixty children at a time, three or sometimes four students squeezed onto a bench beside a flat-top wooden desk.

I was a teacher trainer, coaching teachers in efficient methods for teaching English as a second language. I had hardly any direct contact with students, except when I'd go into a classroom to demonstrate a technique. Repetition drills. Substitution drills. Games. Stories. And although I came to know the individual teachers, the students in my school merged into a blur—there were simply too many of them, and in my early days, they all looked alike to me. They wore the same school uniforms—buttoned white shirts and khaki shorts for boys, white shirts and pleated blue skirts for the girls. Boys had similar chopped haircuts, and girls generally wore their hair long and tied back in a ponytail. And around me, boys and girls both had similar shy demeanors.

But it was the kids who didn't go to school who touched my heart most deeply. These were the street kids whose families couldn't afford books or uniforms. These kids slept in alleys or doorways, begged on street corners, wore too-small clothes, and looked as though they never bathed. Street kids were everywhere and pulled at my conscience.

I was attending a training conference for volunteers in the sprawling and sweltering city of Cebu when I decided to live the change. I would give money to a beggar, bestow a gift on a single child, make a difference in one small life. I was walking across the central plaza near a huge, pink Catholic church when a small boy approached me, palm out. "Please, mum," he implored. I'd heard the plea hundreds of times, but I usually just gave out a smile and a greeting in the dialect. But this day was different. This was the day I would make a difference.

I reached in my bag to retrieve 50 centavos, two shiny coins—enough for three jeepney rides, a few cups of uncooked rice, or a bundle of vegetables from the market. Before I had the money out, there were more hands upturned in my direction—two, three, four dirty faces, thin nearly naked, boney kids. I decided to give each only 25 centavos and share the wealth. Sweaty hands closed eagerly around the coins and I turned to go. But I was stopped abruptly by more children, a dozen more, and as I tried to walk away, still more appeared, as if sprouting from the shrubs in the plaza.

"Please, mum," they all shouted, pushing to get near me, eager for coins. I gave a few more coins away but realized that there would be no end. The kids kept coming, pushing at me, little bodies all straining to be near the Americana, to receive coins from my hand.

I looked up, wondering where to go, seeking an escape route. In less than a minute there were fifty kids, and a few seconds later it seemed like a hundred—big ones, small ones, a sea of bobbing black heads. They swarmed around me, some just wanting to touch my dress or rub my arm, and a brave few reached up to touch my hair. I was trying to escape. "I'm going now," I kept saying in the Visayan way, trying to edge my way out of the crowd. But like a giant amoeba, the protoplasmic blob of children followed my nucleus and together we oozed across the plaza. I was sweating, suddenly in the middle of something close to chaos.

It was a fellow volunteer who rescued me. Berting, a six-foot giant among the Lilliputians, came wading through the sea of children on his way to the same conference. "Jesus, what are you giving away money or something?" he asked, taking my arm and pulling me through the sea.

"Uh, well, yeah, I was just trying to help," I offered.

"Where have you been," he scolded, "on the moon? You'll start a riot." Berting was a Brooklyn boy, and he knew the ways of the world. He pulled me toward the steps of the church, and we sat on a bench looking out over the now dispersing mass of children.

"Where'd they all come from?" I asked, incredulously. "I thought there were just one or two—and then, there were so many so fast."

Berting shook his shaggy brown head at me. "You can't just give away money like that. You'll have every street kid in the city on you. Jesus, girl!"

"What am I supposed to do? Never give to beggars? They look so needy," I said.

"Naw. But you gotta be smarter. Look, what I do works pretty well."

"What's that?" I asked, wiping my face with a handkerchief. I was feeling calmer, but very thirsty.

"On days when I feel benevolent, I buy a bunch of bananas, a big bunch, and when a kid approaches me, I just give him a banana. That way, I figure the kid at least gets something to eat that day, and when the bunch is all gone, all the other kids can see it, and that's it. I just keep walking. Kids seem to like it pretty well, and it works. No sweat."

I liked Berting's idea, but tried it only once. I ended up with a smear of banana goosh on the side of my teacher's uniform. I reverted to acknowledging the street kids with a big smile, a wave, and a greeting shouted in Visayan. It wasn't much. It didn't fill any bellies.

My calluses grew thick. One evening I was having dinner with other volunteers at the home of my regional rep when a volunteer told me that he'd heard that in the old days each new building project—a building, a road, a bridge—was christened with the blood of a newly slain child.

"Where'd you hear that? Don't believe it!" someone hooted at him. I too doubted the truth of it, but my own bias popped out of my mouth.

"Great idea!" I retorted. "There are too many kids and not enough bridges in this country anyhow." The laughter of the moment eased the pain of what was really an ache. I never quite got over all those kids, the hundreds of children's faces desperate, yet hopeful, and their wide brown eyes that looked to me. I internalized the guilt, finding that I couldn't really change a thing.

◉◉◉

Yesterday, another example of how peculiar things can be. I got a note from Alan and Nan to meet with them and a Filipina woman at a Butuan City restaurant, because the Filipina needed help with something important. So I went and this older lady started talking about her "big problem" that only an American could help with. Turns out, she wanted us to call in the American Marines to liberate a plot of land that she said was hers. She said the squatters wouldn't move, so we were supposed to help her by calling the Marines. She said she knew the Marines would come, because during the War (that would be World War II) she had dated a US Marine. We tried to tell her we were merely teachers, with no military influence. And Alan went on to try to explain that the US Marines weren't likely to intervene to get her land back, but his explanation went right over her head, and she kept insisting that we call the Marines. I wonder who she thinks we are? We drank tea, paid the tab, and left. Politely, I hope.

— Journal, November 14, 1970

◉◉◉

I hate how everyone keeps telling me how wonderfully fat I am. This, to me, is such an insult, because I try to lose weight, but with my ravenous hunger and the heavy, fatty, greasy food (which is the only food available!), I am expanding. But folks see my expanding girth with pleasure and pride — as a sign of good health, an indication that I am being well cared for in my household. Intellectually, I can understand their comments from their cultural point of view, but still, it hurts both literally and figuratirely as someone pinches my arm and loudly reports, "Oh my dear, you are so FAT!"

⦿⦿⦿

I still want to do something positive in this country, but my energies are waning. I might soon throw my hands up in frustration and go home for a salad, a bed, a bath in hot water. But, there's a fiesta at school this afternoon, so I'll get the little smile out and paste it on my face so everyone can see the smiling, blonde Americana. And I'll make it through another evening being on display.

Do other volunteers feel like I do? Am I the only one? Is this the Peace Corps experience that will, in the long run, prove so valuable and worthwhile? Or is this just me, being stupid, gullible, and entirely exhausted.

I'm at the bottom of the well, can't see any way up and out.

—Journal, March 27, 1971

⦿⦿⦿

The Chief of Police

The food situation in my home leaves a lot to be desired. I can't understand how I could be gaining weight. I've yet to feel full at any meal. After each meal, I'd still like a sandwich or something. And I feel guilty about eating too much meat, because the others eat so little of it. They eat piles of rice with a little puddle of vegetables and minuscule slivers of meat in a sauce. I find the vegetables nauseating—greasy and mealy. The rice is fattening nothingness to me. But ah, the bananas—I eat one at each meal, sometimes two. It's embarrassing to eat so many bananas.

I still don't know how much rent I'll be paying. I've asked, and merely get a vague answer. I think they're waiting to see how much I eat. I've been here four weeks.

I've figured out that this is sort of two big houses joined together. The family lives on one side; that's the side I live on too. The other side is filled with boarders. The boarders have meals with the family, which is why I've been so confused about how many people are here and how they come and go. The boarders are all men.

I'm craving popcorn. I was hoping for some at the movie theater, but it's not even remotely available in movie houses here. All you get is the smell of urine and sweat. And lots of rats, rats that will bite your toes if you keep your feet on the floor so you have to prop your feet up on the balcony rail, or the chair in front. And certainly, don't put your purse down on the floor. You might put it in a puddle of pee. But I love the movies—the stories, the escape.

I was wondering what would happen if I brought some popcorn back to the house to pop. But it's a moot point. There's no popcorn in Butuan City.

—Journal, November 25, 1970

⊙⊙⊙

I had dinner every night with the Butuan City Chief of Police. He was one of the boarders who ate at the long family table at the Bila home. As Ced stood behind Mrs. Bila swooshing strips of newspaper pinned to the end of a bamboo stick, fanning away flies from the piles of steaming rice and vegetables, the Chief dominated our conversation.

He was big for Filipino man—solid, round, and beefy, like a well-fed steer. And he was loud, his voice rising in commanding tones when he asked for the platter of vegetables. He was a man accustomed to getting his way.

I stayed clear of him and expressed no particular opinions one way or another, until one night at dinner the discussion turned to World War II.

"And your family," someone asked me, "were they in the War?"

"Yes, my father was a training pilot. He taught other pilots how to fly B-52 bombers."

"Did he serve here in the Philippines?"

"No. He never left the United States. He stayed there, training other pilots." I didn't tell them that because of his German family name, he hadn't been allowed to serve overseas, although he'd wanted to.

"Have you heard the stories of the War here?"

"I know Japanese soldiers came here."

That's when the Chief of Police took over: "They are angry, brutal people, the Japanese," he boomed. "They have no conscience. No conscience at all! When I was a boy, I saw what they did. The came to my village in Zamboanga. They took all the men of the village. All of them! My father also. They put them in the center of the plaza and killed them all. I saw it. They cut off my father's head. As if he were nothing but a piece of ripe fruit. I will never forget!"

His words ricocheted like bullets. "And if I ever see a Japanese person, I will kill him. I will take my sword and hack his head until it opens. I won't hesitate. These people deserve to die."

I swallowed. "But that was wartime," I suggested. "Surely, now, it was so many years ago…" In my own mind, World War II was history, a time before my birth, an era that lived only in stories. And I knew there were Japanese volunteers in the Philippines, young people who were helping in peacetime projects, just as we US Peace Corps Volunteers were. Young Japanese people, like me, born after the war, who had no personal memories of the war. What if things were only slightly different, what if I had been born in Japan, what if I were from the enemy nation? Would the Chief of Police have chopped off my head, even though I'd had nothing to do with his father's death?

"*Any* Japanese," he boomed. "I will kill! I will *not* hesitate!"

I got the picture. This man carried hatred. Justified, perhaps. But for a public official, a man in a position of authority sworn to uphold law and order in the city, his vehemence seemed over-the-top.

I quietly pondered the split between this man's political position and his personal politics, and later I had another glimpse into his character.

One evening, a young Filipina joined us at the dinner table. The Chief of Police introduced her to us as his wife. She was beautiful in a round and soft way, but she looked frightened. I thought she might be scared of me, the Americana. I tried to calm her fear by talking to her.

"Oh, you live in Zamboanga City. It's one of my favorite places. I traveled there last year to a Peace Corps conference in Zamboanga City. The market in Zamboanga is wonderful; so much beautiful black coral jewelry."

She looked at me as if she'd never heard of Zamboanga City. But I knew that was where the Chief of Police's family lived. He had often spoken of how lonely he was for his wife. The young Filipina ducked her head and mumbled "Yes, beautiful," and the Chief quickly changed the subject.

She stayed with us about a week, and hardly said a word. Then she was gone, as quickly as she had come.

"What happened to her?" I asked Ced. "Did she go back to Zamboanga?"

We were in the kitchen, just Ced and me. Ced glanced around, then whispered to me. "She went back to the Sultan Hotel."

"Huh?" I asked. I now knew that the Sultan Hotel was the local din of iniquity, a nightclub of gambling and prostitution.

"She is not his wife," Ced whispered. "She is a comfort girl. The Chief of Police just borrowed her."

"Oh," I whispered. Was I the only dense one around here? Did everyone know this but me? Probably. That's why everyone else was so quiet with her. Dumb old me, not catching on, trying to get her to talk about her "hometown" of Zamboanga.

Then came the night of the shootings. About 3 a.m. I was awakened by gunshots and shouting below my window. In the room next door, I heard Ced hissing to the kids to get under their beds. I heard the scrape and creaking of beds, and Aloy whimpering in fear.

But me, I raced to the window to look from my second floor vantage point. There was enough moonlight for me to make out a figure on the street below, a figure holding something shining, something the size of a handgun. Then more quick shots and the dark figure ran. From my window, I could see a second figure walk boldly into the street. He was a short, beefy man wearing a nightshirt and firing a pistol in the direction of the retreating dark figure.

The next morning at breakfast, I was told not to worry about gunshots anymore, that the problem had been taken care of, that we were lucky that the Chief of Police lived in our house. Law and order had been restored to the streets of Butuan City.

Uh-huh, I thought, lucky us. We have in our midst a man ready to behead innocents, a man who lies about his family and abuses women, a man with a gun who blatantly fires into the dark city streets. Boy, are we lucky.

◉◉◉

A Philippine jet was hijacked on its way from Manila to Davao and flown instead to China. It was on the national news. By now my parents have probably heard about it and are assuming I was on it and am now being held prisoner in China. People say it's only the second time a plane has been hijacked from the Philippines. The other time, they say, was in about 1952. If I were a hijacker, I certainly wouldn't select a Philippine jet as my carrier of choice. The airlines here seem sketchy at best. On a recent trip north, I was buckling myself in and the seat belt came out of its rusted rivet on the cabin floor, and I was just holding a loose strap in my hand. Not confidence-inspiring.

— Journal, March 31, 1971

◉◉◉

"I don't know what your destiny will be, but one thing I know, the only ones among you who will be truly happy are those who have sought and found how to serve." Albert Schweitzer said that. I've been decorating my room, and these words are on a Peace Corps recruiting poster that's now on my wall. I see the words every evening as I blow out the lamp before sleep (I'd rather look at the poster, than the weird golden crucifix!)

Nice words Uncle Albert, but I can't quite figure it out.

I am seeking, and attempting to serve, but it's not work-ing in terms of finding happiness, for I'm not happy, and to tell the truth, I can't see how I'm serving anyone at all, not even myself. Did ole Albert get it wrong, or am I going about things the wrong way?

— Journal, January 27, 1971

◎◎◎

Pirate

Local Peace Corps legend says that seven or eight years ago several female volunteers here in Butuan City came across a pitiful little girl, beaten by her relatives because, they learned, she was epileptic. She was twelve years old, yet only in grade one. The volunteers took her into their apartment, and as time went by, they took in four other Filipina girls who needed help, putting them all through school and paying medical bills. Even after the volunteers left the country, the next generations of Butuan City volunteers took over, helping out this group of girls. The terminated volunteers have continued sending money to them too. Betsy Lusa was one of these later volunteers and she has remained something of a champion for the girls because Betsy married a local boy and stayed here in Butuan. Now, two of the girls are in college, one has graduated from college and is a teacher, and the epileptic girl is in high school. The oldest of the girls is 24 and is getting married. All of us Butuan area volunteers are going to the wedding. Even though I haven't personally done much for the girls, they seem to appreciate me—I guess I am a stand-in for former volunteers. It's a big day.

—from Letter home, April 1971

⊙⊙⊙

I'd never seen a dog smile before, but Pirate definitely smiled. You could approach him with a biscuit and he would sit and grin a big happy-dog grin. He loved biscuits. In fact, he grew quite round in the belly.

Pirate was a rare kind of dog. Ordinary dogs roamed Butuan City streets in packs—scrawny, mangy beasts, desperate, angry, aggressive, and far more malevolent than the wolf in any fairytale. We volunteers learned to carry matches if we were walking after dark. If we threw flames at a pack of the snarling beasts, they would back off.

But Pirate was a family pet living behind high walls in the compound of the Lusa clan in Butuan City. Matriarch of the clan was Betsy, an ex-volunteer married to local boy Molong. Betsy was something of an enigma to me, because she had chosen to stay in Butuan City and build her life there.

Her house was a refuge for us volunteers, especially for me, because her compound was just a few blocks from Butuan Central Elementary School. I could drop by for lunch, and she was always glad to see me. We'd go upstairs, to her private sanctuary, an air-conditioned room with floor to ceiling books—row after row of American novels, big soft chairs, and a plush recliner. It was a marshmallow of a room. Silent. Secluded. A perfect place for us two Americans to talk about literature and love, and safely rant about the injustices of life in Butuan City.

Betsy's idea of American life was different from mine. She'd been raised in the rural flatlands of the high Western plains with no indoor plumbing, and she'd had to struggle to get an education. At fifteen, she had to leave home in order to board in a more populated city where there was a high school. Betsy was bright, and she got through college on an agricultural scholarship. When she volunteered for Peace Corps, she was already used to physical hardship. Then she was wooed by Molong, a handsome and attentive young man from an upper-class mixed Spanish-Philippine family in the logging industry. When they married, she felt as if she had arrived in the promised land—a huge living compound, household servants to cook, do laundry, maintain the manicured yard, drive the car. There was a round-the-clock guard at the front gate and a dedicated house generator for the many nights the city's electricity was out.

It was Betsy's idea to get Pirate. I saw his puppy pictures, a roly-poly guy, mostly white, with a black patch circling one eye. So cute. He was an indoor-outdoor dog, and it was his job to bark at anyone approaching the gate. There might have been some bulldog in him, because he was short and stocky and intimidating when he barked. But after several biscuits, he didn't bark at me anymore, he just smiled.

One time Pirate stopped eating, and Betsy was worried about him. She sent me out to the downtown grocery for a can of American tuna to tempt him. I walked to the store in the afternoon sun and found a few rusting cans on a shelf. Twelve pesos each! Any American-made product would be expensive, but that was outrageous. Surely Betsy hadn't intended to spend that much on a can of tuna for her dog. So I walked back to her house to report, and Betsy just sighed and laughed, and asked me to "go back and get that tuna." Clearly, she lived in an alternate financial universe from mine. So I dutifully bought the tuna, wincing at the price even though the money wasn't mine. And I watched Pirate sniff, then lick, then gobble the goods. I was jealous; I never could have afforded the luxury of American tuna. Pirate ate better than I did!

One noon I walked to Betsy's house and she was crying. "He's gone. What will I do, he's just gone."

I assumed she was talking about Molong, because they'd recently had a spat. Molong, like many Filipinos, was a gambler and he spent many evenings playing cards in the back room of a local sari-sari store. Betsy told me she got tired of playing the role of the waiting-at-home wife, and she'd snapped. She did the unthinkable. She stormed into that store and burst into the smoky back room where the men were sitting at tables, cards sprawled among bottles of San Miguel beer.

Betsy was fluent in the language and in a blast of high-plains American-style brazenness, shouted in the dialect for a showdown. "Who do you love—me or the cards?"

Molong was stunned. No long-suffering Filipina would ever commit such a brash act, such a public confrontation. And Molong, surrounded by his peers, was in a tight spot. Who did he love? His wife? Or the cards? Betsy stood there, hands on her hips, waiting for his answer. Shrugging, Molong grinned his sweetest little-boy grin. "Both of you." The men burst out laughing and Betsy went home alone.

But that day it wasn't Molong who was gone; it was Pirate. Three guys came just before dawn and pounded on the locked gate with some sort of important message. Pirate came out barking, and as soon as the gate opened, they rushed in, put a rice bag over the dog's head, hoisted him over a shoulder and ran out to a waiting vehicle.

Just like that, dear old Pirate was gone. We all knew his fate. He was a fat dog and would bring a fine price. He would be a meal for a feast.

Betsy gave up on dogs after that. Instead, she became pregnant and had a baby girl she named Jennifer. No one would dare steal little Jenny.

◎◉◎

Finally, a letter from home! And it got here in only seven days, which is really fast. Even better, it made it through the international mail—slipping past Mister First Class at the Butuan post office—with a $10 bill tucked inside! Ten strong, husky, green American dollars I can save for my trip home. Funny thing though, I had $40 when I got to Butuan and have gotten $30 from home since then, which means I should have $70. But I only have $50. I can't figure out where the other $20 went, but I moved my secret hiding place to a new location in my room.

— Journal, April 7, 1971

Six Fingers for Luck

Here's a short crocodile story I recently heard from a teacher at school:

In the old days—well not that long ago, actually—when there were still crocodiles in the Agusan River, a big croc was captured. He was a novelty monster, enormous, twenty feet long as I heard it, weighing hundreds of pounds. He was taken to a cement enclosure, a swimming pool of sorts, which was touted as a zoo, although it held only the one lonely croc. People came to gawk and assault the creature with rocks and bottles. Then came typhoon season, and the flood waters of the Agusan rose and ripped. Old Mister Croc got lucky. His pool flooded, the fence around his enclosure was swept away, and out he went. As the story goes, he appeared briefly inside *the flooded elementary school (Nan's school) across the river—perhaps, after his months of captivity, he was searching for tasty young nibblets. Then Old Mister Croc was gone again, back into the wild Agusan.*

This is supposed to be a cautionary tale, to keep us away from the banks of the river where the old devil might still hide out. But I'm a Texas girl who cheers when the unjustly maligned old outlaw escapes, and I can't help but root for him. I'm the only one on his side, but I'm hoping he still lurks somewhere beside the big river.

— Journal, November 14, 1970

⊙⊚⊙

When Betsy and Molong's niece was born in Butuan City, I was invited to the christening. A driver picked me up at home, and I was escorted past the big iron gates into the Lusa compound. I squinted in the bright sun reflecting off the cement as I passed the eight-foot garden wall topped with jagged bits of broken glass. Two security guards sat in the shade of a flowering *ilang-ilang* tree just inside the courtyard, holstered guns at their waists. I was granted entrance with a quick lift of chin and eyebrows.

The marble floors shone and the spacious dining room and *sala* were dark and cool with mahogany walls and ceiling. Heavy shelves along one wall held leather-bound books in English and Spanish. There was a television too, and I figured it for a show of affluence and wishful thinking, because there was no TV reception in Butuan City. And there was a telephone—and like the one atop the credenza in my own host family's home, it was connected to the fourteen other phones in the city, but not to the outer world.

I don't think I'd met the baby's parents before, but they seemed to know me. I was accustomed to being the highly visible Peace Corps Americana in the city. I uttered the proper niceties in the local dialect, then made my way to the wide buffet table laid out with dozens of dishes. In the center was the *lechon*—the body of an entire roasted pig with crispy golden skin, crackly on the outside and warm, stringy, succulent meat below.

"You take the ear," Molong's younger sister Tita was saying to me. I knew it was an honor, being offered the crunchy pig's ear.

"Oh, no thank you. Ears are for the family, the uncles and aunties. It's yours," I gestured to her. It was an attempt to gracefully avoid the ears. I loved the skin, the layer of sweet fat beneath, and the pork meat itself, but there was something about pulling parts off the head that I found repulsive—the dark deeply vacant eye sockets, the grimacing white teeth. I pulled instead at a hunk of pork skin, fat, and meat from the ribs. Then I scooped fried rice mixed with sweet peas, onions, garlic, and flecks of cabbage and parsley.

I was sitting with Tita when the baby's mother asked if we could all be in a photograph together. I agreed. I stood beside the baby's parents with Betsy, Molong, and Tita for a few flashes of the big camera, then they asked if I would like to hold the baby.

To tell the truth, I didn't want to. Babies frightened me. They're so fragile, they might cry, or worse, pee on me. But how could I refuse. Besides, the baby was sleeping, and was attired in a spotless white gown, and—I gratefully noticed—a diaper. I held the baby and was photographed again.

It was while I was holding her that I took my first long look at the sleeping infant. A big round head with wisps of dark hair. Light brown skin the color of milk and cocoa, a squished up perfect little Asian-baby nose, small frail arms hardly bigger around than my thumb, and hands with perfect miniature fingers.

Then I noticed it.

"Tita, what's this?" I said looking at the baby girl's right hand. I knew what it was. It was an extra finger. A small weakly developed sixth finger grotesquely protruded beside the normal pinkie finger.

"Oh yes," she said. "She will be very lucky in life. She has been blessed at birth with the sixth finger."

"This is good?"

"Oh yes," said Tita, apparently amazed at my ignorance. "Is it not so in your place?"

"Um, well, no. Not really. A baby born this way would probably have surgery, to remove the extra finger, so she could be like other children."

"How sad," said Tita shaking her head. "To remove the good fortune of a lucky birth."

I couldn't agree. I felt sorry for this child who would grow up being different when it would take only a simple surgery to remedy the problem. Then I remembered where I was—that despite the rich Western trappings, I was in another culture. I examined my narrow-minded opinion on birth defects versus lucky anomalies and finally considered the fortunate possibilities of having an extra finger in life—perhaps she would find it useful for playing guitar. Hadn't I often wished for more fingers myself?

Handing the child back to the arms of her mother I said, "She is both lucky and beautiful." She truly was.

◎◎◎

I'm not sure what I ate to make me sick, but I've had diarrhea for days. Did I ever mention that I still haven't found the toilet at school? That's crazy, I know. The kids just go outside. I see them peeing in the schoolyard. But the teachers? I thought I'd spotted a toilet in the home economics department, but it turned out it to be a fake bathroom to show the students what one looks like, so they can learn protocol for using it. The toilet isn't hooked up to water or sewage, it just sits there for lessons. When I have to go, I walk back to my house, which is only a block from the school. Unfortunately, I'm leaving school and scurrying home far too frequently today.
— Journal, April 13, 1971

◎◎◎

I just watched one of my teachers doing a second-grade TESL lesson. I'm supposed to be teaching the teachers how to improve their skills in Teaching English as a Second Language, but that lesson was so perfect it could have been on TV, much better than I could have done. It turns out this teacher has a master's degree in TESL—while I have a ten-week Peace Corps crash course in TESL. This teacher knows TESL better, knows the kids and the culture better, and is an experienced professional teacher trainer. I'm not needed at all, really! What am I here for, decoration?

— Journal, January 27, 1971

◉◉◉

I've never been so close to terminating as I am this very minute. My regional rep has told me I can't transfer out of Butuan City Elementary School. I don't know what to do. I don't want to quit and go home, but it's so stupid to waste another year in this place. I just can't stand my nonexistent job!

—Journal, June 21, 1971

◉◉◉

Manila Movie

Another thought. I'm starving to be touched. At home, Daddy would rub my feet while we watched TV, or Mother would brush my hair sometimes. Those were human touches. But now I'm never touched. Maybe I would like a boyfriend. That sounds really odd coming from me, as I'm the one who can get along fine without boys, without a relationship. But somehow, now I really would like to find a companion. Filipino men are generally so repulsive to me, small and skinny and short and leering and syrupy and overly eager. Well, I guess I shouldn't be so hard on all Filipino men, but really, I haven't found an exception yet, although I keep trying to find a real person who can see me as a real person—but Filipino men see only my skin color and don't care about the inside-me person. I don't think they even realize that there is a real person inside the white skin. My other options are the three volunteer boys here around Butuan, but well, just not my type. Besides, they have dozens of beautiful, un-sweaty Filipina girls to flirt with, and you can tell the boys are just gaga over those girls. So it's just me and Nan, she's my best friend. Thank goodness I have her to talk to, and that'll have to do for now.

—Journal, January 10, 1971

◎◎◎

We were in Manila for a training seminar and language evaluation. I was grateful for the break from Butuan City, because it was rainy season in eastern Mindanao. The dank grayness, day after day, week after week, was depressing.

Manila was a wonderland of opportunity and adventure. I shopped at the nation's most Westernized shopping center in the elite Makati district. There I found new sandals to fit my American-sized feet. I bought a woman's blouse that didn't buckle and constrict at my arms and shoulders. And best of all, I found an honest-to-goodness, Western-style supermarket, where I got real cheese, a box of Cheerios, a quart of cold milk, and several rolls of true Kodak film—with the pull date not yet expired.

There were museums to see in Manila. The National Museum. The Museum of Traditional Culture. There were stores and boutiques for buying gifts to send to my family back in Texas. Some stores would even ship them with guaranteed delivery. Wood carvings. Woven fabrics. Cast bronzeware.

And there were movies to see in Manila. The entertainment district of the city was a maze of placards and billboards, towering ads of recent releases of American, European, and Asian movies.

Nan and I picked one. *Friends* it was called by its Asian release title, but it was an American movie. I'd been hearing about it, the story of a boy and girl marooned together on an island as they grow into adulthood. A touching story, I was told. Sweet, poignant.

The line at the ticket office was long, and when we finally got inside, I could hear from the lobby that the movie had already begun. And I could smell the crowd before I could see it. Sweat, urine, and dirty feet. Nan and I entered the theater's darkness holding onto one another, unable to see where to go, until I could discern the silhouettes of people, a lot of people, sitting, standing, packing the theater.

More people were still coming in behind us, and the crowd pushed Nan and me forward. As my eyes adjusted to the darkness I could tell there were absolutely no seats left, and the aisles were jammed with standing viewers. Wherever we stood, people were standing in front of us, and now, people were behind us too. Pressing. Everyone was pressing forward for a better view.

I grabbed for Nan's arm, and we stood together while behind us people pressed. I could feel an elbow at my side and warm breath at my neck, I moved forward by an inch, grasping my shoulder bag in front of me until it brushed the person in front of me.

"Let's get out of here," I whispered to Nan.

"How?" she said. It seemed impossible to move. "Maybe it's almost over and most of the people will leave," she said hopefully.

With my American height, I could easily see over the heads of the people in front of me. I watched the screen. It became obvious that the movie wasn't over. I tried to relax, but I was sweating. I held my bag and Nan's arm even tighter and stood there.

I must have been conspicuous in that crowd. My blonde hair and five-foot-six height must have glared like a lighthouse on a black rock coast. When I first noticed it, it was no more than a tickle at my back, the crowd was pressing, and I tried to move, forward or sideways, but could hardly do more than shift my weight from one foot to the other. I dismissed the tickle as an accidental brush.

It came again, a tickle at my right thigh, something brushing against me. A bag perhaps. A hand? No, a blunter touch.

I looked to Nan. She was watching the movie. I shifted my weight and stood there.

It came again. A certain brush this time, a rub, something small and lightweight. I could feel the breathing all around me, especially behind me, at my neck, hot air, moving the hair at the nape of my neck.

I couldn't stand it. I knew that this is their country, that crowds aren't unusual here, that I should just watch the movie and ignore whatever's going on, but I couldn't stand it. I turned around. There was a a a man—short, sweaty, slicked-back greasy hair, and he was close, too close. I touched his shoulder with a finger and pushed him back.

"Too close, no air," I said in the language, but he probably didn't hear over the sound of the film. Yet for a moment it worked, he moved back, and I felt freedom at my back.

Then, too soon, the press resumed. And there was the tickling feeling again. Firmer. Unmistakably not an accident now. He was doing something. Trying to steal my bag? I grasped it more firmly at my belly and held on.

It continued. A tickling. A brushing. A rubbing. Like a rubber toy against my pants leg. What was this? It didn't exactly hurt, but was horribly unpleasant. If only the movie would end. If only I could leave. If only I could move.

It went on. Then stopped. Then started again. Stopped. Started. It was dreadful. Am I imagining this? Maybe he has an itching disease and he is scratching. I hope it isn't contagious. Stop. Start.

I didn't want to think about what else it might be. I sort of knew about penises, and that it was said that men would take them out and play with them. But for all I knew, like much of my sex information, that could have been misinformation. I didn't know the mechanics of penises. I pushed such thoughts away. Unlikely. Impossible. Why would I think such a thing?

Then there was another sensation. Dampness. My first thought was that I was sweating so much that the perspiration was running down my pants. But I wasn't sweating that much. And the dampness soaked only the back of my right leg.

And I started to think that maybe it was that most terrible of things, that maybe that awful man had done something unthinkable to me. Maybe I could even get pregnant from this awfulness. And I hated myself—for my compliance, my ignorance, my light skin and light hair. I cried, silently, in the darkness of the theater. No one saw, no one knew.

Then he was gone, and I could move. I took a step back. My right foot squashed in something moist and slippery and supremely vile.

I was still wiping my tears of anger and sadness and shame when the movie ended and the lights came up. Nan looked over at me. "Sad movie, huh," she said.

I nodded. "Let's go." I didn't tell her. And because I felt I had done something wrong, that I had somehow caused that man to do the awful thing, I never told anyone.

◉◉◉

Lady on bus yesterday holding her daughter, about five years old, on her lap. The mother was smoking, uncommon for a woman, and the cigarette was dangling dangerously close to her daughter's hair, so she flipped it so the lit end was inside her mouth, filter end out. She continued to smoke, the smoke wisping from the corner of her mouth, and she was still at it, with dragon-like puffing, when I got off. This country is full of weird-nesses, some interesting, some stupid, some positively painful.

— Journal, March 3, 1973

◉◉◉

The most traumatic thing—the worst thing in my life—happened in Manila. Co-volunteer Judy and I were walking to the PC office just before sundown and this creep was walking toward us on the sidewalk. It was a wide sidewalk alongside a wall, and all along the wall there were many what we call "Yellow Rivers." Pee. It's common for men to pee against walls. The rivulets start waist-high on the wall and run yellowish across the sidewalk. We were wearing sandals, cautiously stepping over each rivulet. As the creep walked by, he reached out and grabbed and twisted between my legs, then he took off running like a streak of lightning. I was so stunned I couldn't speak. It really hurt, and I was crying. Judy, who has dark hair and slightly darker skin and wasn't the target, saw it, put her arm around me, and we just walked on, side by side, going on to our meeting and party. I get physically ill and want to vomit every time I remember this horrible thing. Why do men treat me this way?

— Journal, May 9, 1971

⦿⦿⦿

The Worm

Nan and I went to visit a teacher's friend's family who lived in a little barrio named Pulangtubig (Red Water). Their house was a nipa hut, constructed on poles and made entirely of bamboo and palm fronds, and set far off the main dirt road, down a small pathway near the ocean. To feed us, they killed a chicken, giving us the best of what they had. We stayed talking so long that it got dark, very dark. It was a moonless night and I could hardly see my feet at the end of my legs.

As we were about to walk back to the road, the most amazing thing happened. The boy from the family took his guitar, and we started singing and strolling, step by step along the narrow pathway. And from the other houses, people would lean out their windows or stand

in their doorways with candles or little lanterns. As we sang—and Nan and I joined in the Visayan folk songs that we'd learned in training—our way was lit by the kindness of neighbors. It was a great feeling—the community helping one another. You'd never see this in Amerika.
                                    – Letter home, October 28, 1970

⊙⊙⊙

Toward the middle of my second year as a volunteer in Butuan City, I moved out of the Bila house into an apartment to have the freedom to cook my own food and escape the fishbowl of scrutiny. But after living there just a short while, my apartment was robbed. Not that I had much worth taking, but my tape player was gone—music, my one luxury, my link to American youth culture.

When I told my landlady, she said, "Oh, too bad."

"Shall I call the police?" I asked her.

She shrugged. "If you want to."

I knew already. The police were unlikely to do anything but come and stare me. It was no use.

Even though I was now cooking on my own and eating better, I still had the constant dull thud of hunger in my body. One day I went to the Butuan City market intent on finding the one thing that I knew could satiate me—meat.

I visited an open-air meat stand with flaccid headless chickens hanging from hooks and blood-red sausages strung along the wall like birthday streamers. And there was red beef under a glass hood, like a Baskin-Robbins counter, open to the air on one side. Black flies dotted the side of the trays and the *tendero* shooed them away with a stick with newsprint streamers on the end. Maybe...if I cook it thoroughly...

"Is this fresh?" I asked the skinny *tendero* behind the table.

"Oh yes, mum. Just this morning. Very fresh."

"Cow meat?" I asked. I wanted to make certain. Water buffalo meat would look the same.

"Oh yes, mum. Very fresh cow meat."

I bought a hunk and back at the apartment I cooked it; for three hours it simmered atop a gas burner in a pot with salt, pepper, and an onion. The aroma drove me wild with anticipation, and when it was tender enough to fall apart with gentle prodding, I sat down and ate every morsel of it, tearing it apart with my fork straight out of the pot. I ate like a wild thing and relished the thick sweet warmth of its juices, the chewing, the swallowing, and the lump it left in my belly. And when the meat was gone, for dessert I downed a whole papaya drizzled with fresh citrus.

I was full, but still not sated. I still craved *something*. Looking in the mirror I saw myself, pasty and round, like a sausage stuffed too tightly into my clothes. I was fat and feeling guilty for every bite I'd put in my mouth, and yet I was still hungry.

It was sometime during those constantly-hungry days in the city, I began to notice that I felt odd, a kind of sick feeling that crept up over a period of weeks, a general weakening of body and spirit, a growing sense of not being able to cope with life and not caring. Then came the fever and the puking.

I took down the Peace Corps medical kit to see if there was anything that might help. Anything to kick the sickness. But then, I didn't know what was wrong, so how could I know what medicine to take.

Antibiotics. They ought to help just about anything. I took one. And the next morning, another.

I sent word to school that I would be absent until I felt better, and I spent hours sitting on a cushion with my back against the wall, trying to read. The mosquitoes zeroed in on me, first a day-biting species, then their nocturnal cousins. I lit mosquito coils to keep them at bay, but the smell of the pungent smoke made me barf even harder. I went to bed and huddled under the mosquito net, sleeping until the diarrhea and stomach cramps hit.

And then, a stunning bowel movement. There in the toilet was what looked like a ten-inch earthworm—a long, round-bodied worm, not moving. Apparently it was stunned or dead, or of a particularly lethargic disposition. I stared, not quite believing it could be real. A joke. Perhaps a rubber toilet toy. Yet I knew the truth.

Incredible! That disgusting creature was in *my* body? I puked on top of it and crept back to bed feeling sick and ashamed. Ashamed for whatever I had done to allow myself to host that disgusting parasite.

I'd sat through hours of medical instruction during Peace Corps training. I could hear the Peace Corps doctors, their words shaming me, for I had failed.

"Be vigilant!" they said. "*Never* eat raw vegetables. Do *not* eat green salads. *Always* boil or purify your water. *Watch out* for ice in your drinks if the water comes from an unknown source. Magnolia and Silver Bell are the *only* safe brands of ice cream."

I had slipped up and somehow ingested an egg that had come from the fecal material of an infected person. The larva hatched inside my intestine, migrated through my bloodstream to my lungs, up the bronchial tubes, and then one day I coughed. Just a tiny cough and the larva was in my throat, and I'd swallowed it again. Then it anchored in my intestines and grew to be the enormous monster that I'd just expelled.

I became weaker and sicker just thinking about it, and I threw up again. Was it the worm or some germ-based illness making me sick? Leaning against the wall for support, I made it back to bed, the image of the giant creature permanently etched in my memory.

What had made me expel it, I wondered. Must have been the antibiotics. Were there more vermin lurking in my gut?

When I felt better, I went to the local pharmacy and bought a bottle of Padrax, the common deworming tonic that affluent parents gave their kids regularly. I read the instructions and, calculating dosage based on body weight, I downed the entire bottle of this disgusting black-tar gorp.

Then I watched the toilet. Nothing. Days went by, there were no further signs of worms.

I read the Peace Corps medical literature. Ascariasis, "very common," it said. "producing feelings of hunger." Yes, that was true enough. "Infection is often found after a patient passes an adult worm in the feces, or through the nose or mouth."

The *nose* or *mouth?* Maybe I was lucky after all.

After that, I *always* boiled my drinking water, twenty full minutes. And I *never* took ice in a soda, even when it was an option, which was hardly ever.

And shamed, I kept the secret of the worm, never forgetting the image of that leviathan in my toilet.

◉◉◉

Butuan City Elementary School is, for all practical purposes, out for the summer break. I'm still at school making final reports, but there are no classes. Some kids come to school just to hang out because they like being here, and many teachers are still here, working without pay.

You wouldn't believe the chaos around the school at the end of the term. Did I tell you the latest from the bureaucracy? Mass promotion. Every student must pass to the next grade, no matter what, even if he hasn't attended a single class. So teachers are going back and changing failing grades to passing. It's ridiculous! Supposedly, it will save the public school system money, since there will be no repeaters. No one seems to care about education—well, some of the teachers care, but they have to do as they're told. We volunteers in educa-tion have long thought that teachers need to organize into a union to fight for some rights. This "organizing" thinking is so American, I know better than to suggest it out loud. I would just sound like a pushy, foreign, cultur-ally insensitive dolt.

— Letter home, April 21, 1971

◉◉◉

Fely, a teacher friend, had been diagnosed with a heart problem and was told by her doctor she should never marry or have sex, because the excitement might cause a fatal heart attack. But, as fate would have it, Fely fell in love, and she was forlorn that she couldn't marry. When I got to know them, I saw how great she and her friend were together, a very loving couple, yet both realized that marriage could not be in their future. So they dated and had good times, and sometimes I accompanied them to the movies. One day Fely's purse was snatched right out of her hand as she was exiting a store. She screamed and chased the guy for quite a while, finally losing him in a crowd. After that panicked, heart-pounding excitement, Fely and her truelove blew caution to the wind and went ahead and got married. And Fely hasn't died from having sex. At least not yet. Happy ending (so far).

— Journal, April 20, 1971

Soldier Boy

This heat's a killer. I can't remember ever being this hot. My skin feels like grease. I took a bus from Butuan to Davao. Thirteen grueling hours of jostling, thumping, bumping, and being numb on my butt. All with a thick layer of dust—like Mamaw's flour coating on Sunday's fried chicken dinner. And we had three overly long unplanned stops, one for engine trouble and two for soldiers.

— Journal, July 1971

☉☉☉

"Eggs, still hot," came the call from the kid with a shallow basket resting on top of his head. It was the middle of the night, and the thought of eating an egg, or anything else, made my stomach curl.

But the day ahead would be a long one. I faced an at-least eight-hour bus ride, and that was if it went smoothly. Sometimes the unexpected happened on the unpaved national highway that led from northern Mindanao to Davao City—vehicle collisions, mudslides, collapsed bridges, flat tires, or luggage that got so jostled on the rutted road it tumbled off the roof of the bus, splaying open in the dust. Then the bus would stop and passengers got out to help gather the bag's contents. "Wow, panties!" a man would shout, holding up some poor woman's underwear like a trophy catch.

"How much, the eggs?" I asked the vendor.

"Ten centavos, one" he responded, his eager face looking up to mine in the bus window.

"I'll take two," I said and gave him twenty-five centavos. "Keep the change," and he grinned his thanks. The eggs were comforting. I held them for a while in the palms of my hands, feeling their warmth before sticking them into my duffle beside a bottle of Pepsi. By mid-morning we'd be along the road somewhere and those boiled eggs would taste great. But for the moment, I craved sleep.

It was not much past three in the morning and I'd been on the bus since midnight, securing my seat. Now I could sleep. I folded forward with my duffle as a lap pillow and closed my eyes, waiting for the bus to depart.

First light was spreading orange and pink above the corrugated tin rooftops when the bus roared and shimmied me awake. There was a skinny figure in the driver's seat and the horn bellowed three long wails. The driver leaned wide out his window, pounded the flat of his hand on the side of the bus, and shouted to the milling crowd to get on board or out of the way.

The morning was sunny, the weather dry. That boded well for making time along the unpaved, washboard highway that stretched southward nearly 300 miles. But the dry weather brought dust, and it poured in through my open window, blown in from under the wheels, as if a vacuum cleaner decided to blow instead of suck. I pulled up my handkerchief cowboy-style to keep my nose and throat covered, but the technique seemed to work better in the movies. In real life, nothing worked.

When the bus stopped, the dust settled. We were en route, stopped along the side of the road in the middle of nowhere. I drank the Pepsi and ate an egg while our bus sat motionless in the baking sun. Our driver was gone for a while, and when he returned he wasn't alone. Three soldiers in mud-colored fatigues and high lace-up black boots, each carrying a shining black semi-automatic rifle slung across his shoulder, boarded with him. My fellow passengers fell silent and still, as though trying to become invisible. Even the pig under the seat up front stopped grunting. Our driver, I suspected, had been bartering with the soldiers, bribing them for safe passage. I hoped it would work.

Two soldiers sat right behind the driver, while the third walked up then down the aisle, looking everyone over closely. People stiffened as he passed by, gazing out the window, careful not to make eye contact with the soldier. Then he was beside my seat. Even covered in dust, I knew I stood out. He anchored himself beside my bench, his hand gripping the back of the seat in front of me.

I looked up at him. "Sit down?" I asked him in Visayan, and I scooted over as far as possible to make room for him. He sidled on to the bench beside me and the bus engine roared to life. We were moving again.

His rifle was on his left shoulder, muzzle hanging in the aisle.

He was gawking at me. Glaring. An unfriendly look. Inscrutable. Perhaps hostile.

"Where are you going?" I asked him in Visayan. He just looked at me harder, like he was trying to figure out what to do about me. I could feel his surprise that the Americana spoke the language. He gave a noncommittal grunt.

"Where are *you* going?" he asked me.

"To Davao. To visit a friend, to work in a school." I said.

"You are a student?"

"A teacher. Peace Corps. Do you know Peace Corps?"

He nodded. "In my town before, we had a Peace Corps teacher," he said. "A man. From Boston."

I nodded. "What town are you from?" I asked him. He told me. I'd never heard of it. "In Davao del Sur," he said. I nodded, recognizing the province, but not the town.

"What's your age?" he asked me.

"Twenty-three," I answered. "And yours?"

"The same," he said and we stared one another in a new way. I saw a young person not so very different from myself, but on a different life path.

"You are a soldier in the national army. Did you always want to be a soldier, even when you were a little boy?"

"No. I had to become a soldier."

"Why?"

With a shrug and a gaze out the window he said, "There was nothing for me in my town. My family is poor. The army will take care of me. I can send money to my family."

"But it is a dangerous life," I said.

He shrugged again. "Not so dangerous really. Anyway, my friends and I are the ones with the rifles," he grinned.

"But it seems like here in the Philippines, many people have guns. Not just the soldiers."

He nodded. "I've been lucky so far."

"And you ride the buses, back and forth on the roads? That is your work?"

He nodded. "Checking for bandits."

"But some would say the soldiers are bandits. Is that true?" It was an audacious thing to ask. Like everyone else in Mindanao, I'd certainly heard the stories of the massacres of bus passengers, robbed for their jewelry and luggage and left on the roadside as carrion for wild dogs. Some said they were Communist bandits, some said it was the national army. Maybe it was bandits dressed as the army. Maybe the army dressed as bandits. Who knows? Yet there was something about this boy that made me feel easy. "I think the Philippines is a confusing place," I said it with a grin, but I was only partly joking.

And he looked straight at me, youth to youth, across a broad cultural chasm. "I agree, it is sometimes a confusing place." The soldier boy asked me about myself. My family. My work in the Philippines. If I was anxious to go back home.

"No. I'm not ready to go back yet. I want to learn more about the Philippines."

"Be careful," he said finally. "These roads can be dangerous. There are bandits in these places you are traveling."

After a few miles, the soldiers up front beat on the side of the bus for the driver to stop and the three of them disembarked. From the side of the road, I saw my soldier glance back over his shoulder in my direction. I raised my hand in a small wave.

He was a boy not unlike the boys I knew back home, not unlike my classmates who were now soldiers in Vietnam. Here was a boy trying to find his way through life, caught up in a world I could hardly fathom, an impossible world of military power, kickbacks, bandits, guerrilla warfare, rifles, and sudden death.

He turned toward me, gave a small jerk of chin and lifted eyebrows, a barely discernible gesture of farewell. Our bus rolled on, great puffs of dust rising as we shuddered and thunked along the rutted national highway, the road taking me southward to Davao City.

◉◉◉

The bus station in Butuan isn't much more than an open dirt field with a few three-sided shelters. You have to wander around looking for a bus that has your destination posted in the window. Then you have to ask people, because it might or might not be the one that leaves next. It had been raining. It was muddy. It was dark, although there was electricity, so there were a few bulbs dangling from wires strung between shelters. The seats on the bus were just wooden benches with backs, but no cushions. And since they're benches, you might have three or more people squeezed in.

The engine revved up at 3:30 a.m., and we were off. The road through town was paved, but in just five minutes, we were on the unpaved, potholed, muddy, slippery, and dangerous national highway. I was able to half-doze in a stupor till dawn. The speeding bus was sliding around and fish-tailing in the mud, and every time we hit a bump it would send us soaring upward, then back down smacking ours bottoms against the wooden seat, just as another bump sent us soaring again or lurching left or right. Having other passengers squashed in close buffered the lurches. It was like being in a popcorn popper, except it was very cold. The plywood bus windows slide up to close and down to open. Passengers were getting carsick when the windows were closed, because you can't see anything, and all the lurching and bouncing and rocking can be nauseating. And when the windows were open, the cold air and rain came roaring in. This went on for more than twelve hours. I wonder if this is what it felt like to ride a stagecoach across the North American continent in the old days. At least I don't have to wear a corset.

— Journal, December 2, 1970 (7 months prior to the trip described in the chapter above)

There are still things in this country I want to do before I terminate. For one thing, I want to learn more about the way the Manobo mountain people live. Being with them might be the most interesting—and relevant!—thing I've done in this crazy country.

— Letter to Nan, never mailed, June 21, 1972

PART III

◎

In Manobo Land

Counting to 100

Yesterday I tried some social studies work. My Bigs looked at Egypt, because there were some pictures of Egypt in one of our Life magazines. This was way, way beyond them. These mountain kids have no concept beyond the river, and perhaps a little bit downriver. They've never seen pictures of the rest of their own province, or their own island, or their own archipelago, let alone Egypt. The idea of a desert, a place without water—"The people don't drink?"—took more explaining than I could muster, and it left them in confusion. On Monday, I'll start over and make it simple, drawing a map of our river. Even the concept of a map will be new, as though seeing from the sky, like a bird. I'll try that and *see if I can stretch the world for them one small step at a time.*

—Letter home, April 29, 1972

◉◉◉

I sat quietly on the hard bench at the end of another school day in Madga. The kids were drawing, the last activity of the morning and one of their favorites. My favorite too, since it takes only a little energy from me and the results are instant and gratifying.

I passed around the box of crayons. Each student chose a color, then kneeled on the bamboo slat floor to use the long bench as a desk. I watched, never knowing what images the kids would create. Sometimes they simply made circles and swirls and colored them in. Sometimes it was something more—houses on stilts, people at the river, pigs in the forest, a fish trap.

Teaching math had been a challenge. It needn't be so hard, I thought. I was trying to describe numbers beyond ten. The kids seemed to have their own concept of numbers, but I couldn't tell how high their numbers would go. What happens in their minds after, say, twenty or fifty or one hundred? At what point does it just slip into "very many"? To describe greater quantities, I'd heard them at times use metaphor images: many, like the seeds of a papaya, or the leaves on a tree. Perhaps their language lacked precise counting, but more likely what was lacking was my own ability to understand how they thought, how they conceived quantities of "very many."

I developed a strategy to teach numbers to my Bigs. I cut a bunch of bamboo sticks using our bolo machete, each stick about six inches long. I was able to cut about thirty pieces out of one bamboo stalk, enough to get us started.

We counted them out, one to ten, using the Visayan words. That part was easy enough, as that's the number of fingers they had, and the concept was quickly solid. We looked for things around us of which there were ten or fewer. Three chicks were following a mother hen across the yard, so we put out three sticks. There were seven Bigs on the porch that morning: seven sticks. In just a few minutes, they had the idea. At counting from one to ten, they were entirely competent.

Eleven to twenty was trickier. I bundled ten bamboo sticks together and we counted the number of sticks past ten, and learned to say the numbers in Visayan, which uses Spanish words for eleven and above. And so it went, day by day, until we got to thirty—at which point I ran out of bamboo sticks.

Find a bamboo. Cut more sticks. My goal was to get to a hundred.

Or, maybe I won't teach math at all, I wrote one day. I'll just teach reading. Since this little school is well beyond the realm of the public school system, we're entirely on our own out here and can do whatever we want. What would help these kids be able to communicate with the outside world, if they ever need to?

I watched Big Norma, Penang, and Serhio—my best and brightest students. They were able to learn anything — these kids were daring, clever, creative, and happy. They were young people who could become whatever they wanted to but were unlikely to be anything other than what they already were. Not likely to go anywhere, ever. They would have children of their own, and they would teach their families to survive with the skills of hunting and planting and harvesting. There was really no place in their lives for reading and writing despite their bright and inquisitive natures. I sighed, knowing these kids were probably getting in our little school the last the worldly education they would ever receive.

At the other end of the bench, among Janet's Littles, sat little Jeorge, about three years old. He was at the beginning of his life and full of potential. What did the world hold for him? He sat drawing with a pencil, squiggle circles and scribbles. He was taking care of his little sister, who sat bouncing on his leg. Then, for no apparent reason, his baby sister started screaming long and loud, and George pushed her away. He was intent on drawing, and the baby just screamed louder. Older sister Tarsilla, about six, put aside her drawing to pick up the baby, and bouncing her little sister on a small thin hip, Tarsilla then returned to her spot at the bench to continue her art work. With one hand she held a teal-blue crayon and with the other, she supported the baby on her hip. Tarsilla was not at all disrupted. Still focused on her art, she jostled and soothed. Until the baby pooped. Darna went inside to retrieve a cup of water to rinse the porch, while Tarsilla ran down to the river for a quick rinse of her body and dress. She was back, dripping, and refocused on her art in five minutes.

The outside world. It was hard to image that it was actually out there, or that these kids would ever see it. Yet some part of me knew that however unlikely it might seem today, things could change. In this river place these young people were entirely competent. But I had the feeling that *just in case*, I should get them counting to 100.

I made a bamboo microscope for the kids this week. I used my penlight flashlight, broke the bulb, and got the little glass magnifying bead at the tip of bulb. Then, using a node of bamboo and a piece of tin from a can as a reflector, I put it all together and it's a microscope. We looked at a leaf and a butterfly wing. This has been an amazing thing for the kids and they have been entirely engrossed day after day. Unfortunately, I no longer have a little flashlight, but then, I had no batteries anyway.
      — Letter home, April 29, 1972

Kamote Mountain

Our nextdoor neighbor Amalya is very pregnant, looks like she's due any moment now. She still climbs the mountain trails to the sweet potato fields every day and carries 20 or 30 pounds of kamote home on her back. And she pounds rice every day too. She has a humongous belly, so big she can hardly reach past it. She doesn't wear many clothes, just a kind of sarong wrapping below her belly to her knees, so I can clearly see that her breasts are also heavy. But her belly! I can't believe how big it is.
—Letter home, May 11, 1972

☉☉☉

"How do you think she does it, being so pregnant and all?" I asked Janet one Friday morning. I hoisted our cardboard box of school supplies onto my shoulder and sidestepped gracefully down the pole ladder. The morning was warm and bright. It was not yet 7:30, and I was already sweating. The heat would be debilitating by noon. I was hoping to get a nap during the hottest midday hours.

"Dunno," Janet said with a shrug. She grabbed the metal rebar and started striking the hunk of iron below our house to call the kids to school. The clanging set my teeth on edge. We walked side by side across the dusty path to Datu's porch.

"But I mean, how can Amalya even bend to the ground with that gigantic stomach? The kamote don't leap from the ground and into her basket." There were so many surprises at Madga, maybe I wasn't kidding about the leaping kamote.

"Dunno. Why don't you ask her?" Janet said coldly. I let the ice slide by, knowing Janet. I sat on my end of Datu's porch, organizing papers, expecting the kids to appear at any moment. I contemplated some other tactic to find out how Amalya was physically able to bring home enough kamote each day to feed not only her own family but two Americanas as well.

I could hardly ask Amalya anything and Janet knew that. Amalya spoke little Visayan and talking with her was not easy beyond the basics. To communicate with Amalya, I resorted to fragments of the Manobo language I'd picked up, woven with Visayan words that Amalya seemed to understand, along with pointing and gesturing. And when possible, I asked her kids to interpret. Her oldest, Serhio, spoke Visayan as well as I did.

Later, when my Bigs were copying board work, Amalya walked across the dirt path to Datu's house, then balanced her front-heavy bulk up the notched pole and sauntered through the schoolroom into Datu's house. She wore only a length of grayish fabric tucked under her enormous belly, covering her to her knees. I tried not to gawk, but her belly button had all but disappeared in total expansion. I didn't know anyone could be that big. In the Old Country where I came from, pregnancies were hidden behind closed doors and layers of pleats and fabric, a secret shame. No polite mention of the word *pregnant* was ever made, no reference to impending birth was spoken in public, and in polite company eyes were averted. Pregnancy was invisible until the Blessed Event passed and the newborn could be openly inspected and ogled.

Amelia was the first openly pregnant woman I'd ever seen. And her rapidly changing body frightened me. How can the female body take such stress? At what point will the skin just rip open? And how can she possibly function with that watermelon on her front side? Was this the fate of all women? The thought of my own body grotesquely betraying me with gigantism sent shivers down my spine.

The next afternoon as Amalya, Poring, and Darna were returning from the kamote fields, I shouted across the yard, "Did you find sweet potatoes today?"

"Yes," said Poring.

"Was it hard work, with Amalya being so big?" I asked.

Poring looked at her mom and they said something to one another. Both grinned, Amalya with the wad of red-brown tobacco between her lips.

"Yes," said Poring.

"Maybe Janet and I could help," I offered. "We want to learn to dig kamote. Can we go with you sometime?"

More talk. Then Poring said, "Tomorrow. Come with us tomorrow to the kamote place."

Word of our adventure spread, and the next morning there were two *kajad* headbaskets and a gaggle of kids waiting on our porch. Amalya led the procession as we crossed the river and headed up hill. In no time at all, I was panting.

"Mud balls," I muttered, hating my worthless rubber slippers as my heels slipped off one side or the other in the mud. I could get no traction from the rubber and every step forward, I'd slide back half a step.

I watched Amalya and the kids. Their wide, bare feet and strong toes gripped the mud and they climbed surefootedly. My slippers were sucked into the mud, then would release with a squish, flicking muddy splats up the back of my legs.

I'm taking these things off and throwing them to the wild pigs, I thought. Then I reconsidered. Hookworms. Schistosomiasis. A poking stick or sharp rock under my tender feet. Well, I'll keep them on, but the next time I come to this country I'm going to bring sturdy sneakers, with cleats!

Every step was uphill, each a little harder than the one before. I was breathing hard and sweating. We passed through dense forests, layer upon layer of greens and golds and browns, tangled and woven, a dappled mosaic of sunlight and shadows.

Amalya paused and turned back to us. "Pig trap," she said pointing with her lips down a faint trail to our left. I noticed the perspiration on her upper lip above the wad of tobacco. I looked where she pointed and saw only trees.

"Where?"

"There," said Serhio. "At the end of that trail. Donkilyo and Tripon set the trap and are out hunting today."

All right, maybe I could just make it out. In Texas it would have been called a box canyon, a river trail running into a dead-end cliff, but this one was a vague tunnel of vegetation heading through walls of greenery. As we turned to go, I mentally wished good hunting to Donkilyo and Tripon. Fresh meat would be wonderful.

Up and up, and up some more we climbed. The trees grew thicker around us, the trail narrower, until the forest opened in blazing sunlight. We were in a clearing of vines. They hugged the ground, growing over one another, a tangle of heart-shaped, blueish-green leaves reflecting the heat of the sun.

Darna gave us our first lesson in finding kamote.

"You find a vine as thick as your finger, then follow it to where it goes back into the earth. There," she said demonstrating with a vine she'd found, "is where you dig." Darna poked the earth with a long, pointed stick, something like a spear, and turned up a fist-sized purple tuber. "Now, you try it." The kamote made a solid plop into the bottom of her basket.

I looked for a thick vine, but they all seemed the same to me. Well, if they are all the same, I thought, I'll just dig… here. I took my stick and dug where a vine went into the earth, and out popped a peanut-sized tuber.

Darna laughed. "That's just a baby. Put it back and try again." Darna set her basket near me and dug nearby. I looked around, searching for the perfect fat vine. When I looked back at Darna, she had a small pile of kamote beside her.

I tried again and again. A few times I got lucky and found kamote of modest, edible size. Mostly I found nothing. I was sweating, salty beads running down my face and across my lips, turning into rivulets trickling down my neck and belly.

Amalya and Serhio were on the far side of the clearing, Amalya digging with her thick stick, Serhio bending over to pull out the tubers. That solved the mystery. She had the kids do the bending.

We'd been digging for a little while when Lando and Junior appeared with a load of sugarcane stalks. Lando brought me a piece. I ripped into the pithy core with my teeth—sweet and moist.

"You are a good hunter," I told Lando, grateful to the four-year old for the cool, juicy sweetness as I tore the fiber from the stalk, chewed it for a long time, and sucked out the sweet juice before spitting the macerated fiber into the bushes.

When I set to digging again, I found little or nothing. I checked Janet and Penang who were working together nearby. "Finding anything?" I asked.

Janet looked up. "Hey, this is easy. We've got enough for a meal already. How are you doing?"

"A light meal maybe," I said. I tipped the basket to look inside. Three purple potatoes the size of chicken eggs rattled loosely against the walls. A downright measly meal.

I dug a while longer in the baking sun till even my earlobes were sweaty, my head started to buzz, and I was feeling dizzy and nauseous. Heat stroke coming. "I've got to sit down a while," I told Darna. She nodded, sweat running down her face as she dropped her potatoes into the basket with a thud.

I plopped down on my back in the shade on the edge of the clearing. Good grief, I thought, watching the patterns of sunlight through the broad leaves that gently stirred in the breeze. I can't believe this is so hard. If I had to do this to feed myself, I'd starve or die of heat stroke.

Janet was standing beside me. "You alright?"

"Sure, just a mild heat stroke." Janet's neck was covered with sweat, and her face was red.

"It sure gives us a new respect for those sweet potatoes we've been eating."

I sat up and looked across the clearing. Serhio, Penang, Dita, and little Mordino were working alongside Amalya, Darna, Tessie and Aida. Lando and Junior were nowhere to be seen.

"Can you imagine if everyone in the world had to work this hard just to get enough food?" Janet asked.

"There'd be a lot more skinny people in America," I said.

Lando and Junior appeared, carrying a huge bunch of fruit. "Try one," Junior offered. "Very sweet." They looked like bananas, but each was no bigger than my pinky. I peeled one and took a bite. Sweet pulp, with crunchy black seeds.

"Is this a banana?" I asked.

"Maybe half passion fruit, half banana," Janet said.

"Weird." I said.

"Tasty," Janet said.

I ate four of them, whatever they were, and tossed the skins aside. One peel hit the trunk of a tree and bounced off some leaves, revealing a flash of orange and yellow. I investigated.

"Hey look," I said to Janet. "It's Alice in Wonderland time. Take a look at the size of this caterpillar. It's bigger than the kamote I've been finding." There was a red, black, and orange creature more than four inches long and covered with protruding hairs. "Hey Junior, look at this. What is it?"

Junior came over, took one look, shouted something at me in an imperative tone, and ran away. I took the hint. It was dangerous. I backed off, adding the caterpillar to my ever-growing list of Madga mysteries.

With a sigh I picked up my stick and went back out into the sun. I stuck close to Darna and again she showed me how to find food.

By mid-afternoon our group had quite a mound of kamote—very few of which I had found—when Amalya began dividing the potatoes equally among the baskets.

"Alright, let me try to lift it," I said hoisting the head-strap kajad basket onto my back. "Hmm, not bad." I adjusted the weight. The way the head strap aligned the basket along my spine, distributing the weight low and close, made it comfortable. "Try it," I suggested to Janet.

"Hey, yes," she said. "We'll be the ones to carry these baskets," she told Amalya. And to me, in English, she said, "After all, if she can do it pregnant, we big old milk-and-cornflakes Americanas should be able to manage this."

I found it easy walking downhill, even with thirty pounds of potatoes on my back. Something felt good about the balanced load in the center of my back and having my hands free to grab roots and limbs for balance. When we reached the river, we squatted in the cool shallows holding the potatoes underwater and rubbing away the soil with our fingers.

"What we need here is a vegetable brush," I whispered to Janet.

"Oh sure. And maybe a pressure cooker too," she whispered back.

Darna and I delivered my load of kamote to Datu's house, while Janet took her load to Amalya's. And an hour later, Dita appeared at our door with a mounded plate of steaming kamote.

"There it is," I said as we sat down to dinner of sweet potato and canned fish. "It certainly gives one a feeling of living close to nature, close to the source."

"Yep, now we can write a cookbook," she said, "with recipes for kamote hash, kamote chips, and kamote casserole— we'll call it *The Complete Kamote: From Field to Table in Three Easy Steps.*"

"The operative word being *easy*," I suggested. Janet and I looked at each other, eyebrows raised. "Uh-huh."

⊙⊚⊙

Breakfast: *Skyflakes Crackers, 2 each, and now they're all gone.*

Tea (and we share the teabag till it's beyond dead. Tea is nearly gone too.)

Lunch: *macaroni and cheese (or, more accurately, that canned, yellow, foodlike substance they call cheese) and water to drink.*

Supper: *more macaroni and cheese with a meat sauce*

(our next-to-last can of corn beef, in ketchup) with water to drink, which was, ugh!, still hot, cuz we'd just boiled it.

And then, just when we thought we'd had another bleak food day and that was all we'd get, some super-good, fresh sweet corn was brought to us from Amalya's house.

And then—amazing!—there was a post-supper addi-tion. Tagleong's house just sent over some kamote with little pieces of cooked chicken! It's turned out to be a good food day after all. Great! I wonder which chicken got offed. Okay with me!

— Journal, September 18, 1972

◉◉◉

Letters from Home

The guys from Silco are due up anytime now. We requested cookies and bread from the camp bakery, as well as fruit, instant coffee, and canned milk. And, most important of all—MAIL. I sure need some word from a friend or family person. If my family could grasp how much I need to hear from them, surely they would write. But it's been two years and I've asked and begged, I've written letter after letter and waited weeks, sometimes months. Once I went on strike, but eventually ended the strike because it made no difference. I write to them, but they don't write to me. I try to understand that they are busy, that writing letters simply isn't something they do. I know they like me. Or at least, they used to like me.

So how could they just forget about me? Why don't they write? I don't understand.

— Journal, August 13, 1972

⊙⊙⊙

Tessie and Aida reported in morning class that the logging guards were back. But it wasn't until after lunch while Janet and I were prepping lessons for the next day that a pack of kids ran up to our porch, their bare feet making little explosions of dust and muffled slapping smacks as they shouted, "They're coming, they're coming!"

I could hardly contain my joy. Trining and TingTing had been gone nearly two weeks this time. And it had been two weeks before that since they'd brought the last batch of food and mail from the Silco logging camp. I was imagining the taste of cookies and fresh fruit long before I saw the two figures coming in from the trail south of Datu's house. Trining carried a lumpy rice bag slung across his shoulder.

I could tell by their grins and the way they waved long before they reached our porch that they were glad to see us. I poured some cool water into our enamel "company" cup and set it out on the bench. Trining hoisted the bag onto the porch, climbed up, took the water with thanks, and sat down to bring us the news from Silco. TingTing crossed the path to Datu's house for a similar debriefing there. I heard Ricarda greet him as he sidestepped up the pole ladder into Datu's house.

"How was your trip? What's the news?" Our questions tumbled out.

Trining laughed, and I poured him a second cup of water. "The trip went well. The river is low so it took us two days to get upriver to you from Silco camp. There has been no rain, and the load in the banka was heavy. I'm sorry, but we were not able to bring your water barrel this trip."

"That's okay," Janet assured him. "We're doing fine without it." I had given up ever seeing the rainwater catchment barrel from Mr. Guatno. It would never make the trip upriver to Madga. My mental image of such a huge barrel atop the little river banka was laughable, like an elephant on a canoe. Although I appreciated Mr. Guatno's concern and generosity, I knew the barrel would stay forever at Silco Camp.

"What's the news?"

"Mr. Guatno sends his regards and invites you to his home for the Silco fiesta next month. Dr. Troucio says he will try to come up to visit you, but he is occupied with the health clinic at Silco Camp now and cannot make the trip upriver at this time."

"Is the logging work going well?"

"There has been some trouble. That is why we were gone so many days. We were called to work in the lower Umayam section where they are cutting many logs now, and we could not return to Madga until we were released from our duty there. All the concession guards were called to duty since there are logging pirates in that area."

"Pirates?"

"Yes. Those who come at night and take away the trees. We had to sleep in the forest with our guns."

"Did you shoot anyone, Trining?"

"No. I saw no one. But other guards had trouble on their watch. I was lucky."

"How about in this area? Is there any trouble near Madga?"

"No. This area is peaceful now. The trouble is all there, below, where there are many roads and ways for the pirates to get in and out of the forest with trucks. But Mr. Guatno was anxious that we should return to Madga to check on you, so we have returned," Trining grinned. "And we have brought you mail and food from Silco."

Janet was opening the rice bag. An entire pineapple rolled out.

"Ooooh, Trining, how delicious! Thank you!"

"It is Mr. Guatno who sends this to you."

"Good ole Mr. Guatno," Janet said, lifting the pineapple to look at its golden skin and cropped crown. I wanted to hack into it that instant and eat until I'd gorged. But I knew better. We would share it with our neighbors at dinnertime.

Janet pulled out a hand of yellow bananas, a brown wrapper of fresh bread, and a second wrapper of the bland cookies from Silco Bakery. They looked delicious. I imagined slathering one with peanut butter, setting a slice of banana on top of it, and nibbling it slowly, morsel by morsel, with afternoon tea. The fresh bread smelled wonderful.

The rice bag also held canned foods—mackerel and sweetened condensed milk and corn beef—and our plastic Baggie from home.

Wrapped tightly with a rubber band as a precaution against unanticipated plunges in the river, the plastic bag had become our precious mail pouch. It had gone downriver weeks before protecting our outgoing mail, and now it returned to us, fat with incoming letters.

Trining left to go to Suat and Amalya's to continue spreading the news from Silco as Janet and I turned our attention to the mail pouch. To say that I was starved for news from home was an extreme understatement. My yearnings for news from home, from friends, from the world outside of Madga, were even stronger than my cravings for fresh food. Janet snapped off the rubber band and untwisted the Baggie. The top letter was addressed to her. So was the second letter. And the third. And, in fact, all eight of the letters in the pouch were addressed to Janet. My throat tightened and I gulped a breath, not wanting my hurt to show. Janet looked up at me, her own excitement evident, yet she was not oblivious to my pain.

"You know, you'd get more mail if you would write more letters," she said.

I couldn't speak. My throat would crack. I would cry. I would scream my rage and anger and sadness. I went into the house and sat down to write in my journal.

But I *do* write, I poured it out on the page. There must be at least ten people who owe me letters—friends from college and church and my family. I write long, friendly, upbeat, happy letters, even when I'm not feeling friendly, upbeat, or happy. I try to make them interesting, telling stories of life here and asking about their lives. But it's getting harder and harder to write, to explain anything when I have to keep backing up to explain what I'm explaining. Things are so different here from what my friends and family know or care about. And even when I write, I get no response. It's like I've just vanished from the earth and no one cares.

I was half-crying and trying hold it in, trying not to think about facing another month without mail. After all, this should come as no surprise, I continued in my journal. My family doesn't write. After nearly two years in-country, I have gotten a total of maybe five letters from home. Why should I be surprised not to receive any letters today? Grow up. This is reality. My friends and family just don't write. It doesn't mean they don't like me. It just means they don't like to write letters.

"Listen to this," Janet shouted. "I'm an aunt. My brother's wife had a baby girl! She'd be two months old already. I just can't *believe* it!" I slumped, my journal across my lap. I didn't care a bit about Janet's brother or his child. What about my own baby brother? He must have really grown up in the years I'd been gone. He was fifteen when I left, and now what? He must have graduated from high school this year. He hasn't written to me *ever*! I haven't heard from him even once! I have no idea what college he'll be starting this month or what he'll study. I don't even know him anymore. We used to laugh together. I miss him.

I'll be a surprise for them too, if I ever see my family again, I continued to write. I can't exactly pinpoint how I've changed, but I have. For one thing, I'm fatter. My hair is longer. I have more zits than ever. The only thing that's the same are the clothes that I'm wearing—exactly the same ones I left home with more than two years ago.

I'm not like Janet. I'm not perfect. I'm not beautiful. I don't have a Pepsodent smile and a lanky tanned body with fluffy, flowing hair. I get messy menstrual periods and cramps so fierce they make me puke. I'm not smart like her. I'm not neat and tidy like her. I don't have deep questions about philosophy and anthropology and culture like she does. I can't make a white sauce or a one-egg omelet. And no one writes to me!

I have changed. I used to be a regular person, with some cleverness, humor, charm, some worthiness, some skills. But Peace Corps has changed me. I've become a fat, worthless hunk of nothing, a protoplasmic blob of empty reasoning, with zits. I've become a person not only lacking answers, but now unable to frame the questions.

Janet was looking at a snapshot of her new niece as I leaned past her to grab the bucket. While Janet read and reread her eight letters, I would wash my hair at the river. That way no one would see my tears.

◉◉◉

During afternoon class on Datu and Richarda's porch, I was watching Ricarda in her house weaving pandanus leaves with little Lalak by her side. When Lalak cried, Ricarda propped the baby over a broken place in the floor and Lalak pooped between the slats. The pig under the house sauntered over and scoffed up the yellow-green runny mess. Then the dog took up where the pig left off as Ricarda poured a dipper of water over Lalak's butt.

Later on in the morning, Lando, naked as always, leaned sideways out over the porch rail, clinging, one foot on the porch, one hand on the rail, the rest of him suspended in midair as he peed onto the ground below. The stream was strong, and from that height made a splattering splash in the dust. He bounced back onto the porch and went on his rascally, flighty way. Like a monkey, that child.

And later on, it was Poring who took a break from class to scamper down the pole, squat a couple of feet from the bottom of the pole and—without missing a beat in her conversation with Ricarda inside the house—peed into the dust with a great gush that seemed beyond capacity for her small body.

The young kids seem to pee just about anywhere. I'm the only one who notices these things, and I notice that I too am beginning not to notice.

— Journal, September 16, 1972

◉◉◉

Dear Buck

Perhaps I already told you that our mail was lost by the logging company. When we arrived in Davao, we found out that the Peace Corps office had forwarded our last batch of mail on one of the logging trucks going to Silco Camp, to be put on a banka heading upriver to us. But the mail got lost. Maybe it was full of your letters to me.

—Letter home, August 30, 1972

◉◎◉

"Dear Buck" her letter began. Buckshot was my nickname from my long-gone Roy Rogers cowgirl days, when I'd don tall rubber boots and gallop around the backyard on my palomino stick pony named Trigger.

Some days, riding that same sock-headed broomstick, I called her Buttermilk and imagined her a dusty tan color. I tried to encourage our housecat to run along with me, calling, "Here, Bullet. Come, Bullet," but Bullet wouldn't play with me.

> "I'm so ashamed of myself for not writing in so long, but my life is so different now and I never get to do the things I should. I haven't cleaned house in many months so you can imagine what it is like. I do pick up the necessary items and wash the clothes and dishes, but that is the extent of it."

In her written words I could hear the silky, ruffled cadence of Texas talk. I'd almost forgotten the comfortable rhythm of it.

> "My work at Montgomery Ward is exhausting," Mother wrote. "I come home each day and fall into bed, too tired to do anything, then on weekends, your daddy and I go out to the lake, which I thoroughly enjoy, but there is much work to be done at the lake too. I awoke this morning thinking of you and vowed this day would not pass without my writing."

Her handwriting, so precise, old-style cursive, with rounded curves, and the ending t's that look like r's, because ending t's were taught that way in the generation before my own.

> "First let me say I am very concerned about your health. I am afraid your diet is not sufficient to give you the strength to combat complications, and I worry how will it affect you later in life.
> "I know this is the first time I've written since Mother died. I like to have never gotten over that—then finally I got all her things moved out last May."

My grandmother Effie died in April, while I was living in Butuan City. She'd had a form of paranoid dementia, in those days just called "senile," and she lived her last months mostly bedridden in my old room. Mom and Dad were her caregivers. But before she died, my grandmother wrote me a note in her shaky hand, telling me how proud she was of me, and how she wished me much happiness in life. Before I packed up to leave Butuan I memorized her words and burned the card, because I didn't want anyone else reading, or stealing, it. It was a beautiful American greeting card and had blackmarket resale value.

> "We love our mobile home and fishing out here at the lake," Mom wrote, "but there is so much yard work to do. I have a garden. I have black-eyed peas, peppers, tomatoes, squash. Why today I picked 20-30 tomatoes, beautiful ones. I give many of them away, but mostly I just sit down and eat them. That's the kind of living I like."

Her letter stops, then she picks up later.

> "September 9, 1972. It's been almost a month since I started this letter. While writing the above, a terrific rain started while we were at the mobile home. We had never been there when it rained so much. The wind blew very, very hard, but we seemed secure. However, we didn't get to leave the mobile until around 10 o'clock at night when the rain finally stopped. We did notice a lot of activity at the sales office when we left out, but didn't think too much about it. Anyway, when we got home to Fort Worth, the telephone was ringing. It was sales office calling. There had been a funnel cloud that completely demolished the marina and the boats. Our boat was sunk. And some of the mobile homes out there were damaged. I was so glad we had been out there because I would have worried myself to death had I not known ours was safe. Anyway, they found our boat many yards away from the marina. It was totaled. We have insurance, but not enough. We can get the motor fixed, but not the boat. We will have to come up with the extra. The boat had big holes in the side, and we lost the windshield, and the battery, the lights, and all the stuff in the boat too, such as the minnow bucket, fish net, and the fish basket. But they say they can fix the boat. Anyway, 'The Buckshot' was a sad looking sight."

They'd named their fishing boat after me. I was touched, even if it was now a sunken ship.

> "We received your recent letter and pictures last Friday and I've already re-read it three times. I say Bravo! You are doing exactly what I would like to do this very day. I am so tired of 'keeping up with the Joneses.' Of course while you children were growing up I always wanted the best for you and that took both

of us working and I am very proud of all of you kids, but I do want to stop for a little while, but it seems as though we just keep going deeper and deeper, and my income is needed too. I'm almost willing to just live in a tent somewhere if only I could enjoy life for a while. I would like to garden, in a real garden, and raise flowers and just be in touch with nature, the birds, the sky, and all living creatures around me. But no, I have to go to Montgomery Ward every day to work, and I am so very tired.

"So I say if you are happy doing what you are doing, fine. Also if you want to travel and you feel as though there will not be any danger in the way you will be traveling, enjoy it, but do be careful, because other countries may not be so friendly.

"Well, next week is your birthday. I hope you have a very Happy Birthday.

"Love, Mother"

Finally, a letter from home had reached me. And I was crying again, this time because her words took me back to a homeland and people I loved, the same homeland and life that I was grateful to have escaped.

⊙⊚⊙

I have enormous, runny, skin ulcers on my legs that don't ever seem to heal. Lots of them. I'm going to take an antibiotic for a while, to see if they improve. I'm very tired, physically and mentally. Madga is, I think, getting to me—the isolation and the endless work just to stay a little bit clean and moderately fed.

As I wrote the last line, I knocked over the tin can kerosene lantern and started a small fire on the porch. The worst part is wasting kerosene. Geez, I'm clumsy.

—Journal, September 18, 1972

⊙⊚⊙

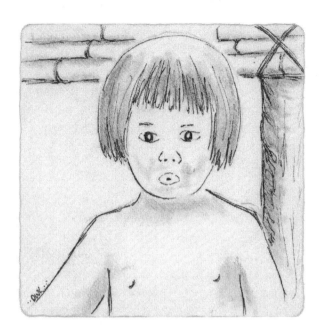

Tata

Today is Spirograph day in school. It's really fun. A Spirograph is a two-dimensional set of gear wheels within wheels. You put a pencil through a hole, roll the meshing gears and circles, and draw amazing patterns. It's simply mind-boggling and mesmerizing for the kids—and for me, too.

On another note, I'm beginning to worry that I might have head lice and maybe bed bugs too. I itch constantly, and I'm clawing at myself incessantly, although I'm trying not to. My itchy head might be from sweat; it seems better after I wash my hair. I found a bug in my bedding yesterday that looks like what I imagine a bed bug might look like, but I've never actually seen one, so all I have to go by is Mamaw's stories of growing up in East Texas in the

⊙⊙⊙

At first it was hard to tell how many children Datu Tagleong and Ricarda had, because kids were all over the place and every child seemed to belong to everyone in the village. But the general rule I came to use was: Where does so-and-so sleep? Generally speaking, kids slept at the home of their parents, so that was how I determined families. But that hypothesis led me to some inaccurate assumptions. Understanding the tangled familial relationships in the little village of Madga wasn't easy.

As I tried to sort it out, I asked and kept asking questions. Even when I had already heard the answers, the second and third times I asked, I was likely to get new information. Contradictions were common. Was it my inept language skill, or were people deliberately misleading me, or were things complex in ways that were so foreign to me that facts were multidimensional?

One day, I learned that twins Tessie and Aida, along with their siblings Kassio and Romeo, were Datu's kids by wife number two. These children were among the older kids in my class. I hadn't suspected they were closely related to Datu, since they all slept across the river.

Datu's wife number three, Ricarda, had six children, three from a previous marriage, including one who was studying in Sagunto with Joe and Flor, and Darna who lived across the path. And then there were Ricarda's three little ones who had Datu as their father—Lando, Tata, and Lalak. Too young to regularily attend our classes, these little ones were more like school mascots.

It had taken me a while to notice Tata at all, for in the early days at Madga, I was doing well to hold on to the faces and names of the kids in our school. The little ones in the village were a blur of runny noses and dusty baby bodies.

But Tata's physical disability set her apart. She limped. I started giving her special attention, a few bites of leftover pancake, a little hug when she came to lean over my lap to see what I was doing. One day, Tata wandered from inside her house to sit at my feet during class—and then pooped, a diarrhea greenish-yellow odoriferous river that nearly made me wretch. It got worse when the hunting dog ran over and began lapping up the mess with great smacking sounds. I was trying to keep from puking, breathing deeply to regain composure, but wasn't doing a good job of it until Darna came to the rescue with water to wash down the porch.

With an impulsiveness uncharacteristic of myself, one day on our porch when I thought no one was watching, I cleaned Tata up, taking a damp cloth and rubbing her face.

"Ohhhhugggggg," I said, "let's get rid of those green elevens." Like the number eleven, one green numeral hanging thick from each nostril, mucous ran from her nose to her lips. It was her trademark. When I wiped her cheeks and chin, she grinned back, as if I had done her the biggest favor of her short life.

"Look at that," I told Janet. "Dimples! I hadn't even seen them through the dirt." Tata giggled and grinned over her tiny white teeth. Then she crinkled up her nose and snorted a laugh that made me laugh, and I whispered to her with a smile, "You're a funny little bunny."

"I have a theory on that," Janet said.

"On kid dirt?"

"Yeah. The children stay dirty until they are old enough to walk down to the river and bathe on their own."

I considered the hypothesis. The tiny infants in Madga were pretty clean, for their immobility kept them out of the dirt and their mothers poured water over their butts from time to time. But the toddlers were abysmally dirty. Then, from about three-years old, they were moderately clean again. "Yeah, could be," I acknowledged.

One Saturday morning I was sitting on our front porch washing the breakfast dishes when Tata wandered across the path from Datu's and climbed our ladder. Her little body leaned against me as I squatted rinsing the enamel cups, and she rested her arm on my shoulder. She didn't say a word, but I felt her curiosity. I talked to her, telling her in Visayan that I was washing dishes and that the water in the basin was cool. "Would you like to feel the water?" I asked her. She didn't answer, but her big brown eyes looked at me with happy anticipation.

I took a dipper of water and poured it over her protruding round tummy. She rubbed it over her stomach and the trails of water left brown paths against the dusty gray of her torso and legs. She grinned, wanting more. I resisted the impulse to just plop her in the bucket and bathe her, but I did take a damp cloth to her face once again smearing away the green elevens.

Then I sat her down beside me and began the ritualistic lice-hunt the way I'd observed so often among families in Madga. Tata sat very still, enjoying the attention, as I slowly fingered my way through her dark hair. I had never exactly seen lice, but I knew they were small, grayish spidery things that moved quickly, sucked blood, and tickled. There was so much to see in Tata's hair I couldn't tell lice from the ashes and mud and bits of leaves and twigs. After a while I gave up, handed Tata a book to look at and got on with my chores, not without recognizing my own growing affection for her.

A few weeks later during class, Tata sat on Datu's porch ripping at a stalk of sugarcane with her strong, small teeth. Flies circled and landed at her mouth and nose. She scratched at them; they circled and landed again. I was teaching, but could hardly keep my eyes off her, the flies, the green elevens, her dirty brown body, and the brightness of her dark eyes.

"I gotta do something," I told Janet. "Back in a minute." While my class copied their letters, I bolted across to our little house and brought back a damp cloth and wiped Tata's face. She gave me a rubber-mouth grin and a snorty laugh, then in a gesture of toddler love, she stretched out a hand and offered me her sugarcane.

While I laughed and told her no thanks, inside I melted. I knew it then, in a remote part of myself, that if I were ever to have a child, I wanted it to be a girl child like that one. I wanted to scoop her up and take her away to a place she could be clean, loved, and cared for, where she would have a chance for a bright and beautiful life.

Get real, I told myself. She's a little girl among a million little girls in a dirty Third World country. She'll be lucky to live to adulthood. Yet from that day on, I did what I could for her—bits of food, hugs, and stories she probably didn't understand. Despite my own advice, I loved little Tata.

◉◎◉

Then there are the little kids, who have Ricarda as their mother: Lando, the monkey-child about 4 years old who never stops moving; Tata (one of my favorite kids!) whose real name is, I think, Merle, about 2 years old, with a limp, making her slightly crippled; and baby Imelda, known as Lalak, still a babe in arms, not yet walking on her own.

— Journal, April 12, 1972

◉◎◉

My Bigs have quite a repertoire of songs I've taught them at school, mostly in Visayan, but some I haven't been able to translate so I taught them in English. We talk about the meanings, and they seem to like the English songs as well as the Visayan songs. The newest one is:

I've something in my pocket
That's very nice to see
I take it out and put it on
It's a S-M-I-L-E (and everyone smiles, BIG)

Cute. We began talking about pockets and who had a pocket. Some of their shorts have pockets, and one of the girls had a dress with a pocket. So we were going around the porch, asking, "May doon 'pocket'?" (Do you have a pocket?) and it came to Tata, an always-naked toddler, who was hanging out with us on the porch that morning. Not wanting to overlook her, I asked her, and she was so cute, grinning shyly. She didn't say anything, but I think she was sort of understanding and was happy to be included. Anyhow, the kids all laughed and she got a big hug from her sister. It was a sweet and funny moment in school.

— Journal, September 20, 1972

Soap

I have only a few clothes—and five pair of panties—
so normally I do laundry every few days. That usually
works out okay. But sometimes, like now, because of
rain or because I'm sick, the laundry piles up. Once I've
worn all my clean underwear, I start over again, wearing them inside out. That buys me five more days. And
if I still haven't done laundry, I start over again. But the
third time is really disgusting, especially when I've had
a period and there's been leakage. This is one of those
details of life that no one will ever know about, and
probably I shouldn't even write about it. I'm glad I can
erase these embarrassing parts of my journal.

— Journal, August 18, 1972

◎◎◎

Bath time in Madga usually began after the noon meal, when it was oppressively hot, the flies were droning, and there was little or no breeze to cool things off.

"Who's first today?" Janet asked.

"Me! I gotta wash my hair," I said. "I've got enough oil on my head to fry *kamote* chips."

"Okay, you win. Gross, go on."

I grabbed the plastic bucket from under the cooking platform, slipped on my yellow rubber slippers, and headed to the river. Washing hair had become a mix n' match activity—sometimes it included laundry at the river, sometimes not. Sometimes I'd haul the water back from the river and wash in our little shower room under the house. That meant more work, but the advantage was privacy. Sometimes I washed my hair at the river, which meant having a gaggle of kids around me.

This day I opted for the private bath. I crossed the dry river stones alongside the channel, then headed out through the sun-warmed shallows until I was shin deep, where the water runs clear and cool. I put the bucket into the river and lifted—too heavy, so I tipped a third of it back in.

Toting the sloshing bucket back up the slippery slope in wet slippers was the tough part. No wonder everyone else goes barefoot. Toe-grips. So I cheated. My feet slipped off the side of my slippers, and I grabbed in the mud with my toes. Useless rubber slippers! But I'd heard too many Peace Corps warnings about schistosomiasis: the larvae that live in shallow waters and enter a person's body by boring through the skin between the toes, flow through the bloodstream, lodge in lower limbs, and cause elephantine swelling. In training, we'd seen photos of obscenely deformed legs and feet from the tropical parasite. Preventable by wearing flip-flops, we were told. So, despite their inadequacy, I hung on to those yellow slippers and wore them most of the time. Did they really do any good against disease? I doubted it. But at least they provided some protection against sharp-edged river rocks. The kids in my class laughed at my American feet, soft like a baby's, they said, while I envied their leathery bare soles.

"You want to bathe after me?" I asked Janet as I toted the bucket to our bath house.

"Um, no. I'm thinking of going down to the river to do laundry after you finish with the bucket."

"Okay, I'll bathe here, then I'll go with you to the river. I've got some clothes to wash, too." Experience taught us that the most practical way to keep up with laundry was to wash in small, frequent batches.

Janet returned to writing while I headed under the house to our "shower room," the only one in Madga and a welcome addition to our home. After his last trip upriver to check on us, Joe Habana oversaw its construction. Nipa fronds spanned our house supports, like leafy planks, creating a private cubicle. The dirt floor was covered with fist-sized river rocks placed closely together, and the result was a private room where I could take off my clothes and splash water all over myself, while my feet stayed un-muddy. Luxury!

Not that anyone else in Madga was concerned about nakedness. They might have been curious about my white body at first, but generally most people were mostly naked most of the time. I still carried American-girl modesty.

I thought myself clever for devising a bathing system using only a couple of gallons of water. I used the bucket, along with our shallow dish-washing basin and a dipper cup. I recycled the water repeatedly—poring it, catching it, and reusing it as it became soapier and dirtier, and setting aside a last bit of clean water for the final rinse.

When I finished my cold, dip-and-pour, river-water shower, I was pleasantly chilled. I'd learned the hard way how important it was to wash my hair midday, or I'd spend a miserable night shivering with wet hair.

I sat on the porch brushing my hair dry while Janet gathered her laundry and claimed the soap, shampoo, and the bucket and basin.

"Ready to go?" she said.

"Um, I'll come along in a little bit. I want to dry my hair first." Janet left me sitting on the porch brushing my hair.

By the time I got to our upstream, low-lying, easy-access laundry and bath spot, Janet had washed her clothes and was in the river bathing in the Manobo way. I had to admit, her method looked like more fun. She swam out to the deepest part of the river while I squatted on the river rocks along the bank, rubbing my T-shirts and underwear in soapy water in our plastic basin.

"How is it?" I called to her.

"Terrific," she shouted back, diving under head first, and reappearing with her hair streaming down her back. She wore a T-shirt and shorts into the water and a few minutes later she was standing beside me, dripping on my shoulder.

"Hey, I already bathed." I laughed.

"Yeah, my turn now. I need the bucket. You finished?" We had worked out a system for modest bathing at the river while keeping our soapy residue out of the current. Janet used her Balinese *tapiz*, encircling chest to knees. Once covered, she shucked her soaking shorts and T-shirt. Taking a bar of soap and a bucket of river water, she walked behind me to the edge of the forest vegetation, where she lathered up and rinsed off inside her tapiz. Then she headed back to the river for a final dip. No one ever said anything to us about soaping up our bodies in the river, but still, we tried to keep our soapy wash water out of our neighbors' cooking pots. She put on a dry T-shirt and wet shorts, and I was still wringing my last shirts when three little kids appeared, giggling and sidling up to me.

"Soap," they begged, eyes bright. It was one commodity that set us apart. I gave each of them a squeeze of shampoo, a bean-sized dollop, and they waded out to the river, dunked under to wet their heads, then lathered up, giggling and shouting cheerfully. Watching them, I could just imagine how good it must feel—clean hair, maybe fewer lice.

Janet was beside me. "So, we don't soap up the river, but we give them the soap so they can do it themselves. Is that it?" Her tone was gently scolding.

"I can't not share. And it's too hard to explain about getting soap in the river, especially when they use the river as a toilet. It's complex." I looked up at her, thinking she might have a logical solution.

"Probably we shouldn't use soap ourselves then," she said.

"Well that might be what happens. We're nearly out of shampoo, and I'm not keen on washing my hair in Tide. Anyhow, we don't have much of that left either," I said, shaking our nearly empty, plastic detergent bottle.

"Time for a Davao supply run, I guess."

"Uh-huh. Wonder what's on at the movies."

I started home, crossing the river cautiously, balancing the basin of clean clothes and thinking. I'm here, a part of this place, living the life, and yet I'm not. I have choices. I have ways to step out and back in. I leave when it's convenient, drifting in and out of a lifestyle that for me, is purely optional—unlike our neighbors, who have no choices. They have no other life to slip into. And our neighbors have no soap, ever. What must they think of us?

And as I balanced cautiously on my soft American feet across the slippery river rocks, thigh-deep in the cool Madga waters, the two little kids appeared beside me. One took my bucket of laundry, balanced it on top of her head, and walked beside me. The other held my hand and steadied me across. Their long black hair, sparkling clean, glinted sleek in the afternoon sun.

I don't know how we look to the adults of Madga. I don't know if we are doing the right thing by touching this culture and maybe changing it in some small way. I don't know how history will judge Peace Corps or us. One thing I do know: These kids love us.

And I felt the same about them. I'd share my soap anytime, down to the last beany dollop.

◉◎◉

I've always been a people-watcher. My daddy taught me. I remember how I used to moan when my parents would insist on taking us kids to the downtown post office every Sunday night, without fail.

First Mother and Daddy would sit down at the kitchen table on Sunday evening, after the dishes were done, and together they would pay bills, deciding which ones would be paid, which ones would have to wait another week. Then, when the checks were written and the envelopes sealed, they would bundle us kids up and put us in the car. Sometimes I was already in my jammies, and Daddy would wrap me up in a blanket, carry me out, and put me in back seat. And off we'd go, downtown, at night. The post office was big, old-style, next to the train station, a fancy stone building with cattle-headed rock gargoyles topping round columns. And while Mother went inside to buy stamps and mail the bills, Daddy and we three kids would wait in the car. That's when he showed us how to watch people, how to observe them carefully—the way they walk, the way they dress, what their clothes say about the weather or how their walk shows how they're feeling. Sometimes you could even tell who they love by watching their faces, their smiles, the way they touch or hold hands. Daddy would make up stories about these people, and an ordinary trip to town turned into an adventure.

If I could do it again today, I'd try to get Daddy to stop by Griff's for a burger and french fries and a chocolate malt on the way home. Geez, I'm hungry.

— Journal, September 11, 1972

◉◉◉

Drink More Water

Lately I've been having trouble telling dreams from reality. I get mixed up. And there is the continuing clumsiness and forgetfulness. I also forget what I did and did not tell someone. Maybe I have a brain tumor. Janet says I got this way because our life is so dull.
—Journal, September 15, 1972

◉◉◉

In Davao City, I went to see a doctor. Things weren't right. I was off-kilter and unable to straighten. I had no fever or pain, no broken bones, earache, headache, sprains, or strains. Just oddness, an increasing disconnect with reality.

The waiting room was full, and some of the patients looked truly ill. One skinny old man with sunken eyes, unable to stand or walk, was leaning on the arm of a younger man, perhaps his son. I felt stupid for being there; what was I going to say to the doctor — "I feel weird?"

He was not the regular Peace Corps doctor, but a substitute, young and skinny in the typical Filipino way. "What's the problem?" he asked.

I began the litany. Zits, really bad zits that seem to come from someplace deep inside my face and emerge like enflamed budding horns, forehead, chin, nose, cheeks, neck. Zits far beyond the superficial whiteheads or blackheads of normal greasy skin. What was this plague?

Boils. I'd had a boil on my thigh and one on my butt.

My period was becoming increasingly irregular and heavy. I used to be very regular, and I'd get mild cramps signaling my impending period. But more recently I was getting no warning, and last time a giant midnight gush left me at the river washing out two huge sheets and a cotton blanket because of the surprise. My body rhythm had changed. And now I experienced cramps like being squeezed in a vice, pulling my guts till I puked.

I couldn't tell dreams from reality. I got mixed up. Did I do something or just dream that I did it? Did I say out loud what I was thinking, or not?

I dropped things. My hands didn't remember their job. A cup of water slipped through my fingers; fortunately, my cup didn't go under the house and fortunately, it was almost empty so I only wasted a little splatter of our precious boiled water.

Finally, my toenails. They were washboard rough, splitting and rotting.

The doctor said next to nothing. He looked me over, listened to my breathing, to my heart, looked at my toenails. His recommendation: "Drink more water."

Over the next days in Davao City, along with drinking plenty of safe water, I ate ice cream, barbecued pork, roasted sweet corn, a ton of fresh fruit, a banana split, slabs of grilled tuna, a hot dog, boiled eggs, *pancit, adobo,* fresh lobster, blueberry muffins, steamed ricecakes, and more safe water. And I felt better. I could focus and laugh again. Doc must have been right. But I gained weight. My shorts were tighter than when I'd arrived. Must have been the banana split.

◉◉◉

We're finally on our way upriver to Madga after ten days in Davao. It was a really enjoyable stay, with movies and conversations and shopping and good food and hot showers. And I got a letter from best pal Jane in Fort Worth, although she didn't really have much news and her life actually sounds kind of boring. Her big excitement is a guy, and I get the feeling she's looking to marry him. I couldn't live such an existence, where the big events are going out dining and dancing with a guy and thinking about him all the time. I think she's in love, whatever that might be.

— Journal, August 1, 1972

◉◉◉

I'm pretty sure I can't live in Texas anymore. I want to tell my family and friends about this, but I'm certain they won't see my viewpoint. Having never lived anywhere else, they see Texas as the best and only place to live. What I see is that there are too many stifling expectations put on a Texas girl, expectations about how her life should be. I won't live life as I am supposed to. I want to talk with my family and friends about these thoughts, but I can't think how to say these things in a letter. So I am putting this conversation off. Indefinitely.

— Journal, August 1, 1972

◉◉◉

Fire

We were supposed to leave Davao today by pickup truck back to Silco Camp and be on our way upriver to Madga tomorrow. So we got all our supplies together here at the Davao guesthouse, loaded the red company pickup, and left the guesthouse at 1 p.m. At 5 p.m. we were still in Davao. Our driver had stopped by the maintenance shed to get the spare tire for the truck, but the maintenance people searched for hours and couldn't find it. So we went back to the guesthouse for the night, and we'll try again tomorrow.

—Journal, September 1, 1972

☺☺☺

Janet and I were in Davao prepping for another return upriver to Madga. We'd just spent a week and a half eating at restaurants, seeing friends and movies, and shopping—bug spray, body soap, laundry soap, shampoo, and—a personal luxury—American-made, expensive, roll-on deodorant, a lucky find in the city. We'd bought toilet paper, writing paper, and carbon paper, a bundle of new pencils and some rulers, and a new pair of scissors for our school. And for our neighbors, we had rock salt, red fabric, and after a long search, some shiny plastic beads and thin needles for Amalya for her bead-weaving. We had medicine to share in the village. I had new rubber slippers. We had two corked Coke bottles filled with kerosene, nails, string to fix our door, and a new *plangana*, a plastic tub for washing dishes and clothes to replace our broken one. We had canned goods—corned beef, beans, corn, mackerel, pineapple, condensed milk, teabags, instant coffee, flour, sugar, fresh garlic, potatoes, carrots, fresh fruit, bakery buns, and cookies. We would share the baked treats with Trining and TingTing on our trip upriver. Most important of all, our Care package from Manila had arrived with real gardening tools—a shovel, a pick, a spading fork, a hoe, and trowels. Heavy, unwieldy things; I was already plotting how to fit the tools into the little river banka. Packing took me two days; consolidation and weight balance were the keys to success.

It was after dark and the water was finally back on at the Santa Inis-Melalie Guesthouse in Mafori Heights, Davao City. I had been showering when the water suddenly went frigid, then stopped entirely. This happened all too often, and early on I'd learned to suds and rinse my hair quickly. I'd been burned more than once with soapy eyes when the water abruptly quit. This time, I didn't even squeak when the water went icy and then stopped. I just grabbed a thin little Philippine towel— one that would have been a dishtowel in the Old Country, but here was a practical climatic adaptation. The flimsy towel would air dry quickly, while a thick, soft, fluffy American towel might mildew in the humidity before it dried.

Janet was at the bathroom door. "Better hurry. There's a fire, we've got to evacuate."

"Huh?" I heard footsteps running in the hallway and a male voice shouting. "*Sunog!*" Fire. "Get out." I had a choice, exit in the skimpy towel or get dressed first. I opted to dress. I preferred to chance a close encounter with flames rather than face certain shame, laughter, gossip, and an enduring legacy as the Americana who ran out with only a thin, flapping towel.   Janet was checking the hallway. "Nothing yet. We've got time." We'd been together so long I knew that she meant we had time to get our personal gear out of the building.

I put on shorts, a T-shirt, and rubber slippers—skipping the underwear to save a moment— and started down the hall and out into the yard carrying my duffle, purse, and camera bag. Janet was behind me with her goods. We could smell smoke. We stood side by side in the darkness under a sprawling *ilang-ilang* tree in the side yard and were joined by two houseboys. No one had seen flames. Everyone smelled smoke.

"We're going back in." I heard Janet say. I knew exactly what she was thinking. We'd just spent a couple of months' living allowances on supplies, not to mention a week of shopping and months of waiting for the arrival of the Care package. We were going in to bring it all to safety.

"But Mum," a wide-eyed houseboy said. "Mum! The fire!" Janet was the first one to the door, I was right behind her, and behind me were the two whimpering helpers. "But Mum. *Mum!*" They followed us, nonetheless, through the smoky, dark hallway and into our room. And in one giant, overloaded, adrenalin-fueled trip, the four of us brought out ten heavy boxes of supplies, a bundle of tools, and one unwieldy blue *plangana* basin that kept slipping off the top of my stack. In the darkness, the four of us sat on the boxes beside the tree, breathing hard and waiting for flames to consume the guesthouse. I knew not to hope for a fire department. I'd been in-country long enough to temper any expectation of help. But from inside, I heard the guesthouse manager searching for a telephone number for Davao Light Company.

"Where's that number? Does the phone still work?" I could hear him scrambling and shouting from the front office.

Then, "Turn off the current! Watch out for hot wires! *Pull the breaker!* I can't see the phone!" There were shouts, running footsteps, and crashes from inside.

We waited. The smell of smoke got stronger, and there was something familiar about the smell. It was a high-pitched smell, like burning metal, like the smell of lightning in the West Texas desert before a gully-washer. The smell of toasted ozone. The taste of airborne electricity.

And we waited some more, swatting mosquitoes, hearing only our own breaths, and the *kwerk*-chirp of some night cicadas. The skies turned darker and cloudier as the moon moved higher. We continued to watch for flames.

None came. Mr. Bañez came to sit with us and sent a runner out for bread from the bakery down the street. For a while, beneath cloudy moonglow, loggers Raul and Pedong, Mr. Bañez, Janet, and I shared buns and cookies while the Davao City Light Company checked the guesthouse. They found overloaded and shorted-out wires in the radio room, directly beneath our bedroom.

Finally, the shout came, "You can go back inside now."

The boxes seemed heavier as we toted them back upstairs. It was Raul who spotted two sprawling bodies in the dark corner of the downstairs meeting room. He kicked at the foot of one of the bodies and a sleepy head rose. Two drunk logging guys had slept through the entire episode.

I lay down on my squeaky-spring bed, clothed, not daring to undress, restless in an all-night semi-sleep. I could hardly wait for morning so we could finally leave the crazy city and begin the two or three-day journey through the mountains and up our river to the quiet safety of Madga village.

◉◉◉

While we were in Davao, Janet and I went out to dinner with Mr. Hilario Bañez, administrative officer for the logging company, along with logging foremen Pedong and Raul. We went to the Marakesh Club, the best night spot in Davao City. Janet and I received a note from the next table, scrawled on a yellow paper napkin: "I Rey. You are all very beautiful and friendly. Can I join you?" Rey and his buddies at the next table, no doubt, thought we were white whores and they wanted in on the action. We were properly offended and ignored it. There were 13 San Miguel beer bottles on the table with the three very drunk Filipino men. So typical. So tiresome.

— Journal, August 1, 1972

Mister Redford

We arrived at Silco Camp at about 4:30 p.m. The pickup truck is definitely the most comfortable way to get from Davao City to Silco. On other trips, I've ridden in 18-wheeler logging trucks, and they're incredibly slow, like lumbering beasts. The Manobo people from the lower parts of the logging concession are always hitching rides on the logging company vehicles, and it's good PR for the trucks to pick up the Manobo passengers and carry them back to their home areas inside the concession. But it's crazy, because there's no passenger space on the 18-wheelers. The Manobo hang on to chains and ropes and balance themselves precariously on the steel beams on a truck designed to transport big logs, not people.

The Manobo men and women have to be strong and have terrific stamina to hang on for hours as the wheeled beast crawls up and down deep gullies, and carefully inches forward on the edges of steep precipices beside harrowing ravines, and fords fast rivers as the cab plunges deep (up over the headlights! The rule is never stop or the truck will stall out!), and passes through low-hanging, slapping, scraping trees that are trying to reclaim the roadway for the forest. It's dangerous, but the Manobo hang on, because if they let loose and slip beneath a wheel, they'd be dead. I'm glad they don't make us ride like that; I would fall off. We ride in the cab next to the driver, and even that is frightening at times. So compared to a trip in the big trucks, the ride in the little pickup truck today was pure luxury. Manobo passengers still got a ride, but were able to climb in and sit in the back bed—jamming in, all crowded—and they'd jump out while the truck was moving slowly. If the truck was going too fast, someone in back pounded on the cab and the driver slowed down so the passenger could jump out. I don't think jumping out of the pickup truck is too dangerous, and I'm sure the Manobo today were grateful they didn't have to cling onto the chains and rails of a logging truck. Today was an easy ride for all of us.

—Journal, September 2, 1972

⊙⊚⊙

The Santa Ines-Melale Logging Company Guesthouse at the Silco Camp outpost sat near the river at the edge of cleared forest. Silco Camp was the terminal end of a dusty, washboard road running into the mountains a long day out from Davao City and was populated by dusty, behemoth, chain-bellied, eighteen-wheeler trucks, and bulldozers with blades that could eat a mountain. Civilization either began or ended at Silco Camp, depending on which direction you were coming from.

Silco was hot and dusty except in the air-conditioned office of logging superintendent Pedro Guanto. I was so accoustomed to tropical heat that the coolness of his office chilled me as I entered. He sat behind a massive Philippine mahogany desk, a product of the old Mindanao forests. Polished to a high gloss, the beautiful, enormous carved desk probably weighed a thousand pounds. Mr. Guatno was about one-sixth the size of his desk, a smallish round man with a kindly face. Delighted that we Americanas were living in his logging concession, he wanted to help. When we'd first arrived, it was Mr. Guatno who had assigned his concession guards Trining and TingTing to watch over us and help with transportation up and down the Madga. Janet and I checked in with Mr. Guatno every time we came downriver, giving him updates on our mountain school. It was he who helped us with our mail, dispatching our baggie-wrapped bundles when we sent them downriver with Trining and TingTing. He would also send fresh fruit or bakery bread upriver to us and he offered us open accommodations at the Silco guesthouse on our journeys in and out of Madga.

The Silco guesthouse was a low-slung, unpainted, tin-roofed building with a wide veranda, a sunny kitchen, a noisy generator, and an attached wing of guest rooms with two squeaky twin beds in each. It was the permanent residence for a lanky teenage houseboy named Isco, an aging American named Mister Redford, and a spidery monkey who would sit on my shoulder and pick invisible lice from my hair. I didn't have lice, but the monkey would rifle through my long hair with great patience, thin fingers, and long tiny fingernails, plucking out nothingnesses and delicately placing them between his dark rubbery lips. This monkey's tickling head massage felt wonderful.

"You're up early," Mister Redford said, running a thick hand over his gray grizzled chin.

"I thought I'd do laundry before it gets too hot," I said.

"You don't gotta do that stuff. Isco'll do it for you. Give him your dirties."

It wasn't my style to have someone else do my work. Besides, I didn't want the houseboy touching my underwear.

"I'd rather do it myself," I told him. I was actually looking forward to the cool slosh of soapy water, and the rinsing and wringing at the outdoor hand pump.

He nodded and turned his back, taking a cast iron frying pan and metal spatula down from ceiling hooks.

"Rats can't get to 'em as easy if you hang your pots. Remember that. Your friend, she still sleeping?"

"Guess so." I'd left Janet earlier on her twin bed in the room we shared, sprawled beneath a slow, circling ceiling fan stirring the heavy air.

"She's a real pretty one, she is." There was something unnerving about this old man thinking about Janet as pretty, and the way he said it, sort of dreamily. "You both like eggs for breakfast?" He glanced over his shoulder at me. I wasn't the pretty one. I was safe. He was tall, thin, bent in the back, and old, fifty at least. "Scrambled okay with you?"

"Scrambled eggs would be great," I said. Actually, I could barely tolerate eggs, but I was learning to appreciate their nutrition. Scrambled or hard boiled was the only way I could eat them, because there was no squishy, eggy texture. "Do you do all your own cooking?" I asked him.

"Most times. Easier that way. Used to be a cook you know."

"Really? When was that?"

"Army days. Cooked for the whole company." He was cracking eggs and whipping them with a fork in a big ceramic bowl. "Them days, the hard part was finding fresh food. Eggs fresh like these was hard to come by."

"You were here during the war?"

"Yep."

"And you're still here?" World War II had been over for twenty-seven years.

"Decided I liked it better here than back home."

"What about your family? Where are they?"

"Don't got much family. Had a wife. But hell, she went along with someone else soon as I left. Time come to go back stateside, I didn't go. Hid out for a while in the mountains. Drifted for a while. Been here at this guesthouse now going on fifteen years."

I let that soak in. Fifteen years. He'd been in this outpost since I was in third grade. A lifetime. Mister Redford was chopping garlic, wielding the knife in quick bursts. He scooted the pulp into the hot oil.

"Think you'll ever go back home?" I asked.

"Don't reckon. Army chalked me up as dead. Lost in action, or maybe deserted. Wrote me off."

The smell of garlic filled the room, making my mouth water.

"Is there anything about America you miss? The scenery, the music, the food, movies, anything?"

"Nope. Nothing." He poured the eggs into the skillet and started stirring with the spatula.

"Get that knife and help yourself to the bread over there. Made it yesterday."

"You bake bread?"

"Sure thing. Got to. That or eat soft rice twice a day. Me, I like bread I can sink my teeth into. Now where is that long-haired girlfriend of yours? These eggs is just about done."

"I'll see if she's ready," I said jumping up. Janet was on the veranda writing.

"Mister Redford says breakfast is ready. You want to come?"

She looked up. "Is he in there?"

"Yes. Scrambled eggs. Homemade bread. Looks pretty good."

"I don't think I want to see Mister Redford this morning. Did you hear the racket last night? With Mister Redford and Isco?"

"Guess not. I slept pretty solid."

"They woke me up, thumping and running. So I looked out here. They were both here on the veranda, naked, chasing one another. Isco laughing like a wild turkey. Mister Redford, playing with himself, kind of teasing and chasing. It was sick and spooky. He gives me the creeps."

I was silent a moment, imagining the scene Janet described. "You mean, totally naked?"

She looked at me like I was stupid. "I think what was going on didn't require clothing."

When I got back to the kitchen, he was tilting the pan and scraping a mound of hot eggs into my plate. "Janet's up, but not ready for breakfast yet," I offered.

"Fine. Maybe we'll save her some. Got plenty. You just help yourself to as much as you want."

I was hungry. I forked eggs onto a tear of bread and chewed. "They're good." I told him with the surprise probably apparent in my voice. "Really good. The best I've ever had. Really."

Mister Redford was next to me, elbows on the table, shoveling down eggs and bread.

"I'll tell you one thing. A secret." He leaned close and raised one bushy eyebrow. An egg crumb hung from the corner of his mouth and I smelled garlic and stale breath from between his yellow teeth.

"What's that?" I was not one bit sure I wanted to hear his secret.

"You gotta get them off the fire before they look done. Eggs is like that, they just cook themselves a little bit more, even after they's off the fire."

I looked at him. "Eggs."

"Uh-huh. You remember that now. Take 'em off the fire just a little bit early. That's how you make perfect eggs. You got that now?"

My eyes lowered to the pile of eggs on my plate and I nodded. "Yes. Your secret is something I'll definitely remember."

☉◎☉

> Here's something different—I grew up seeing the "man in uniform" as desirable. My daddy was in the US Air Force, and there are a lot of pictures of him, handsome and proud in his World War II uniform. But a man in uniform has an entirely different connotation in the Philippines. People remember the war, and it seems that there is an innate fear of soldiers, at least here in the southern interior mountains. Horrendous stories of cruelty, torture, murder, and starvation by Japanese soldiers live on. All soldiers, it seems, have a bad reputation. "They ate our chickens and took our eggs," I've been told. But it's hard to tell when these things happened or which army it was. The invading Japanese? The liberating Americans? Or the Philippine National Army at the time they occupied the area? There doesn't seem to be any difference. All soldiers trigger fear.
>
> — Journal, October 3, 1972

Pools Russ Een

It's so incredibly hot and breathless at the Silco Camp, it defies description. I want to lie in ice water, but there's no ice, or water for that matter. Sweat is pouring down my face, back, chest, and legs. My shirt is soaking wet. I can't eat. I can't even move. I tried to sleep, but the bed was like a heat cloud radiating around me, making me feel even hotter. I got up to shower, but there isn't any water at the guesthouse this time of day. It will come back on later, I hope.

—Journal, August 1, 1972

⊙⊙⊙

I sat alone on the bare plywood bench inside the Silco Camp General Store and Bakery. The smell of baked goods filled my head, and beside me were my bundles of fresh buns and cookies I'd purchased to take upriver to Madga. On my table was my half-full bottle of warm Pepsi.

A preadolescent girl at the counter folding brown paper wrappers for bread. Every few minutes, she'd glance up at me, smile, and then duck her head back to her work.

She's embarrassed, I thought. She probably would like to ask me something but is too shy. I could start a conversation, but I don't really want to. I'd rather just sit here silently and finish this Pepsi. What I would give for some safe ice now!

Outside, the midday temperature soared. Sweat dripped down my backbone and circled my armpits. It was siesta time. The logging camp was eerily still. Only a few flies seemed to have the energy to move.

I just want to sit here out of the sun in the relative coolness of the store, waiting for Janet, waiting for the afternoon breeze off the river, waiting for life to move a little further down the line.

My eyes roamed the unpainted frame building and the shelves stocked with the goods of daily life, and for a few moments, I watched the young woman. Backlit by the doorway, her long black hair glowed, so deeply black it was nearly purple, tied back with a baby-blue ribbon.

How can she not be sweating? Why am I the only one in this country who's a sopping sponge of sweat?

I scratched a tickle of perspiration running behind my ear as a man stepped out from the back of the bakery.

"Cita, any customers?" he asked the girl.

The girl pointed with pursed lips toward me.

"Only one," she said. "Americana."

He grunted his approval and leaned against the counter, openly staring at me. He was old, in his forties I guessed, with graying, greasy hair. He had a short wiry body, the typical Filipino man weighing less than a hundred pounds. I didn't want to talk to him. I didn't want to smile or answer the questions I knew he would ask—about eating rice and finding a Filipino husband—questions I'd been asked a thousand times before and would be asked a thousand times again. I wanted him to quit staring at me.

I looked out the door, squinting into the sunlight. The dirt road was deserted. Nothing moved. Even the wood-frame buildings across the way leaned into each other, as if collapsing from the heat. Where the dirt road sloped downward, a dark ribbon of river lay flat and lifeless against the raw, red-brown, hard-packed earth.

I should have brought my book, I thought. I could sit here and read. Or my journal, I could write. Anything would work, I just don't want that man talking to me. He's still staring, gives me the creeps. I took another sip of warm Pepsi and looked at the pile of brown paper wrappers on the counter.

Then I asked the girl, "Please, could I have a piece of paper?"

The girl nodded and scooted a wrapper across to me. I placed it in front of me on the table and got out a pen. I'll just write. He'll see I'm too busy to talk.

The man walked slowly out from the counter toward me.

No! Please don't start talking to me.

"You like another Pepsi?" he asked, his Visayan words slow and melted, like the over-warm, too-sweet syrup I was drinking.

"No!" I spit the word out, stomping any flicker of invitation. I didn't even add, "Thank you." I was deliberately being rude.

He walked past me to the table at the far end of the room and perched on the back of a wooden bench beneath two homemade ukulele and a plywood guitar. From where I sat, I faced him directly. Now I was uncomfortable, deliberately avoiding eye contact. I looked down at the table, at the blank wrapper, at the Pepsi.

The man slowly lifted the guitar from its hook and began to strum. It was out of tune. It sounded like the guitars I used to make when I was a kid, using a ham can, a stick, and some wire. It was a flat, toneless imitation of music. And he strummed ineptly, plodding, using his whole hand like a paddle stirring at the strings. Down, down, up. Down, down, up. He was humming.

I wrote. I described the Silco General Store and Bakery.

Front counter: fresh cookies and loaves of bread. Cookies, five centavos each, loaves sixty centavos each. All are tasteless. I think they deliberately leave out any ingredient that might have a flavor. A whole bag of hard cookies, two pesos.

I looked up. The man was staring at me. His eyes tugged at me, grasping at me to respond. I shivered at his look and turned back to the brown paper.

Against east wall: twelve cans of Baguio cooking oil, canned cuttlefish, canned mackerel, canned pineapple, canned pork and beans, canned wieners, canned milk, canned corn beef.

From ceiling: Enamel cups in four sizes, plastic gallon water containers, enamel coffee pot, plastic egg carrier, metal coat hangers, tin ashtrays, two umbrellas, rolls of nylon fishing line, tin ladles, six metal skillets, hemp ropes, five straw hats, three plastic thermoses.

I glanced his way again. He was still staring hotly at me, his eyes tracing against my sweaty skin. I focused on the store, and I wrote.

Behind counter: Bags of hard candy, bottles of soy sauce, tins of crackers, jars of peanut butter, tins of Star margarine, baby bottles, plastic tubs, enamel bowls and plates, and two entire rows of *pancit* noodles in various sizes.

The man was singing now. It was a familiar English love song. I ignored it. I wrote.

Stacked by the walls: seventeen woven mats, five short-handled brooms, and a rice bin covered with a gunny sack. Probably full of rice. Or maybe empty.

Beside door: Paper notebooks, pencils, toothpaste and toothbrushes. Soap: Lux and Palmolive in bars. A wire-bundled bunch of metal zippers. Candles. Brillo-style pot scrubber pads. Baby powder. The two ukulele and the guitar.

In the middle: An old refrigerator. Empty, of course. There's no electricity. Wishful thinking on the part of the store owner.

Well that's it. That's everything in the store. Then I began to sketch the layout of the shelves, the tables, the counters, and benches.

The man sang on, watching me, singing to me, pulling at me with butchered English and a toneless guitar.

> "Wais men say
> Only pool russ een
> But I can hep
> Palling in lub... wid... you"

I was sketching the bread counter when Janet walked through the door.

"Hi, what are you doing?"

"Oh, just writing."

"Writing what?"

"Oh, just writing down the things in the store."

The man was still singing, finishing up his song.

> "But I can hep
> Palling in lub... wid... you."

Janet examined the brown wrapper. "You really did. You listed every item in here. Honestly, sometimes I think the heat must have gotten to you. You're crazy, you know."

I smiled, very glad to see Janet. "I know. Guess I'm just peeling poolish."

"Huh?"

"Nothing," I said, rising and gathering our bundles of fresh breads tucked into my woven shopping bag. "Let's go."

◉◉◉

FOUR KILLED AS TRUCK FALLS

DAVAO CITY, July 22— (PNS) — Four lumberjacks died instantly and 51 others were injured, 13 seriously, when their service bus plunged into a 57-meter-deep ravine in Sabud, Asuncion, Davao del Norte, Thursday afternoon.

The truck was en route to the Santa Ines Melale logging camp in Davao del Norte when the accident occurred.

Charles Opena, manager of the logging firm, identified the fatalities as Andres Gokun, Romeo Quijano, Alfredo Lacayen, and Francisco Daloy.

The injured, whose names were not immediately available, were taken to hospitals here.

Opena said the truck developed engine trouble, causing it to go "wild."

Comment added in my handwriting: "Those 51 name-less 'others' were likely Manobo riders —as always, the unimportant, invisible people."
—From torn news clipping tucked inside my Journal, July 1972

⊙⊙⊙

From Silco Camp, we took the banka heading upriver. The boat was full of our supplies, and us, and one more passenger, an adolescent Manobo girl named DayDay who was trying to get upriver to her family. She'd gotten word somehow that her father was very ill, and she had been trying for several days to get transportation. We said she could ride up with us. It started raining, hard, and for a while I held my camera on my lap, trying to keep it out of the water that was sloshing in the bottom of the banka. I bailed. A lot. And still the rain came and I bailed even faster. Finally, the rain stopped.

We had lunch on the side of the river, near where the little girl wanted off. She ran into the forest, then came back to tell us that her family had moved—something about their crops being washed away by a recent flood. She said that her house was still there, but other people had moved in, not her family. But she told us the people in her house said that her father was well again. The girl cried. I'm not sure what she's going to do. Hope she will be okay. We moved on. Upriver.

—Journal, April 8, 1972

⊙⊙⊙

Speaking

Peace Corps language training—it's more like bombardment—is ongoing and irritating, like being pelted with a thousand snowballs. No single moment hurts, but taken all together, it's overwhelming. Hour upon hour, day after day, not a moment's rest from those phrases ringing in my ears. Maayong buntag! I think my trainer stays up nights making this stuff up, goofing on us with the most illogical and impossible syllables she can imagine. I feel utterly inadequate.

— Journal, July 12, 1970

☉☉☉

Our dugout banka moved cautiously up the shallow river. From my seat on the narrow bench in front of the noisy outboard motor, I watched the forests of Mindanao roll by. Trees towered above us, some a hundred feet tall— massive, ancient giants. Beneath them grew a tangle of smaller trees and shrubs in endless green-to-yellow hues, alongside patches of teal and jade, umber, indigo, crimson, and sienna — jumbled whorls and dappled splotches of color, some shaded, some lit by sun. Closest to us, peeking from the eroding shoreline, were occasional shining lavender orchids, the little kind, wild and wonderful, nodding gently on pencil-thin stems stirred by the river's breeze.

The river was running low, less than a foot of water in the shallowest channels. Smooth river rocks exposed their slick russet, silver-blue, and gray-green faces. And under the water in the places where the forest shadowed our passage, the stones glistened dark and rich — impassive, enigmatic, and mysterious sunken orbs. Trining and TingTing were sweating, maneuvering our boat through the shallows as we continued to make our way upriver toward Madga.

Then we scraped bottom and came to an abrupt halt. "Walk now," Tringing said. And Janet and I hauled ourselves out of the little boat into the shin-deep waters. Trining tugged us forward with a bow rope, TingTing tilted the motor up out of the river as he pushed from the stern, while we two Americanas pushed and pulled from the sides. Then the river deepened, and we all climbed back in. Trining steered from the bow with a long pole, guiding the little boat toward the deeper parts of the river. TingTing kept the motor going, propelling us forward.

Then, with a sudden clank and shudder, the motor died. The abrupt silence was welcome.

"*Lansang!*" TingTing said. Nail. The propeller had hit a rock in shallow water, snapping the pin that held the propeller to the motor. TingTing was asking Trining for a nail to fix it, and Trining had a pocket full of nails. The delay was nothing unusual.

The sudden stillness allowed me to listen to the forest and the river. The water slapped gently at the sides of the banka, while birds chattered in sparkling bursts. The wind rustled the leaves in the tallest trees. Sometimes, when the river ran deep, the trip from Silco Camp to Madga took half a day. When the river was shallow and the going was rough, it could take as long as two days. I didn't mind if this trip would take extra hours. The day was glorious and the company good.

As TingTing worked on the motor, Trining asked if we would like to eat something. "*Gigutum ba kay yo?*" a phrase I'd heard hundreds of times: Hungry you?

My response was simple. The words fell out easily in Visayan. "*Deli pa. Wala pa udto. Unya na lang.*" Not yet. It's not yet noon. Later on.

Trining nodded and waded through the shallows to the shoreline, then merged into the forest and disappeared. Nature break.

I was comfortable with Trining and TingTing and Janet as co-travelers, comfortable with the river, comfortable with my knowledge of the place and the river people. It had taken two years, and I was finally comfortable with the language. At last, everyday conversation flowed. I'd even come to think of Visayan as superior to the cumbersome, convoluted English language. Visayan was simple and straightforward, linear in its syntax with the verb or adjective at the beginning of the sentence so the listener knew right away what was happening. And I appreciated how in Visayan, a verb could become a noun by the addition of a syllable or two at the end. "To sit" becomes "that which is sat upon" by adding a couple of syllables, and you can do the same trick with nearly every verb. "To eat" can become "that with is eaten"; "to ride" becomes "that which is ridden."

There were other tricks in creating tenses. To say something like "the water is heating"— you'd express something like "heat-erizing is the water." These were clever tricks with prefixes. After hearing the patterns often enough and figuring out the langauge consistencies, understanding and speaking had become simple and fun.

Of course, Visayan had not always been easy for me. During Peace Corps training, I was in the slow-learner section, and even then I was among the slowest of the slow. My mind couldn't retain the meaningless syllables, and my tongue felt like a cow's hoof in my mouth as I tried to wrap it around those rapid-fire syllables.

What a hurdle it had been to learn to say in Visayan, *I'd like to introduce you to my companion, Mister Smith*. I could get the *Mister Smith* part all right, but the rest of it was a jumbled-up sound like the flapping of gulls' wings.

Petite and perfect Alma Nera, a native speaker from Davao City, had been my language trainer, and her patience was remarkable. She'd say a few syllables at a time, and I'd repeat them. Then she'd say them again, adding a few more syllables until the whole phrase was, more or less, in my mind. Then she would dramatize the introduction, and we trainees would act out the parts of the introducer and the introducee. Four to eight hours a day, six days a week, we worked on dialog, repetitions, drills, and vocabulary, for three months. All lessons were oral, never written, as our ears learned to distinguish syllables and our tongues learned to roll with awkward enunciations. By slow degrees, my mind began to hold the gibberish.

The goal was a language rating of S-1 on the government language rating scale by the end of training. I should be able to give and receive location directions and order a meal at a restaurant. I was nervous and sweating the day I took the dreaded language test. It was oral, and I sat at a table with one of the trainers. I could tell he wanted us all to pass. He spoke slowly and deliberately. He pretended to be the waiter at a restaurant.

"What would you like to eat?" he asked me in Visayan.

I was so nervous, even if the test had been in English, I might not have been able to think of what to order.

"Papaya," I finally said. And then added, trying to show that I knew something about speaking Visayan, "please."

"What else?" he asked me. "Are you hungry?"

"What else," I repeated. There must be something else. Some food. I couldn't think. "Pig," I said finally.

"Yes, pork. How would you like it prepared?"

"Pig. Cook pig." I offered.

My tester looked disappointed and made a note in his book. "And what to drink?" he asked.

I knew I was failing. All those weeks of labor on this language and I was losing it. "Water," I said.

My tester smiled. "Um, with ice?"

"Yes, yes, with ice. Water with ice. Cold. Cold water with ice."

He gave me another chance. "You are in a city. What do you think about this city?"

A city. What would a person see in a city? "Cars," I said. "Many cars in city."

"And what else?"

"People. Many people. Many people walk."

He looked at me blankly. My words were few, my sentences too simple. I wasn't doing well and I knew it. I needed more words. Something flashy. Something to show him I could say something intelligent.

"Anything else?" he asked.

It came to me like a gift—a word that wasn't among our vocabulary lessons, but I remembered it from a conversation I'd overheard between some volunteers who were heading out back to illicitly smoke marijuana—because when I heard it, I thought I heard a volunteer say "asshole," and I was shocked. But then, it was another word entirely. "*Aso,*" I said, "*Daghan aso.*" Smoke. Much smoke in the city.

The language trainer grinned big. Ooh, good! Smoke!

It was my last chance, and I'd pulled off a big finish. A fancy word.

I passed the language test with a zero-plus. Almost a 1. It was a dubious success, and my trainer could have failed me, but he took pity. Perhaps he saw potential, because he passed me to the next phase: in-country training.

Once I was in the Philippines, I had little choice but to increase my understanding. I learned early on that much of my formal training was moot, because in the place I was assigned, the "pure" form of Cebuano Visayan that I had learned was not spoken. I needed to relearn, to blur and slur pronunciations, to shortcut words and phrases for everyday use. One day, as I was heading out to market with a teacher friend, I was trying to ask one of the kids in my house, "Would you like to come with us?" Rearranging the thought into Visayan syntax, I began searching for the words—"like, you, go, companion..." My host stopped me with a short phrase: "*Uban ka?*" Accompany, you? It was a shortcut. I got it.

Many times in the early days, my lack of fluency was positively painful. Like the time I was visiting another volunteer at a small college where she taught. I had just received a package of clothes from my family in Texas, and I was proudly wearing a new white polyester shirt.

While waiting for my volunteer friend, I was chatting with one of her students. In Visayan, of course. "*Nindot ang lawas mo,*" the boy observed. My mind clicked out the translation. Pretty my—something. What was that word, *lawas*? I quickly concluded they were admiring my new shirt.

"Thanks," I responded in Visayan. "It's a gift from my parents in Texas," I added, looking down at the gleaming whiteness of the blouse.

The student grinned and walked away. Then another student came to me and said the same thing. Again, that word, *lawas*. I responded the same and he too smiled in an odd way. Then I saw the whole group of students grinning. I had said something unintentional. But what?

That evening I asked my host family. "What is that word *lawas*?"

"Oh, it means body. Did someone say something about your body? You are becoming very fat and beautiful, you know."

Ah. My body, a gift from my parents in Texas. It shamed me to replay my stupid response, and every time I remembered that incident I flinched. I'd come a long way with the language since those days. There remained occasional moments of uncertainty, but they were increasingly infrequent. I might not have been native-speaker fluent, but I could cope comfortably in just about any situation, and I usually understood local metaphors, humor, and implied innuendo. Once a male acquaintance touched my arm, noticing the fuzz of light-colored hair, and told me in Visayan with a wicked-playful grin, "If there is so much in the barrio, how much more in the city." A teacher friend had explained that he was referring to my pubic hair. Again, the Texas girl had been embarrassed, but encounters such as those spurred my comprehension.

The outboard motor roared, and we four river travelers were on our way once again. The noon heat was pressing down, and the cool Madga River breeze refreshed. At another bend in the snaking river, the waters deepened between the high banks of a narrow gorge. Here the current was strong and the little outboard puttered valiantly against the flow. The strength of the current set our banka rocking, and I gripped both wooden side planks, holding myself steady in the churning waters.

To my right, the river bottom fell away and I looked down into water that was perhaps ten feet deep, impossible to tell...

Then there was a shout from behind, "*Tudlow!*" The word came to me not so much as a sound, but as a jolt. I jerked my left hand away from the side of the boat a fraction of a second before we lurched with a thud against the cliff wall, precisely at the place my hand had just been. If I'd been a millisecond slower, my fingers would have been smashed.

I looked over my shoulder at TingTing. "Thanks," I said. He lifted his chin and hoisted his eyebrows in silent acknowledgment as he gunned the motor, maneuvering us back into the main stream.

Shaken, I pondered the moment. I'd been close to disaster, saved by TingTing's shout of the word *finger,* to which I had responded reflexively, even before the word reached my ears. Looking back at the receding cliff face, I felt in my chest a flutter of fear at the near-miss disaster, and a slowly dawning realization that the truest communications lie beyond vocabulary, somewhere past culture and language. It was as if I'd *felt* his warning before I could hear and process his spoken word. The more I thought about it, the less I could see into the mystery of what had just happened, as the clear Madga waters danced us onward, shimmering, enticing, mesmerizing.

⊚⊚⊙

On this side of the river, the logging concession guards are Trining and TingTing. They are friends, and I trust them entirely, even with our lives. They've proven themselves to be entirely reliable and have helped us over and over again.

— Journal, August 6, 1972

⊚⊚⊙

It was a nice evening last night. Trining and TingTing and Saldi came over after supper. We passed the guitar around for music, and chit-chatted until it stopped raining, about 9 p.m. Janet had a sick stomach so retired early, going inside to lie down and shutting the door, while the rest of us sat on the front porch. There were no hassles. No trying to cheer her up or offering her home remedies or saying that surely she needed medical *treatment, drugs or injections. Just letting her go rest. Easy. So very unlike the usual lowland attitudes I've found in the Philippines.*

— Journal, September 5, 1972

◉◉◉

The kids are writing (copying from the board) a story about TingTing coming up the river and bringing bread and pomelo *(similar to a grapefruit) and onions and a cabbage—foods that will be shared in the village. I call these things that I write "stories" but they are just two, maybe three sentences. They are not much really, but the kids do seem to appreciate seeing themselves and their friends in the stories. They copy these stories into their composition books and seem to treasure their books. Sometimes I see them re-reading or re-telling these stories and laughing together.*

—Journal, September 12, 1972

◉◉◉

Balbid

We're back in Madga, and the first thing I notice is the sweet smell of this place. Maybe it's the betel nut spit permeating the dust, perhaps it's the houses, or the life. For my first ten minutes back, things seemed smaller and dirtier than I remembered. But now, three hours later, I've already adjusted. Tagleong's little girl Tata has a bleeding skin ulcer on her buttock, where she sits on it. We'll have to put medicine on it and try to keep a bandage on—but keeping a bandage on a naked toddler's butt for any length of time is unlikely.

Ricarda came rushing over to us when we arrived, and I think she was really glad to see us. Tagleong himself hasn't said much to us one way or the other.

— Journal, August 4, 1972

◉◉◉

It's been an unusually quiet day in Madga. There were only a few voices of children playing and some splashes from the direction of the river, and then came Ricarda's harsh, somewhat screechy, and definitely bossy tone as she ordered her family around—commanding them to bring wood, take care of the baby, bring water, build the fire. She is loud and authoritarian, and when I hear her shout, I too have an impulse to jump up and do whatever she commands! Poor sweet, uncomplaining Darna, the eldest daughter. She catches most of the workload at Datu's house.

— Journal, August 19, 1972

◉◉◉

There was whispering, and our little nipa house jiggled as someone, no, several people, climbed the notched pole onto our front porch. It was past dawn, but still early for visitors. I pulled tight into my sleep to keep it close, not wanting to acknowledge the day, the clucking chickens. or the neighbors who had just come up to visit.

More whispers, then Janet stuck her head around our door. "You might want to wake up. Amalya is having her baby."

The powerful pull of sleep continued to hold me, and drunk with the need for more rest, more dreams, more silence, I muttered, "You mean right now, or sometime today?"

Janet shrugged. "Don't know. The kids just said that she's having the baby now. Suat has gone to the forest to gather some herbs, and Ricarda is next door helping."

I leaned up on one elbow. I knew it was time to get up, but gravity had increased exponentially overnight. "Do they need us for anything?"

"Nobody has said anything about medicine," Janet said. "Besides, I don't think I would be much help in this situation. How about you? How many births have you assisted?"

I sat up inside the mosquito net, trying to rub life into my hip. I'd slept on my side again, a holdover from the days when I had a bed. Now I usually woke from the sleeping mat numb in my shoulder and hip. If truth be known, I probably understood less about the facts of life than six-year-old Dita, who I glimpsed sitting cross-legged on our porch, a magazine in her lap.

"Anyhow," said Janet, "I think Ricarda has things under control. I hear them talking. Something's definitely happening over there."

I rolled up the sleeping mat and mosquito net while Janet got the fire going and fixed flour-and-water pancakes. Amalya's four children— Serhio, Poring, Dita, and little Mordino—sat looking through *Life* magazines from our schoolbox. Serhio glanced back at his house.

"Do you remember when Mordino and Dita were born?" Janet asked him.

"Yes, Mother fell through the floor the day before Mordino was born. That scared him and caused him to be born," he said.

"Amalya fell?"

"Yes, there on the porch," he said, gesturing with puckering lips and a flip of his head to the bamboo-and-nipa-palm house on stilts across the dirt path. "She was very big, like now, and it was hard for her to walk. The bamboo broke, and she fell through the floor."

"Was she hurt?" Janet asked.

"Not so much. And then Mordino was born."

"He cried. Mordino always cried when he was a baby," Dita added with a glance at her three-year-old brother.

Mordino was absorbed in the magazine's color photographs and seemed not to notice that he was the topic of conversation. His round, naked belly pooched out over the pages on his lap. "Ball," he said, pointing with dirt encrusted fingers at a picture of Earth from space.

I sat beside him, took a breath, and readied the words to explain the concepts of Planet Earth, space travel, and the round planets in our solar system. Then I stopped myself, and the words dissolved. For a three-year-old river child living in the upland forest of an island near the equator, for a child who will likely never see a telephone, a movie, or a pair of shoes, for a little boy who only a few weeks ago when we arrived had seen his first rubber ball, yes, this was a photograph of a ball.

"Yes, Mordino, that's right," I encouraged.

Janet handed around a plate of hotcakes sprinkled with sugar. The kids rolled them up and gobbled them like hungry puppies.

"There was another baby too. It died," Serhio told us between smacking lips.

"Another baby? When?"

"I don't remember. But Mother says there was another baby before Dita. It was a girl. She died when she was born." Serhio took the last pancake, rolled it, and ate it in two quick chomps.

I looked to Janet and saw her concern. For the first time, we both considered that this birth could be dangerous for Amalya and for the new baby.

"Seems like Amalya has a baby every three years. I wonder how that works, biologically. Why every three years?" I asked.

"I guess because she breastfeeds. I've heard that you don't get pregnant right away if you're breastfeeding. Maybe that's why."

For the zillionth time, I wished I knew more. With a liberal arts college education, I could analyze Shakespeare's iambic pentameter and play badminton by tournament regulations, but could I find a sweet potato, catch river shrimp, or navigate overland through the forest for days? When the river was low or dirty, could I find a mountain stream for clear drinking water? Could I plant or harvest upland rice, or cook it perfectly, steaming it in a node of bamboo over a fire I built myself—without matches or kerosene starter? Could I catch, kill, and clean a wild pig? Could I hack bamboo with a machete and build a raft, lashing it together with rope I'd made from forest vines? Nope. None of these things. Six-year-old Dita was educated far better than I at the things that really mattered in this place, including reproductive biology.

Suat returned from the forest with an enormous bundle of leafy branches across his shoulder. He was sweating, even though the morning heat was still mild. He nodded briefly to his children and to us Americanas as he carried the oversized load up the notched bamboo pole.

The draping rice-bag door to his house widened, and I glanced inside. The interior was smoky and shadowy, but I could clearly make out the figure of Amalya squatting in the center of the room, her belly an overinflated beach ball. She leaned heavily, pulling hard on a rope that was hanging from a ceiling rafter. Her long black hair was loose, and I got only a glimpse of her face, eyes sunken and tired.

The kids looked at magazines while Janet and I did household chores. Janet burned or buried the week's garbage while I made four trips to the river for water, for showers and household cleaning. I planned to wash my hair, a project that took extra water and extra time. I also brought up a bucket of water to wash down the kitchen platform. The bugs were particularly pesky lately, and I was trying to discourage them.

From the house next door, I heard low moans and Ricarda's coaxing voice. Then Datu Tagleong emerged from his own house cater-corner across the dirt path, wearing his red kerchief head covering and carrying himself upright with an aura of dignity and respect. He entered Amalya's house and chanted, long and loud, a monotone patter of rushing syllables falling like rain on a tin roof. The tone was cheerful and enthusiastic, perhaps a peptalk for a safe and speedy birth.

Suat came out to sit on the porch. He was pounding some of the leaves he'd collected.

"How is Amalya?" I hollered across the path.

He looked up with a worried expression. "Soon," he said, then he stepped inside to the continued sound of moans and deep, low breathing.

"I always thought women screamed and raved when they give birth," I said to Janet. "Amalya is pretty quiet."

"Maybe because she's had other children, maybe it's not so bad this time."

"Or maybe it's just American women who scream," I suggested.

"I don't know," said Janet.

"Me either."

There were more groans, scary ones, like an animal in pain, and a deep-down-inside awful kind of moan.

What came next was a whimper, more of a squeak than a squall. The whimper got louder, breathless little gusts of a new voice. It crescendoed with a cry, strong and sure, then faded to whimpering gasps. Something fell through the bamboo slat floor of the house next door, splatting on the ground. A flock of chickens ran to the dark blob and a rooster grabbed it, picked it up, and ran in circles with it. Other chickens chased him, squawking and flapping, grabbing for the loot. I got a good look at the chicken treasure—a dark sack, dripping blood, an oozing pouch of tissue.

"What's that?" I hissed to Janet. "The baby? Was that the baby? Is it dead?"

"It didn't look like a baby," Janet said tentatively. "It might be the afterbirth."

"Does that mean it's over?"

"I don't know," said Janet.

"Me either." It was a whispered apology for all I didn't know.

The village pig was under the house, rooting and grunting, looking for more treasure.

Suat stepped from inside. "Boy," he shouted across to us, and the children scampered across the path to their own bamboo house. I beamed back at Suat. I couldn't have explained it, but tears came to my eyes.

"And Amalya is well?"

"Tired, but she is well," Suat said.

"Good. Very good," I said.

A little while later, Janet and I were invited to the little house next door to see the new baby. "I wish we had something to take, some sort of present," I said looking around at our few belongings, searching for something appropriate for a newborn. My hand rested on my soft Cannon towel from home. But I had only one towel and I really needed it. No, I'd better not give it away.

"It's not like we can run down to Sears and charge a layette," Janet joked. "Come on, let's just go."

Serhio, Poring, and Dita sat on their porch, while Mordino played in the dirt under the house. Janet and I stepped through the rice-bag doorway into the dim room. Slanted streaks of morning light filtered through bamboo slats. Amalya leaned against a wall, a small bundle in her arms. She looked smaller, frailer than before. Her hair was knotted up with sweaty tendrils trailing.

Her eyes were dark and tired, yet peaceful. Between her lips was a red wad of tobacco. As she moved the bundle, I saw her belly, a slackened, wrinkled bag, a deflated balloon. Amalya was naked, but for a cotton blanket across her lap and around her waist, a thin hand-braided fiber rope holding a wad of green leaves against her navel.

She slowly opened the bundle, revealing a small wrinkled pinkish blob. It was the smallest living person I had ever seen, tiny ears and nose on a head the size of my fist, miniature fingernails on miniature fingers.

Is it real, I wondered? More like a newborn marsupial than a human. Dark hair fuzzed above big dark eyes. The baby pursed its lips and jerked a tiny hand. A very cute marsupial, I thought.

Suat was positively beaming, a glowing smile on his face.

"We are asking you for a name for our new boy," he said.

"What? You want us to name the baby?" Janet said, astonished.

"Yes. A name for a boy."

I was embarrassed. "Should we do it?" I asked Janet. I didn't want to impose, it seemed too much of an honor to accept.

"Of course, silly. They asked us. Do you have any favorite names?"

"I've always liked the name David," I suggested. "A name for someone calm and gentle and smart. How about you?"

"Eric is a good name," she suggested. A warrior's name, I thought. Strength and endurance, worthy attributes for a mountain life.

"Eric or David? Which shall it be?" I asked.

"Well," Janet considered, "David might be easier to pronounce in Manobo."

"Great."

Janet turned to Amalya and Suat. "David. We like the name David."

"Balbid," they repeated. "Balbid."

Amalya smiled at me through the tobacco wad, then looked down with glowing black eyes on the new boy child, Balbid.

The striped shadows of sunlight through bamboo slats and the smell of smoke and sweat. It was Madonna and Child, Manobo-style. And there we were, two not-so-wise women from a faraway land who offered the only gift we had, a name. I wanted to give more. I wanted to give this child health, the chance to grow up. It shouldn't be too much to ask. But somehow, there, amid the dirt and sickness in the tiny river village of Madga, deep in the interior mountains of the island of Mindanao on a warm May noon in the year 1972, it seemed like a lot.

He was born yesterday morning, and now Janet and I are thinking of making him some sort of birth certificate so he'll know how to spell his name in the future, and know his birthdate and be able to tell his age—just in case he ever needs to know. The people here have no idea of birthdays or age. It's irrelevant to them, and they had the strangest looks on their faces when we used to ask how old someone is. We've learned not to ask.

Today is Monday, and there's no school, which is why I have time to write this letter. There's no school because Tagleong and Suat and Donkilyo have gone hunting for wild boar. Early this morning they were singing and chanting—loudly!—at Datu's house, and then the three of them went charging off into the mountains with their spears. Datu put up bamboo posts with dangling twine at the entrance to his porch. We were told that no one can climb into the house until he gets back from the hunt this afternoon, or it will break the spell (or something like that). And since our schoolroom is on Datu's front porch, our classes are cancelled, at least for the morning. I hope that whatever they're doing brings good luck, because we all sure could use some meat! I'm not sure if the pig hunt and Amalya's delivery yesterday have any connection—probably, but no one talks about it.

— Letter home, May 22, 1972

◉◎◉

Amalya and Balbid —
As she leans against the bamboo slats of the house, gently she guides her infant to her breast, relaxing, holding close the preciousness that he is. Her blackest-black hair is pulled cleanly from her face, knotted on itself at the base of her neck. Ear to ear hang woven Manobo beads, echoing the round of her face and brightening the brown of her skin. The ever-present ball of tobacco protrudes

from her lips, yet still she smiles and whispers to him, a mother delivering wisdom and love in a language I don't understand, yet I know just what she says. I watch from between slats in the wall of our house, shamelessly spying, yet I stare, breathless, and can't turn away.

I sear this image into my brain—this moment, so special and beautiful. And so entirely ordinary.

—Journal, August 21, 1972

⊙⊚⊙

Weaving Lessons

Cockroaches are thriving in the no-longer-new nipa fronds of our roof, and they're overrunning our lives. They prance across our food as we eat. When we sleep, at least one roach will find its way under the mosquito net to walk across me in the night. They leap into my hair while I'm reading. They burrow into every nook of our supply boxes and even into my clothes, which are zipped in my duffle. It's beyond exasperating! We've tried a thousand ways to discourage them, but so far, nothing's worked. We tried Raid, which only kills them if we spray the bug directly, but doesn't put a dent in the population. We've washed and washed with soap and water, kept the floor and walls immaculately clean, and even swept at

the nipa roof, but we don't dare do too much, because if the leaves fall apart, we'll be vulnerable to the rain.
— Journal, August 12, 1972

⊚⊚⊚

We also have termites. Sawdust falls like snow, leaving a thin layer on everything. So we cover everything when we leave the house. I think they're in the crossbeams, the ones that are holding up our roof and walls. What happens when the structural integrity is compromised? It'll all come tumbling down. Yikes!
— Journal, August 13, 1972

⊚⊚⊚

Trining and TingTing came up from Silco Camp yesterday and brought us a few supplies, then this morning had to depart quickly. A bundle of logs has gotten loose on the river, and all the loggers and concession guards have been called in to try to round them up. Like in a cowboy movie, only instead of rounding up straying little dogies, they're rounding up stampeding little logies.

I didn't get a chance to give Trining and TingTing my letters to mail. And it will be weeks before I see them again.
— Journal, August 17, 1972

One Sunday afternoon as I got back from the outhouse, Janet was gathering her beadwork. "Amalya says to come over for another lesson. Want to go?" I did. It would be my third lesson on the Manobo bead loom.

Amalya rested against the bamboo slats of her porch with a wad of tobacco between her lips and the sleeping baby Balbid atop a scrap of fabric by her side. In her lap was a handmade bead loom, a bow of wood held taut by twenty-five waxed, stringlike fibers. Suat had made similar looms for Janet and me, and I carefully unwrapped mine from a handkerchief to prepare for the lesson. The length of a completed necklace would have a couple hundred beaded rows set tightly across the warp of the loom, with about twenty-five beads across each row. I was on my sixth row.

Amalya sat without speaking, but in her calm presence I felt welcome. I sat beside her, my back against her bamboo wall. I watched her hands, thick, dark-stained fingers moving deftly. With a long needle she picked up several beads, one at a time, and placed them between the taut waxed warp strings of the loom, then nudged the needle through the entire row and pulled the thread tight, securing the row. Then she started back across the warp threads in the opposite direction with the next row of beads. I watched, knowing she could see a pattern of colors, determining which beads to choose for her weave. I mimicked her, one bead at a time, trying to see ahead to the pattern I was creating, but it boggled my mind.

These times working alongside Amalya were special, not only because this was one of the few recreational activities I had, but also because of Amalya herself. She spoke little Visayan, and I spoke only a smattering of Manobo, so our communications were mostly non-verbal. Unlike Ricarda who might shout and gesticulate wildly, Amalya was peaceful, and her calm radiated to me.

The beads were not much individually, specks of plastic traded from downriver, but when seen as a whole, her work was stunning—bright and vibrant with the colors of sky and sunset, alive like the flow of the river under a silver moon.

As I sat beside her, I became silent too. I looked at my small pile of beads, wondering if I could ever make anything as perfect as hers. Perhaps, if I kept trying—trying to keep the beads straight and evenly spaced across the waxed strings, trying to keep the tension in my thread neither too taut nor too lax, trying to choose the next color wisely, trying to visualize the pattern. I looked at her loom, then back at mine as the sun sank lower on the mountainside. She rose to care for Balbid and start the evening fire to boil the sweet potatoes she'd collected earlier in the day.

Amalya was a good mother. I could see her reflected in her kids.

Serhio—competent, bright, respectful, clever, good-natured, and always willing to lend a hand. Poring—beautiful, quiet, with the shyest sweet smile, always quick to help. Dita—strong beyond her years, wide-eyed, and silently absorbing everything around her. And Little Mordino—curious, with a touch of mischief and a bubbly giggle. And now baby Balbid, a calm infant with a big belly and bright eyes. It's as though he knows he's safe in this family, that he'll always be fed and cared for. Amalya exuded gentleness and competence to everyone around her. She moved like a whisper, a rustle of a cotton skirt swishing by. I could smell the mingling of tobacco and sweat, her own sweetish perfume. Her feet—wide, strong, shades of brown, tones of the earth—passed near my hand. I felt rested, whole, as I picked up my beads, wrapped my unfinished project in a faded yellow handkerchief, and walked back home across the dirt path.

In the end, I never did finish my own bead project, although I tried. I got tangled and confused and frustrated. But Amalya persevered. Before we left Madga, she gave us gifts. She called me over to her porch and presented me a bead necklace that she had been weaving over the past weeks. There was one for me and one for Janet. It was a choker band, about two inches wide all the way around my neck, with more than twenty long, dangling streams of beads that hung down across my chest. I tried it on, felt the weight of it, and admired the brightness of the beads sparkling in the sun and glittering with every breath I took. Here, against the backdrop of forest and river, the simple beads sparkled like rare jewels. She smiled, the wad of tobacco between her lips, pleased with her work.

"Like a Manobo now," she said. I offered my heartfelt thanks and at that moment, I knew there was still much I wanted to learn from her. I truly wanted to be like Amalya, the calm, creative, beautiful mother of Madga.

◉◉◉

I see pictures all around me, my mind recording the images. These words on paper are trying to catch up. This is what I see from my porch this evening:
There is Tata, the bare, brown-skinned baby who

clambers on the back of her ten-year-old sister, Darna, and they take off like lightning, darting, dipping, jumping, and screeching as they play. Baby Tata, who limps and may be crippled for life, hollers with joy.

There is Lando, a commanding presence whose naked figure leaps in the evening shadows. He's never still, cajoling, enticing the little ones to follow him in jumping, tumbling, and running.

There is Lalak, a baby barely walking, huddled in a soggy, torn, and stained yellow dress, hunching over her serious work. Too busy to follow the others, she meticulously hammers a bamboo stake into the soft earth with a stone. Her baby hand and short fingers are caked with grime, and she grasps tightly the black rock and pounds again and again and again, until the bamboo stick vanishes beneath the dust.

— Journal, August 21, 1972

◉◎◉

I might have discovered another universal value. It might be true that everyone needs something in life, an object perhaps, that brings a certain calm, or joy, to the spirit. I have watched Amalya with the bone bracelet and beaded ear and neck pieces that she keeps in a beautiful woven basket. I see the way she touches them, as if she is taking in their calm, their beauty, as if she is internalizing their timeless peacefulness. I'm thinking about my mom—her calm comes, it seems, from washing dishes. She once told me that the warm sudsy water makes her lose her thoughts. A best friend in high school had a fuzzy dead-animals pelt collar that she wore a lot, fuzzy at her neck, and she said it was like having an old friend close by. I wonder what it would be that calms my own restless spirit. Real food maybe.

—Journal, September 18, 1972

◉◎◉

I'm sitting here after supper with a cup of tea—finally!—a treasure from the supplies we brought upriver last month. And special tea it is. I was so hungry this evening, I would have eaten anything! I ate rice and some canned fish covered with what was supposed to be a garlic white sauce that Janet made. But it was actually quite runny and a little too salty. We were out of water and didn't have any to drink with the meal. I was so thirsty! So I went down to the river for water, but first I had to clean the rice pot (which is also the water boiling pot, which is to say, our only pot). The rice was stuck to the bottom, and some bits remained stuck no matter how much I dug at it with my fingernail and scoured it with river gravel. Finally I gave up and just boiled the drinking water. During the twenty minutes of boiling time, many of the stuck rice pieces floated off in the water. Yuk! Now, finally, I've got something to drink—a cup of hot tea, complete with rice floaties. Is nothing ever easy?
—Journal, September 20, 1972

◉◎◉

Lost

I had a nice afternoon "conversation"—in Manobo, of which I understand very little, but the kids helped translate into Visayan—with Amalya, who was taking care of baby Balbid, and with my student Penang, Amalya's younger sister. Amalya told us at length about little Mordino being lost in the forest while she was getting kamote, and how he was finally discovered asleep under a tree. She told the story in a light way, because it had a happy ending, but I know how worried she was when it happened. I think this story is now a family legend from the way the kids knew the story and enjoyed the telling.

— Journal, August 18, 1972

◉◉◉

It was mid-September of 1972 and the long months I'd spent in Madga were shrinking my energy and enthusiasm for this project. The best I could do many days, was merely to make it through the day, dawn to dusk. Yet there remained occasional bright spots. The best part of each day was in the evening, when I climbed under the mosquito net with a tin-can kerosene lamp, my journal, and my pen. I could sit, think, and sketch or write. Sometimes I recorded an event of daily life. Sometimes I noted some small beautiful thing I'd seen. Yet frequently, I wrote out my frustrations, pain and questions. Why was I doing this thing?

The words and images would rise of their own accord, spontaneously cluttering the page. Uncalculated. Unguarded. Like those noisy, scratching chickens impulsively searching for sustenance, the words formed images of this and that, here and there, then and now.

Those words on the page came ever seeking, yet rarely finding, satisfaction.

A few days before my birthday, there was this.

> I've become emotionally exhausted, ignorant, and inept. There was so much I wanted to do, and time has slipped by as my wheels spin, splattering plenty of mud and getting nowhere. Almost twenty-four years old, and I've lost touch with all that came before.
>
> *I want to be home.* I'm hungry for the music of my own culture. I want to sleep in a real bed, where I can feel safe from leering strangers, biting bugs, and horrible dreams. I want to have a good supper and know there'll be a good breakfast in the morning. I want to have good breakfast and not worry whether we'll have anything at all for supper. I want to stretch out on a carpeted floor and watch TV.
>
> I want to keep my clothes, not in a duffle bag. I want to use a clean towel. I want to read a new book. I want to have friends, laugh, and have a good time. I want to drive *long* distances along superhighways in an air-conditioned car and not have my kidneys bruised by hard bounces on the wooden bench as we jolt across potholes and rat-a-tat washboard ruts, and I want to *not* have to wear a bandana across my face to filter the choking dust. I'm tired of wearing a sweatsuit of mud.
>
> I want to find a toilet easily when I need it, preferably one that flushes.

I want to write real poetry and maybe write a book, not merely doodling these random meanderings of a sick mind. I want to go to school and learn things, and discuss literature, and hear some new ideas that make me think.

I want to be normal, not an oddity, a specimen constantly under a microscope. I want to feel some self-respect. I want to think I might have a strong and good character. I want to look pretty.

I read *Newsweek* and *Time* cover to cover when I can get them. I don't know what to make of the Vietnam War anymore. So much is happening in my own culture, and I'm missing it all. I'm hardly even a member of my own generation.

I've lost my place, maybe forever. I'm lost. Truly lost.

◉◉◉

There has been a small disaster: on this trip upriver— a kerosene bottle leaked all over our food supplies. The main casualty was the sugar, which was doused. I won- der if it will poison us to still use it? Do I remember that oldtimers put kerosene in their homemade cough syrup? Or was that whiskey? Oh, I don't know. But we're not going to throw out that sugar, that's for sure.

— Journal, August 4, 1972

◉◉◉

It will be too bad when this pen runs out of ink. It's getting weak. And I'm getting weak, running out of the inky stuff of life—words, thoughts, creativity, and energy. I, my very own self, am running dry, just like this ghostly-globby, daut na (worn-out already), draggy old ballpoint pen.

— Journal, October 1, 1972

◉◉◉

Making History

This journal isn't what I had in mind when I started. I thought life in the Philippines would be interesting, but my experiences don't seem exciting at all. There's really nothing to write about. So I write, but it's circular, inconclusive, murky, obscure, and minuscule. My writing is a poof, an illusion, a wisp of smoke, almost a waste of time—but for the relaxation and renewing focus of merely moving the pen.

— Journal, February 1971

⊚⊚⊚

It was night and silent in our little bamboo house. Outside were evening whispers—the distant lapping of the Madga against stones and the occasional high-pitched chortle of a night creature. Janet lay under the sheet on her side of the mat reading *Nicholas and Alexandra* by the dim glow of the tin-can kerosene lamp. I sat beside her, writing, sharing the half-light, my head brushing the top of the mosquito net as my thoughts tumbled onto the pages.

She paused, resting the book on her chest, then asked me in a quiet voice, "Do you think we might be making history here?"

"Huh?" I asked. "Making history? Us? ...Well, sure, I guess so. We all are. Everybody is always making history all the time, right?"

"That's not what I mean," Janet said. "I'm talking about real history. Do you think it will ever matter to anyone else that we're here with the Manobo now, in 1972? The world is changing so fast for them. And here we are, actually helping the change happen. It's like at this particular moment they have one foot in the old world, one foot in the new, and we are part of their change. History."

"Um. I don't know. Change is so slow here. Seems like nothing ever changes, not really. Even with us here, teaching them, we're like one stone in the river. I'll bet that in twenty years everything will be just the same. A new crop of chickens, of course." I glanced at her with a grin. She looked serious.

"You think so? I'm not so sure. I think...." her voice trailed off. "Oh, I'm too tired to think any more tonight." She rolled over and pulled the sheet to her neck. "Goodnight."

I sat up for a few more minutes, finishing my journal entry. I wrote the conversation about history. If this is a historically significant moment, it sure does feel like regular life, I wrote. This wouldn't be the stuff that makes up history; it's too ordinary. The Manobo are people, like people everywhere, with hopes and ideas and survival instincts— just the methods are different. As for me, the observer, I'm merely a person feeling tired and hungry, with too many itchy bites on my legs.

If this were history, I'd be doing it all better somehow. My lesson plans would be more together. My language skills would include the Manobo dialect. I wouldn't be so tired and grumpy and hungry. Janet and I would get along perfectly. And I would always be smiling. If these times were historically significant, there would be politics or wars or tribes on the move to report in my journals. History happens in Manila, not in Madga. No, this couldn't be history. This is regular life among a tiny band of humanity on a minuscule patch of planet earth. Nobody particularly cares about these people now; nobody is likely to care about them in the future.

I blew out the lamp and set it outside the mosquito net. Then I tucked the net under the mat all along my side of the bed and pulled up my side of the sheet. I lay in the darkness, hearing the river and Suat snoring from his house next door. I'd struggled through history classes in college. It was all dates and documents, kings and presidents, peasant rebellions and naval battles. I learned that real history is set by national politics, by events that matter on a grand scale, not by afternoons of bead weaving on a bamboo porch beside an unremarkable meandering mountain river. I heard another long, rattling snort from the little house next door.

In the stuff of real history, I thought, nobody snores.

⊙⊚⊙

Voice of America is coming in clear tonight. It's great to hear news of the outer world. They just said Peace Corps Volunteers were arrested in Uganda, and one was killed and the other injured. The dead boy was twenty-three, from Houston. I'll bet my family hears about this and worries about me.

— Journal, September 20, 1972

⊙⊚⊙

Yesterday afternoon, Janet and I gave away prints from a roll of black-and-white film we had processed in the lowlands. Sus! These prints were a huge hit! Suat and Amalya's family got five, Tagleong got two, Maria got two, Donkilyo got two, Tessie got one, and Darna got one. Of course, there's no way for them to take care of the photos, so within a short while they'll be dusty, damp and bent. Considering the river, the environment, the life, these prints won't last very long. But they're certainly good while they last!

Just now little Poring and Aning came over to ask me to take their picture. So I did. I guess it's because they saw the photos we gave out and they didn't get one. It's tough, not being able to do everything for everyone. Normally, I don't take photos simply because someone asks me to—or that would certainly be the end of my film supply. But for these two kids, it was, "Aroglado"—sure thing! These little girls just carried load after load of river rocks on their heads for the floor of our new bath stall under the house and they deserve so much more than just a snapshot—which they'll probably never see anyhow, because I'm using color slide film which I have to send home for processing.

Through Daddy's business connections in New York, Kodak is processing all my slide film for free. Daddy sends me film—sometimes—but I don't have much. I can buy it here—sometimes— but it's very expensive and usually past the expiration date. But the processing is free—thanks, Kodak!

And someday, I hope I'll get to see all these slides I'm taking!

— Journal, August 5, 1972

◉◉◉

The Garden

It's the end of this season's corn harvest. The crop was small, and Janet and I hardly got any, just a taste, but it was sweet and good. They tell us that the rice harvest will come in September and October. Meanwhile, watermelons are ripe now, and they're delicious. Kamote seem to be available all the time, although sometimes our neighbors don't find tubers, but only bring in the leaves — which taste like grass clippings but are better with soy sauce. Bananas, including the big fat red ones that they boil, are an infrequent treat. Papayas grow on the edge of the forest, but most of them are eaten by birds unless they're picked very green. Lansones, nice grape-like fruits with thick skin, will ripen in October and November we're told.

Also from the forest, there are occasional fat, finger-sized passion-fruit-type things with crunchy seeds, or a stalk of sugarcane. Sometimes we're offered a new and unknown food—like the pasty, mealy substance that tasted like dirt. But we appreciate all they bring us. Usually it's Janet who eats the really weird stuff.

— Journal, August 4, 1972

⊙⊙⊙

It's Sunday morning and Datu is getting over-the-top loud, shouting, not exactly angry, but really loud. Perhaps it's enthusiasm. I can't understand his words at all. I think he has had Vino Kalafu, or tuba—i.e. he's drunk.

Trining and TingTing are supposed to be up tomorrow, which may mean mail and cookies and bread and fresh fruit and coffee and salt and canned milk from Silco. But the way things go, I won't get my hopes up, won't expect them till later in the week or maybe next week or the end of the month, or even later. That's just how it is.

Today's menu:

Breakfast: instant coffee and a spoonful of peanut butter for me. Janet had leftover cucumber salad.

Lunch: more cucumber/melon salad, which gives me a stomach ache. I hate cucumbers. Even slathering the cuke with peanut butter doesn't help.

Supper: kamote/canned corned beef hash and more cucumber, and some un-jelled Jello, the red kind. I heard the red dye is carcinogenic. Along with peanut butter, which if made with tainted (moldy) Philippine peanuts, is also supposedly carcinogenic. What's worse, I'm not even remotely satiated by eating this risky food. Hunger gnaws. Bummer.

— Journal, August 16, 1972

⊙⊙⊙

When the gods of the forest are generous, the hunters might bring in a pig for everyone in the village to share, but there is no relying on those capricious gods or the luck of the hunt.

That left us with a kamote purple sweet potato as our dietary staple, filling, yet boring meal after meal, day after day. One time we worked for days to finish off a football-size tuber we'd been given. So, Janet creatively diversified the cuisine. I thought her a brilliant chef, knowing secrets for stews and sauces and casseroles. Sometimes we ate plain boiled kamote, taking big bites from the warm and sweet fist-sized tubers. Sometimes she sautéed kamote chunks with canned corned beef. "It's hash," she told me. She fried kamote slices and sprinkled them with sugar for dessert. Or she thinly sliced boiled kamote, covered the slices with a flour-water-oil white sauce, and "baked" them in our kettle over a slow fire— "scalloped," she called it. When we received a green papaya from our neighbors, we ate our kamote topped with thin slices of steamed green papaya.

One day we were presented a new food, a small melon. Janet opened it and took a bite.

"It's a watermelon," she pronounced with a wide grin.

"With white meat? Never heard of such a thing!"

"Well, here it is. Try it."

I tentatively took a bite, hoping that it wasn't just an overgrown cucumber. Trial and error dietary experiments were proving that I had unpleasant gastric reactions to cucumbers. But this was different. "Good grief, it is incredibly sweet. Wonderful!" I said in wide-eyed surprise.

"Ummm," Janet said, taking quick bites.

We Americanas craved dietary diversity. So from the office of the United States Information Service in Davao, we requested a Care package of gardening tools. Some weeks later the tools arrived, so Janet and I were shopping in the city for vegetable seeds.

"I don't know about this. I'm not sure the concept of a cultivated garden is in their culture," I told Janet as we looked over the seed packets.

"Okay, so we make a project of it. We'll teach them how to grow a garden."

"I'm not sure I know how to grow a garden. I've never done it before," I said.

"Me either. But how hard can it be? We've got tools. We'll get the kids to help us. It'll be fun." To Janet, it probably would be. To me, it sounded like hard labor in the hot sun. Yet I was willing to try.

"Okay, I guess so. And it'll be nice to grow some food we can share with them for a change. But here"—I took the eggplant seeds out of her hand and replaced them with a package of mung beans— "at least get something I like to eat."

Back in Madga, we commandeered an empty San Miguel beer crate from the base of Datu's front porch—it had formerly been a step—and filled it with soil from under our house. We sprinkled in the seeds, placed the crate in the shade on our front porch, watered it, and waited. By early August, tiny sprouts began to emerge en masse.

"We're mothers!" I exclaimed, leaning close to examine the tiny seedheads. Janet leaned over from the door stoop.

"Cute!" she grinned. "I can taste the vegetables already! Sautéed, baked, and steamed."

"How much longer till we harvest?"

"I guess we better start working on the garden plot. Where should we put it?"

My mother put her backyard garden in a sunny spot. "Somewhere close, so we can keep an eye on it and somewhere it can get plenty of sun."

"How about behind the outhouse?" Janet waved to a weed plot in back.

"Sure. Looks good. We'll get the kids to help us prepare the soil. Let's start tomorrow, early, before it gets too hot."

The next day, we brought our classes over to our porch to see the seedlings.

"These are baby beans, cabbage, and squash," Janet explained.

I added, "It is food for all the people of Madga, but first we need to help the little plants grow." I made a charade of it, "growing" myself from a seedling into a big strong plant. The kids punched one another and grinned at my silliness.

"So, all of us together are going to make a home for the vegetables, a garden, a place where they can grow strong," Janet summarized.

We took the kids under our house to where we kept the Care package of garden implements—a hoe, a rake, a spade, a pitchfork, and some hand tools. "We will use these. Come on, let's make a garden."

Janet grabbed our machete from the porch and we traipsed out behind the outhouse to a level spot of ground covered knee-high in weeds.

"First, we get rid of the weeds," I announced.

I laid into a spot with the hoe. Janet started chopping with the machete. Serhio, Darna, and Big Norma ran home to get their machetes, and in a few minutes, we had a small clearing. It was already hot. I was sweating and my head pounded. I handed the hoe to Penang. Janet must have felt the same. She passed her machete to Junior. "We'll take turns," she explained, sitting at the back of the outhouse in the shade.

I watched Serhio shallowly turn the soil with the spade. These tools are made for people who wear shoes, who have a big strip of hard leather on the bottoms of their feet, I realized. But even though barefooted, Serhio kept at it. He turned over a clod, revealing an enormous robust earthworm. Lando grabbed it and dangled it menacingly at the *mga gamai* girls. I laughed and could hardly help noticing that the fat earthworm jiggled like Lando's dangling penis as he cavorted naked.

The kids vied for a turn with the new garden tools, and in half an hour we'd cleared a small plot. "Okay, that's good for today. We can continue tomorrow. Let's go to the river and wash up," I called. The cool river water never felt better, and we passed around a bar of soap for the hardworking kids.

We started studying farms in class. I had solicited farm pictures from the US Information Service in Davao, illustrations of an American farm with picket fences, a big red barn, a white farmhouse with lacy curtains in the windows, healthy cows and horses and pigs and chickens, and fields of corn and wheat. I showed these pictures to my class and we talked about growing crops.

They recognized first the animals, which they said were "fat." We all laughed, for no one had ever seen animals as robust as the ones in these pictures. Then we looked at the farmhouse. "Big house," they said.

"Yes. There is one room for cooking and eating. Another room for sitting together. Another room where the parents sleep. Another room for the children. And in the winter, there is a place for a fire inside the house, to keep the family warm."

Silence. This was a too big a stretch of imagination for these kids. It simply didn't compute. Then we came to the picture of the boy fishing beside the stream.

"What's he doing, mum?"

"He is catching fish," I explained.

"He is hitting the fish with a stick?"

"No. He has a fishing pole. It is a long stick, with a little rope from the end of the stick. On the end of the rope is a…a…" I couldn't think of the word for hook. "A piece like this. I drew on the blackboard the shape of a hook. Made from…" What was the word for metal? "… something hard," I said, "like a bone, or a rock, or the sharp part of a machete. But small and shaped like this," and I pointed again to the hook. Was this concept getting across? I forged on.

"And then, there is a worm on the end of the hard thing. Maybe this fishing boy needs Lando to help him find a worm." The kids laughed.

"Then the worm on the hard thing is put under the water, and a fish comes along, sees the worm, and tries to eat the worm. But the fish gets his mouth caught by the hard thing, and the boy pulls the long stick, and the fish comes out of the water. Then, fish for supper. Yum, yum."

I realized how far-fetched this must have sounded to the kids. Most of the fish in the Madga were tiny, mere minnows by Old Country standards, and a worm would outsize them. Madga river fish were caught most efficiently in bamboo fish traps set between rocks where the current flowed strong. That system worked here, and a fishing pole would be ludicrous. But those were the pictures I had to work with. So, we continued to tell stories about how fences were built to keep the cows and pigs away from the corn and how a tractor is a like truck that tears up the soil to make soft places for seeds to grow.

The kids sat listening, asking questions, and were interested in how things worked in the strange land of America. I tried to soften the differences between these all-too-squeaky-clean American pictures, and the reality of how things were accomplished by the simple methods that worked well in Madga.

"And we will have our little farm too, here in Madga," I said. "Tomorrow we will continue preparing the soil. Come to school early, before it gets hot, and we will work again."

Word got out about the garden. The next morning several parents arrived with toddlers, and a group of us was out hacking at weeds and turning the soil before the school bell sounded. Suat was a leader. He seemed to know all about making a garden, and Big Norma and Ben did a lot of the digging. In a few days, we had a plot about twenty by forty feet.

As the seedlings grew, I began to realize that we had planted far too many seeds in the beer crate. They were crowded, their little heads nodding against one another, tangling in vegetable chaos. With so much confusion above ground, I could only imagine what their roots were doing beneath the soil. We'd never be able to separate them if we let them get much bigger.

"I think we'd better plant them pretty soon," I said.

"Do you think they're big enough?" asked Janet.

"Well, they've got leaves. They ought to be able to photosynthesize on their own now. And I guess they can grow in the ground just as well as they can grow in this box." There was excitement in the air. "Tomorrow we'll plant the vegetables," we told the kids.

Parents, students, toddlers, and friends arrived early the next day. We showed them how to plant in neat rows. Some people dug holes in the newly turned earth, some people carefully separated the entangled seedlings, some people set the plants into the holes and gently patted on the soil. Kids brought water up from the river and sprinkled each new plant.

In an hour, we had planted half the garden. I looked back over the rows of nodding green heads and knew something was wrong. Our robust seedlings were looking positively droopy. I went back to the first row and conferred with Janet.

"Golly, they look all wilted. Do you think they're just getting used to their new home and they'll perk up?"

"Um, I don't know. Let's wait awhile and see."

After school we checked again. They looked worse than before. I called to Suat who was sitting on his porch making rope.

"Suat, the plants look tired." I didn't know a word for wilted. "What do you think?"

Suat strolled out to the garden and nodded. "*Lawas nga saging*," he said—body of the banana—and he shouted something to Serhio.

"It's the sun," he said to us. "The sun is too strong for the little plants, and he went hurrying off with Serhio into the forest."

"Too much sun? I never heard of such a thing. They are plants after all. Plants are supposed to like sun," I said to Janet.

"Well, people are too, and we certainly do get droopy if we are in the sun too long," Janet suggested. "Must be the tropical sun, too much of a good thing."

Serhio and Suat were back in minutes. They each carried an entire banana tree across their shoulders.

"*Lawas nga saging*," Suat said. "Like this." He hacked at the stalk of the banana tree. The banana tree stalk is built like an onion, layer upon concentric layer of moist, fibrous material. Suat hacked the banana stalks into foot-long sections, then peeled apart the layers. Meanwhile, Serhio had gathered sticks. And over each little vegetable plant, Suat made a lean-to: the *lawas nga saging*, one layer of the banana plant held up by a stick. In an hour there was a little shady vestibule for each plant.

"Thank you, Suat," I said as he returned home. And to Janet I mumbled again, "Gosh, I didn't know a vegetable could have too much sun."

"Live and learn," she said, an understatement.

The vegetables got on pretty well for a while. A few times the kids had to tote water from the river to the garden, but soon it started raining in the late afternoons and evenings. I ran out to remove the *lawas nga saging* so that the rain could reach the little plants. They grew.

The serious rains began in September. For a while they were gentle, evening showers, then it started to really pour. The river rose and was running muddy brown. The clouds hung dark gray and ominous over the hills, and each evening another cloud would dump on our village.

Finally, one night, the bottom fell out of the sky. We'd gone to bed as usual but were awakened when enormous claps of thunder shook our house like blasts of a cannon.

Better bring in the school box from the front porch, I thought through a dream. But I was tired, and I just couldn't move. I heard Janet get up and retrieve the box. At the next clap of thunder, the lightning flashed so bright I sat bolt upright.

"What's going on?" I asked still half-asleep.

"Storm," Janet said. She was pulling her duffle away from the bamboo slat wall that the rain was blowing through.

The rain on the nipa roof turned to torrents. The wind pushed and shook our little house. It came from one direction, then another, and lifted the thatch from our roof as if shuffling the pages of a book. Rain pelted *inside* our house. Buckets of it.

"Get the cameras," I shouted over another roar of thunder. I wanted my camera, at least, to stay dry. I set it in the middle of my zipped duffle, cradled among my dry clothes.

We took down the mosquito net and pulled our bags and school boxes to the middle of the room, away from the walls that had become little more than sieves. I had a plastic poncho and Janet had a raincoat. I wanted to put the poncho on myself, but sacrificed it to covering the school supplies, my guitar, and our two bags of clothes. Janet sat on one side of the poncho, I sat on the other, and with our bodies anchoring the plastic against the wind and Janet's raincoat stretching to barely cover our heads, we sat. My head collapsed to my knees as I curled inward like a stressed armadillo.

The wind howled, buffeting our house, and I began to feel like a peppercorn in a shaker. When I looked up through our flapping roof, I saw gray sheets of rain hurling from dark skies. By now my hair was plastered to my head, and even when I shouted to Janet, just three feet away, she couldn't hear me. Through closed eyelids I could see the lightning, and I tensed instinctively with each percussive blast that followed. There was no place to go, no shelter, no relief. I sat in the darkness, shivering. I was cold. And scared. Would it last all night? What if our house fell or washed away? What if my guitar, or worse, my camera got wet? What if my mom was right and I died of pneumonia?

The storm slackened for a while, and Janet and I were checking on our goods when our front porch rattled and voices spoke. It was Darna and Poring with Dita. The kids were scared and had run to our house for shelter. We took them in, and when the next big blow came, we all huddled, our arms around each other, sharing the raincoat over our heads. And when the rain slowed, we sang songs. We tried to turn on the radio, but of course, got only static. The kids didn't care; they danced to the static and our singing, pretending it was radio music, until the torrential rain started again and we scurried under the raincoat to wait it out.

Time crawled at an excruciating pace until the storm gradually calmed. When there was enough light to see, I looked beneath the poncho. The school box was soaked, and the kids, peering into the box with me, were obviously saddened at the soggy state of their composition books. I mustered an it-can-be-fixed attitude — "We just need a good day of sun to dry them out. No problem," I said. But really, I wasn't sure. I hoped their precious books wouldn't disintegrate.

As the sun came up, the last of the night rain passed and the wind died down. The nipa palms lay flat on our roof once again. My guitar was damp, but not drenched. I dug for my camera inside my duffle and found it mostly dry inside its leather case, although the clothes around it were pretty wet.

Janet and I walked to the river in the early-morning light. The turbulent, churning waters roared past us, not contained by the riverbanks but flowing out, above and beyond, thundering like a wild thing, dark and fierce. There would be no classes today—no one could possibly cross that river.

We walked past the outhouse. It lay on its side, blown over by the wind and pounded by the rain. And in the early light we saw what was left of our garden—a brown hollowness on the flats beside the river. It was gone, washed away by the rain and the wind and swallowed by the teaming river.

"All that work," moaned Janet. "Gone."

"All that food," I said. "What a waste." I wanted to cry, but it seemed that any more water at that moment would be beyond senseless. Janet and I stood silently for a long time, staring at the empty garden patch, eyeing the woolly gray clouds that still clung to the tops of the hills, feeling the chill of our wet clothes and hair, and listening to the menacing roar of the river.

"Live and learn I guess," sighed Janet.

Once again, an understatement.

◉◉◉

From Amalya's house, the kids brought us two river fish, fist-sized, which is pretty big as they go. I've never had to clean a fish before. Kind of gross, but we managed, and we cooked and ate them. Not exactly tasty, nothing like the delicious bass that my grandmother used to catch below the dam at Lake Whitney in Waco. Mamaw was quite the fisher-woman and she'd catch a mess of them, then crisp them up, coated with cornmeal and quick fried in hot oil. Delicious. These fish today were boring. At least Janet and I could add salt. I'm not sure our neighbors even had salt.

Our Jello fermented. I guess it was the canned pineapple we put in it. It tastes like vile cough medicine and is probably the reason for my frequent runs to the outhouse today. But I feel compelled to eat it. It tasted good yesterday, but today it's beyond dreadful. Janet kind of likes it. After bringing it all the way upriver, we can't just throw it away, so we eat it. No refrigeration, so it's runny and continues to ferment. I think our experiments with Jello are over. At least I hope so.

—Journal, September 16, 1972

⊙⊙⊙

A while back, I was working in the garden, and didn't think about the intensity of the sun, and I got a sunburn on the back of my neck and arms. The kids saw the redness and brought me a glop of mud that they smeared on me. It cooled my skin, and when it dried, it made a crust that protected me from the sun. They said my skin is like a baby's skin, and I need to put the mud on when I work outside. I would like to find out if it is regular river mud, or some special kind of mud.

—Journal, September 2, 1972

⊙⊙⊙

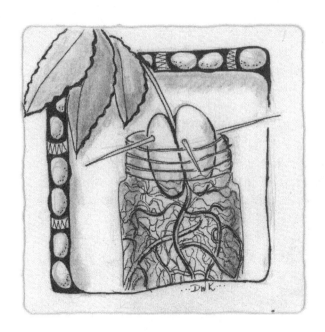

Noontime Heat

The river finally cleared enough so I could wash and rinse my clothes, and I just did a humongous load. Now it's cloudy and I can see the rain on its way, probably within an hour. There's thunder in the distance. Janet is "showering"—actually, dipping and pouring. I'm next. While it rains, I'll work on lesson plans; then it will be dark. Suat is singing to baby Balbid on their front porch. Amalya has gone off to dig kamote, and I think she took the big kids with her, I guess to help her finish before it rains. I hear Ricarda at her house, shouting at her kids. I see Datu there too, shaving in the kitchen doorway. He has a regular double-edge razor! I've never seen anyone shave in Madga. He has no soap, water, or mirror, just

*pulling the razor across his chin. I wonder how (or if?) he
gets fresh blades. Yet another mystery.*
—Journal, September 16, 1972

◉◉◉

*Here's a piece of the mystery puzzle. Trining told us
that Datu sometimes gets money from the logging company for helping keep the concession safe, which means,
I think, leading the Manobo and keeping things calm.
That money might explain how he sometimes comes in
with store-bought Vino Kalafu, and a razor too.*
— Journal, September 18, 1972

◉◉◉

The noontime breeze off the Madga lifts the oppressive heat for
an instant and lets me breathe. It's quiet in the village, except for the
clucking and peeping of hens and chicks and the low hum of Amalya
next door. I sit on the porch bench, too hot to move except to scribble
thoughts into my spiral composition book with the cover photo of Nora
Aunor, the wildly popular teenage screen star of the Philippines.

Noontime heat smells of rotting fruit skins and sweet forest trees,
kid sweat and the clear waters of the Madga leaping on a long, twisty,
eastward journey. It smells of the fresh leaves and new roots of the little
avocado tree we're hatching from a seed suspended over an old peanut
butter jar beside our stove platform.

The breeze opens the pages of the book beside me and blows off
course the white cabbage moth that's nearing my shadowy front porch
perch. Ever-present flies thrive in the heat and take advantage of my
stillness to crawl up my legs with sporadic little jerks. To them, it's a
game, I think. I shoo them away, they circle and land again, only to pick
up where they left off, tracing drunken patterns on my perspiring skin.

The ants also find me suitable company as they race in circles on my
legs. Occasionally one finds its way to my neck or shoulders and stings

me, a sharp prick. The black wasp drones menacingly near. The steaming noontime heat smothers my breath and fogs my mind. It will rain within the hour.

◉◉◉

This morning we deodorized our outhouse, which means we cleaned the walls and threw some Lysol down the hole. Not sure it really helps with the stench, but knowing we tried does help psychologically. We washed clothes at the river—but the water is still muddy, and I'm not sure the clothes come out cleaner. Well, the colors may be duller, but the odoriferousness is gone. We changed our routine from taking showers in the afternoon, when it's already rainy and cold, to taking them late mornings after we get out of school, while the sun is still shining.

—Journal, August 6, 1972

◉◉◉

I've had stomach cramps, semi-diarrhea, and a general body weakness for almost a week. What's going on? Intestinal parasites? Cucumber? Ricarda has just brought over dinner: two giant talong eggplants, along with some unidentified, mealy, cooked forest vegetable, and—another—cucumber.

—Journal, August 18, 1972

◉◉◉

Today, my stomach is fairly okay. Last night I made some vegetable soup (without cucumber!), because I had diarrhea again. And today so far, I've had only oatmeal. We'll see how I am later, after I eat that cucumber, which doesn't agree with me, and I hate it, but it's what we have, so I'll eat it anyhow.

Later: They brought us wild boar for supper! Ya-hoo! I think Donkilyo caught this pig! He's a really good hunter. Our portion is three cubed pieces of fat, two pieces of liver, and several pieces of meat. I don't like the fat or the liver, but I appreciate the gift and will certainly eat it! We'll barbecue it all over the fire.

— Journal, August 19, 1972

◉◉◉

We are lucky to have the salt that we bring up from Davao and share with our neighbors. We call it rock salt, evaporated from the ocean. It took me a while in the beginning, to understand the work of the salt flats beside the ocean. They are like low corrals, piles of rock or knee-high wooden walls, with a gate. The gate is opened to the sea water, then blocked for days or weeks, and the sea water eventually evaporates, leaving a mushy crust of salt across the floor of the corral. The mush is turned and raked, collected in baskets and spread out on mats in the hot sun, and raked some more, until the white sea salt becomes entirely dry and crusty. The little chunks of salt are bigger and more coarse than our round-blue-box salt at home, and the sea salt is entirely more tasty, almost sweet in its saltiness. I have developed a new love for this un-ordinary sort of ordinary salt.

— Letter home, July 1972

◉◉◉

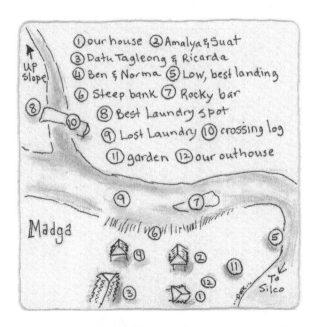

1 our house   2 Amalya & Suat
3 Datu Tagleong & Ricarda
4 Ben & Norma   5 Low, best landing
6 Steep bank   7 Rocky bar
8 Best Laundry spot
9 Lost Laundry   10 crossing log
11 garden   12 our outhouse

UP Slope

Madga

To Silco

Laundry at the Madga

With all the rain there's much to do, so Janet and I gave the kids the afternoon off, even though I think they'd rather be in school. But we are busy trying to dry things out in the few minutes of sun that might come at midday. The river is still running dirty and we're boiling and drinking river water that is silty from the rains. It doesn't get clear, even after sitting in our bucket for half a day. This morning I was waiting for my turn with the teabag while Janet's tea was steeping, and my cup of plain boiled water was the same color as her cup of tea.

Not only is the water a challenge, but even the Black Cat tea itself is only marginally desirable. The bags seem to hold mostly twigs, stems, and roots, not a lot of leaves. When the mesh falls apart, the little twigs swim out into

our cups. To be fair, we do use each teabag a few times;
it probably isn't designed for multiple cups per bag. Still
though, the tea is bland with a bitter and dirty aftertaste,
even when the bag is new. I just pretend to appreciate
our morning tea, because of the psychological benefit;
it's a very thin facade of civility.

—Journal, September 19, 1972

◉◉◉

The heavy seasonal rains stayed with us. Torrential downpours came at night, along with thunder that bullishly shook our tiny nipa house. My days were busy attempting to keep the school supplies and home dry and clean, and at night I fell into a netherworld semi-sleep — frightened of all the thunder and lightning, yet dreamy enough to escape into concoctions of other realities.

The days were calm and dark. Low gray clouds wrapped the treetops and intermittent rain pounded Madga and everywhere around. Few students came to school; many feared crossing the rushing river, and frankly, I was grateful for the respite. It was impossible to communicate during the downpours; the pummeling of the rain on the nipa roof and the heavy splashing and gurgling of surging rivulets across the mud made any attempt at verbal instruction or conversation next to impossible. So, we practiced writing alphabet letters, making art, and looking quietly at the semi-soggy magazines and picture books from our library box. Then, when the rain slackened, we'd discuss our work briefly before the gully-washers began pounding again.

Meanwhile, life went on, especially during the interludes. There was wood to gather and chop, fires to build, meals to cook, and every few days, Janet and I would tote muddy water from the ever-rising river so we could dip and pour a bucket over ourselves and call it a bath. It helped to bring the bucket up from the river early in the morning so we could let it sit a few hours before bathing. Much of the silt would settle out. We'd bathe at noon, when the day was as warm as it would get—which wasn't really warm at all when you are splashing naked under dippers of cold river water.

Neither Janet nor I had the heart for laundry. Day after day, we'd let it accumulate. I knew the problem was getting serious when I had worn all my five panties for two days each—then turned them inside out and wore them again. T-shirts and shorts were mud-flecked and smelling of mildew and body odor. My only towel looked and smelled as if it had rubbed down Datu's hunting dog. The clincher came during a rainy night when I started my period. I woke to find myself lying on blood-smeared sheets. With Janet sharing the same bed, the time had come to do laundry. Luckily, a spot of sun was breaking over the trees.

At noon one Friday in mid-August 1972, just after school let out, Janet and I loaded our arms with plastic buckets, laundry soap, bath soap, and a duffle bag of laundry, climbed down the new runged porch ladder that our neighbors had built for us, and headed for the relatively clean waters upstream, a bit of a walk.

"Wait," said Janet. "If we're going all the way up there, we may as well wash the pot too." True. Our only cooking pot was now a filthy crusted mess, needing to be scoured with small gravel and fine river sand. And we desperately needed some cleanish drinking water, too. We would still boil it before drinking, but it would be nice to have drinking water that was less gritty.

Traversing the Madga proved difficult. In normal times, the river crossing was knee-high and flowing smoothly, in a cheerful sort of way. But these were not normal times. The waters that day were thigh to waist-high, brown, and angry. Getting across the river was a challenge. It was hard to find footing on unseen river rocks beneath coffee-brown waters. Rubber slippers want to float, so every time I picked my foot up to take a step, my slipper would try to escape downriver. I gripped tightly with my toes. I considered taking my slippers off, but I was a tenderfoot, and I knew some of the river rocks were sharp. So, I took baby steps, balancing my load, and made my way cautiously across. Then we walked up a hill, across some flats, and finally, balancing like tightrope walkers, down the length of a fallen log to one of the clearer upstream tributaries that fed the Madga.

Janet and I spent a couple of hours there, washing load after load of laundry. When we were done, we took baths. We were lucky; it didn't rain.

But the clouds were darkening the trees overhead by the time we gathered our buckets. Janet carried a basin of wet laundry and the tote bag of soaps. I carried a blue plastic bucket of clean, wet laundry and the scoured kitchen pot filled with cleanish drinking water, and we began our trek back to the village, walking slowly under the weight of our loads. The wet laundry was a lot heavier than the dry clothes we'd hauled upstream.

I took my *chinelas* off and used my toes as grippers to make it up the slippery fallen log without tumbling into the abyss below. As we neared the river, the rocks began to hurt my feet, so I put the cursed rubber slippers on again. Instantly, they were muddy and unmanageable, slippery as roller skates, and my feet were squishing off one side, then the other. What would I have given for a pair of rubber-soled lace-up canvas shoes! I took the worthless slippers off again. Ouch! My progress was slowed by the edges of river rocks. But I'll make it, I thought, eventually. As usual, Janet was way ahead, making it all look easy. She balanced the basin of laundry on her head and carried the tote bag of soaps over her shoulder. She was nearly to the Madga already, her slippers firmly attached to her feet.

I was barefoot and in the shallows of the Madga and Janet was well into the strong brown midriver current when I heard her shriek. I looked up and saw one of her slippers wisking away on the current. She cried for help—I was about ten seconds away—the stones, the current, and weight of my two containers slowed me down. As she reached for her first— then her second— rubber slipper, the laundry basin slipped from atop her head and bobbed on the surface of the river for a moment before a swirling gush flooded it. From that second on, it was pure chaos.

The basin submerged and our individual garments were starting to be swept downstream. I caught up with her, threw the kitchen pot and my own bucket of laundry atop her now half-full basin. I was holding the basin at the surface with one hand while grabbing for floating laundry with the other. But the basin was sinking, and we both pulled at it, trying to keep what was left of our clothing above water, while together we pushed the plastic basin slowly to shore. There we assessed our losses. We'd lost the precious cleanish drinking water, Janet's slippers, and much of our laundry. What laundry we still had was muddy.

"My Balinese tapiz!" Janet wailed. "It floated away. And my shorts. Your T-shirt. They're gone." She was practically weeping.

Janet sat along the riverbank to wring muddy water from the remaining laundry. I headed up the hill to the home of Amalya and Suat for help.

It was Serhio who stuck his head out the door to hear my story. Before I could get back down the slippery slope, he was naked and up to his waist in the muddy water. He swam downstream in the deep and swift waters and came up instantly with a bobbing white soap container and one rubber slipper. Janet and I hooted with delight, and he dove further, particularly in an area where several dead trees lay across the streambed.

"Mum!" came his triumphant shout as he held aloft a pair of green panties.

"*Yahoo*, Serhio! Atta-boy!" I shouted. Serhio dove again. In the roots and tangle of the trees he found more panties, my T-shirt, my towel, and Janet's precious Balinese tapiz.

A few more dives turned up empty-handed. The first light sprinkles began. Within moments it was raining intensely; the heavy fat drops were cold and pelting. We all headed home, Serhio helping us carry the soggy load.

Janet and Serhio were already up the ladder and onto the shelter of our porch when I arrived. They took my bucket from me, and Janet offered a hand up. I stopped for a moment at the base of the ladder and looked up at our nipa roof. Rivers of rainwater rolled off the roof and onto my head, and from between tendrils of my stringy, dripping hair, I saw Janet, soaking wet. I burst out laughing at the futility of it all. Nothing was easy here. Nothing worked. Nothing was ever warm or dry or clean. We survived—barely it seemed. The luxury of clean clothes, and in fact, all creature comforts suddenly seemed silly, trivial even, senseless energy-sucking exertions against the mighty currents and muddy waters of life. The more I thought about it, the sillier we strugging living creatures seemed. Still laughing, I flung myself onto the porch like a flailing wet tuna.

My yellow rubber slipper, which has been through so much with me, including almost getting swept away in the great laundry misadventure, has finally and permanently broken. Now what? I'm patching it with string and a stick, but it really doesn't work.

At school, I'm bored and tired. I'm not cut out to be a teacher. I have no new ideas and can't even muster the energy to care. These kids deserve better.

— Journal, August 21, 1972

◉◉◉

Okay, here's a secret. I never knew how boys' penises are really different from one another. I've had the opportunity to see many around here and I can tell that they vary in size and structure. When I mentioned this to Janet, she said that's how you know you're in bed with your husband. It's one of so many things I notice around here that I wouldn't think about in another place or time. I still haven't figured out what circumcision is. I get the idea, that a flap of skin gets cut off, but what flap of skin? I know the penises around here are uncircumcised, so I need to see a circumcised one, to compare. I don't think I know anyone I can ask for a look.

—Journal, September 27, 1972

◉◉◉

Sweet and Sour

News! Janet's long-lost cutoffs came home! Tarsilla's mom was washing dishes down around the bend in the river and found them snagged in a branch. Amazing! The great laundry hulog (fall) happened three weeks ago, and now her shorts appear. Considering the place and the people, I suppose it's not surprising that Tarsilla's mom knew whose they were. The story of our laundry misadventure will live on in infamy, as everyone within miles knows all about it—much to our embarrassment.
—Journal, September 8, 1972

⊙⊙⊙

I had a sick stomach again and declared definitively the culprit must be the cucumbers. Yet, ever hopeful, assuming I must be wrong, I ate them again; after all, they came to us daily.

With the recurring gifts of cucumbers and the chilling afternoon rains, my frequent jaunts to the outhouse left me shivering. Even though it was early evening, I put out the sleeping mat, stretched out on the bamboo slats, and wrapped myself in the cotton blanket. I rolled sideways to write in my journal, and as a challenge, I decided I would fill one page with things that are positive about my life here. No complaining. Just this once.

* I love lying under the mosquito net at night, watching the incredible super-nova lightning bugs that dance inside our house under our *nipa* roof.

* I love watching village life, peeking through the bamboo slats of our walls to observe silent, peaceful, everyday moments—kids playing, Suat making cordage, Amalya tying up her long hair. I find these things beautiful.

* I love listening to the patter of the non-menacing rain on the *nipa*. It is a gentle clatter of leaves stirred by the breeze, punctuated by raindrops, like music with depth and texture and rhythm. As long as the rain is gentle, the sound is soothing.

* I love the calls of the forest birds in the early mornings. Their warbles are quite clear and their voices diverse—some short pips, some cackles that begin on a high note and go low. There are so many calls I can hardly distinguish one from another. I'm not talking about the awful chickens.

* I love the river—the clarity and coolness of the water, the way it keeps on moving and is never the same twice. I love the sound of the water moving over and around the rocks, like cheerful laughter, an encouragement to keep on with life, to keep trying. I'm not talking about its angry moods, which can be terrifying.

* I love trying to learn the Manobo language. I say "trying" because I'm not getting very far very fast. The Manobo seem to have words for only four colors: white (or light-colored), black (or dark), yellow, and red. No words for blue, green, brown, etcetera—it's all "dark." When the sky is blue, it's "dark." When it's rainy and cloudy, it's "light/white." This is exactly the opposite of our concept, yet makes perfect sense. I know they see differences among colors; it's obvious in their beadwork. But there seems to be no differentiation in their language. Interesting.

* I love watching the kids play with the aluminum-can logging truck that Serhio made from our rubbish. In the evenings, they leave the truck under our house, where it waits till the morning chores are done. Then the kids squat in the shade and play together again, pushing dirt into piles and making stick forests to knock down and haul away.

* I love the crack of bolo and the screech of splitting wood and the smell of wood smoke in the evening. It means warm sweet potatoes will be ready soon.

* I love hearing Tagleong and Ricarda sing and tell stories to their kids at bedtime. Some of the stories, I'm pretty sure, are about us, the Americanas here to teach the Manobo. Yikes, is this how legends start?

* I love listening to Amalya and Suat chant/sing to their kids in the evenings too. Low and slow and sweet—comforting sounds.

* I love the sunset over the mountains to the west. Red and gold and pink before it fades to stars.

* I love how life is so simple, the way the people are willing to see us as people, kind-of-ignorant people, but they don't have preconceived stereotypes about us. I like the way they patiently teach us things, even the kids teach us things, and the way we can all laugh together, never hurtfully, just alongside one another. Laughing at yourself is easy here. And believe me, we give them plenty to laugh about.

Perhaps this sounds naive. Actually, life is much more complex than these comments make it seem, and I don't laugh much. In fact, I can't remember the last time I really laughed with true joy. Life is downright hard most of the time. And I feel sick a lot.

I've got to go to the outhouse. Again. In the rain. Again.

⊙⊚⊙

It's still morning. Probably. I forgot to wind our watch, so we have no idea what time it is. So I <u>feel</u> the day, and it seems like it is nearing, but not past, noon. Anyhow, we're the only ones here who care about tracking the time of day by specific hours.

— Journal, August 20, 1972

Zoon

Saldi made us a kubing, a musical instrument, from a piece of bamboo. It's played with the thumb and mouth, the sound resonating in the open mouth, modulated by the position of the cheeks and tongue, like a jaw harp. He made it for us, but now he's borrowing it back. I would prefer to keep it clean, since it's played at the mouth, but I can't say no since he made it and is kindly teaching us how to play. So, we asked him if he might make another one, and he said yes. He also told us to put the kubing near a flame to improve the tone. I guess the bamboo kubing has a short lifespan, since this one already seems daut, worn out—although it might revive when it dries out. At first it was punchy; the sound was sharp. Now it sounds muddy and slow. Who knew there's music in a

single bamboo sliver? This is today's simple pleasure, on
this day when I cherish any simple pleasure I can find.
—Journal, August 17, 1972

◉◉◉

I climbed the notched pole onto Datu's porch, crossed the porch, and stepped up into his house, the creak of the bamboo slat floor announcing my arrival. Something was wrong. Children were standing quietly on the porch and inside among the shadows, silenced from their running and jumping games. A group stood in the far corner of the house, adults mumbling under their breaths. Only the harsh bark of Datu's hunting dog tied in the back corner of the house broke the silence.

It seemed the whole village was there, gathered around Datu Tagleong, who squatted on the pandanus mat, peering at the form of a baby boy wearing only a dirty gray shirt. The small legs were pulled up tight with knees spread wide, as if muscles had suddenly shrunken, contorting the little body into a small human pretzel.

The child breathed in short raspy bursts, his eyes caked with film and rolled high in their sockets. The eyes terrified me at a primal level. His black pupils were wide, dark marbles in their sockets, staring fixedly up. The infant was Junior, Eddy and Alang's only child, Datu's only grandson. Everyone called him Zoon.

On the left sat Eddy, tightly grasping his son's small clinched fist, as if hanging on to keep his infant on earth. On the right sat Alang, a quiet young mother with long dark hair and sad eyes. Zoon was her firstborn.

I approached cautiously, not knowing what to expect. The people looked up from a crouched squat around the baby, and a few moved aside so I could reach in.

Zoon's eyes, staring blankly into space, his rasping baby breaths, emaciated frame, the silence of the crowd—it all frightened me but I moved in closer. Could this be the same baby boy who a few weeks ago had played—and pooped—on my front porch? I didn't recognize him.

I felt the small foot and noticed the heat. A fever. A small blob of liquid green feces lay under him. Eddy apologized for the mess and explained that Zoon had been having diarrhea.

"*Sige lang*," I said. That's okay, I don't mind. And I proceeded to examine Zoon. I touched him gently, tentatively. His muscles were tight, his stomach soft and sunken, his tiny hands clinched in hard, tight fists.

My hands moved over his small frame, searching for something, anything, but not knowing what. I asked Eddy what had happened.

"Zoon has been sick for a long time. He has loose bowels. We took him to Silco Camp to the doctor, but the doctor was gone. We saw the midwife. She gave Zoon an injection and some medicine."

"What kind of injection and medicine?" I asked.

Eddy didn't know.

"We brought him back home, and yesterday he became much worse. Now he's like this. He didn't fall, and he doesn't have any wounds or sores. He just has diarrhea, and he's been vomiting Alang's milk for a long time," Eddy told me.

My mind clicked through what little I knew of medicine. Hepatitis? Typhoid? Amoebic dysentery? A reaction to the injection? Malaria? Tetanus? These were all possibilities, but I had insufficient knowledge to distinguish the symptoms, make a diagnosis, or suggest treatment. Eddy and Alang looked to me, waiting with anxious eyes for a miracle. I was not trained for this. I gazed silently back to Eddy and Alang in helplessness.

My heart was breaking, my mind was racing. I knew that the situation was critical. Zoon's dark, staring eyes were unblinking, intense, and I felt them deep in my gut, like a low scream, primal, disquieting. I concocted scenes of rescue.

Getting Zoon to a doctor was imperative. The nearest doctor might be at Silco Camp downriver to the south, or perhaps at the sometimes-occupied Dongalyo logging camp to the north. But each of these camps was at least two hours away, either by logging truck to the north through impassable mud roads, or by river *banka* to the south, down the currently deep and fast-moving Madga. Zoon surviving an arduous trip seemed unlikely. And even if he made it to the logging camp, there was no guarantee a doctor would be in residence.

I considered sending Zoon downriver by speedboat, maybe even as far as Butuan City where there was sure to be a doctor, even a hospital. But in Madga there was no speedboat, not even a *banka*.

If I had a radio, I could call for help. What was needed was emergency medical evacuation by helicopter. But there was no radio. And certainly no helicopter.

My mind screamed—something *must* be done. It's an emergency!

As my thoughts tumbled, Zoon stared into nothingness, breathing in sporadic and shallow jerks, punctuated by occasional tiny hiccup coughs. Meanwhile, the people of Madga were demonstrating concern in other ways.

Laurentina had built a small bier of sticks and leaves that burned near the boy's head. The pungent smoke filled my nostrils and coated my tongue. Eddy still tightly grasped Zoon's hand and wrist, and he mumbled under his breath. A wad of wet leaves sat atop Zoon's forehead and stomach.

Maria came rushing in, perspiring heavily, as if she had just received word of Zoon's condition and had hurried across the mountain. She took one look at Zoon and took control.

"Move over!" she commanded Alang. Beads of perspiration dotted her face as she mumbled words semiaudibly near the face of the child. She spit three times on Zoon's head, little red splatters of spittle mixed with tobacco juice. I gasped slightly, with an impulse to tell Maria to stop defiling the child, but months among the mountain people had taught me to be patient and trust their good intentions, to watch, listen, and try to understand.

Maria mumbled again and spit three times on Zoon's stomach. With callused and gnarly fingertips she rubbed the redbrown spit in small circles on the baby's skin. The ritual was repeated for each of his hands and feet. As she finished, her head dripped with perspiration, as if she had strained to the very core of her being to pull Zoon through this crisis. Then she smiled, relaxed, and sat back against the flat worn boards of Datu's house and began the betel nut ritual: Crack the nut with her teeth, sprinkle on white lime powder, roll it all in a leaf, and stick the whole glob in her cheek. She smiled at me, the smile of one who had no particular worry or burden. Maria had done her best.

Tarsilla came in to announce the arrival of Joe and Flor Habana, the ones who originally brought me to the Manobo village. I hadn't seen them in months. We'd heard they were planning to visit us and had been expecting them for weeks. Their arrival at this moment was, to me, nothing short of miraculous. Surely, Joe and Flor would know what to do.

A few minutes later, Joe and Flor walked up the dirt path to the village from the direction of the river and they climbed the pole ladder to Datu's porch. Flor came immediately to Zoon's mat. For the next half hour Flor worked over Zoon. She asked for our medical kit—the only Western medicine in the village—and placed the thermometer under his arm. It was 101. She sent a runner across the mountain to Dongalyo Camp to see if the doctor was there. She opened the bottle of rubbing alcohol and began to rub down the child. It might bring the fever down.

I should have thought of that.

For the next hour, I sat with Flor, Alang, Eddy, and the infant Zoon as everyone else drifted slowly back to daily work. For a while, little Poring came to sit beside me, resting her head on my lap. With gentle fingers, I stroked Poring's head. I touched her hair, smoothing it, stroking it, taking comfort in touching the child, and Poring relaxed, her long dark eyelashes fluttered heavily, then closed in sleep. I continued to stroke her head, listening to her slow, smooth, sleeping breath.

Outside, children played and cried in the dusty earth. Dogs wandered in and out; one came over to inspect the baby with a sniff and a flick of a tongue on Zoon's foot. Ricarda prepared supper of sweet potato vine tops for her family. Zoon continued to stare blankly heavenward and to rasp short sporadic gasps.

Flor and I kept up the alcohol baths, and Flor gave him solutions of aspirin for the fever, diarrhea medicine, tea, and cough medicine—minuscule amounts of medicine, in a spoon, drops placed between his lips every few minutes, but he didn't appear to swallow any.

"Flor, what do you think is wrong with him?" I asked.

"I don't know. But he's dehydrated from the diarrhea," she said.

There was another question I wanted to ask. Sometimes these questions brought looks of scorn or vague unintelligible utterances from people. But I wanted to know. Long quiet moments of concerned silence passed as Flor, Eddy, Alang, and I kept vigil. In a quiet moment, I finally posed the question.

"Flor, a while ago Maria was here. She was spitting on Zoon and mumbling. Do you know why ... why she did that?"

Flor looked at me as if gauging how to reply. "She was praying. She thinks the spittle carries the power of the words."

It made sense. What had appeared a barbaric act now seemed a gesture of utmost care and concern. I knew Maria cared and was trying to help. I just hadn't understood.

The runner returned from Dongalyo Camp. There was no one there. My heart sank.

Evening set in, and I finally returned to our bamboo house for a dip-and-pour bath and a meal with Janet.

We both returned to keep the night vigil. I'd never been in Datu's house after dark, and the space was eerie. The floor was nearly full with mats and sleeping bodies. Eddy and Alang were lying with Zoon between them. A tin-can kerosene lamp glowed from the corner, casting a soft golden half-light. Zoon's eyes were caked in mucous and stared unflinchingly skyward. His temperature had decreased to 100.4 degrees, and during the night hours he blinked several times.

Flor continued to give him drops of medicine from a spoon. His breath was sporadic, with long pauses, and there were moments I thought he was dead, then he would rasp again.

The night hours dragged on. Alang and Eddy stretched beside Zoon, sometimes drifting in a fitful sleep. Alang, looking not much more than a girl herself, slept in the Manobo way, with a marble-sized ball of red tobacco between her lips. I stroked the child's head or held his small foot in my palm, feeling as though he were my own, a boy child I loved, for whom I had great plans and wished a full life. The next instant, I would see the child was a foreign entity, a strange blob of human tissue in limbo between life and death, beyond my reach.

My mood changed effortlessly, as if it rode the gentle night breeze that rattled the dry nipa palm fronds of the roof above our heads. I felt detached, floating. I felt the immense value of this small life, this person who could grow to help this village, this single life that might prove a catalyst for much-needed change. Grandson of the chief, Zoon might one day lead these people into the twenty-first century.

And I felt the simple ease of his early death, an escape from the dust and harshness of life, a happy release from the burden of human existence and growing up poor. As the night hours slipped by, feelings swirled through me like the clouds that wrapped the moon in silver-gray tendrils, then vanished. In confusion and pain, I shared the long hours with Eddy and Alang.

It was deep in the night when I returned to my own bamboo hut. I only half-slept, tossing beneath the mosquito net with dreams of my friends Eddy and Alang. In the darkness, I woke to hear muffled sounds from Datu's house. It was Alang, weeping.

Sometime after eight o'clock the next morning, I again crossed the dirt path to Datu's. A crowd of villagers had gathered. "He's dying," someone whispered.

Alang was sobbing loudly. Eddy was wiping his own eyes with the back of his hand, cooling Zoon's head with a damp cloth, then pressing gently on Zoon's deeply sunken belly as if to help him breathe. Zoon's breath was now more of a twitch than a real breath. His body muscles, yesterday rigid, today were slack. Was he dead? I wondered. No, another twitch. Now? When? How does one know? In silence, the villagers of Madga, Flor, and I watched.

During these moments of Zoon's transition, my mind indelibly imprinted the scene, the tiny details of life around me suddenly took on enormous proportions—the safety pin with a dangling bobby pin that hung like a cherished broach from little Tarsilla's tattered gray-green dress. The rooster crowing on the porch rail. The old opaque wine bottles hanging in the wood-frame windows, catching the morning light and scattering dull rainbows of grays and greens. The hunting dog barking in the corner. Datu's black and gray peppered hair and the red bandana he wore as a declaration of authority. Ricarda's wild hair and round body and rolls of flesh beneath her too-tight dress. The creaking slat floor. Zoon's long, dirt-encrusted fingernails.

It was Eddy who finally shut his son's eyes. For the first time since he arrived, the child looked as if he were asleep. But still there came another twitch and a tiny rasp.

My head swam. Finally Eddy held his hand over his son's nose and closed the baby's mouth and held it closed, until every twitch was still. The little life ended.

The first tear streaked my cheek. Only Eddy, Alang, and I cried as the people of Madga turned slowly back to the daily tasks which would ensure survival of their own families for another day.

I couldn't understand why I was crying. It wasn't because I had loved Zoon. I cried for friends Eddy and Alang. I cried at the senselessness of the death, at my own ineptitude and helplessness. I cried for the little life that never really started. I cried because I had never before watched someone die.

I walked to the window to stare into the forest. It was little Norma *gamai* who came to me, to comfort me. The two of us hugged for a long time, finding solace in each other. I held tight to the little girl, to someone alive and protected and safe.

Poor Norma *gamai*, I wondered how much of this she understood. Then I paused and considered, how much of this do I understand?

◉◉◉

I think the Manobo see Zoon's death as caused by evil spirits, not by medical conditions. The thought has crossed my mind that they might blame us, the strangers among them, but it doesn't feel that way. Eddy and Alang are among our friends, more than mere acquaintances. We've been in Madga five months and have been a part of birth too. This is the first death. Now I'm at Silco Camp. When we arrived this morning, Inday was quick to ask about Zoon. She was Zoon's ya-ya caregiver while she stayed with us at Madga a while back. I had to tell her that he died yesterday, and she seemed nearly unaffected, but then, what did I expect? She too is Manobo, and they don't easily demonstrate their emotions. But I know Inday, and I saw how she cared for baby Zoon, how she watched over him and loved him. I know she cares. She cares a lot.

—Journal, August 26, 1972

◉◉◉

Tirzo and Laurentina are characters. Freeloaders, as my grandmother might say. Tirzo is always the last one to jump out of the boat and help pull it through the shallows, the last one to show up for rice-planting work, the first one to sit down for a community feast, the first one to take his share of the community rice or corn. And Laurentina is "Miss Fashion" of Madga. She has more clothes than I do – actually, they are my clothes, the ones I gave Ricarda to disperse to people who needed them. Seems like most of them ended up with Laurentina while everyone else in the village still wears the same clothes they were wearing when we met them. This says something about community dynamics. The Manobo don't seem to notice, or perhaps they don't mind the disparity. It's only me, the Americana, who notices and gets irritated. Although I certainly don't say anything out loud. I put my opinionated observations here, quietly tucking them into this journal.

— Journal, September 5, 1972

◉◉◉

Janet and I were supposed to take this Madga job for a couple of months, as a final summer assignment before we were scheduled to terminate. But we've been stretching the temporary assignment, and Peace Corps Manila has begun asking why we're still there. So now we're officially asking for an extension of our service, asking for a third year, so we can go back into the mountains. I'll never have another chance to live this way, the way the Manobo people live. It's a rare and unique experience, even for a Peace Corps Volunteer. The Manobo live outside normal Philippine culture, and we've been invited in, accepted into their community, living in the old way. I guess there are scientists, anthropologists, who go into remote places to study cultures, to dissect and quantify and publish about the people. But we aren't studying the Manobo, we're living beside them, day after day. It feels different, important on a human level, and I want to stay longer.

— from Letter home, June 9, 1972

◉◉◉

Davao City

It's been nice staying in Davao City with our regional Peace Corps representatives Phil and Lynn. Great food, cooked by their house helpers who know how to cook for Western taste. And we met some neat people. Phil and Lynn always have people coming or going, and we just went along with the swirl of activity in their house. We met Kelly somebody from Peace Corps Washington, who stayed for two days. She was anxious to talk to us, to hear stories from "real" volunteers. I get the feeling that Peace Corps Washington is pretty far removed from the real life of volunteers. I told her stories of doing laundry and our great laundry misadventure and what we eat, and I showed off the beads that Amalya made. But I didn't *tell her about Zoon. Unlike our other mountain tales, the story of Zoon just doesn't seem like evening entertainment, easily told, easily heard, over coffee and cakes.*

We met Mr. and Mrs. Ashbrenner, an older couple who were very active in Peace Corps during the Sargent Shriver Days of the 1960s when Peace Corps was new. I felt like a country bumpkin, clueless about world issues. It's as if I float through time encountering life by chance, like a helium balloon bumping along the ceiling of life, wafting along on the drafty currents of sketchy information and my emotions.

— Journal, August 30, 1972

◉◉◉

Our trip downriver began just before noon on Friday, after morning classes. Janet and I hiked the footpath from the Madga to Trining and TingTing's concession camp half a mile away. The Madga kids walked with us, or ran ahead on the path, giggling, warning us of holes and pushing aside branches for us. I'd learned to trust the kids in the forest, and I enjoyed their enthusiasm and cheerful companionship. They sang our songs from school and stopped to point out fruit or insects or pig tracks. In a spot where the vegetation thinned, I could peer over the steep bank and check the depth of the river below. Shallow today. The Madga was running low, in some places maybe inches deep over the rocks—meaning the trip downriver might take longer than usual.

When we got to their camp, Trining and TingTing were waiting for us, their banka's outboard motor gassed and ready, so we quickly loaded up and pushed off, leaving the kids on shore waving goodbye. I soon fell under the spell of the river. I loved watching the shadows of overhanging vegetation playing over river rocks, mesmerizing golds and reds and browns under the water in dappled patches of sun and shade. Only twice did we have to get out and walk over the rocks as Trining and TingTing pulled the banka and we pushed from the sides. It took five hours to reach the Silco Camp dock; there was still daylight remaining so we briefly checked in with Mr. Guatno who was just finishing up dinner at his house. We spent the night in the Silco Camp guesthouse, luxurious in beds, with crisp, clean linens. Saturday morning, we got an early start into Davao City, catching a Jeep ride with a logger, and we arrived at the Santa-Inis-Melalie Guesthouse six hours later. But this time the place was empty. No staff. No helpers. Electricity shut off. Utterly deserted. We couldn't stay there. Now what?

Phil Lilienthal was the Peace Corps regional representative in Davao City. It was his job to give support and keep track of the volunteers in the Eastern Mindanao region, all thirty or so of us.

Although Janet and I were a part of the flock, we saw little of Phil and his wife Lynn, usually just a quick check-in while we were in Davao. We'd usually drop by the Peace Corps office to assure Phil we were okay, bring him up to date on our school, then shop for supplies and leave the city.

But that Saturday, since the Santa-Inis-Melalie Guesthouse was closed, we arrived unexpectedly at Phil and Lynn's house and asked if we could stay a few days. They welcomed us and put us up in a spare bedroom.

"I'm glad you came down this week," Phil said. "We're hosting a visitor from Peace Corps Washington, Mrs. Ashbrenner, an old-timer with Peace Corps, been around since the Sargent Shriver days. You picked a good time to be in town."

On Sunday morning, Janet and I headed out early to purchase supplies for the mountains: food, soaps, salt, and new rubber slippers for me. We stashed the goods in our little room at Phil and Lynn's, then set out for some fun.

We went to a movie, *Duck, You Sucker!* It felt good to laugh, to escape into American scenery, American language, and American humor. "Ever notice how we're the first and sometimes the only people to laugh?" Janet asked.

"Sometimes I think we're the only ones in the theater who understand the movie at all, let alone the humor," I said.

"Yep," Janet agreed. "Just goes to show that humor isn't universal. What's funny to us isn't necessarily funny to Filipinos."

"And vice versa. Ever notice how the audience will laugh at things we don't see as funny at all?"

"Just goes to show."

"Show what?"

She shrugged. "Just shows. Cultures. Differences. You know."

I knew.

After the movie, we ate roasted sweet corn from a sidewalk vendor who stood beside a glowing charcoal brazier, turning skewered ears of golden corn until each was roasted to bursting perfection.

"This has got to be the best corn in the world," I said. "Back in the Old Country, I'd put butter and salt on corn, but here that would ruin it. It's incredibly sweet just like it is."

"Umm," agreed a chewing Janet.

On Monday I talked to Phil about seeing a doctor. There was a red lump on my eyeball, and my left eye had been aching "like a headache, but in my eye," I told him.

Phil got me an appointment. "It's nothing serious," the doctor said. "Are you out in the sun a lot, in glaring situations?"

I thought of all the hours on the glaring river and the way my eyes ached. "Yes."

"Do you wear sunglasses," the doctor said.

"Sometimes, but they distort my vision. They warp the shapes of things, which gives me a headache so I don't wear them much."

"You need a good pair."

"I'd like to have a pair from America, but all I can find here are junk ones."

"Look around," the doctor said. "Be sure to get the kind that are polarized."

I did look around Davao City and found a pair of American-made Polaroid sunglasses in an upscale boutique at a Western-style hotel on the edge of the city. The price was sixty pesos, which, in American money was about ten dollars, yet on my Peace Corps salary was a significant chunk. So I didn't buy them.

That evening, Phil asked how my eye appointment had gone.

I told him what the doctor had said, and my search for an affordable pair of sunglasses.

"So, did you fine some?" Phil asked.

"Yes, but they cost too much."

"Well, if the doctor said you should wear them, seems like we could consider it a medical expense. I'll give you the cash tomorrow and we'll write it off as medical. How's that?"

I knew that sunglasses would not routinely be considered a medical expense. But I purchased them the next day. They were wonderful, big and fashionably round, and they calmed and cooled my eyes like a good night's sleep.

On Tuesday, Janet and I visited an ex-Peace Corps volunteer who had married a Filipino seven years earlier and remained in-country. Now Kay lived in the ground floor apartment of a Western-style home on the outskirts of Davao City.

She insisted on taking us swimming at the Luzon Hotel pool.

"But won't they mind if we just walk in to swim?" I asked.

"No, they like having Americans around," Kay assured us.

The little hotel looked clean and the pool was deserted. We splashed and swam for most of the afternoon. "Do Not Expectorate In Pool" read a sign on the veranda.

"*Expectorate* is not a common word. Would one who might actually spit in the pool be someone who could read and understand the sign?" I asked.

We agreed, probably not. I eyed the water warily for floating globs.

Kay enjoyed hearing about our life in the mountains. "What other errands do you have while you're in the city?" she asked.

"We're looking for school supplies. We're nearly out of paper, and it would be nice to have a few new books or magazines for the kids to see."

"I know where you can get some magazines. The Alba family who lives upstairs from us has plenty. She gives them to us sometimes. You ought to ask her."

We did, and she gave us as many old *Life* magazines as we could carry.

Then we visited the offices of the US Information Service in Davao City and asked for paper.

"We've got some paper you can have. It's been mimeographed on one side, but the other side is plain."

"That's fine," we said, "thank you," and we took a stack of paper several inches thick.

"Must be more than a ream here," said Janet.

"Maybe even two!" I exclaimed, feeling quite fortunate.

We spent time selecting gifts for our Manobo neighbors. For Amalya, needles and beads. For Serhio, a plastic truck. For baby Balbid, a rattle. For Ricarda, a bag of sea salt. For Datu Tagleong, a piece of red fabric he could wear as a bandana or a belt.

On Thursday evening, we were invited to a dinner with the Washington guests. I didn't feel much like socializing with strangers, but the promise of good food lured me. Janet and I bathed, lay across our beds reading and writing for a few hours, then put on our only nice-enough dresses and went downstairs as the guests arrived.

The food was spectacular, with roast beef, American-style macaroni *and* vegetable salads, *pancit* noodles, a Philippine eggplant-garlic-tomato dish, iced tea made from American Lipton teabags, and three kinds of homemade fruit pie, with ice cream. It was magnificent!

Then we all sat in the living room for conversation over coffee, with *actual* cream.

Mrs. Ashbrenner had spent several years in Africa with her husband, working with US AID. Now assigned to a fact-finding project for Peace Corps Washington, she was assessing volunteers and their jobs.

I sat in a comfortable corner, listening to Lynn and Mrs. Ashbrenner talk about life overseas. Mrs. Ashbrenner had many comments on the pitfalls of hiring help abroad, how challenging it was to train good help. I was utterly bored. Then Lynn prodded me to talk about our life among the Manobo. I told them about doing laundry at the river, the food shortage, the progress the kids were making with reading, and the recent windstorm that had blown our outhouse off its foundation.

Then, somehow, we got on the subject of Zoon, and my words began to roll out unstoppably. "It's hard to talk or even think about," I said, yet I couldn't stop thinking about it, telling them things that were never far from my thoughts. "I still can see Eddy and Alang and baby Zoon so clearly, and the staring cold look in his eyes. And the way Alang cried for her baby through the night. And the way the morning light came through the windows and lay across Alang and Eddy and Zoon in the corner of the house. And Eddy, as he watched his only son dying, and then holding shut the tiny mouth and eyes as the little body twitched. And the nonchalance of everyone else in Madga, accepting the death of this child. It's so far away from here, from a roast beef dinner, from shopping and conversations. I just feel so stupid," I ducked my head, averting my eyes, choking.

I felt them watching me, and suddenly I was crying. I wiped my eye on my napkin wishing I'd never begun the story of Zoon. I promised myself, I would never, *never* tell that story again.

Lynn moved toward me and put an arm around my shoulder. "It's a hard thing you've been a part of," she said.

"I guess so," I mumbled, feeling exposed, embarrassed. Mrs. Ashbrenner stared. I felt like I had failed in my ability to hobnob and make small talk with ritzy folks. Yet there was something comforting about Lynn and Mrs. Ashbrenner being there with me, hearing my story. Neither of these two older and wiser women spoke the words that seemed obvious to me—that I should never have gotten myself into this situation, that the pain I was feeling was my own fault. In fact, what I felt from them was just the opposite—in their presence I felt something like understanding and compassion. When I went to bed that night, I felt better, a tiny bit better.

The next day, there was bad news. "I was looking at your record," Phil said. "You and Janet both need to get to Manila for your language tests and medical evals, and the country director wants to see you both. I got your airline tickets. One of you leaves tomorrow. The other next Friday."

I went first.

⊚⊚⊚

I got up early to do my laundry here at Phil and Lynn's house. It's so easy when there's an unlimited supply of handy soap and water. Yesterday Janet and I saw a double feature—two Chinese movies with awkwardly translated subtitles. In these movies, sort of like our Superman stories, the people can do fantastic feats, leaping thirty feet in the air, having superhuman strength, and of course, the hero possesses astounding strength of character. He could kill with a look—the villain dies writhing from the strength of the hero's piercing glare.

These heroic, campy, badly translated, athletic movies are a little secret treasure of Asia and I love them.

I hadn't heard any news from home since last May, but here in Davao I received a letter, an early birthday card, along with a few sentences of family news from Texas. If my family would only realize how much getting a letter means to me, I'm sure they'd write more frequently. Well, maybe.

— Journal, August 27, 1972

◉◉◉

My Lucky Day

Yesterday I few from Davao to Manila. As has happened several times on previous flights, a stewardess came to me and said I was wanted in the cockpit. So, I went forward and when I got there, the copilot exited and the pilot asked me to sit in the vacated copilot's seat. Then, the most amazing thing, he asked if I would like to fly the plane. Well, my daddy was a pilot and I used to fly with him in his company's little Cessna, so I knew about pushing in the wheel to descend, and pulling back on it to ascend, and keeping the wings level as seen on the horizon gauge. It was nuts, but I did, just a little bit down, and little bit back up, as we flew past the Chocolate Hills of Bikol. The pilot said I would make a

good pilot. But it was very uncomfortable, me, flying a
planeload of passengers.

— Journal, September 1972

◉◉◉

I got my hair cut at the salon in the Hilton Hotel in
Manila. I think I look much better, I might even say cute,
if I can stretch the term. My hair is still long, but it's
a little shorter on the sides and longer in the back, in
a curled-under page. Of course, it will never be curled
again. But I think the basic cut is practical and will grow
out and keep a style—as if it really mattered in any of the
places I go.

—Journal, November 7, 1972

◉◉◉

Testing—the annual language exams and medical evaluations—
were parts of Peace Corps service that I dreaded and tried to put off
whenever I could.

Peace Corps Philippines headquarters was on the third floor of a low-
rise in the Ermita business district of the mega-metropolis of Manila.
Manila always brought me a twinges of culture shock as I witnessed
ostentatious wealth juxtaposed with near-death poverty. Ermita was in
the mid-socioeconomic range, modest yet functional. Buildings were
concrete, roads were paved, and telephones worked, but the area lacked
the conspicuous opulence of the Makati central business district, known
for its Hong Kong-style malls and glass-edifice highrises.

As I took an elevator up to the third floor, I wished I had the
mountain kids with me. They would be astonished—the building, the
elevator, the views of the city from three stories up.

The Peace Corps office was staffed by friendly host-country nationals
who seemed to take a special interest in each of us volunteers. They had
watched us arrive years earlier as scared, green recruits. Cely was behind
the reception desk.

I greeted Cely in her Tagalog dialect. I didn't know much Tagalog, the language of the northern Philippines, but I could say hello. She grinned, my linguistic accomplishment not lost on her.

"Paking is waiting for you," she said.

Paking was a Visayan language trainer, a native speaker of Visayan, and my evaluator. He was nice enough, but I always felt inadequate in his presence. I was likely to miss words or misconstrue meanings. Never good enough.

I slid into the leather chair beside Paking's desk, and we began to chat in Visayan. What is my work like? How is my living situation? He seemed interested in what I had to say about life along the Madga. I told him about the patch of vegetables that had been washed away by the floods. I told him about the kids that were learning to read and write in Visayan. I asked him if Peace Corps had any books or learning tools that I might use in teaching the kids to read.

He said, no, not that he was aware of.

I said I would just continue making my own teaching tools, that I only needed a lot of carbon paper and more pencils, and I might "borrow" some from the Peace Corps office. We both laughed.

Something had changed since the last time I sat beside Paking and we chatted in Visayan. No longer did I guess at meanings and fumble for words. I was comfortable. I could understand exactly what he was saying, and I could communicate freely, even joke.

After twenty minutes, Paking said, "Three-plus. Good work."

I was stunned. A rating of Three-plus meant fluency, not quite the Four level of a native speaker, but competent and fluid enough to be easily understood. Me, a Three-plus? I was the volunteer who entered the Philippines at the bottom of my language class, rating a Zero-plus on my first test, barely able to say my name in a sentence or ask the way to the bathroom, fumbling and stuttering. I was the volunteer who got tangled between "good night" and "good afternoon" and who, for a very long time, avoided pronouns entirely because the language called for hard choices: was I saying "we" just you and me; or "we" you and me and all the others? The variable options with multiple pronouns boggled, so for a long time I'd awkwardly structure my sentences to exclude pronouns. I was the volunteer who long struggled to be a solid One, and whose long-term goal was to make it to a Two. I took the Three-plus certificate he handed me and smiled my way downstairs to the medical office.

Medicals exams were different. I hated being poked and prodded and questioned by a stern, skinny male Filipino doctor whose thin lips never smiled. Dr. Agba took one look at the scale and told me to lose weight, as if I weren't already ashamed of the thirty extra pounds I carried since arriving in-country, the pounds that just wouldn't leave no matter how little I ate. He told me I had acne, as if that were news, and he poked at my zits with a pointy tool, to pop them. It hurt. They bled. And I knew there would be more to take their place. He told me to eat more vegetables, as if I had a choice when the mountain menu consisted of sweet potatoes and little else.

"When was your last internal exam?" he asked, looking at my file.

I shrugged, speechless with fear.

"You've never had one?" he asked, flipping through the pages.

I shook my head.

"How'd you get this far without one?"

I shrugged again, my throat dry and my voice gone. I knew that other female volunteers had undergone this examination, but I had opted out. Begged out. And our kindly staff doctor during Peace Corps training had let me go.

"Well I think it is time for your first one. You are, let's see, twenty-four years old, aren't you?" He looked down at my file, flipping the pages.

"Not until September," I croaked.

"Sexually active?" he asked, looking at me with cold eyes.

"No," I whispered, avoiding his gaze. I wasn't proud that I had never found anyone I liked, or who liked me.

"Are your menstrual periods regular?"

"Mostly, yes." I mumbled. They had been clockwork, until lately. But I didn't want to tell him that. And recently they were unusually debilitating. But I didn't tell him that either.

He was silent a moment.

"I take it that you do not want this examination?"

"No."

"Then you will sign this wavier. It says that in the future, you cannot make any medical claims to the Peace Corps for female problems, because you voluntarily waive examination and treatment. Do you agree?"

I agreed. I signed. I would never ask for help for irregular periods, cramps, or anything related to being female. And so, I escaped.

Before leaving the medical office, I asked nurse Elsie to let me into the supply room, explaining, "I need to refill my medical kit." From the well-stocked shelves, I took Band-Aids, gauze, tape, antibiotics, disinfectant soap, water purification tablets, vitamins, cold pills, rubbing alcohol, antacid, aspirin, antifungal skin cream, disinfectant, burn ointment, diarrhea medicine—several packages or bottles of each. Then I picked up a pair of surgical scissors, knowing how handy they would be for dressing wounds. I had more supplies than any Peace Corps medical kit could possibly contain. When I emerged from the supply room, Elsie looked at my bundle with questioning eyes.

"I'm really running low," I explained.

Maybe she knew, because with a lift of her eyebrows and a small smile she bestowed consent.

Mission complete. A Three-plus in language. A traumatic exam avoided. And I had medicines to take back for my Madga neighbors. It was my lucky day.

◉◉◉

> Through some friends in Manila, Janet and I were invited to a cocktail party at the Taiwan Embassy in celebration of the anniversary of Taiwanese independence. The gathering was a huge freak out for me. There were many white people and few, if any, brown ones, except for the wait staff. It was so odd. The guests were interesting, though, with powerful jobs in international governments. Janet and I were a center of interest, but I found it hard to speak, to put truthful words around my experiences in Madga. Good thing talking is one of Janet's skills and she did enough for both of us.
>
> But the food, oh my gosh! A few days ago, I was so

hungry. Flipping between worlds of feast and famine this way could make a person crazy. I'm trying to think of this vantage point as a golden opportunity to sit on a mountain ridge and gaze into the valleys on either side, both into realms of poverty and the worlds of abundance. But really, the disparity and disproportion of these opposite universes makes me want to shout about injustice.

— Journal, October 10, 1972

⊙⊙⊙

I got to explore a gold mine. I met a man at a gathering put on by our logging company friends, and the man asked me if I'd ever seen a gold mine. Of course not, I told him. So, he took me and a couple of volunteer friends to visit a mine last weekend.

We walked down a very long tunnel running deep into a mountain not far outside of Davao City. It was dark inside the mountain, but there were electric lights strung along the top of the tunnel. We walked a long way; there wasn't another person anywhere to be seen. At last we came to a side tunnel, blocked by a riveted steel door with a long sliding bolt. He opened it. I have heard of "gold bars" but had no idea what they looked like. The stack was up to my shoulders and as big around as my entire bedroom at home, maybe bigger. And in the stack were individual bars, each shaped like an oversized Snickers bar, rectangular, and about as long as my forearm. They were stacked cross-ways, so the pile wouldn't topple in an earthquake. He told me to try to lift one. It was really heavy, like cement. They were a dull golden color, not so shiny as you might think.

I didn't like being inside the tunnel, and although the gold was interesting, it actually didn't intrigue me all that much. I didn't ask if I could have one. Too heavy and impractical.

The best part was walking out, because the acoustics in the tunnel were great. I yodeled a Hank Williams cowboy song, and it sounded wonderful, echoing and deep.

Afterwards, I got to wondering. Once gold ore is mined from a mountain, doesn't it have to be melted down to make those bars? Where was the mining and melting part of the operation? Maybe what I saw was just a hiding place for a stash of gold bars, being hidden by a very rich person, perhaps a politician, perhaps one extremely powerful national leader in particular who is notorious for his copious and deviously gotten gains. Or maybe, those were fake bars, made of cement after all. Who knows. This is, after all, the Philippines.

— Letter home, undated

◉◉◉

Typhoon

I know some clean, cheap places you can stay in Manila. If you're willing to forego a room at the Hilton, which costs thirty-plus dollars a night, I can show you a room at a nice little guesthouse that costs ₱8.50 a night (which is a little more than $1.25). If you can do without a private bathroom, you can travel really cheaply here. One hundred dollars is enough, once you're in-country. Airfare getting here is the expensive part. The best time to come to Mindanao is April through June, after the rainy season and before it gets unbearably hot—although you'll find it plenty hot anytime. I hope you come!
— Letter home, February 13, 1971

☉☉☉

The diagnosis was confirmed at a hospital in Manila. I had dengue fever, a mosquito-borne disease, a cousin to malaria. The doctors gave me medication, released me from the hospital, and told me to stay in Manila for a week so I could be close to medical services. They said the disease would likely run its course and I'd be fine. So, I moved into a homey, hostel-style guesthouse in a modest Manila neighborhood. Fele was the guesthouse helper; we were acquainted from my stays there in the past. This time, I paid her a little more, and she cooked me onion-garlic-squash soup and brought me chilled pineapple juice.

I slept. I fevered. Pursued by ugly dreams, I soaked my sheets in perspiration, then shivered myself awake. The slow ceiling fan above my bed became a hideous monster, and I begged Fele to make it go away. She turned it off, slaying the monster. Indoor plumbing at the guesthouse was a godsend. Fele turned on the hot water once a day so I could shower with warm water. It took all my energy to get up and shower, but the warmth restored hope, and the shower became the highlight of my days—before I once again exited consciousness.

Then the rains started. Serious rain in Manila is not uncommon, and there was something calming about the constant pounding on the tin roof. I escaped into my dreams and the deluge became background noise. Then the winds started. Hard winds. But in my foggy state, I hardly noticed that this rain and wind were more than the usual. In fact, they had a name: Typhoon Flossie.

I have a fuzzy memory of Fele standing in my doorway, telling me she had to go home to check on her mother and sisters, that she'd be back soon, and there was soup in the pot in the kitchen. When I became deeply hungry, I made my way to the kitchen, hugging the walls for support, and found the pot overturned and rat footprints through the spilled soup. I went back to bed, my head pounding and spinning while the pummeling rain and ripping winds continued.

Perhaps it was the next day, or maybe the day after, I awoke to stillness, an eerie silence not only without the hounding rain and wind, but also without crowing roosters or barking dogs or shouting children or the motors of passing cars. I felt better, stronger, awake. And phenomenally hungry. I got up to look for Fele, but there was no sign of her—just the capsized pot of soup splattered across the kitchen floor and elaborate footprint patterns of traipsing, feasting rodents. As was common, fresh food was brought in daily from the market so there were no stored foods in the guesthouse except for gallon tins of soy sauce and cooking oil. Without that soup, there was nothing for me to eat. And with the electricity off, the toilet wouldn't flush and the water wouldn't run. But power outages were never unusual in Manila.

Then I looked outside. Downed branches strewed the lawn and a magnificent mango tree lay toppled against the high, cement fence that surrounded the compound. The sky was thick, but it wasn't raining. I put on shorts, got my shopping bag, and prepared for a foray to the nearest sari-sari, a small neighborhood store where I might find a few simple things to eat—perhaps a hand of bananas and a tin of juice. The store was just a block away. If I walked slowly, I thought, I could make it there and back.

I was totally unprepared for what I found outside the compound. The guesthouse and its immediate neighbors were high and dry, but then came the puddles, first just over my rubber slippers, then over my ankles, then knee-high, then thigh-high. I was hungry and committed, so I kept walking. The store was in sight. I was almost there—the water was waist high at this point—when I noticed the objects floating past me in the floodwaters. A bucket. A broom. A chair. A drowned chicken, wings spread, feathers fluttering as they drifted by. I passed through an oil slick and found it rather lovely, the rainbow colors like neon streamers atop the gray floodwaters. Deeper in the water were other shapes, shadows, drifting god-only-knows-what objects.

The front of the sari-sari was calf-deep in water and the door was shut. I shouted at the door of the nearest house and a bewildered face appeared. "May I buy food?" I asked. A teenager hurried out and let me into the store. It was flooded ankle-deep inside and the options were few—coconut-husk floor polishers, rope, a few bottles of soda. I found a tin of Skyflake crackers, three bottles of Pepsi, and a can of mackerel. That was enough.

On the way back through the waist-high waters I saw—first one, then two, and then a third—kittens. One floated face down, another belly up and empty-eyed, and the third seemed only a partial body—

small dead things bobbing in the filthy floodwater. I pushed past them, holding my bag of booty above my head.

Back at the guesthouse, I had enough sense to struggle through a frigid dip-and-pour bath with a bucket of rainwater from a barrel under the back-porch eaves. First, I cleaned with Betadine disinfectant, then with soap. By the time I finished, it was raining again and I was thoroughly chilled, my teeth rattling. I returned to bed with a tin of Skyflakes, a bottle of warm Pepsi, and some cold canned fish beside me. Once again, I slipped beneath the fevered veil, somehow surviving another day or two until the floodwaters receded, until Fele retuned.

◉◉◉

I'm better, but dengue fever is still affecting me. I tire easily and have little energy. If I were a boy, I think I'd be safe from the draft. They say once you have malaria or dengue or amoebic dysentery, the army won't take you. I know a bunch of guys with unlucky lottery numbers who would pay big money to exchange places with me.
— Letter home, July 29, 1972

◉◉◉

My Twenty-Fourth Birthday

On the recent full-moon night, I was bemoaning the fact that I was having my period again, a shorter cycle than ever, with painful cramps.

There's no way to take care of it, I told Janet. I sweat so much, a pad overflows, and half the time turns into soggy little cotton wads, because pads are so crummy here. I would use Tampax, but they don't have them in this country and I'd have to have someone send them to me from the Old Country. It's all so much harder than it should be. I asked Janet what she does, and she said she doesn't have periods! I asked her how that was possible, and she told me she simply stopped having them. That's another point of perfection about Janet. Beautiful.

Lithe. Smart. Funny. Fluent in multiple languages. And no periods! How perfect can one person be?
—Journal, August 22, 1972

◉◎◉

A giant, peeled, purple sweet potato the size of a small football slipped out of my hand, rolled beneath the porch bench, and softly plopped into the dust under our house. The pig came trotting when he heard the hefty plop, then came the snorts, grunts and grindings.

"We're not going to have enough to feed everyone if you keep dropping everything," said Janet. She didn't have to remind me. I knew the work it took to grow and harvest and cook even one kamote.

"I'm trying, okay?"

Silence and a glare from her green eyes.

Half an hour later as I sat in the doorway, my thigh brushed our tin-can kerosene lamp. It tipped and precious kerosene dripped away under the house. This time her glare was frigid, her lips thin. I knew my shortcomings. Fat, clumsy, stupid, and entirely miserable on this, my twenty-fourth birthday.

I wanted a *real* birthday. I would start by getting clean; I'd soak for an hour in a deep tub, my foot languidly turning on the hot water every few minutes so the tub would never stop steaming. I would wash my hair with scented shampoo and conditioner that left it soft and fragrant. I would blow dry it, curl it using electric rollers, and then, when I was done, my hair would cascade to my shoulders in shining curls. I would trim my ragged, dirty fingernails, then file and polish them pink. I'd even paint my toenails to match. There would be a party, a hamburger cookout on the back porch with meaty burgers, store-bought sesame-seed buns, dill and sweet pickles, corn chips, potato chips, and dips of fresh salsa and sour cream. Maybe we'd roast potatoes wrapped in foil on the coals—soft, steamy spuds sweet with butter and savory with salt. There would be Happy Birthday paper napkins, and six packs of Dr Pepper submerged in a chest of crushed ice. Little Hobbit, my fluffy terrier, would entertain with doggy tricks while I sat on the cement steps and laughed. There would be a white birthday cake with roses of blue icing, to match my eyes. I'd go with friends to a theater with no rats and see a movie without subtitles. I would wear a short skirt. I would look pretty. I would feel like a female person again. I'd receive wrapped presents tied with curling, cheery ribbons, and I'd open each gift—books and more books— with a big smile of thanks. And when my party was over, I would lie across my clean, soft bed in my own room with the door closed, an icy Dr Pepper beside me, and I would read late into the night. I would read for weeks. I would read nonstop until my *next* birthday.

Meanwhile, in truth, my broken fingernails were clawing mindlessly at the oozing, itching potholes on my legs as a fat fly circled, seeking a landing near an open sore. I looked down and saw how incredibly ugly my legs had become. Even if the lesions healed, I'd probably be scarred for life.

What I *really* wanted for my birthday was to be another person, maybe Janet. She says what she means and means what she says, unlike me whose words tumble out by themselves. "Maybe we can use kamote leaves," I'd suggested when we were trying to think of substitutes for paper plates. I meant banana leaves, but my brain tangled the rusted wires of language. Not just my Visayan words tangled, but my English ones now too. I was lost in a fog. It was my twenty-fourth birthday, and I was slow and dirty and dull.

As the sun began its downward glide toward the tops of the green mountains and the midday heat dissipated, the kids began arriving at Datu's porch. Party time, Manobo-style. Saldi brought the drum and beat out the syncopated Manobo rhythms we'd been learning to dance to in the mountain way, stomping and jumping with long swirling scarves. The echoes of the drum carried across the hills and more neighbors arrived, their ropey muscled legs glistening from crossing the river. Every student in our school came, most with their families and friends. We danced until sweat ran down Saldi's neck and the dancers were breathless.

"We have a special surprise for you all," Janet announced. "Sit down and rest a while."

I played guitar while Janet, the gifted linguist, sang. I struggled through the Manobo words, but joined her on the choruses. The tune was *Hey Loddie Loddie,* and we had a verse for each kid in our school and for some of the Madga adults too. We sang about Norma *gamai's* missing front teeth and Tarsilla spitting so frequently and with such accuracy; about Junior and Pablito who were always fetching water for their families; about Serhio who chopped wood every day for his family and for us school marms; about Donkilyo the great pig hunter; about Darna who was the "little mother" of her family; about Trining and TingTing who brought us cabbage and pomelo fruit from downriver; about Ricarda who wove beautiful pandanus mats; and about Datu Tagleong himself who got happy drinking Vino Kalafu wine. The song went on and on, each verse greeted by more laughter and hoots than the previous one, especially when Janet threw in Manobo words. Our act couldn't have been more warmly received if we had been on *The Ed Sullivan Show* in New York City.

Janet unrolled a Peace Corps recruitment poster that we had taken from the Davao Peace Corps office, and on the back was my rendering of a tailless horse. Janet tacked it to the wall of Datu's house. We had "borrowed" a box of thumbtacks from the PC office and made paper tails for everyone to play "Pin the Tail." I tied a rolled-up T-shirt over Janet's eyes, spun her once, set her in the right direction, and she made her way blindly to the tailless horse, demonstrating how to play. She stuck her paper tail where she thought it might go and the kids hooted. They loved the game, and everyone had a turn.

Big Norma won, tacking her tail squarely on the horse's rear end. I saw her peeking from under the shirt as she did it—but I kept silent. This wasn't the time to go into the concept of cheating, and besides, no one else seemed to notice or for that matter, care that someone had been declared a winner. Winning is a Western concept, I think. I awarded Big Norma a plastic comb she could take home, and the guests were all thrilled because they knew they too could use it. Private property was also a Western concept.

For treats, we served sugar-sprinkled, fried kamote chips. A mountain of chips that had taken us hours to prepare was inhaled in moments. I watched as great grasping handfuls were shoved into eager mouths. At least everyone got some.

We danced again, the drum's pounding rhythm echoing into the dusk. And when it was truly dark and the rising moon was a smile in the sky, the families returned to their homes for dinner. Janet and I gave out mounds of pancit noodles with bits of the onion and cabbage that Trining had brought upriver, piled high and wrapped with banana leaves, to be carried home, one bundle per family.

Trining and TingTing helped us clean up, and we four had tea together on our front porch. Trining told us his story, how he had fled from his home in the northern islands after a knife fight in which the other man died. He left that night after he saw the blood and the stillness of the body and realized what trouble he was in.

"What about your family?" Janet asked.

"They think I'm dead."

In these remote southern mountains, he had started a new life. It was hard for me to imagine that one of our best friends, the gentle and thoughtful Trining, was a killer—although in a tight spot, I would definitely want him on my side.

"Life is weird," Janet said to me, as we pulled our sleeping mat down and set up the net. I had to agree. It was the end of a long day, September 14, 1972.

Now that I was twenty-four, would I finally feel like an adult?

In the darkness beneath the mosquito net, Janet and I tuned in Voice of America, the music of my homeland. At that moment, I wanted to be home, transported instantly without the stress of getting there.

I'm older now, I thought. Will America still feel good to me? I was twenty-one when I left Texas. I should be old enough now to have answers to some of life's questions, or at least a set of values that can lead me to answers. Yet it seems I have only increasingly difficult questions and fewer firm values. I'm not even sure what it means to be friends with another person. I hear Janet's words every day, but I don't know anything about the person inside. She's close to me in proximity, but far away in spirit. We talk but don't seem to truly communicate. I don't intentionally shut her out, but I feel vacant toward her. We work side by side, yet we're miles apart. I feel confused; I'm crying inside. She has no idea, and I can't tell her. She's competent, knowledgeable, and aloof on the exterior. What is she feeling inside?

What does maturity feel like? All I know is uncertainty. If only I could develop some sense of myself, some personal strengths. Does everyone go through this? Does it ever stop?

I closed my journal, checked that the mosquito net was tucked in securely beneath our sleeping mat, and blew out the kerosene lamp. I pulled up the cotton sheet even though the night was sultry and sill. Saying goodnight, I turned my back to Janet.

Through the darkness of night came the gentle voice of Darna from across the dirt path singing her brother and sisters to sleep. "Make new friends, but keep the old. One is silver and the other gold." It was a song I hadn't been able to translate literally, so while I could explain the lyrics in Visayan, I taught the song in English. Darna sang it sweetly, with a Manobo lilt, yet to me, her voice sounded like home. I made a birthday wish. To have one friend, a true friend, gold or silver, someone who understands me, someone I understand. I wished that friend was with me now, a childish, impossible wish.

In the night there was a rustling and gentle shaking of our bamboo house. I awoke abruptly with a sharp strangling fear, hearing scratching, then silence. The intrusion was stealthy, yet noisy in its stealth. Should I wake Janet? Was it a person? An animal? I lay still, listening past my own pounding heart. The scratches came again, like a brush across stone.

Ka thunk! A crashing clatter of hollow tin. I sat up, fumbling for the lamp and matches, Janet beside me.

"What is it?" she choked.

"Dunno, but it's in our kitchen."

"Guess we better check."

"Uh-huh." My hands shook as I lit a match and touched it to the wick. A pale-yellow glow cast our shaking shadows as we moved to the doorway. There was a scrawny yellowish cat lapping at what had been the last of our cooking oil as it dribbled from the gallon tin and dripped through the slats of the kitchen floor.

Janet laughed, a chuckle of relief.

"Good grief," I sighed. And we leaned against one another.

"At least we got the kamote chips cooked already," said Janet.

"At least it wasn't me that knocked over the oil," I said.

She laughed, I smiled. Friendship. Maybe this is it after all, found in a small, shared moment. It's not all I would have wished for, but perhaps it would do.

◉◎◉

There is a craze here in Madga. Dancing. The Manobo way. Groups gather almost every afternoon—adults, kids, everyone. And they dance and laugh and talk and sit close to one another and pick lice from each other's hair when they aren't dancing. As I sit here writing, there's an impromptu dance on Datu's porch. The drum is a hollowed-out section of log with horsehide covering one end, held tight with homemade ropes.

And they beat on a five-gallon can that used to hold kerosene and on a metal pig trough that appeared from somewhere. They're beating the drum with their hands and the can with rag-wrapped bamboo sticks. It's deafening. On the porch are Ricarda (well naturally, it's her house), Big Norma (whose home is across the way) and Ben (Norma's husband), young adults Tassio and Saldi, and of course our twenty schoolkids, who don't miss anything of interest.

They've been teaching us. The sumbatang is the slow gliding dance for women. The binaylan is the fast, energetic dance for men, evoking war or hunting. The music, the beat, is the same; it's just danced differently by men and women.

—Journal, September 12, 1972

◉◎◉

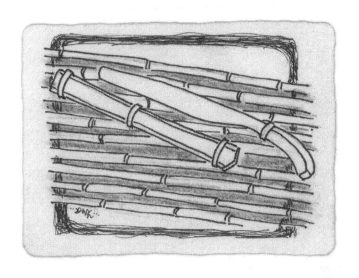

The Bolo Wound

Earlier today I happened to glance into the head-strap basket hanging in our house. The most amazing thing was there. During our daylong absence, we'd had a visitor, and a small chicken egg was nestled in the basket. I can't get over it! An egg! We never see eggs here in Madga, then suddenly one appears inside our house. I chuckled about it all day. Janet and I will share it. I do wish I liked eggs. I've been thinking about other ways to cook it so it won't taste like egg, because I sure could use the nutrition.

Ah, now I see how she's getting in. She came back through a place where the wall doesn't quite meet the

nipa roof. I guess she's looking for her egg. Sorry, all
gone. And guess what! She left another one!
—Journal, September 29, 1972

◉◉◉

In the dust of our yard, a half-dozen scrawny chickens pecked ever hopefully at specks of nothing. They made the cooing and clucking sounds of chickens as I watched them from the shade of our porch. Janet sat in the doorway, and we prepared lessons for the next schoolday.

"School things," Janet offered, triggering a category for our Remember Game. "Mimeograph machine."

It was our game of wishful thinking. Making worksheets, three carbon copies at a time for a class of ten or twelve was repetitive, laborious, and boring. But it was also the only option we had for giving the kids a chance to read and write their lessons independently. It worked as long as the carbon paper held out.

"How about preprinted workbooks, one for every kid, tear out the pages and go," I suggested.

"Okay. Desks," she added. "Each student sitting at one, a level hard surface to write on." In our school, kids wrote on composition books balanced on their knees or they kneeled on the bamboo floor and used the rough, gouged plank bench as a desktop.

"Yeah, and teachers' desks, too, organized, with drawers and a box of Kleenex on top for the kids to blow their noses. Nobody would have to lean out the wall to blow snot in the dust."

"Okay, how about walls, and floors," Janet countered. "Flat floors that pencils couldn't fall through."

"Okay. And pencils," I offered. "Enough for everyone. New, yellow, number-two pencils, with erasers on the ends."

"And a pencil sharpener," said Janet. "The crank-and-grind kind, on the wall beside the blackboard." She glared at her own dull pencil. Since our little toy truck sharpener broke, we'd been using the all-purpose machete. She leaned back to get it from its hook inside the doorway.

"Okay, how about that blackboard, big enough for more than one sentence at a time, and chalk bigger than a pinto bean."

"Umm," Janet was drawing the bolo from its wooden sheath, and as she grasped and pulled, the machet clattered to the floor. She clutched her left hand, and I saw blood ooze from her grip. Red drops splattered on the bamboo-slat floor, and I jumped for the first aid kit, grabbed a bandage, then a second one, then a third. I ripped one open and was at her side. She was pale and silent, clutching her dripping hand.

"Try this. Here, let me see." I didn't really want to look, but then again, I needed to know what we were dealing with.

Janet slowly opened her hand and I could see a slice near the middle joint of her index finger. It looked deep. I wrapped it tightly in the first bandage, which quickly soaked. So I wrapped the second and third bandages tightly and then tied a clean handkerchief around her whole hand. She went inside to lie down on the bamboo floor, and we put her arm up across her chest, elevating her hand. Then we waited. Silent. Wondering. What next?

In a few minutes she spoke in a soft voice. "What am I going to do? I think it needs stitches."

I considered the options. There weren't many. There was no doctor within half-a-day's hard travel, if we had transportation, if the river were running high, if she had the use of both hands to make the trip. And there was me. "Well, I guess I could stitch it up. I've never done it before, but it's like sewing, right?" I tried to sound braver than I felt. The thought of sticking a needle into human flesh made me queasy. "Maybe it won't need stitches. Let's wait and see. Stay where you are. Keep your arm up, and I'll fix us some tea."

I blew on the glowing embers from lunch and got the flame going. I added twigs and blew some more. I filled our pot with boiled drinking water, and while it warmed, I rinsed the blood off the porch and the bolo and returned the sheathed blade to its hook. The water boiled and I poured some over a fresh teabag in Janet's enamel cup.

"Can you sit up?" I asked, carrying both our cups into the house.

She sat, still pale, cradling her injured hand against her chest. With her good hand she dunked the teabag several times before passing it over to me. I set it in my own cup to steep.

We sipped in silence, both of us contemplating the impact this injury might have on our lives. Would we need to send a runner to

Silco to get Trining and TingTing to come up and take Janet back downriver to a doctor? Could we deal with it ourselves? What about infection? What if Peace Corps heard about it and terminated our assignment because of the lack of proper medical support? What if that small slip meant the end of our Madga experience? What about the kids—they were just beginning to read. But how could Janet work with only one hand?

"Maybe we could take a look at it now," Janet said. I nodded. Slowly she unwrapped the handkerchief and took off the three blood-soaked pads. The bleeding had mostly stopped and for the first time we got a good look at it. The gash was an inch long. She moved it ever so slightly and I could see white blobs in the depths. Severed ligaments? Globs of fatty tissue? Bone? I had no idea.

"Do you think you could stitch it up?" she asked.

I wanted to say yes. I wanted to be able to help. I wanted Janet to be all right again. I got out a needle and thread and sterilized the needle with alcohol. I looked from Janet to the needle, to Janet again. Then finally, "No, I don't think I can do it."

Janet just nodded. Maybe she was relieved.

We wrapped her finger and hand in clean bandages and a handkerchief. "But how will I do anything, any work? It takes two hands to do everything around here."

That was certainly true. With Janet incapacitated, the workload would fall to me and would be tremendous. Hauling all the water. Doing all the laundry. Preparing school supplies for both our classes. Doing all the cooking and cleaning and chopping and burning.

"Well, it's your left hand, so maybe you can still write," I suggested. "And I can do the hauling and heavy lifting. Maybe Serhio can help us bring up water and chop wood. We'll make it. Just keep your hand wrapped and don't use it. And don't get it wet. River water might cause an infection and that would be the worst thing. We'll make it. Somehow." I was sounding more optimistic than I felt.

In the late afternoon, I was down at the river washing a few clothes, including the blood-stained handkerchief. The rust-colored cloud drifted in the calm water near shore. Where will these blood cells go, I wondered. Downstream, to be eaten by fish? Or to be caught up in someone else's water bucket, to be cooked into sweet potatoes or gulped in a dipper to quench a thirst?

A day later, I was already feeling the stress of the increased workload, even though Janet was doing what she could. Our focus was to keep her hand dry and clean, so we kept it bandaged in a sling strapped close to her chest. In the afternoon, I helped her bathe under our house in the dip-and-pour style, making sure her hand and arm stayed out of the splash zone. And I washed her hair, then brushed it out as we sat together on our porch in the late afternoon. I was the one who stoked the fire, boiled the water, and fixed our supper of leftover sweet potato, canned wiener hash, a small roasted eggplant, and some unidentified green leafy forest vegetable from our neighbors. It was bitter and—to me—utterly disgusting. The bright spot in the meal was a small slice of melon, a treat from Amalya's house.

For evening entertainment, Janet and I sorted out our travel addresses, people from all over the world we'd met in the Philippines, people who had invited us to come and visit as we traveled home through Asia and across Europe. And by the light of our tin-can kerosene lamp, we listened to Louis Armstrong coming in from Voice of America out of Hong Kong. We listened that night for news of our own culture. Richard Nixon, the Republican Presidential candidate, was expected to carry all fifty states in November.

"Not me," said Janet. "I wouldn't vote for him. McGovern maybe, not Nixon."

"Are you registered to vote absentee?" I asked her.

"No. Are you?"

"Naw. Last Presidential election I wanted to vote, but I was only twenty, not old enough. Now I'm old enough, but not registered to vote absentee. Next time a Presidential election comes along, I'll be twenty-eight. I can't imagine being that old," I said.

"Yeah, if we live that long."

"What do you mean?"

"Living way out here, anything can happen." Janet looked down at her hand, wrapped mummy-style and cradled gingerly across her lap. "Anything."

I'm irritated again. The tiny mosquitos just don't let up. They're as unrelenting as the five kids who are sitting on our porch, including Erlinda, the most demanding and my least favorite. She's always wanting medicine or candy (as if we had some!) or music or just to stare at me.

Then there's the constant howling of Datu's hunting dogs. During class I have to scream sometimes so my voice can be heard above their yelps. And if they pause for even a minute, the chickens chime in, that old fighting rooster crowing in my ear.

And I have a giant, throbbing burn on my knuckle from cooking.

And Ricarda just came over to tell us that Datu Tiklunay has died. Trining and TingTing are making a special trip downriver tomorrow so Ricarda can meet with his widow. Datu Tagleong took us hiking over the mountains a couple of months ago to see Tiklunay, and I was amazed to find him sitting on a pandanus mat wearing one of my old Sears shirts, an original from Texas that I'd given to Ricarda months earlier. It was yellow, with thin red and black horizontal stripes. I think Datu Tagleong or Ricarda gave it to Tiklunay as a show of respect or friendship. And now he's dead. I'll bet he'll be buried in my old shirt—which looked very nice on him.

Life is small, irritating, and difficult, and then you die. Lucky if you end up with some friends who will walk over a mountain to see you, and a good-enough Sears Roebuck shirt to be buried in. And that's all there is to life.

— Journal, September 18, 1972

⊙⊙⊙

Pig Farts

We're trying to arrange for Dr. Troucio, the physician from Silco camp, to come to Madga every so often to help the Manobo with their medical issues. To do so, he'll have to get a ride upriver with the concession guards, work through the afternoon, stay overnight, and then go back with the guards the next afternoon, if the river's willing. Dr Troucio won't want to stay in Madga long as he simply isn't a rough-it kind of guy. He's a friend of ours who wants to take us out only to fancy places in Davao. He dresses nice and doesn't like sweat or dirt, so even though he says he'd like to come up and visit us, I doubt he's actually willing to experience the adventures of upriver field medicine.

Meanwhile, we've had a couple of patients already

this morning. One was little Evangeline, who came to us with a chopped finger. Her hand is swollen and discolored, and it looks really bad. We cleaned and bandaged it and "prescribed" half a tablet of Tetracycline twice a day. Maybe that's not the right dosage, or even the right medicine. I wish I knew more!

— Journal, August 5, 1972

◉◉◉

Little Lando spoke to me for the first time today. He just came up and started talking! Amazing! A front-porch conversation with one of the mga gamai kaayo! After six months of silence and running away, he finally spoke, and what he had to say made me laugh out loud. Such is mind of a four-year-old Manobo boy. Actually, maybe not so different from an American four-year-old.

—Journal, September 15, 1972

◉◉◉

The youngest Madga kids ran in a pack. We called them the *mga gamai kaayo*, the "Very Littles." They ranged in age from about two to four. Their favorite time to come to our porch was late afternoon, just before dinner, to watch Janet and me do afternoon chores and to explore the cardboard library box beside our front door.

They were mostly shy, hiding their heads when spoken to. Even Lando, Datu's four-year-old son, the ringleader of the *mga gamai kaayo*, was quiet in our presence. These kids spoke the Manobo dialect with a bit of Visayan while Janet and I spoke mostly Visayan, with a few phrases of Manobo. It's no wonder our verbal communications with the Very Littles were minimal.

One day, the Very Littles were on our porch looking through the highly prized old *Life* magazines. Lando sat naked as usual, his legs crossed and his extended belly pooching over the pages of the magazine. When he came to the photograph of some farm animals—a horse, chickens, and a pig—I could hear him whispering to the other Very Littles, naming the animals and giggling. I was writing in my journal.

"What do you see?" I asked. I didn't anticipate an answer, but Lando looked at me squarely and answered in Visayan, "Horse."

"Ohhh, yes," I said. "Anything else?"

"Chickens."

"Right. Any more?

"Pig."

"Right, Lando." I was amazed. We were having a conversation, in Visayan. I pressed my luck. "We have animals like that here at Madga, don't we?" I pointed to a couple of scratching chickens.

Lando pointed to the village pig poking around under Suat's house. "Pig eats," Lando said. "Then he farts."

"He farts?" I asked.

"Yeah. A pig doesn't fart much, but when he does, oooh-eee, you better watch out," Lando told me.

I could hardly keep a straight face. "What happens?" I asked.

"It really stinks. A pig fart is much stronger than a human fart," he said. "Pig farts are really big."

"And how do you know when a pig farts," I asked him.

He must have thought me a bit stupid, for he said with perfect matter-of-factness, "You can hear them. Loud!"

From that time on I knew that when Lando hung around school, climbing monkey-like over the porch rail, flitting by to sit for a few minutes before vanishing as quickly as he came, I knew that he was listening. Listening to our stories in Visayan, listening to our reading and writing lessons, and now I knew that he was listening too for a tale-tale rumble from the porker beneath the porch.

◉◉◉

Kids are always around. Lando, Tata, Lalak—the tiny Manobo group. Cute, but a bother sometimes. Yesterday I was scrubbing the floor inside and Janet was bathing dip and pour in the bath enclosure under our house. Lando and Tata sat transfixed in the dirt beside our wall, peeking through the nipa wall into the bath area to watch the Americana bathe. Curious kids, probably wondering why we didn't bathe at the river like everyone else. I told them to go home.

The other day I was at the river doing laundry with a pack of kids. (We never go alone anymore. Since the great laundry misadventure, we're always escorted by a kid-pack, at their parents' instruction, I'm sure.) Dita, who was sitting beside me, took off her dress to wash it in my soapy water. Then she squatted at the edge of the river to rinse her little dress. Then she put it back on and went into the river to play and splash and swim. Lando and Mordino joined, and the three kids started looking under rocks for shrimp. Morino had a three-inch immature melon to use as a toy—it floated—and they tossed and chased it in the water for a while. Playfulness and adventure seem to be built into Manobo baths. Our way of bathing, under the house in a closed-in room, seems boring, even to me.

— Journal, September 6, 1972

⊙⊙⊙

Martial Law

*Look how my handwriting has changed. It used to be
neat and careful, now it's hurried and scratchy. I can
hardly read it. I wonder if that reflects a deep and permanent change in my personality as I become less logical and linear, more scattered, circuitous and random.
Or maybe it reflects that my only remaining ballpoint
pen is junk.*

— Journal, September 19, 1972

⊙⊙⊙

Hunger gnawed like a whole-body headache—constant, pounding,
persistent.

It was September in Madga and the rice wasn't ripe yet, the summer sweet potatoes and melons were gone, and we knew our neighbors needed, even more than we did, the little food that was available from the forest. At least we could fall back on our dwindling food supply brought from downriver. Amalya's family had even less. I'd seen her bringing in kamote leaves for her family's dinner. No sweet potatoes, just the leaves. Times were hard for all of us.

We were due for a trip downriver to resupply. But two weeks earlier, Trining and TingTing had been urgently called back to Silco Camp. TingTing had sprinted over the mountain to tell us. "Logs are loose on the Agusan, and they're floating wild down the river. Everyone's been called to help." A Texas girl like me understood. It was like a stampede, and all the cowboys were needed to ride fast and head 'em off at the pass. "We'll return soon," TingTing said, and they were gone within the hour.

But that had been half a month ago and still no word from our logger friends.

"We've got half a pack of spaghetti left," Janet reported, rummaging through the food box. "You want noodles with peanut butter or this cheese stuff?"

We knew the cheese stuff wasn't real food, but the thought of noodles with peanut butter made me even sicker.

"Cheese," I said. "It's Italian night."

Janet had been oddly quiet the last couple of weeks. We communicated about the necessities, but otherwise we'd stopped talking or laughing. Life was difficult—uphill and heavy. I was short on patience, on curiousity, on humor.

I'd even stopped trying to be sure each child got the best lessons. I just didn't have the energy. It was all I could do to muster the strength to get a bucket of water up from the river twice a day and get through the classes. Walking made my heart pound.

Janet, beautiful Janet, just seemed to grow more beautiful, even though she complained that her hair was breaking off and her fingernails were splitting. My own body was showing changes too. My fingernails and toenails had weird little corrugated ridges on them, like mini-washboards. And my tongue was always dry, even after I drank tea, when we'd had tea, before we ran out. And I was fatter than ever, even though

I was hardly eating anything. It didn't make sense, but I couldn't make sense of a lot of things. I had trouble thinking straight. Words tangled as I spoke, even in English. I dropped things. I lost my train of thought in the book I was reading. My journal entries were brief, disjointed, and most days I couldn't muster the energy to write at all.

I didn't ask Janet how she was feeling. I didn't ask Janet much of anything. She had a tendency to lash out at me these days, scolding me for being lazy and stupid. As if I weren't trying. I *was* trying—at least I was trying to try.

Janet cooked the noodles in the river water I brought up. The wax-cheese-substance melted on top. I gobbled my bowl of noodles, hungry for more. Janet, ever dignified and cultured, ate tiny bites, chewing each morsel fully.

"Yummy," I said as if it were. "Anything else?"

"You can see as well as I can," she snapped, making me sorry I'd spoken.

Indeed, I could see inside the food box. It was low, but not quite empty. Raw oats. And peanut butter. I took a spoonful of each. "Try this. Sort of like oatmeal-peanut butter cookies. Very tasty," I said relishing the salty tang of peanut butter and the satisfying chewiness of the oats.

"Disgusting!" she snorted, walking out to the porch to rinse her bowl. I sat alone beside the kerosene lamp for a few more minutes, having another "cookie" and leaving Janet alone on the porch. I put the supper supplies away and went out to rinse my bowl and utensils. Janet stepped inside as I went out.

Intermittent moonlight between skittering clouds lit my task. I was leaning over to put away my bowl when the first wave of nausea hit. I sank onto the bench, sweating, trying to hold down my dinner. A minute later, another wave hit, and I leaned wide over the porch. It was a quiet, nonviolent retching, a simple splattering of my dinner onto the dirt below the porch.

I was breathing hard, but my stomach felt calmer. What was that? How can I be so hungry, yet throwing up? Was it the raw oats and peanut butter? The thought made my stomach tilt again. I sat there, breathing deeply, listening to the night. The scrawny hunting dog from

Datu's house lost no time devouring the free meal. I watched him in the moonlight lapping at the light-colored circle of puke on the dark dirt. At least someone gets dinner tonight, I thought.

The mosquitoes drove me back indoors, where Janet had set up the mat and net. She was fiddling with the tuning on our transistor radio. We'd attached a long wire to the antenna, trying to improve the reception, but it didn't make much difference. All the stations were mostly static except on the clearest nights.

"Reception's bad tonight," Janet said. "Want me to turn it off? Does it bother you?" She was asking kindly. She must have heard me retching out there and was feeling sorry for me now.

"It's okay. Better than nothing."

Janet sat under the net in our cocoon of respite from the crawling and flying blood-sucking creatures of the night. She was writing. I lay down under the net, a sheet over my head, feeling miserable. Intermittently audible through the static, the Voice of America played music of the 1940s.

I must have fallen asleep, because I was dreaming of hamburgers and dill pickles and steaming baked potatoes with butter and salt, when I was jolted to reality by something on the radio.

"… interrupt program… zkkkkkkkkk … Manila … zkkkkk." The static distorted the reception, the words rising and falling like a coconut husk drifting on ocean waves, just beyond reach. " … Marcos has …state of martial …. curfew and takeover….."

Janet was tuning the dial by minute degrees, trying to maintain a signal. "Did you hear?" she hissed.

"Yeah, I did. Can you get it in again?"

"…triggered assassination … a terrorist … national law enforce …stockpiles… and a government takeover… broadcast … electric … airlines … elections suspended… Marcos ministry officials…"

We listened hard, straining to fill the gaps.

Janet was staring in wide-eyed frustration at the radio, then at me. "That's crazy! What terrorist takeover? What's going on?"

Having no answers, I was silent. From the first days in-country, I'd known that the country's politics were a mess. Democracy was a farce.

The system was inequitable. Power belonged to the wealthy, the well-connected, those who played the game of kickbacks and bribes and backslapping deals with buddies. Democracy didn't work in a place where voters are hungry or chronically uninformed.

"I'll bet Marcos rigged this takeover himself, so he won't have to give up office when his term is over," she hissed. "He's a power-hungry, greedy old man."

"How do you think martial law will affect life here?" I asked.

"How should I know?" she flared. Maybe it was wrong of me to consider Janet the expert, but in truth, she was much more worldly-wise than I. She'd lived on Luzon, close to Manila, and paid more attention to national politics than I did. "Maybe they'll send in the National Army to shoot us all," she said. "One thing for sure, I don't want to travel to Manila right now."

"Wait till my parents hear about this!" I moaned. "Bad enough I'm in this crazy country, but martial law. I wonder if mail will get through."

There didn't seem much more to say to Janet. She turned to her journal and began to write, and I wrote too. I guess we'll just have to wait and see what happens next. Maybe tomorrow there'll be more news on the radio. If the batteries hold out. If the clouds aren't too thick. If we're still alive.

The sounds of the sleeping village lay around me. Next door, Suat snored. The river tossed gently against its banks, a mosquito buzzed determinedly, seeking passage through the net, and I cocooned myself under our sheet, trying to think past my fear of world politics, my loneliness, and the hunger that pressed in on me like a vengeful ghost. Maybe tomorrow things would be better.

◉◉◉

It's been nearly two days since the news, and this morning we heard that Marcos has been bragging, "Not one crime has been committed in the Philippines during the first day of martial law." This morning's Philippine news also reported that Marcos says he'll let the public *know more soon—making me think we're not getting the whole story. It's all so sketchy as the radio fades in and out; it's even harder to get reception in the daytime than at night. If Trining and TingTing arrive soon, maybe we'll find out more. All my kids just arrived at school in a happy pack, so I'll start class now.*

— Journal, September 25, 1972

◉◉◉

Nonsense

Breakfast: crackers, peanut butter (almost all gone), jelly, instant coffee

Lunch: one slice melon (not sweet, not even good), coffee.

Janet had a nipa palmstalk vegetable and some cucumber, gifted by neighbors. I tasted the vegetable, slimy and bland, repulsive actually. And I'm not eating cucumbers anymore, period. They make me sick, a terrible stomachache. We opened a can of milk yesterday, had some, today it was curdled but we drank it anyhow. Like yogurt? Not very good, but we didn't want to waste it.

Dinner: Neighbors gave us some ubi, a root tuber like a yam or taro. We wrapped it in banana leaves, roasted it in the fire, or we tried to till the smoke became more

than we could bear. So, we finished by boiling it. We ate
that, along with some more tasteless, mealy melon.
    As the meals go lately, this was a pretty good day, only
moderately disgusting.

                            —Journal, August 13, 1972

                    ◉◉◉

Ten minutes after the schoolbell sounded, just three kids had appeared for classes. Something was up. Turned out it was rice harvest.

I sat with my three students and quickly revised my class plans. Keep it simple. Keep it short. Charcoal art. Something new and different. The charcoal part wasn't new, because if there were two things my kids knew about, they were sticks and fire. They were familiar with charcoal. It was making marks with charcoal on a sheet of paper that was new— and messy. Of course, they loved it, lines and loops of black, and smears of gray.

Then wash up at the river. Then a story, *Hop on Pop,* a Dr. Seuss book with wacky drawings, donated by the United States Information Service in Davao City. I translated it into Visayan as I read, which meant the rhymes and cadence were lost, but the silly pictures kept the kids' attention. *Hop on Pop* translated into something like Jump on Father.

The first time I'd read this book to my Bigs, all I got was round-eyed stares. Was there a word for *nonsense*? For *silly*? How to explain these concepts. Breathe. Begin. "It's not-true life. It's like a dream, a thought, to make you laugh, an idea to make smiles." Nods from the kids. "Again," they said. "Read it again."

"What part did you like?"

"The flying dog."

"The fish in a tree."

"Do dogs really fly? Do fish live in trees?" I asked

"No." They got it.

"Yes, mum. We laugh. Read it."

So, we read it again. And again.

And again today, with three kids sitting at my feet. One was touching my leg, and I heard her whisper, "Thorns." Okay, so I'd recently quit shaving my legs since avoiding the pothole sores and scabs was problematic. Anyhow we had no new blades for the razor and the old blades were so dull they tore my skin. Now there were thorns on my legs—would that be truth or nonsense? I could see how there might be a thin edge between the two, a mere tilt of the head, a switch of syntax, a shift of perception and truth becomes fiction, or fiction shapeshifts into truth.

After days upon days of hunger and meager rations, sitting on Datu's porch that morning with most of the class out for rice harvest, I had a sudden moment of clarity, a dawning, a palpable *ah-ha* moment when boundaries blurred. Everything in the universe seemed both true and nonsensical at the same time. I stopped seeing a clear line between fact and fiction. I could no longer tell the kids what was real and what wasn't. Reality oozed into fiction. Nonsense became truth turned sideways. And truth was merely nonsense that everyone believed.

In the afternoon I wrote in my journal, "I get it! Today is the day I recognize *Hop on Pop* as a work of nonfiction! Fantasy and reality are overlays, indistinguishable samenesses. I see it so clearly! Is this epiphany enlightenment, or is the constant mental and physical deprivation and malnutrition causing me to slip over the edge and lose my grip on the ability of language to carry meaning. Meaning, I see now, is meaningless."

I closed my journal and considered that I needed a large shot of protein.

⊙⊚⊙

As I understand it, from what little news we can get, these are some of the new laws under Marcos's Martial Law:

1) There's a national curfew. No one can be on the streets between midnight and 4 a.m.

2) No private firearms are allowed by anyone, at any time, for any reason. (This will be a real adjustment for the pistol-packing men of Butuan City.)

3) The government can arrest people for stockpiling anything used in the manufacture or maintenance of arms.

4) There's a federal takeover of certain privately-owned businesses, including Manila Electric and Philippine Airlines.

5) The government has taken over all radio and TV stations in the country. News throughout the country comes only from government sources, which means that Marcos controls all the news. Thank goodness we can listen to Voice of America from transmitters in Hong Kong— when we can catch the signal.

6) The national Police Constabulary, which is the national army, will be the enforcing agent, so that means that the Marcos army is running the country now.

My mom must be climbing the walls by now, sure that Communism is gonna get me.

Here in Madga, things are exactly the same. It's weird knowing that a huge shift is happening on the outside, while things here are untouched. At least for now. There could be a full revolution out there with riots in the streets, and we might not know about it.

— Journal, September 24, 1972

The Flee Bag

People here are scared. Amalya told me that if Janet and I weren't here, they would all run into the forest to flee the advancing soldiers. Rumors are rampant, but facts are few. We heard that soldiers raped a girl at Silco Camp. I doubt it's true. It sounds like a story from the Japanese occupation. Stories tangle over time, facts get twisted, and no one actually knows much. You can't be sure of anything until it happens right in front of you, and then it's too late.

— Journal, October 3, 1972

◉◉◉

Three men with bright beads and brass bells at their necks and machetes hanging in ornately carved wooden sheaths at their waists—strangers from the north, walked across the river and into Madga. They climbed Datu Tagleong's notched pole and traipsed across our classroom as I was finishing our afternoon art activities. An old woman walked behind them wearing traditional Manobo beads at her ears and neck. In our village, only Amalya and her mother, Maria, wore beads in the old way.

The strangers stared at us. We stared back. The men walked into Datu's house, and the old woman paused, squeezed herself onto the bench beside little Poring, and listened with a smile on her betel-stained lips as Janet told a picture story to her class.

From where I sat, I could watch Datu and the strange men squatting, an open bag of betel nut condiments before them. They chewed, talked, and spit red gorp through the slat floor. Their voices were low, the tone serious, but I couldn't understand any of their words. Was it a dispute about a hunting dog or a harvest problem? Perhaps they were telling news of a death or an injury.

We dismissed school a few minutes early; clearly something unusual was happening. Plus, there were buckets to tote from the river, wood to chop, and water to boil. Serhio was helping us since Janet's hand was still healing. He brought us wood. "Serhio," I asked, "Who are those people?"

Serhio shrugged. "From the mountains," he said.

It was later and the village was noisy with a crying baby, a barking dog, and squawking chickens. I was dozing—or trying to—when I heard the familiar "Maayo," greeting as someone mounted our porch ladder, jiggling the house. I leaned out the door and saw one of the strangers squatting on the bamboo slats of our porch.

"Good afternoon, Mum," he said to Janet in Visayan. "We have come to Madga to talk with Datu Tagleong. We are talking of the war."

The war! It had been more than two weeks since Janet and I had heard news on the radio. There had supposedly been an attempted coup in Manila, followed by martial law and a government takeover of private industry and businesses. Curfews, imprisonments, and gunfire in the streets.

"We are telling Datu Tagleong and the people of Madga that the soldiers are in Angeles and are advancing up the river, taking all guns and rifles."

"But surely, even the soldiers know that the mountain people need their guns to get food for their families," Janet said.

"The soldiers are taking all guns. Even from mountain people," the stranger said. "Datu Tagleong is going to hide his rifle in the forest. But Mum," he continued, his dark eyes looking seriously at both of us, "it is important, if the soldiers come here, you must say that Datu has gone, and you don't know where—just that he has gone into the forest."

"Of course," Janet said, and I nodded in agreement.

Early the next morning, before I was fully awake, I heard the strangers leaving. And a few minutes later Datu Tagleong and Donkilyo appeared at our porch. Datu carried a live chicken tied up and slung over one shoulder and his rifle over the other. Donkilyo wore a tattered knapsack on his back and in his arms, he carried his naked toddler sister, Tata. Datu's favorite pig dog sat expectantly at their feet, waiting for adventure.

"You should be ready to go into the mountains," Datu Tagleong told us in a serious voice. "If the soldiers come, you must go with Suat and Amalya. We will all go into the mountains. You will be safe with us. But you must be ready."

I nodded, instantly understanding that our Manobo neighbors were offering us protection from the advancing army.

Datu then paused at Suat's porch, and the conversation was brief. "Watch out, take care of the Americanas." Suat nodded, glancing over at me, his expression placid, firm, concerned.

As Datu, Donkilyo, Tata, and the pig dog waded the river and vanished into the forest, I watched, wondering if I would ever see them again.

I looked to Suat's house. He sat calmly, chewing betel nut, making a basket. From inside came Amalya's low humming and the babble of baby Balbid. Things look so normal, I thought. Yet the undercurrent of unease was stronger than the pull of the Madga during monsoon.

"So then, we'd better get ready. What shall we take?" Janet said.

"We can't carry much if we're fleeing. We'll have a hard enough time keeping up with the Manobo in the forest."

"Right. We can use this," she said, pulling her striped beach bag from a rafter. "It's our flee bag. Let's get ready."

Cameras. One change of underwear each. An extra T-shirt each. One cotton blanket we could share.

"My sunglasses," I said. "I'm not going to leave behind my ₱60 Polaroids!"

"And we'd better take our journals. We don't want to leave any incriminating evidence," Janet said.

"Address book—in case we get out of this crazy country and still want to travel."

Billfolds with Peace Corps identification. A bottle for water and iodine purification tablets. Toothbrushes and toothpaste. A towel. Matches.

"And the beads Amalya made for us," Janet said. "I just couldn't leave them behind for a soldier to take."

"You know, I really doubt the soldiers could be that bad," I suggested. "They're people, after all. And we speak the language."

"Looting soldiers aren't known for their kindness," Janet said.

"Just being Americans might give us some protection," I offered.

"Or, our white capitalist skin might get us shot."

Martial law was never far from my thoughts. As I balanced down the slippery riverbank to get water, I'd glance to the bend in the river. Would the soldiers approach by water? As I climbed the hill back to the village, I scanned the mountainside for movement among the trees. Maybe they'd come across the mountain, stealthily on foot, sneaking into the village with guns raised. Or maybe they would come in tanks, knocking aside trees and plowing through the houses. But I saw and heard only birds circling and trees sighing in the wind.

Datu had been gone for three days, and Janet and I were sitting on our porch, staring off into the darkening Madga evening. The first few bright stars winked above the western mountains. The river shone liquid silver and black silk, flowing southeast. The world seemed at peace.

"You know," she said, "we may never know what's really going on out there." Janet was interested in national politics, world cultures, and great literature—the big things.

I hummed in agreement, but I was really more interested in making rope from plant fiber, weaving beads, playing a Manobo *dimbah* drum, and dancing in the Manobo way—life's little things. Within myself—I couldn't admit it aloud—I was happy for the isolation of Madga because, unlike Janet, I didn't really want to know the truth of the outer world.

◉◉◉

Ricarda gave us a kajad, a head-strap basket woven from rattan, coated with tree sap, durable and nearly waterproof. I think it's for us to use as a "flee bag," although she didn't tell us that directly. But when she was here, we talked about how everyone will be leaving Madga.

Ricarda told us that the people of Madga will be moving to higher ground soon because of the rain. She says it will probably flood here and that they would have moved already, but they didn't want us to have to move our school. Amalya, Suat, and their family will move to their kamote patch up the mountain. Datu and Ricarda will move to theirs. She says some people across and down the river have already moved. She says everyone will come back to Madga later on—she didn't say when. I can't tell if she is talking about moving as the result of a seasonal weather migration, or because of the advancing soldiers. Maybe both.

Eddy brought over a dozen-and-a-half bananas, two big hands—one not-yet-ripe, one of sweet red ones. They're fantastic! We feasted on bananas last night and this morning.

— Journal, September 27, 1972

◉◉◉

Madga Feast

They brought us chicken for supper last night—half of a half of a breast, and we split it, maybe two bites each. I remember Friday nights after Daddy got paid and we kids got him to take us out to the all-you-can-eat chicken place. Golly we ate a lot! Piece after piece of fried chicken, crispy breast after breast, along with hot rolls and butter. A waitress would stroll among the tables, heaping our plates with more, making sure we got full. My brothers and I would stuff ourselves, maybe two dozen pieces of chicken among us, maybe more. And now, here in Madga, it makes me sad—and hungry—just to think about those days.

For breakfast this morning, there was . . . next to nothing until a big steaming plate of rice arrived from

Datu's house. Janet and I scoffed down remaining bits of leftover river fish (tiny minnows!) with the rice, and still had rice left over, so we ate it with the last of our jelly. After that, we were still hungry, but at least we'd had something to eat.

— Journal, September 26, 1972

⊚⊚⊚

That first day Joe Habana motored me upriver to meet the Manobo, he mentioned that Tagleong was a datu, the leader for people throughout the mountains and that I'd be meeting only a few of Datu's people at Madga. I'd nearly forgotten Joe's comment until one day when, without any discernible—to me—method of communication, mountain people started arriving in Madga.

Strangers walked in from across the river and from the mountains, with sweat dotting their foreheads and necks. They headed straight for Datu Tagleong's house, walking through our front porch school to enter the shady interior room. There they sat with Datu and shared the betel nut ritual, retrieving paraphernalia from woven baskets slung at their sides. They cracked the green nuts with their teeth, sprinkled the nuts with lime, wrapped them in leaves, and inserted the globs into their cheeks. Then came the slow chewing and the spitting of reddish gorp through the slat floor, all the while sitting on the bamboo slats, talking nonstop, and gesturing widely with their hands. From Datu's porch, where I was sitting with the Bigs, I watched them. I couldn't understand most of the words, but I was sure they were sharing news.

The strangers had broad, harsh facial features and crazy eyes, a look of wildness. Glaring from these piercing eyes, they'd watch Janet and me as we went about our classes. Those newcomers could have been scary, but I knew they were just curious, watching us as though we were zoo exhibits. When I greeted them with a smile, they seemed spooked. These were the *taga-bukid* people, Serhio whispered to me, Manobo who were part of Datu Tagleong's group but who lived in the interior mountains far from Madga.

There was one very old and very beautiful lady among them. Tessie and Aida said she was their grandmother—which probably meant she was Tagleong's former wife's mother. She had triangular tattoos up the outer calves of her spindly, bowed legs. I asked how the tattoos were done, and Norma and Pinang said with "something like a bolo," but that needles work too, and that it really hurts to get tattoos. This old woman's spine was very bowed. She stooped dramatically—almost entirely bent over—and she could only hobble when assisted. I asked my Bigs how she had been able to cross the river, and they said the men floated her on a bamboo raft. She was wearing beads in the old Manobo way and looked a hundred years old, by far the oldest person I'd seen in the mountains. They told me she lives at Tessie and Aida's and that she never goes anywhere "because she is so old."

With the help of the twins and a man, she was able to get up the pole to Datu's porch. Then she went to Janet's bench, where Janet was telling a picture story to the Littles, and the woman wormed her way into the group, sat next to Janet, and watched, transfixed. I was so busy watching her I could hardly teach my own class. She had few, if any, teeth, but her gums and lips were bright red from betel nut, and she had huge smile. Watching Tessie and Aida's ancient grandmother, I realized the extraordinary effort it must have taken for her to get to Datu's that day, and how important the Madga rice celebration must be to her.

In my class of Bigs, we began to discuss the upcoming event. At first Big Norma and Penang seemed embarrassed to discuss it until I told them we have the same celebration in America, but ours is in November, not September. It's a thanks-to-god time, thanks for food and family. They relaxed when they heard how things in America and Madga are similar—how the gathering happens once a year when the food is harvested, how grandparents and aunts and uncles and old friends come together, sometimes traveling from places faraway, how the youngest kids run a play and make a little trouble, how the food is very good and everyone goes home full.

I knew only a little about the Manobo world view, because the people didn't talk to us about their beliefs. Perhaps because we were outsiders, they assumed that we were Christians and that we wouldn't approve of their spirit gods, even though we had tried hard not to give that impression.

Still, by merely listening and asking occasional questions, I had learned bits and pieces. I knew they had many spirit gods, which they called *diwata*, and that different spirits seemed to take care of different parts of nature, like spirits of the river, trees, and animals. One time at the riverbank, I saw bamboo sticks upright in the mud and the kids told me not to bother them. When I asked what they were, they said the sticks had something to do with the diwata there. I steered clear of the sticks, and though I really wanted to know more, I respected their silence and didn't press for information.

It was midafternoon when we were called over to Datu's house. Ricarda's newly woven pandanus mat was spread across the kitchen floor, and eight plates of uncooked rice were set out. In the center of each plate, a single egg was nested in the rice. A thin white candle was set beside the rice and burned, though it was still daylight.

Datu squatted near the mat in his blue jeans, a whitish T-shirt, and his red kerchief. Then the prayers began. I couldn't understand the words, but my kids told me that it was "*salamat sa ginoo*"—thanks to god, that all the strangers would sleep at Datu's house that night, and the following day the feast would be in the forest.

After we went home, the celebrations and conversations at Datu's became louder and more raucous, and I suspected there was drinking. A bunch of the kids came over, I think to get away from the adults. We told stories on our front porch—Jack and the Beanstalk, one of their favorites, and we told them about Santa Claus. They asked a lot of questions about what it was like being a kid in America and if we would return and bring our own kids back to visit Madga. I said, "No, I'm not getting married. It's too much trouble."

Big Norma chimed in. "I really agree, it's too much trouble. You always have to work, and you can't go around like the young women. It's no fun." My heart broke for the beautiful, bright thirteen-year-old, filled with potential and no options—a married woman who simply wanted to be a teenager.

The next day, the kids came over to take us to the thanks-to-god feast at the edge of the recently slashed agricultural plot, the clearing for next year's rice planting. The vegetation had been hacked down but not yet burned. Young trees lay splintered and drying in the sun. Datu and the other Manobo gathered at the edge, in the shade just inside the forest.

Word of the celebration must have spread, because not only were all the Madga people and the newly arrived mountain strangers there, but also some Manobo who worked for the logging company, conspicuous in their pants and shoes. One wore a hard hat, another wore a wristwatch, status symbols from the world beyond.

Datu Tagleong was at his best. He was wearing his red-striped shirt, the one from Texas, and a bright red kerchief on his head. At his hip was his special bolo with the decorated hilt. A dangling Manobo beaded bracelet, like the bracelets Amalya wove, was tied at the grip. The wooden sheath of his bolo was wrapped in a bright red cloth. Datu carried himself with dignity, and by the way he orchestrated the feast and guided others, there could be no doubt Datu Tagleong was the leader.

Over the open fire hung two iron cauldrons, whose metal handles were suspended from branches of chopped saplings. One pot had fragrant, fresh rice, the other a simmering pork stew. The kids ran freely, while Saldi passed around a bamboo *kubing* mouth harp. Serhio sat in a tree and played the kubing while I leaned in, listening to discern a melody or a pattern in the sounds. I couldn't; to me, the tones and rhythm seemed random.

The women spread banana leaves, snaking them across the forest floor among the trees. Maria and Ricarda lined a kajad head-basked with banana leaves then ladled hot rice from the hanging caldron into the basket. Ben and Norma took the basket, and they scooped mounds of steaming rice onto the banana-leaf table. Tirzo trailed them, placing a dipper of pork stew beside each pile of rice.

Ricarda, wearing her bright red shirt and black straight, tight skirt, shouted, "Come and eat," and everyone did. Like a flock of turkey vultures advancing on a roadkill jackrabbit, like a nest of West Texas red ants surrounding a fallen jellybean, the Manobo came, crowding, sweating, squatting, and sitting along the banana leaf table on the forest floor. Men, women, women holding babies, little kids mostly naked, bigger kids mostly dressed all gathered rice and pork bits with their fingers and crammed it all into open mouths. Datu took handfuls of rice and pork and reached across the "table" to place food into the mouths of others. He fed the blind man who squatted beside him. He fed the beaded and tattooed woman across the table. He tossed a small portion of rice to a dog. I saw it and understood. He was demonstrating his care and concern for all his people. He was the provider, the chief.

When it was over, when everyone had eaten rice and pork and drunk river water from a communal tin can, when everyone was finished and the sun was moving west, the hunting dogs came in to clean up.

All the hard work it took to clear the land, plant the rice, harvest it, dry it, winnow it, cook it, and share it, had all been done for the good of all. Datu Tagleong had seen to it.

And I was among the many who were grateful for the labor and skills of these Manobo neighbors and their constant sharing with us, as Janet and I sat together on the side, sharing a mound of fresh, sweet, upland rice and wonderful pork stew. We'd brought our own spoons.

⊙⊙⊙

A runner just arrived with news that Datu is on his way back to the village with two pigs! Outtasight! Incredible! Everyone is excited. It's taking many guys and a lot of time to get all that meat back to the village, the runner said, but they're on their way. He also said that Trining and TingTing are upriver at their concession camp around the bend and will be coming to Madga soon. I hope they bring mail and coffee and bread and fruit and other supplies we so desperately need. Lunch today was boiled rice soup—just rice and water and salt. At least we had salt. I'm still hungry, of course. Tonight: pork!

—Journal, September 26, 1972

⊙⊙⊙

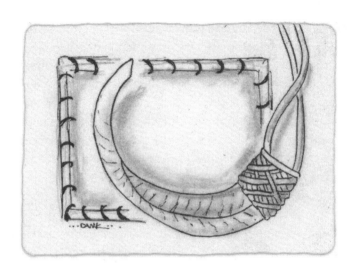

In Celebration of Rice

Janet is on Datu's porch learning the Manobo women's dance, the sumbatang. Saldi is playing the drum with perfect rhythm, and Amalya, wearing a floor-length wrap, is doing a series of small, shuffle-jump steps while waving two scarves—well, in this case, our old T-shirts. The women's dance is so graceful it looks as if she's floating, her feet not even touching the floor. A crowd of neighbors, including our twenty schoolkids who don't miss anything, is hooting and laughing in appreciation as Janet tries the dance.

— Journal, September 12, 1972

☉☉☉

Rice harvest was underway. We'd just had the Madga thanks-to-god gathering, but a bigger celebration was about to happen downriver. Everyone was talking about it. In school, my Bigs created a story about it—as we were working on diphthongs like the *ow* and *ay* sounds.

Naa ang sayow sa balay ni Inday. There is a dance at Inday's house.
Daghan tao muadto sa sayow. Many people go to the dance.
Musayow sila kay muani sila sa humay. They dance because they harvest the rice.

We worked out the story on the blackboard, then the Bigs copied it into their notebooks. I saw Ricarda and her little girls listening from inside Datu's house, as Ricarda sat on the floor weaving pandanus.

On Wednesday morning, Eddy came and perched on our front porch. "It is time for the harvest," he said.

"Good. Will the rice be plentiful this year?" Janet asked.

"Yes, maybe a good harvest. A lot of rice. Maybe soon." Eddy said.

"When does harvest begin? Can we help?" I asked.

"Soon. But first is the harvest celebration. Would you would like to accompany us to the dance downriver?"

Janet and I looked at one another with grins of anticipation. "When do we leave?"

"Today," he said.

Hastily we gathered our overnight supplies, left word with Ricarda that school would resume when we returned, then we pulled our bamboo door shut and tied it with a strip of leather, and hoisted the climbing pole up onto the porch. "There, all locked up," Janet said, as I returned from a final trip to the outhouse.

Suat was on his porch rolling thin strands of abaca fiber into rope. With one bundle of long fibers anchored between his lips and a second bundle in his left hand, he'd stretch and twist and roll the two bundles together, pressing and rolling with his right hand across his bare thigh, and adding in additional fibers as he went along. The result was thin, strong lashing. I'd seen him make thicker, stronger rope by twisting some thinner lines together. The rope was uniformly dense. It was an art. When I'd tried it, my rope turned out lumpy-thick-thin, and it came apart.

"Hu-i, Suat," I called. "Watch out for our house, okay?" Suat looked up from his work, nodded with lifted eyebrows and pursed lips.

The little banka rode high in the water as afternoon shadows stretched elongated fingers darkly across river rocks below. The afternoon heat and dirt of Madga melted off me like Crisco skidding off my Mamaw's hot iron skillet.

The trip downriver took less than an hour. Trining pointed out the durian fruit tree and wild chickens that he spotted along the shores. To me, the forest seemed impenetrable, and I marveled at his ability to spot things that were invisible to me. I looked where he pointed but saw only masses and tangles in shades of green. No fruit. No chickens. I shook my head. No, I couldn't see them.

It was late afternoon when our banka pulled to shore alongside a handful of rafts and dugouts. The house was familiar. It was the we're-almost-there landmark for our trips upriver from Silco. I'd always wondered about this house. It was larger than the others and perched on an embankment overlooking the river. I discovered it was the home of Teodoro Habana.

Shocked faces greeted our arrival. I searched for a smile or a friendly gesture but saw only hesitancy and dumfounded stares. We were on the shore, standing beside our bag and wondering what to do next, when a familiar face appeared from the direction of the house. It was Inday, a teenager who had visited us in Madga, a niece or cousin of Joe and Flor.

"Mum, we did not know you were coming. Our house is very plain and dirty. We do not have a place for you to sleep. Our water is not good for you to drink..."

"It's okay, Inday. We brought our sleeping mats and we brought water. We just want to watch the dancing. We're okay, don't worry."

"Are you smiling?" I whispered in English to Janet. "Keep smiling!" The faces of the Manobo were incredulous at our arrival. Eddy was talking to a group of men, and I caught a few words: "... to watch the dancing." I was embarrassed he had to defend our being there. If it'd been up to me, I would have turned and gone back upriver, not wanting to intrude.

"Maybe we ought to just leave," I whispered to Janet, again in English.

"Relax, just keep smiling," she whispered back.

At last we went with Inday to the bamboo house, walking directly toward a crowd of around fifty people.

"Oh boy, here we go," I said through tight but smiling lips. I knew I was out of place. Skin too white. Nose too long. Too tall by a head. And wearing rubber slippers. I was different, an outsider. And I continued to walk forward, smiling.

As we climbed the bamboo ladder onto the porch, a thick silence came over the yard and house. Kids stopped jumping and running, women turned from their work in the kitchen and yard, and all eyes tracked us.

"Wait here," Inday said, vanishing to the back of the house.

Then a large man stepped out from the crowd and offered his right hand in the Western gesture of a handshake.

"You are welcome," he said in booming Visayan. "Welcome to my home. We are happy you and your friends have come from Madga." He was a distinguished-looking man, graying, and larger than any Manobo I'd seen—taller, broader, heavier. He had the bearing of a man in command, and he spoke to us in a warm tone. For the first time since we'd arrived, my smile became genuine as I shook his strong hand.

Inday reappeared from the kitchen with a large dipper of water. "Your feet," she said, and she poured, washing off the river mud.

"Come," the man said. "Bring your things this way, inside. Sit. The dancing will begin later. Inday will help you." He walked outside again.

"Inday, that is your father, Teodoro Habana?" Janet asked.

"Yes."

"And this is your house?"

"Yes."

The tensions in the house eased. Conversations resumed and the children returned to their games, racing across the yard and through the house, whooping and launching themselves off the side porch into the dust below. Young men stood in groups, their heads together, the smell of tobacco smoke wafting in from the porch. The women worked, nursing infants or preparing food. The smell of garlic drifted from the kitchen.

Inday devoted herself to us and sat talking, explaining the Manobo rice celebration and pointing out some people in the crowd. "There, beside the door," Inday said, "is my mother." She was a small, tired-looking woman I thought, with unusual Asian eyes, as if some Japanese ancestry lurked in her heritage. She had long, straight graying hair pulled into pigtails that were knotted in place on the sides of her head.

"And there is my eldest brother," Inday said, pointing with her lips to a young man on the porch. He was a tall, skinny teen with short kinky hair, as if he held some African genes. Manobo, yes, but it looked to me as if some ancestral mingling had taken place among these people.

Teodoro Habana was building an altar of bamboo in the corner of the room near where we were sitting. Long narrow plant stalks were brought in, and Teodoro struck one against the slat floor. Again and again he smashed it, and on the fifth strike, the stalk split into long fibrous strips, like crepe paper streamers, and he tied the stalk to the altar.

Then sugarcane stalks were tied upright to the base of the altar. Then betel nut stalks and berries were added, along with the wooden sheath of a bolo, an old-looking bell and bead necklace, and a delicately embroidered blouse. Finally, a long stalk of grain was placed along the altar.

"Is that the rice?" I asked Inday.

"It's supposed to be like the rice, but really it's a weed," she said.

The room was filling with people, and I kept moving toward the altar, making room for new arrivals till the room was packed and I was squeezed alongside the altar, the streamer-plant and pseudo-rice tips brushing my shoulder.

Then the dancing began. Eddy had brought a drum from Madga. A gong, a little bigger than a basketball hoop and made of solid brass, was suspended by homemade rope from the rafters of the house. The music was unbelievably loud—pulsating and deafening, pounding through my body like the roar of a jet engine. Two women beat on the gong with fabric-wrapped sticks, while a man played the drum. The rhythm was fast and steady like the flow of the river with no beginning or end, over, under, and around river stones.

Inday's brother was the first to dance. He wore a long sarong-style skirt and his dance was male-style, the *binaylan*—stomping, jumping, and lurching to represent war or hunting. Then he relinquished the striped skirt to a toothless old woman who grinned with appreciation. She danced alone, circling with small stomps and flutters, the *sumbatang*, the feminine dance, just as the women of Madga had been teaching

Janet and me. In her hands, she carried bandanas, swirling and flapping, creating an illusion of flight.

She danced toward us Americanas. Oh oh, here it comes, I knew it. A bandana flipped out and came down on Janet's shoulder. Janet was ready. She jumped up with the bandana and began to dance in the little stomps that she had practiced in Madga. The crowd roared, cheered, hooted, and laughed.

I wasn't surprised when the lady in gold flung the second bandana on my shoulder. I had to do it. I didn't want to dance, to flaunt myself in front of all these people, but it was no time to be shy. I danced, doing the best I could, trying to remember what Amalya and Ricarda had taught me, making little stomping circles to the clatter and rumble of the drum and gong. The music somehow carried me like the river carrying a twig downstream. I rode with it, in it, and on it. I danced as the crowd cheered and then I didn't hear them any longer. It was just the rhythm and my body, and I turned and swirled and stomped and flew.

I lost track of how long the three of us—the woman in gold, Janet, and I—danced, but when at last I felt my legs weakening I cast the bandana on the shoulder of a young woman and sat down with rapid pulse and heavy perspiration. The music rolled on and on; the gong players traded positions with fresh players, not missing a beat.

"How long has it been?" I wondered. "An hour? Two?" Then the music became more subdued and after that, stopped abruptly. The silence was eerie.

Teodoro Habana spread a colorful mat on the floor near the altar and someone brought out eight plates of uncooked rice and three white candles. On top of each mound of rice was a delicately arranged dried leaf—perhaps tobacco—and several split betel nuts. Teodoro stood at the end of the mat watching the candles burn and began to speak in low conversational tones.

Inday whispered to me. "He is praying for health for our family and for friends. He is asking for safety from war and famine. He is asking for food to continue to be plentiful."

I looked around the room. Not exactly a reverent group, I thought, as I watched men spitting over the porch, mothers giving orders to children, and the continuing preparation of betel nut chewing by individuals in the crowd. This group was different from our Madga group, I decided. More cosmopolitan, more groomed and clean. This group could almost pass for city barrio people except for a few conspicuous tip-offs. Their clothes, although somewhat cleaner and newer than the ones we were used to seeing in Madga, were discolored and worn. Men smoked hand-rolled cigarettes. Among the women were the ubiquitous tobacco wads between red-stained lips and the naked babies and snot-nosed toddlers sucking at breasts. Most evident of all were the remarkable feet of the Manobo, feet that had never known shoes, wide and bare, with long, strong toes that looked as if they could pry open coconuts.

Teodoro Habana closed the prayer and placed the plates of rice on the altar. Then he came to sit beside Janet and me and spoke to us in Visayan. "Do you enjoy the dancing?"

"Yes. Our friends in Madga have been teaching us," Janet said.

"We will dance again later, after the meal."

"Here," he said, brushing at the altar ornaments that dangled against my shoulder, "these are bothering you?"

"No, they are all right," I said. I hardly noticed the tickling anymore, and besides, I felt somehow safe there tucked up close beneath the altar. "This blouse is very beautiful. Who made it?" I pointed to the embroidered Manobo blouse on the altar.

"Ah, my daughter-in-law. It is not yet finished. Here, see," he said taking the red shirt from the platform. "She has been working on it for many weeks but isn't finished yet. Do you know how to sew like this?"

I examined the fine needlework. Threads of yellow, black, and white were worked in a cross-stitch pattern on the red material of the shirt, little x's making up a greater pattern that resembled stars and animals across the shoulders and chest.

"I sew a little, but not like this," I said honestly. "How does she do it? Does she use a pencil or draw the pattern on the cloth before she sews?"

"No, she just knows what to do," he said proudly.

As I continued to examine the blouse, Janet asked about other Americans who had been to this area. "Do you remember when Grosbeck came upriver?"

"Yes. That was maybe 1956 or 1957. He was the first. But later came Weaver and Downs."

"Were they missionaries too?"

"Yes. But they stayed only a few days. You have stayed the longest."

"But we are not missionaries," Janet said.

With a dismissing gesture of his hand, he said, "You are teachers." I knew that he thought missionaries and teachers were the same, and I sighed. It would be fruitless to differentiate.

I could feel the listening silence of the people around us as we spoke with Teodoro. A woman sitting nearby spoke up.

"There were other Americans here also," she said.

"When?" I asked.

"It was during the time of war. I was just a little girl, but two American men came to our house. They were wearing tall shoes and long pants. They asked for food. My mother gave them boiled chicken eggs. I can still remember."

"Then the soldiers reached this far during the war?" I knew she was remembering World War II.

"Yes, a few. But not many," the woman said.

The conversational ice had been broken and many people began to ask questions of Janet and me. They used a mixture of Visayan, Manobo, and even a few English words.

"Are you sisters?" they asked. "Where are you from? "Are your families complete?" They were asking if my parents are still living. Yes, I answered. How many brothers and sisters do you have? How long have you been in the Philippines? How long in Madga? How long will you stay? Will you fly home? How long does it take? How long does a boat ride take? Is there a road from Manila to your place in America? Will you get married when you return to America? Will you ever come back?"

I was surprised by the awareness these people had. These people were definitely more exposed to the outside world than our Madga neighbors. They knew about Manila, they knew that America is far away, and they knew about ships and oceans.

"How is it that you know some English?" I asked Teodoro Habana.

"During the war, I learned from the Americans," he said. "And some people have been to school," he added pointing to two women in the crowd. "This one is from Butuan, and the other is from Bohol. "

I was intrigued. How could it be that a girl from Bohol would end up with a Manobo family in the hills of Mindanao. I wanted to ask, but the moment passed in the onslaught of questions.

They didn't even stop to breathe, shoveling and swallowing as fingers scooped load after load of rice. Some people used two hands to shovel faster. Did they even taste it? Did they know what they were eating? Did they care?

Janet and I had been served separately, on enamel plates, with tin spoons.

"I feel like we ought to eat with them," I whispered to Janet. "All this special attention makes me feel funny."

"I think they feel better with us eating like this," Janet said. "Anyhow, I don't think I could keep up with their pace."

It was true. The second round of diners had swarmed around the mat and were scooping mounds of fresh rice and boiled pork from main platters. We'd been served first and still were only partway through our bowls of food.

"This is incredibly good," Janet observed. "Did you notice?"

"Ummm. I think it's the rice." The rice had a fragrance, a sweetness, a pungent bite, a flavor that must be a secret to the rest of the world. If it weren't a secret, surely this incredible rice would be demanded by the world market. It was the flavor of fresh Manobo upland rice.

"The pork is good, too. Thanks to TingTing." Janet said. TingTing had spent part of the afternoon roasting meat especially for us.

"I think this is the best food I've ever had. *Ever*," I said, my mouth still half-full as I took another bite.

"I'm glad we don't have to scramble for our share," Janet said, with a tilt of her head toward the feeding frenzy before us.

"Why do they eat so fast? Don't you think they would enjoy it more if they slowed down, maybe talked as they ate, maybe took time to breathe between mouthfuls?" I asked.

"You might gobble too if you had to compete for food the way these people do. And if this were the only good meal you'd had in a while, and if it might be your last good meal for a long while."

I watched a mother chew a mouthful of food then take the wad from between her own lips and place it into her baby's toothless mouth. And I watched a mother stuffing small globs of rice into the mouth of her toddler. The child looked wide-eyed and overwhelmed, chewing as fast as it could, as the mother pushed more rice to the child's lips. "Eat now," she was saying. "Eat, eat."

When the flurry of feasting subsided and folks went to the river to wash up and drink, Inday swept the mat and brushed the scattered rice crumbs through the slat floor. I heard the chickens below clucking and squawking over the spoils. Then Inday spread a large, clean mat, and the dancing began again.

"Oh, I see. What we had earlier was the warm-up exercise," Janet shouted over the din of gong and drum.

Inday sat beside Janet as her father donned the long sarong of the dancer, wrapped a bright bandana around his head and placed the beaded and belled necklace from the altar around his neck. He began the stomping, jumping steps of the male dancer. In the fading light of evening, TingTing strapped a kerosene lamp to a support post, and it cast a yellow glow over the crowd.

"Watch," Inday said excitedly. "He will dance for a long time, then he will shake all over. It is the spirit of the dance taking over. You will see," she said.

Teodoro Habana was joined by his son, also wearing a long tube skirt. The two of them twirled and jumped in broad strong movements, warlike, masculine, forceful. Their faces were tight—intent masks of concentration. Their dark eyes glowed in the lamplight. Their stomping feet shook the floor.

Perhaps half an hour later, Teodoro began to pant heavily and lean against a support pole, his eyes glazed, unfocused, and he began to shake. At first, they were mere trembles in his limbs, then larger shakes that nearly knocked him off balance. The crowd cheered and someone helped him to the side. More male dancers joined the frenzy, and over the next hours every man in the room danced.

I liked TingTing's dance best. Always a bit of a clown, TingTing modified the Manobo dance to include ludicrous gyrations and modern dance steps. The crowd loved it and shouted encouragement. TingTing grinned. As the evening progressed, women danced the fluttery female dances of flight.

Several hours later, my back was breaking and my legs were numb from sitting cross-legged on the floor for so long. Janet propped her head against a pole, and her eyes drooped and glazed.

"When will it end?" I asked Inday.

"Sometimes it goes until dawn," she said. "But tonight, I think it will end soon." She pointed to people already sleeping in the corners of the house.

When the music finally did end, I was beyond caring. I was leaning against the altar, drifting in and out of sleep.

"Come," Inday said. "You can sleep there." She had scooted a few people aside and made room for us to spread our sleep mat.

"I don't want to brush my teeth. I'm too tired to even pee," I muttered to Janet. I pulled a brush from my plastic travel bag, stroked a few tangles from my hair, and rubbed Clearasil on my pimples. I barely noticed the people watching and was beyond caring.

"Should we put up the mosquito net?" Janet asked.

"I'm too tired," I said. I stuffed a towel into a travel bag and gave it to Janet for a pillow. I used a wadded-up shirt.

The yellow lamplight glowed, and I was aware of some men playing cards on the opposite wall. I fell back to sleep immediately. The next thing I knew, I was dreaming of raucous chickens. It was morning.

◉◎◉

I would note how useless it seems for us to keep insisting that we're not missionaries, that we're not preaching about a god, but that we're TEACHERS helping the Manobo people learn how to read and write in Visayan. The difference between the two—being a missionary and being a teacher—doesn't seem to exist in their brains. So (sigh) we've given up. We just keep smiling.

They know about missionaries because there is, somewhere I've heard, a portion of a bible that's been translated into Manobo. Flor told us about this, but I've never seen it. But everyone seems to know that it exists, and the Manobo seem proud of that fact.

All during our conversation with Teodoro Habana,

Janet (especially) and I kept throwing in Manobo words and phrases. This is tremendous for public relations! It's a real crowd pleaser when we use their language. We'd say a little something, then they'd jump to the conclusion that we are fluent in Manobo, and many people started talking to us. It became an open forum—halo-halo, mix-mix Visayan/Manobo talk. We got enough to understand their questions and continue the conversations. Janet is truly a linguistic wizard! Me, I'm hanging on.

— Journal, September 29, 1972

◉◉◉

I've been watching Ricarda sitting in the doorway of her house, weaving mats from the long pandanus leaves. I'm like the kids—watching is how we learn. Ricarda doesn't say much, but she shows us how, sometimes weaving slowly so we can see clearly. I still don't get it, but her daughter Durna, who stands beside her watching, picks up bits of cast-off leaves, plaits them, and seems to have the idea solid.

I think these mats are for drying the rice harvest that's coming soon. The grains have to be laid out in the sun to dry after they're harvested. When they're dry, they're pounded and winnowed for cooking. Pounding makes the outer husks easier to remove. So mats are critical for having a clean place to spread out the rice. After rice-harvest season, I think they sleep on the mats, so they need new pandanus mats every year.

Donkilyo is mounting and hanging the horns of the deer from yesterday's catch. They will be coat racks (so to speak, as there are no actual "coats" to hang), really catch-all racks. We have a rack of deer horns in our little house, from Donkilyo, the great hunter.

— Journal, September 27, 1972

The Dancings

The kids just found a picture in one of our Life magazines of natives in New Guinea. Naked women. The kids were laughing and pointing to the breasts. I thought it was so weird, because they see naked breasts around here every day. But then they told me that the women in the magazine had nipples that were very large and dark. So, these kids know breasts so well that differences in nipple size and skin tone make a difference to them. I never saw a naked breast till I was in fifth grade and went next door to watch TV with my friend. Her mom was breastfeeding a new sister, and I had no idea what was happening. My friend had to tell me that milk came from her mother's breasts, which I found astounding. I didn't see another breast until

years later when I looked down and I thought some-
thing was going drastically wrong with my own chest.
Funny, huh! Or really, sad. These kids know more about
anatomy than I do.
                                    — Journal, September 27, 1972

◎◉◎

Next came what was certainly the most memorable
part of the entire dancing event. I'll try to describe it in
detail, not because I want to be gross, but because it is
a cultural experience that one doesn't come across very
often. Okay, I'll try. Here goes...."
                                    — Journal, September 29, 1972

◎◉◎

I woke up in Teodoro Habana's home and whispered to Janet, "I've got to pee. Now!"

"Me too," she said.

We walked toward the river, passing a gang of men chasing a pig. The men had encircled it, their arms outspread, *hooing* at it and slowly tightening their circle, the pig trapped inside. Dogs barked, men shouted, and the pig squealed. It was a great circle of excitement, and we walked the other direction, thinking maybe we'd find a secluded spot along the riverbank. But there were people everywhere, washing and using the river as a toilet, butts exposed to the morning air. I just couldn't do it, so we walked back past the house and along a path toward the forest. A tangle of youngsters followed us. I heard the whispered words "teachers" and "school" in excited tones, their small faces grinning and giggling whenever we looked their way.

Janet tried talking to the kids in Visayan but got no response except giggles. "Either they only speak Manobo, or they're too shy," I said.

"I wish my Manobo were better," Janet said.

I wish my Manobo existed, I thought. Most sounds of Manobo flew past my ears like fat June bugs heading for well-lit screen. I could hardly make out syllables, let alone meanings. After all these months, I probably knew a few dozen words and phrases, not enough to make conversation.

"Where's your house?" Janet, the linguistic wizard, asked in Manobo. A smiling girl gestured with a wave of her arm into the forest. She giggled and pulled on the arm of her smaller companion.

"Sister?" Janet asked.

The girl ducked her head and giggled.

"This looks like a good spot. Janet, will you watch the trail while I do my business? See what you can do to keep the traffic down."

While Janet chattered to the tangle of children, I went into the bushes and returned.

"My turn," said Janet. "Now you entertain them."

"Sure." I said, as if I had a plan. Thinking quickly, I used my hands. I'd learned a simple finger game as a child's rhyme: Here's the church. Here's the steeple. Open the door, here's all the people! But now I changed the words—"Here's a house, here's the roof, inside, the family," I said in Visayan. The kids giggled and tried to mimic my entwining fingers.

"Again," I said, and I tangled my fingers illustrating the story, then bent to help a child get the hand position, linked fingers inside pressed palms, then the quick turn of wrist, and the magic of wiggly fingers topside. I could smell the sweat of childhood on the boy as small brown fingers worked awkwardly, lines of dirt like dark crescent moons beneath his pale fingernails. An intent expression of concentration came into his black eyes. He wiggled and entwined his fingers, and quickly turned them inside out. Success! He looked up at me with a huge grin of accomplishment.

"Good, good. All together. Again." I used Visayan words, and perhaps they understood.

The kids laughed and elbowed one another in pleasure as they mimicked my hand game.

"Ready," Janet said. "Have you entertained enough?"

"Yep, but I'm not sure who was more amused, them or me. We walked a bit further along the path, the kids following, their fingers playing the game, until we stopped at the sound of drums and gong.

"Music. Let's go back."

We walked toward the house, like pied pipers followed by a string of small bodies. These certainly are the most beautiful children in the world, I thought, watching their round faces, bright dark eyes, and honest smiles. And hands that learn quickly.

As we approached the house, I saw the pig, now trussed up with its feet lashed to a bamboo pole. It squealed repeatedly, while the crowd ate a morning meal of rice. By the time the crumbs were brushed through the bamboo slat floor, the pig had been hoisted into the main room.

"How big do you figure it is?" Janet asked.

I thought of the size of my father, who weighed one hundred seventy pounds. The pig was bigger, much bigger. "At least two hundred pounds," I guessed. "Maybe more. Two fifty."

The teenage boys brought water in and rinsed off the pig. It squealed louder when the cold water splashed on its skin, then it lay quietly on the slat floor as the dancing began.

Teodoro Habana donned the beads, skirt, and kerchief, picked up the dancing handkerchiefs, and whirled himself into a bleary-eyed frenzy. Then someone handed him a spear. He danced with the spear, jumping and jerking and lunging with feints toward the pig. It lay there, sometimes squealing, like the voice of a razor blade, slicing even over the din of the drum and gong. Then Teodoro danced the spear over to his son; and while Teodoro whizzed and jumped, leaped and twirled to the pounding gong and drums, his son in two thrusting strokes, stuck the pig completely through at the neck. It squealed hysterically a moment and the blood came gushing out the underside. Someone rushed forward with a metal washbasin to catch the blood, and the music intensified as the pig twitched.

Teodoro Habana and his son were both dancing, whirling and spinning and jumping, wielding the spear as if in battle, when someone stepped up to offer them the basin of pig blood. Both of them stared at it with glassy eyes, then they drank from it, blood dripping down their faces and chins, and they danced some more. Then the basin of blood went around the room, each person taking a sip. When it came to me, I wanted to participate, wanted to drink, but I just couldn't. Not raw blood still warm and frothy from the pig. I passed it on. No one seemed to notice my decision, nor care. But I figured I'd failed some sort of test.

The dancing continued, becoming more frenzied and even louder, and I crouched deeper into the shadows beneath the altar. Teodoro Habana was sweating, exhausted, and still bleary-eyed when he signaled for the music to stop. The silence was a knife, sharp and painful. He danced-stepped over to a group of women and put his hand on one woman's head. "You're heavy," he said. She squealed a happy squeal. Then he did the same thing to two other women, and I suddenly figured what he was doing. He was predicting pregnancy.

Teodoro's son joined him as the gong and drums started up again. This time Teodoro danced holding up a tiny baby. Teodoro lifted the infant as high as he could, up and up as he whirled around the mat. It seemed he was blessing the people, a dance of happiness for fertility and birth among the Manobo people. Then Teodoro Habana danced to the mother, placed the baby gently in her arms and the baby sucked from her breast.

The woman who brought the basin of pig's blood offered her baby to Teodoro. This child was bigger, heavier, and Teodoro danced with it for only a few minutes. Then more people danced, one or two or three on the mat at a time. They danced until they tired, then the bandana was passed to another person. This time, even the children were allowed to dance.

The morning dancing was still going on when a young man brought the head of the pig and placed it on the altar above my left shoulder. I could see the severed spinal cord, like a thick rope cut through, stark white against the red meat surrounding it. There was not a heavy stream, but an occasional drop of blood fell from the altar, splattered against our water container, and bounced a mist in my direction. I wanted to move, but there was no place to go. I was wedged in beside the altar like a seed in a pod. I looked up at the pig's head, its eyes staring blankly toward the nipa-frond roof, its tusks curling from grimaced lips, its blood speckling my arm in drying flecks.

Teodoro Habana had been drinking alcohol. Probably the homemade brew from coconuts or rice, or maybe cheap wine from downriver. His voice was loud and his face red. I could smell the alcohol. As he began dancing, the crowd roared and hooted exuberantly. He was squatting in the middle of the mat in what Janet and I called "the old Asian squat," feet flat and comfortably separated while the buttocks hung just above the floor. It was a position I had never seen in the Old Country, but in

Asia it was standard resting position for old men talking in the shade, women digging in the garden or washing at the river, and kids playing in the dirt. It was also the standard toilet position for all.

Teodoro Habana squatted and motioned with his hands. He mimed something falling from between his buttocks. He mimed a flow from his penis.

Could it be, I wondered, is he dancing about bodily functions? I watched more closely. He mimed the running river, the squatting, the defecation, the urination. He scooped up some of the river water to wash his rear. His left foot stomped in time to the music. The crowd cheered. Then he did it all again.

Unmistakable. Incredible. Appalling. And, totally embarrassing. The dripping pig's blood had been enough to make me wish I'd stayed home, but now this charade threatened to send me comatose. But the crowd was loving it, hooting for more. I wasn't sure I could stand any more, but more was to come. Once more, he repeated the unmistakable story, only this time with embellishments. The drums and gong roared on. The crowd cheered even more loudly.

He scooped up water from the imaginary river and rubbed his rear, then lifted his hand to his nose, took a whiff, shook his head and repeated the process. Three times he washed his rear until finally the whiff test proved that he was sufficiently clean. He then put his imaginary pants back on and danced off into the crowd.

He was met with hoots of approval. I wanted to melt, to be anywhere but there, and was too embarrassed even to meet Janet's eyes. I said not a word and stared fixedly at the bamboo floor. I wondered if I could leave now, just go out and sit in the banka. Surely the worst is over, I told myself. And yet a part of me remained interested, as if I were looking through a window of time and culture. I leaned heavily on my journalism training—observe and record the facts, set personal judgments aside. I held onto each detail—the dancers' clothes, the faces in the crowd, the sun and shadows through slat walls—and if I concentrated on remembering the details of what I was seeing, I could push aside my own emotions. I stayed absolutely still beneath the dripping pig's head. Watching.

Inspired by the crowd's enthusiasm and probably the wine, along with the pulsing vibrations of the drums and gongs, Teodoro Habana took a T-shirt and a long skirt from a hook on the wall and laid them carefully on the floor, elongating the mound of fabric, lovingly tucking in edges. Then he covered the fabrics gently with a white kerchief. I watched and breathed a sigh of relief. This story would be about doing laundry at the river.

He danced around the elongated bundle and knelt down beside it, still dancing, still keeping the rhythm of the gong and drum, and he gingerly touched it, stroked it, caressed it with his fingertips and his cheek. He lay down beside it, still keeping the rhythm with an arm or a foot, and he entwined his arms around it, and rubbed his face into its softness.

It's a "her," I realized. My stomach clinched. I looked to the doorway, jammed with people, laughing and clucking in approval. The music intensified, louder and more pulsating. Keeping tempo with his feet and shoulders, Teodoro Habana mimed removing his pants and he sat astride the bundle. Unmistakably, he pumped his into hers. Again and again, his face radiating pleasure, until he collapsed in spasms atop the bundle, still keeping tempo.

I was in tears, straining to become invisible, to unsee what I'd just seen. My breath came in short gasps as I sat immobile, unable to look at Janet, unable to look at the crowd. My brain short-circuited.

The crowd was hooting for more, still cheering as Teodoro Habana retired from the floor. The music lessened, lightened to a ripple, and an old woman stepped out from the crowd. Please, please, let this one be something simple.

The woman wore the long skirt of a dancer and her hair was tied back in a bun. She danced twice around the mat in the male style stomp and thrust. Then she began to quake with a wide-eyed stare. Her limbs shook and she leaned against a pole for support. She stopped, grinned at the audience to signal this too was part of the story, then again leaned against the pole, quaking.

Her hands moved to her groin area. I wasn't sure, but yes, she was miming an erect penis, flapping her hands up and down. I'd never seen an erect penis and had only heard rumors of such conditions, yet the illusion the dancer was creating left no doubt.

The crowd knew, and they loved it. The old woman danced about the room, flashing her erect penis into groups of women, who screamed in mock fear. The penis chased a young woman who laughed and ducked into the kitchen. It pulled the old woman around, inflating, deflating in anxious cycles. I got it. She was spoofing on men. The crowd laughed, cheered, and begged for more. I just wanted out. I was embarrassed and frightened by things I didn't understand. Yet my mental recorder was running, and I was holding on to each image, etching details into my mind.

Teodoro Habana returned carrying a cup of water. He danced into the middle of the room and the kids at the edges scattered. This time he danced calmly, and as he went around the room he sprinkled water on the crowd, droplets propelled from his fingertips. He danced to Janet and me and flicked water into our faces. It was a calm blessing, a benediction, a gesture of friendship. I tried hard to smile at him.

The music swelled and his dancing intensified. He danced faster, in stomping circles at the center of the mat and as the intensity peaked he slung the water into the crowd. The music stopped abruptly and there were gales of laughter and shouts. The dancing had ended.

There was one last meal, a giant feast of fresh rice and pig meat. Teodoro Habana made a special show of calling the people from Madga and feeding us with great hospitality and celebration. He was jovial and friendly, and made sure that TingTing carried a leaf-wrapped bundle of pig meat to take to Tagleong and the people of Madga. In the afternoon, as our bankas pulled away from the shore with bows pointed upriver, a hoard of kids and Manobo adults were there to wave us off. I waved back, glad for the fresh air, the clean flowing waters of the river, the chance to leave the rice celebration, and not to have to think about what I'd just seen—at least not right away.

On the trip back to Madga, neither Janet nor I mentioned the dancing. Trining and TingTing stopped at the durian tree that Trining had pointed out on the way downriver. Eddy shimmied up the tree and cut eighteen football-size fruit, unripe, but I liked them better that way because the fruit was less mushy and smelly. Janet and I sat in the shade on the riverbank wiggling our toes in the cool water and not discussing what we had just seen, sharing durian with the guys.

It was several days before I could deal with the rice celebration. First, I wrote about it in my journal, scrupulously trying to describe in exact detail what I had seen. Then I allowed myself to write about my reactions, about the red-faced embarrassment I'd felt, and how my own American girl lack of information at age twenty-four was a hindrance in this culture where anatomy and sex were so open.

Several more days passed before I could open the subject with Janet. "Do you think that is really how they do it?" I asked.

"Do what?"

"You know. Make love like that. Like he was riding a horse."

"I don't know. I guess so."

"But that's not how it's done in America. I mean, I think not. I've seen movies. It's not like that. He made it look like the woman didn't matter. Like she was some horse in a rodeo. Like she wasn't a person at all."

"Maybe it's different here. Maybe the women don't share as much as Americans have come to expect. It would fit with a lot of other abuses of women in this country, don't you think?"

"I guess so," I said. "It just seemed like the woman was no more than an animal, the way he made it look." I paused and asked quietly, "It isn't like that. Surely it isn't. Do you think?"

There was no response.

◉◉◉

Lots to report! Flood! The river is at the highest point I've ever seen, almost up over the cliff bank that protects Madga. Scary!! Last night after an extreme torrential rain, I was brushing my teeth as the moon shone upon the rapidly moving river. Janet and I went out to check it out, and then walked around in the moonlight. It was 12:30 a.m., and we were really worried. In the darkness, the sound of rushing, leaping water was entirely disconcerting. We thought about waking up Suat or Datu to tell them the houses were in danger, but in the end, we decided to keep our concern to ourselves and let them figure it out. The water was all the way up the hill that we usually have to walk down to get to the river. This morning we asked Datu and Ricarda if we should be worried about being washed away, and Datu says it's not really close yet, and that it's receding now.

There's no school today, because the kids can't cross the river. I'd call it raging—deep and swift—nothing like the sweet, thigh-high Madga we have come to know.

Since there was no school, we brought out the basketball from the Care package, but it was deflated. A pump had come with it, but someone had taken the pump across the river. Serhio insisted on crossing the frothing river to retrieve the pump. He took off his clothes and swam across, got the pump, and swam back with it, arriving on our side of the river naked. He was shy, but got his clothes on, pumped up the basketball, and had fun bouncing it in the dirt for hours, and rolling it off our nipa roof, which, unfortunately, breaks the fronds and causes the roof to leak even more than it already does. I had to ask him to stop throwing it on the roof.

— Journal, September 27, 1972

⊙◉⊙

Now it's late evening and I've spent most of this day trying to write an account of the rice festival dancing. I had to write in snippets, as it's all so daunting, so if my account seems disjointed, that's why. I also did a huge load of laundry today—sheets, blanket, and towels, things that are really heavy when wet. The river isn't exactly limpid yet, but it is calmer and clearer than it was a couple of days ago. Since Janet's hand is still delicate, I did most of the heavy work today. At least her hand hasn't gotten infected, we have survived the rising waters, and with help from our neighbors, we've had fresh rice to eat today. Life goes on.

— Journal, September 29, 1972

⊙◉⊙

Thanksgiving 1972

Despite all the rain and the muddy river currents, I was at the river today, trying to get the blood-splatter dots off my cut-off jeans, tiny droplets of blood from the baboy head on the altar at the rice festival. I kept washing and washing and washing. I was glad I had soap.
— Journal, September 27, 1972

☉☉☉

The dance of the two men and one woman went on for quite a while and was frenzied. It seemed as if they were becoming the pig or taking on pig-like energy by drinking the blood. I don't know for sure, it's just the feeling I

got as I watched their wild, glazed eyes, their jerking and
jumping movements, their powerful, crouching dance.
— Journal, September 29, 1972

◎◎◎

His was a precarious life
in the forests of these old hills
above the jungle river.

Hunted by tough-skinned
Manobo men
who built traps
and carried spears,
he hid by day and
foraged by night.

When the dogs and men came,
he tried to run for his life,
crashing through slapping, scraping branches.
Yet in the end,
those quick trotters didn't help a bit.

I met him as he dangled upside down
feet lashed together
straddling a stout pole
shouldered by warriors.

He grunted, snorted, and shouted
as six men hoisted his hulk
up the ladder and into the bamboo house.

Suspended upside down, he was
seeing us for the first time,
we, his downside-up enemies.

They laid him on the floor
and he looked around
with wide, dark, angry eyes.

The whirling, leaping leader
handed the spear to his son.
The man-boy felt its weight,
then jumped and plunged.

The pig screamed and lurched,
but lived.
The leader nodded,
and his son leaped and lunged again.
The spear lodged in the pig's throat
and shrieks turned to gurgles, then
to murmurs, and to a final twitching rasp.

The crowd cheered.

They hoisted him up,
dead weight,
and cut his throat.

The blood ran out,
was caught in a shallow basin
and passed around the room,
each person sipping of the sacrifice
as gongs and drums rattled.

The head was hacked from the body
and placed reverentially on the altar
amid offerings of uncooked rice
and a single boiled egg.

Sitting cross-legged on the bamboo floor
I could look into the nostrils of the boar
and examine his old, battle-scarred ears.
His eyes were black marbles,
startled, but no longer angry.

Where I sat, blood dripped from the severed head
and fat drops splattered
into droplets fine as sea mist,

speckling my duffel, my jeans,
my arms, my neck, my hair, and my cheek.

The feast of thanks was delicious.

My gut is still digesting this sacrifice.
So is my mind.

⊙⊙⊙

Most times, people danced alone on the floor, or perhaps two or three people at a time danced, like Teodoro
and his son and the lady who collected and was first to
drink the pig blood. The three of them all danced wildly
together for a long time. I'd expected mass dancing, but
at no time did that happen. It was always just one or
two, maybe three dancers, and they would go on and on
and on until they became exhausted. Teodoro Habana
had a lot of stamina and stayed up dancing a very long
time.

— Journal, September 29, 1972

Janet and the kids are on Datu's porch dancing right
now. The poor "dimbah" drum is falling apart. The wood
is splitting, and the hide head is slipping sideways. Some
kids colored the hide blue with Crayolas "borrowed" from
the school box! The fact that it's now blue is disconcerting. Is this vandalism, or beauteous embellishment? No
one else seems bothered by the blue drum, only me.

— Journal, September 28, 1972

⊙⊙⊙

Wild Upland Rice

In the afternoon, Datu and Ricarda, Darna, Lando, and Little Lalak, as well as Maria, Tessie, and several others went downriver to Teodoro Habana's house to help with the rice harvest. We went to the celebration and they went to work. Janet says we should just relax and let that obvious inequity be. At Datu's house across the path, only Tata and Donkilyo stayed behind. Donkilyo will cook for baby Tata. I'm going to keep an eye out to be sure sweet little Tata is taken care of. I trust Donkilyo as a great hunter, but less as a babysitter.

— Journal, September 30, 1972

☉☉☉

It was rice harvest time in the fields near Madga, and Janet and I had been hinting to our neighbors that we wanted to help. On Saturday, three days after the rice festival at Teodoro Habana's home, Big Norma came to our porch and offered us the chance. We slipped out of our shorts and into jeans to protect our legs from the itchy irritation of rice leaves.

"Can we ride the *gakit* to the mountain?" I asked eagerly. A recently constructed addition to our community, the river raft looked like fun. Eleven fat bamboos, each about ten feet long, were lashed together with rattan strips. Built as transportation for crops headed downriver, these rafts rode low in the water, heavily laden and precariously balanced, poled by a single, highly skilled raftsman.

Everyone knew the river etiquette—a motorized boat would pull to the side and wait till a raft was well past so there'd be no wake washing over the precious cargo. On a trip upriver the previous summer, our banka pulled to the bank to wait while a raftload of watermelons passed us heading downriver. The melons were stacked in a four-foot tall pyramid, the load so heavy the big gakit rode barely above the river. The raftsman tilted his weight one way or another and pressed the pole into the river with incredible precision. Well-muscled, wearing just shorts and a sheathed bolo, he danced the river with intense concentration. The image of him poling that melon-laden raft seared into my memory as the most profound expression of athletic grace and skill I'd ever seen. Now I wanted to try the raft experience for myself.

Our adventure was way less elegant. With the weight of Baleriano, Janet, and me standing, the gakit rode so low that the river lapped over my slippers and the raft tilted and skittered. The slightest movement was amplified exponentially. I considered squatting to lower my center of gravity and stabilize the raft but I couldn't easily manage the "old Asian squat" on the tipsy raft with no handhold. Our ride was short, as Ben, Norma, and Tassio pulled us along the edge of the river. Ben was out front, chopping overhanging branches with his machete, as they led us up a shallow side stream until we could go no further. After that, we climbed hand-over-hand up the steep and slippery embankment. Ben helped me up, and Big Norma helped Janet. We had to balance across gulches on fallen logs and pass through tangled vines that were so thick

I could barely see my feet. Ben was chopping the vegetation so we could find our way, but even with his help, I tripped and stumbled more than once and slowed everyone down when I had to retrieve my slipper from the grasping vines.

The view from the top of the hill was spectacular. We looked down and saw the river winding around our little village and disappearing into the forest. The forest roiled in capricious shades of golds and yellows, greens and deep umber, while the ribboning river shone blue-black and silver under the glaring sun. In a clearing alongside the river were the toast-brown, coconut-frond roofs of our village. We rested there, enjoying the breeze, the birds, and the view—I told Janet I was experiencing an epiphany—what I'd come to the mountains to find.

"Well, enjoy it," she grinned. "Let's see how you feel after we harvest the rice."

Of course, she was right. The work was about to begin.

The rice field was on the slope of the mountain. The standing snags of charred trees reminded me that this was the site where, months earlier, I'd seen fire and flames. I was teaching school that day and saw smoke on the mountainside. I asked the kids about the fire, would it spread toward our village, and they assured me we were safe, that the fire would stay on the mountainside and we'd have rice later in the year. Well, that day had arrived. This was the first time I'd seen a plot of upland rice—shoulder-high grass with heavy tassels of ripening seeds. Rice, that most precious of foods, I realized, was actually gigantic grass. Amazed, I suddenly understood we were about to gather grass seeds.

Big Norma gave me my first lesson. "Look at the color of the grain," she said. "Like this, don't pick," showing me unripe greenish grains not fully emerged from their sheaths. "These are ready," she said, showing yellowish-brown plump grains. "Like this," she showed me, slicing the rice head where it joined the main stalk of the plant, using a sharp scythe-like tool she held in the palm of her hand.

Then she gave me a tool—a fist-sized, crescent-shaped blade set in a short wooden stick. Norma could pull the rice stalk over her blade with one finger, slicing the head cleanly and quickly. Harvest for her was a one-handed operation, leaving her other hand free to work the *kajad* basket at her side. It took me two hands, sawing each rice head from the mother stalk.

Janet and I worked side by side and nearly filled one kajad, while Big Norma singlehandedly filled two. Ben appeared with slightly unripe, but delicious lansones. We rested, and Ben pointed out the lansones tree.

"You can see the fruit," he said.

I couldn't. As always, the forest to me was an impenetrable wall of yellow, green, brown, and black.

"And there, the *kamoting kahoy*. See the dark, like blood?" Ben's voice was gentle, as one might teach a toddler. Then, suddenly, it came into focus, the small kamoting kahoy tree, I could see it! It reminded me of poinsettia, with long green leaves that quiver even when there's no perceptible breeze. And the stems were bright red. I grinned at Ben, "I see it!" He nodded in a kindly way. Baby was learning to see.

Back to work in the sun, and my arms were getting itchy from the long blades of the rice plants. Sweat made my arms both tickle and sting. It was still morning, and my productivity rate was already slowing.

"Let's go now," Norma finally said. She had beads of sweat on her upper lip and her kajads were full.

On our way back to the gakit, Ben disappeared for a few moments and returned with two stalks of sugarcane, two fat kamote, and half a basket of lansones.

Back at Madga, we continued the work, because the rice had to dry. Big Norma unrolled a pandanus mat and spread our harvest across it. Kids were deputized to keep the chickens away while the rice dried in the sun. It would take a couple of hours.

Janet and I had lunch, lugged buckets of water from the river for afternoon dip-and-pour baths, then rested, but not for long. It was time for the pounding.

"Can we try?" Surely our neighbors were becoming accustomed to this question from us, and each time we'd ask, they did their best to accommodate and teach us.

A mortar and pestle were the tools for this project. The mortar was a knee-high, hollowed-out tree-stump bowl. The pestle was a heavy three or four-foot-long pole, about as big around as my upper arm and slightly thinner in the midsection, like an elongated hourglass. Several handfuls of fresh rice were scooped into the bowl, then pounded with the pole. Wham. Wham. Up and down. Over and over again.

Janet took a turn to the amusement of our neighbors, especially the kids. She was tall and had to bend her knees on the way down, which threw her aim off. She repeatedly hit the side of the mortar, missing the rice and provoking good-natured laughter.

Then came the winnowing. The chaff, the outer sheath of the rice kernels, had been loosened by the pounding, but the rice had to be separated from the husks. Pounded rice was scooped into a shallow, wide, beautifully woven bamboo and rattan basket the shape of a garbage can lid. The basket was held at the waist and the rice was tossed into the air, then caught in the basket as it came down. On the way down, the lightweight husks were blown away. It took skill to toss the rice up and catch it again, and the women made it look effortless, their hips rolling and skirts swishing to the swaying rhythm of the toss-and-catch dance.

They didn't let us winnow. I was relieved, because I knew how much work it had taken to get that rice grown and harvested, and for an unskilled Americana to let it fall to the chickens would have been painfully wasteful. So Janet and I watched. A few grains did fall, even from the expert winnowers, and the chickens got a bit of rice and a lot of chaff.

A few hours later, just at sunset, Big Norma brought us a steaming plate of fresh rice. It was delicious. I hadn't even known upland rice existed during my first two years in-country. I'd been indoctrinated by images of the ancient, engineered, stepped, flooded rice terraces of the northern islands. Or the wet flatland paddies of the central archipelago, where carabao—the lumbering, laboring water buffalo—turned and smoothed flooded mud fields for planting, and laborers planted by hand each young shoot, punching it into the mud. It was back-breaking— bending for hours in the blistering tropical sun.

There was even a 75-centavo First Class stamp that I used for all my letters home in 1971 with an artist's depiction of President Ferdinand and First Lady Imelda Marcos side by side working the flatland rice fields. Ferdinand was depicted wearing a fine Spanish-style *barong tagalog* with his sleeves rolled up, alongside Imelda. We volunteers laughed at the utter improbability of this image, the president and first lady getting their hands dirty in a rice field, yet we kept our scoffing among ourselves, not wanting to offend the many people who remained staunchly loyal to the Marcos government.

Apparently there were many Marcos supporters in the Philippines at this time. Inside almost every home I visited, there was a prominently displayed portrait of Imelda and Ferdinand, usually framed and hung high on a wall in the *sala*. I assumed these families were supporters, and I kept my critical political opinions to myself until one day a teacher friend whispered to me that the photographs had been distributed to all workers throughout the country, and they were required to display them in their homes.

So, for many months I thought all rice was a product of flooded rice paddies of the lowlands or steep flooded terraces of the north. Now that I'd tasted the wild dryland rice of the southern interior mountains, I found it superior in every way—easier to grow and more fragrant, sweet, and satisfying. How would I ever go back to bagged white rice? Yet once I left Manobo-land, I never saw mountain rice again, and when I spoke of it, no one knew what I was talking about.

◉◉◉

It is certainly something of a national character trait of the people of the Philippines to make-do, to re-use things, to take what you have, manipulate it, and make it work in new ways. (My Mamaw, right out of Great Depression days, would be pleased with this. She always thought me too needy of new things.) But really, the Manobo take this make-do concept to new heights. Using what is at hand is an integral part of their way of seeing the world. In the forest, they seem to not merely see a tree, but they see the tree and know what it is useful for, even down to the shape of branches. They'll remember a particular tree and the way a branch crooks in a certain way. Then when a need arises, they'll remember, and return to that tree to harvest that particular crook for a particular use. Like the J-shaped bend of a tree *limb that is used to suspend a caldron over a fire. That branch's unusual angle of growth was visualized for that specific use. This way of seeing the forest seems brilliant to me. To them, it is simply living. I only catch occasional glimpses of how they might be seeing the world, but I find these smatterings very interesting.*

— Journal, August 15, 1972

⊙⊚⊙

We don't hear much about martial law, but it's a constant undercurrent. People know something is happening in the outer world. Yesterday afternoon, the Madga women and kids were working frantically, cleaning all the harvested rice. They said they were going to hide bags of it, so they'd have food when the soldiers come. They gave us uncooked rice too, so we could hide it. Where am I going to hide rice? Folded into my underwear in my duffle? That's the first place soldiers will check— Americana underwear is a trophy item. Shall I hollow out my rubber slipper and stuff some rice inside? The situation edges on ludicrous, but it's really not funny.

— Journal, October 3, 1972

⊙⊚⊙

Janet and the Chicken

I was sitting on the porch writing and Janet was in the doorway beading the way Amalya taught us when we heard a huge, sudden crack and then a crash from our kitchen. Janet was startled, and her beads went flying, rolling between the bamboo slats and into the dirt below the porch.

The supporting pole for the stove platform had snapped, and tins of oil and kerosene, the cooking stilt, and all the sand, came crashing down, along with the avocado seed we were sprouting in a glass jar. Seems the termites took one bite too many, and the structure gave way. We called out for help, and Datu and Donkilyo came over to assess the damage. They cut a new support pole from the forest and lashed it onto the platform frame *with rattan strips. The flat-bottom, woven-bamboo section of the platform was still good, so they reused that and replaced the sand as best they could. We stuffed the avocado rootlets back into the jar and gave it fresh water, and I think it will survive.*

While the guys were fixing the platform, Janet, Tata, and I were under the house searching for scattered beads. The stupid chickens ate the ones they saw first.

— Journal, October 1, 1972

⊙⊚⊙

Janet and I were beginning to formulate plans to leave the Philippines, to travel homeward together the long way, through Europe. "I've always wanted to see Rome, haven't you?" she asked.

"I guess so." I thought I should want to see Rome. Maybe it'll be interesting. But I really just want to rest. And eat. Pretty much anywhere.

"Rome seems so far away," I said. "I guess it's real."

"What *is* real to you?"

I looked to the cardboard food box. "Supper." I knew it would be rice again, and little else. There was half a can of wieners, and for dessert, maybe a spoonful of sweetened condensed milk, if any was left and hadn't gone sour, not that curdling or spoilage would stop us.

Janet's gaze lingered on the food box a long moment. She might have been considering the meager prospects for dinner, too.

"I've been thinking," she said, slowly.

"What about?" I asked

"Maybe we should have a party. In honor of our Madga friends. Before we leave. Invite all the kids and families, and concession guards, everyone who has helped us. We can ask Datu if we can use the drum for dancing. Saldi can play the *kubing*, and you have your guitar. We could get Trining and TingTing to bring some extra food up from Silco. Whaddaya think?"

"I like the part about extra food. Let's plan." That's how the idea of a party got started.

A few days later, she said again, "I've been thinking."

Dangerous. "What this time?" I asked, looking up from creating the second set of carbon copies of fill-in-the-blank sentences for tomorrow's writing lesson. The carbon paper was worn through and copies were increasingly faint, the words barely legible smudges. This might have to be the last individualized writing lesson. We were overdue for a Davao supply run.

Janet was rinsing off our lunch dishes in the basin beside me on the porch. She stood up straight, lifted the plastic basin, and with a quick jerk tossed out the rinse water. The sound of it splattering in the dust alerted the chickens, and they came running, competing for morsels of rinsed-away food.

"It's about our life here, how dependent we've been on Datu and Ricarda, and Suat and Amalya. Even the kids. You know, I don't think we'd have made it without so much help from our neighbors."

"That's true," I said. "Our skills weren't honed for a hunting-and-gathering life in the forest wildlands. I never learned wild pig-butchering at home or in college."

"There are still a lot of skills we don't have."

"But we've learned a lot, too," I added. "To harvest sweet potatoes, build a fire, and cook over it. To slash and burn the forest, plant, harvest, pound, and winnow rice. To track a pig and butcher it. To tie together a bamboo house or a raft with rope we made ourselves. To build a fish trap, catch and clean river fish." I grinned. I was more than half-joking, of course. "Well, maybe we're not proficient in these areas, but we've learned something. Another year and we'd be ready to go it on our own. Don't you think?" Janet didn't answer.

A few days later she announced she was going to kill a chicken.

"Why?" I asked incredulously.

"Because I never have and I don't know if I can. I want to believe I could actually learn to survive the way people here do, at such a basic level. Real survival. Like tracking down an animal and killing it and cleaning it and cooking it over a fire and eating it so I could live another day."

"Without canned wieners?" I joked.

"I'm serious. If we're going to serve chicken at our party, I'm going to kill it."

I had to admire her. I thought of chiming in, "Me too!" but the thought was fleeting. "I'll build the fire and make up a song about your exploits."

I wasn't kidding. I went for my guitar to create some sort of extemporaneous headless-chicken ditty, when I noticed a mysterious buzzing coming from inside the body of my guitar. There was a mud wattle wasps' nest inside, and I could hear the wasp rattling for battle. I set the guitar aside in something of a panic and began to think. It took a while, but I devised a strategy. I soaked some gauze from our first aid kit in rubbing alcohol, hung it from a thread, attached the thread to one of the guitar strings, and dangled the alcohol pad inside my guitar. The next day, I replenished the alcohol. And the next. Finally, the wasp decamped, and I punched at the mud nest with a stick till it disintegrated and I could shake out most of the dirt. Then I played my guitar again.

A couple of weeks later, Trining brought up a scrawny gray rooster from Silco camp, trussed up in an old rice sack. He let it loose in the village and for days I watched it wander around companionably, squawking and scratching and rattling its feathers like its comrades.

The morning of the party, Trining came over early.

"Janet," he said, accenting the second syllable as he always did. "Are you ready to kill the chicken?"

She was. Trining and the kids cornered and caught the gray chicken while she changed into an old yellow T-shirt and khaki cutoffs, hitched her braid atop her head, and fixed it with a triangle bandana. She took our bolo out from its sheath and with a fleeting backward glance, balanced down the ladder and walked with Trining toward the river, her rubber *tsinelas* slippers raising dusty puffs.

Would she do it? I was hungry, as ever. I wanted barbecued chicken and noodles, but could I actually bring myself to chop the head off a living creature, even one as obnoxious as a scrawny Philippine rooster? I knew the sad truth. I couldn't.

I was in the outhouse when Janet returned from the river. When I climbed back onto the porch, she was washing her yellow T-shirt in the plastic basin.

I looked at her for a long moment before I spoke.

"Did you do it?"

She gestured with her lips toward the stove platform where two skinny chicken legs stuck out from a rice sack.

She didn't say a word while she rinsed and hung her shirt.

"Blood?" I asked.

She seemed pale, but maybe I was imagining it. She nodded with a steely expression. "You got that song ready?"

◉◉◉

I couldn't watch the beheading, but I sure did eat that barbecued chicken. I feel a little ashamed, but there it is. After all these experiences in the mountains, I think I'll look into vegetarianism. But first, I want a few dozen hamburgers. I'm so hungry for deep, thick, juicy, gnaw-able serious animal protein, I think I'll postpone vegetarianism for a while, but I'm pretty sure it is in my future.

— Journal, October 2, 1972

◉◉◉

Fishing

Last night, I heard on the radio that under Marcos's martial law, all government employees in the Philippines are being forced to resign by October 15. I wonder if teachers in the public education system are considered government employees? I wonder if all the schools in the country (except ours) are still closed? I wonder if the country's incoming and outgoing mail is being censored or stopped? I wonder how people are doing out there, outside of Madga?

Meals continue to be rotten. We've had rice with nothing. Well, some of Janet's flour-water-curry sauce on it. Bleak. Piteous. Seriously insufficient. But I'm glad for the fresh rice.

— Journal, October 4, 1972

◉◉◉

I was at the river. My load of laundry was half-done when Big Norma came over.

"Would you like to go fishing with us?"

"Of course, yes!" I finished the laundry hurriedly and a few minutes later I was following Big Norma to the spot downstream where the river narrows and runs chest deep. Our regular crossing site usually ran shin to thigh-high; at the fishing spot the river narrowed between steeply cut banks and gushed chest-high and strong enough to knock me off my feet.

Big Norma and I joined three women who were already in the river up to their elbows, holding open the edges of a mosquito net that spanned much of channel. I hooked a corner of the net over my big toe and anchored my foot to the river bottom, ready to stand my ground. Then Norma came over and put a river stone on my corner, lightening my task. I just had to hold up the top part of the net. But still, it was a challenge to keep my balance against the bucking current.

A pack of men and kids were working upstream. Eight men poked under logs and rocks with long sticks, walking in a row slowly, working their way downriver toward us. They were corralling the fish. When the men almost reached us, they went back upstream and did it again.

After the second sweep, it took all of us to pull up the heavy net. I was surprised at how many fish we had caught, several dozen, half a kajad basket. I wanted to ask the names of the two kinds of fish in the net, but the noise of the river was too loud. There were three-inch silvery fish with long, pointed bottom lips. I'd never seen such creatures and I spent several moments examining one. What was that bottom-lip probe for? How could it eat with such a long spear as its lower lip? These long-lipped fish were the catch of the day. A second kind of small silver fish was only an inch or two long. At home, these would have been bait. And there were a few tiny river shrimp in the net. All in all, it didn't seem much of a return for all that effort, and with so many hungry people to feed.

Later that afternoon, Big Norma came over to give us a share of the fish. I really didn't want them, but wouldn't refuse as we were, in fact, hungry. So they sat beside the stove, the catch of the day and the minnows, awaiting inspiration. First I sketched the odd long-lipped fish in my journal. Then I took on the challenge of the evening—how do you clean and cook a minnow?

Only Big Norma and Aida were in my class this morning—everyone else was harvesting rice. So I gave them the choice of reading, writing, or coloring. They asked for the Spirograph set, and they were contentedly drawing circles within circles and exploring the relationships of the whirling gears in various sizes. I always love the Spirograph too.

Tata and Mordino took some pieces from our old, cardboard school box—the one that got soaked in the storm—and were "sleeping" under our house during class, their little naked bodies on the dirty cardboard in the dirt.

Playing house is the big pastime among the mga gamai kaayo. They always make stoves of sticks and dirt and put a tin can from our rubbish pile on top. Or they make little lean-tos of longer sticks and big leaves and then crawl underneath to "sleep" in the shade. Cute.

— Journal, October 2, 1972

News

Early this morning, a group of Manobo travelers from downriver passed through our village carrying large bundles strapped to their backs. A man, a woman, and two children. They were heading for the dense mountains. They talked with Datu, bringing news, and then kept going.

— Journal, October 3, 1972

◉◉◉

It was just after two o'clock on a Wednesday afternoon in early October 1972 when a sweating Baleriano ran in from the south and headed up the pole ladder onto Datu Tagleong's porch. I could hear Datu and Baleriano's voices but couldn't understand any of it.

"Serhio, what is the news Baleriano brings?" I asked. "Can you hear?"

Serhio stopped chopping wood to listen. "They talk about the war," he said after a moment. "And Baleriano says that Trining and TingTing have arrived at their concession camp today and will come soon, after they eat."

News and food supplies and mail were coming! It had been weeks since we'd seen them, and we were almost out of food. Lunch had been "rice pudding"—soggy rice topped with semi-curdled canned milk and sugar. Perhaps worse, we were running out of toilet paper and I wasn't anxious to resort to leaves.

Madga village was quiet. Too quiet. In my morning class there had been only two students. Serhio told me that Suat and Donkilyo were up the Madga net-fishing, so I knew we'd have some minnows for supper. Amalya and her kids were still in the village, but Big Norma and Ben, Ricarda, and all of Datu's kids were missing.

By the time Trining and TingTing arrived, I had tea ready. TingTing went straight to Datu's house, and Trining came to our porch. He looked tired and even thinner, though he'd always been little more than muscle and bone.

"I'm sorry, we have no mail for you this time. And only this bread. Things are not the same at Silco Camp."

"What's the news?" Our questions tumbled and jumbled. We craved information.

"There are reports of fighting in Manila, the national army of Marcos against the NPA Communist forces." He was talking about the New People's Army, a loosely banded fighting force, supposedly formed to take the side of the common folk against corrupt politicians but said by some to be carrying out the repressive, antidemocratic Communist agenda that was spreading throughout Southeast Asia.

"Uh huh. That's what the radio said too," Janet said. "How bad is the fighting?"

Trining shrugged. "I heard only the radio, and who knows, perhaps they are reading the press releases from Marcos, so what is true? Maybe Marcos is just creating the story to support his claim that martial law is necessary. But Mr. Guatno has called all of us concession guards and forest workers in from the field and told us to hide our arms in the mountains. That's why we are here, to tell Datu and the people of Madga to prepare. You too. Are you ready to leave?"

Janet and I showed him our Flee Bag and told Trining that Datu had told us to go with Suat and Amalya into the forest. We were ready.

"It's good that Datu has made preparations," Trining said. "The last time soldiers came to the area, they confiscated Datu's rifle and it was never returned."

"When was that?" Janet asked.

"Many years ago, in the big war. But Datu hasn't forgotten." Trining lifted our striped beach bag. "Heavy." He looked inside and smiled but didn't say anything. I thought he might have been amused by our toothpaste.

"People are wondering how long this war will last," Trining said.

"But there is no war," Janet said. "This is the army of their own country. This is the Philippine Army that is advancing."

"Yes, but all the schools and government offices are closed, and people everywhere are running. It is like a war. Marcos has laws now against guns. He has imposed the death penalty on anyone who kills with a gun. And there are fines and imprisonment for anyone who possesses a gun."

"But this is the Philippines," I protested. "Guns are everywhere, all the time, at least with men. I've never known a woman with a gun, but women are always protected by men who have guns." I'd known a few guys without guns, teachers and office men, but they were generally away from their place of birth and I'd bet there were guns in the family compounds back home. I was sure that people all over the country were hiding guns. It wasn't only a Manobo problem.

"But the Manobo can't leave the village now," Janet said. "The rice isn't all harvested. They won't just leave it in the fields. Not after all that work. They need rice to survive."

"Maybe yes, but they can speed up the harvest, and they can hide the rice," Trining said. "That's where your neighbors are now. They stay in the rice fields, working all day, into the night. The children too."

Oh. I'd wondered where everyone was. I sipped tea, confused. Who are the good guys, who are the bad guys? What will happen to this crazy country? To our friends? To us?

Class roster. I found this class attendance roster stuck in my journals from Madga days. All twenty-one kids have great attendance—until October 3, 1972. After that, there are practically no kids in school. October 3, only Serhio, Poring, and Dita—and Baleriano, who was tardy. That was when things changed in Madga. That was when martial law touched us. That was the beginning of the end for us. And the end came quickly.

— Journal, November 15, 1972

⊙⊚⊙

Last Days

It looks like my Peace Corps days are coming to an end. I'm stepping out on the Termination Trail. It's all so beautiful here in Madga, yet horrible too. We're planning our final trip downriver, but it's impossible to manage time. So much is happening—odd things, weirdnesses, hard things. Sometimes I can't breathe, like I'm being crushed.

— Journal, October 9, 1972

⊙⊙⊙

October 5th and 6th were horrible. On Thursday evening, the men of Madga all got drunk. Not that they didn't occasionally get drunk, but all of them at once was something I hadn't seen before. And they weren't happy drunks. They got rowdy.

The biggest surprise came from Donkilyo. Donkilyo the mute. The great hunter who never spoke but used his own invented sign language. But drunk, Donkilyo was shouting and dancing in the moonlight. I stepped onto the porch to check out the noise.

"Janet, you gotta see this. Come here." I said.

"Is it really him?" she asked, incredulous.

"Yep. How is that possible? Now he can speak? Not just speak, but shout!"

"He's been fooling us all along?"

"It's the vino. Gotta be the liquor. Magic stuff."

She grinned at me. "Uh huh, magic, like out-of-your-skull, skunk-drunk, crazy magic."

Even solid, level-headed, responsible Suat had a rip-roaring squabble with Amalya. Their kids traipsed over to our porch to get out of the way. Serhio led sleepy little Mordino by the hand, and Poring carried baby Balbid in her arms up to our porch, while little Dita sleepily trailed behind. I got my guitar off its rafter peg. We put the kids down on our mat and sang "Twinkle, Twinkle, Little Star" to drown out the angry shouts. It went on past midnight.

"I think they were fighting about us, you know," Janet told me later when the kids were asleep under our net, covered by our blanket. Janet and I were sitting up, discussing departure plans, making lists, sorting out household goods, what we would take, what we would leave behind.

"What makes you think that?"

"I understood part of their shouting. Amalya thinks they ought to leave here, take the family to safety in the mountains. Suat thinks they need to stay and take care of us. They don't know what to do about us. I think that's what they were fighting about. Seems we ought to go downriver for a while, till things return to normal. After martial law, or war, or whatever this is."

"Uh-huh," I agreed. "Whatever this is."

Late the next afternoon, a giant military-style truck came roaring up the old Dongalyo Camp road through the logging concession on the other side of the river. The rumor was instant: Army coming. Run! Datu and Donkilyo—the only ones occupying their house across the path—hightailed it like streaking deer, leaping off their porch with spears in hand and heading west behind the village, away from the river and into the hills. Suat was out hunting for the day, and Amalya, with five kids and us two Americanas to take care of, was slower to act. By the time we were rounded up, Serhio had gone across the river and was back with word that it wasn't the military after all. It was the Dongalyo loggers. Dongalyo Logging Company hardly ever used their camp clearing on the other side of the river, but that day, they arrived.

"Bet they're here to hide their rifles in the forests. What do you think?" I asked Janet.

"Makes sense. They sure did scare everyone. We could be dead by now if it'd been the real army. We didn't get out very fast."

"Datu and Donkilyo made it, but not us. I think we're slowing them down."

A few hours later, in the late afternoon, Datu and Donkilyo returned and Suat walked into the village from the south. I glanced up to greet him as he passed our porch, but the words never came. Something was wrong. Suat was chalky, his lips pale, his body silver with sweat. His right foot was wrapped with gray-green leaves and he leaned heavily on a walking stick. He hollered to Serhio some rapid words that I couldn't catch. Serhio shouted back to his father and headed to him double time. I caught only one word of their exchange: *snake*.

I'd heard there were snakes in these forests, but I'd never given it much attention. After all, I grew up around water moccasins, copperheads, and rattlers and found them generally to be shy creatures. In Madga, more visible daily hazards took my attention and I'd forgotten about snakes.

"What do you think happened to Suat?" Janet asked.

"I think I heard Suat say something about a snake. I guess his family has the situation under control." I glanced toward Suat's house. There was no activity on their porch, and I'd turned back to my chores when Serhio was suddenly beside me.

"Mum," he pleaded, "do you have a blade?" I glanced worriedly to Janet.

"A knife?"

Serhio said something about getting something from his father's foot. There was a bite, he said. A snakebite.

"Get the snakebite kit!" Janet barked. "Quick!" It was a fist-sized unopened cellophane wrapped bundle in our Peace Corps medical kit.

Suat sat stiffly on his bamboo-slat porch, Amalya by his side. My nervous fingers fumbled with the cellophane while we tried to get the facts.

A snake. In the pathway. Suat stepped on it. It bit him.

"Are you sure it was poisonous?" I asked. I wanted it to be a grass snake, a garter snake, a rat snake. Something harmless. Please.

Suat spoke rapidly and I caught little except yes, he was certain. He'd gotten a good look at the snake. The sweat beaded on his forehead and upper lip. Amalya offered a hank of tattered fabric and wiped his face. Both of them looked to us, wide-eyed with fear, expecting a miracle from us.

Janet was bent low over Suat's left foot.

"There! Two holes. Fang marks," she hissed, pointing to the outer rim of his foot, not quite on the sole, not quite on the top.

I had the cellophane off. Out tumbled a set of instructions along with a rubber suction cup, a couple of fat strips of rubber, some razor blades and bandages.

"I don't suppose you've ever…" I looked at Janet.

She glared back. "Are you kidding? Of course not! You're the one from Texas."

I remembered the cowboy movies: The victim would tie on a checkered bandana, pulling the knot tight with his teeth, then slice his arm with his bowie knife and suck the blood, spitting red gorp to the ground. I unfolded the directions. They were in multiple languages. I found English.

"First. Tourniquet."

"Right," said Janet. And she tied one of the rubber strips at Suat's calf. "What's next?"

"Umm." I was reading. It didn't make sense. I was trying to translate, trying to give instructions that we all could understand. But if it didn't make sense to me in English, how could I give instructions in Visayan.

"What's it say?" Janet pushed. "Just tell us what it says!" She was holding Suat's foot, keeping the tourniquet tight, but not too tight. We all were sweating and Suat looked panicked, his eyes wide, his face tight in a grimace of pain.

I was reading. "Cut the skin. Make an X. You want a lot of blood to come out." At least I thought that's what it said. The directions were hard to follow. Was the X at the wound, between the puncture marks, or somewhere nearby? How much blood is a lot? Nothing was clear.

Janet unwrapped one of the single edge razor blades from the kit. It was a new blade yet I could see specks of rust.

"Go on," I urged her. "An X. Do it at the fang marks."

Suat stiffened, sucked in his breath and nodded.

Janet jabbed the blade. Nothing. She tried again, dragging the corner of the blade between the fang marks. No blood. The blade didn't penetrate. She looked up at me and said. "It's too tough. His skin is too thick."

"It's just got to work!"

"Okay, you try!" She eagerly handed me the blade.

I had never touched the foot of an adult Manobo man before. It was tough as tanned cowhide. I unwrapped a second razor blade, also slightly rusty, took a breath and pushed it hard into Suat's foot. He jerked. The skin severed slightly and a drop of thick crimson blood appeared.

"Good!" Janet cheered, but I felt a wave of nausea in my gut. I'd cut a human, intentionally inflicted pain. I almost cried out for my own hurt, but Janet was hissing in my ear, "More! Cut the X!"

I tried again, but I may as well have been wielding a red Coca-Cola pencil. The blade was dull and would not penetrate the skin.

"Try the suction cup," she coached and passed me the oversized rubber thimble. I put it on top of the small oozing incision and squeezed. There was no seal against the leathery skin, no suction, and very little blood.

"We'll never get the poison out like this," she moaned.

"I've never seen anything like it," I whispered back. "This is the toughest skin I've ever seen."

We tried. There on the bamboo slat porch we repeatedly pushed and jabbed, trying to get Suat's foot to bleed freely. We failed.

Datu appeared with a small bundle of leaves wrapped in a rag.

Exhausted, Suat leaned against the bamboo wall as Datu tied the compress on his foot. There was much talking and gesturing. I understood nothing but my own abysmal failure.

Finally, we all sat back against the bamboo wall, Suat's foot an icon in front of us. There was nothing more to be done. Suat looked ill. Was he dying? Was it my fault? Serhio brought up cool river water and offered his father a drink from a tin cup and Suat closed his eyes. Amalya sat beside him, supporting his leg against hers, her eyes dark and worried.

In a while, Janet and I returned to our house across the path where we talked in hushed voices about Suat's chances for survival. We had questions but no answers. How long does it take to die of snakebite? What are the symptoms? What were the leaves that Datu brought? Maybe the leaves will suck out the poison, do you think? Why are we sitting here with a snakebite kit with rusty razor blades? What else in that medical kit is no longer any good?

In the dark of early evening, we headed to the river. "How is Suat?" I called out to Serhio as we passed their porch.

"Still alive. Sleeping," Serhio said.

Janet and I looked hopefully at one another.

Next morning, first thing, as I headed to the outhouse, I saw Suat limping toward the river.

"I guess he's okay," I told Janet. "I think he'd be dead by now if he had been poisoned."

"Looks that way. But he walks like his foot sure is sore."

"I guess my foot would be sore too if there had been two people tearing at it with rusty razor blades. So what do you think really happened?"

She thought a moment. "I have a theory," she replied. "I think the snake was poisonous, and it did bite him. But I think that snake had just as hard a time getting its fangs into his foot as we had getting a razor blade in. I think the fang marks were superficial, like our incision. I think the poison didn't really get into his bloodstream. I think Suat was saved by the toughness of his feet."

I nodded. It made sense. "I have a theory too." I offered. I paused to give her the full brunt of my theory: "I think all of us were pretty durn lucky."

◉◎◉

The Peace Corps snakebite kit was a big fail. Are we the first volunteers who ever had to use it? Why do they give us something so worthless? I'd rather have a checkered bandana and a sharp bowie knife. Those dull, rusty blades and the stupid rubber thimble and inscrutable directions were ridiculous, a completely unfunny story that could have turned tragic!

Hooray for the tough, bare feet of the Manobo!

— Journal, October 9, 1972

◉◎◉

Departure

It was a long morning of extended goodbyes to each person in Madga. We didn't get into the boat till nearly noon. I'll never forget the sight of all those faces, all our kids, lined up in the grass by the river, waving to us as we pulled away, and the waving continued as I looked back—me waving to them, them waving to me. I was crying. Those are my kids, my bright and beautiful Manobo kids, the river kids of Madga.

— Journal, October 10, 1972

⊙⊙⊙

Our twenty-one kids were all at school on Friday, and we had a going-away celebration. We made a ceremony, giving each student his or her notebook and a red Coca-Cola pencil they could keep. And we told them they had all graduated from the Madga school, but that they should keep practicing and keep learning, because the world downriver was very big. I gave them back their artwork—their drawings of houses and pigs and logging trucks and their colorful Spirograph circles and curlicues.

All my Bigs and most of Janet's Littles could write their names, and some could create and write out stories. All my Bigs could read, some quite well, others could at least sound things out. We emptied the school box, leaving with Ricarda the now-broken, toy-truck pencil sharpener that the kids loved. We had lucky drawings for the books, knowing full well that the "winners" would share the books with everyone. Knowing too that the books would most likely end up battered and river-soaked. We gave the magazines to Ricarda and knew she would share them with the village. We gave the Care garden tools and basketball and pump to Datu Tagleong.

We had a pile of worn-out T-shirts and some household goods—a bucket, a basin, pillows and two sleeping mats, sheets, blankets, matches, tin cups, and spoons to give away too. That's when the trouble began. Word got out, and people showed up at our porch asking, wanting, begging. The crowd became too much, and Janet and I had an idea. We would *trade* our household items for baskets. "Come tomorrow, early. Bring baskets to trade," I told them.

"They can make more baskets. They can't make a water bucket or a sheet," Janet said, "so it ought to work for them. At least if we trade things away, we can spread the goods around a little bit. Better than just giving things to the loudest asker."

"I know who that would be," I thought aloud.

"Laurentina." Janet said.

"Yep."

And the next morning neighbors came. Janet and I ended up with five finely woven head-baskets each, some very used, some newer, all of them beautiful. "Museum-quality," Janet said, and I agreed.

Laurentina, having made no baskets and having no baskets to trade, gave us a chicken in exchange for a pair of Janet's cut-off jeans.

"Really? A live chicken? What are we gonna do with that?" I asked Janet.

"We're gonna eat it," Janet-the-chicken-slayer said. "Tonight. At Silco Camp. You watch."

"You really think it was their chicken to give away?" I knew Laurentina and Tirzo. They were the kind of folks who would give away someone else's chicken. Despite their quirks, though, Laurentina and Tirzo were tolerated in the Madga community, because, it seemed, Laurentina knew about forest herbs and mountain medicines, while Tirzo sometimes worked for the logging company.

"I have no idea where that chicken came from. But it's ours now," Janet surmised.

We had honed our goods down to two duffle bags, a small zipper case, ten woven baskets, my guitar, and a chicken. We were ready to go.

While Trining and TingTing were bringing the banka to the shallows near the village, Janet and I went over to Datu's house to say goodbye. I gave him my still-good red T-shirt and a red tie belt I'd been using as a guitar strap. He didn't say much, but I think he liked the gifts. Ricarda did the talking, asking us to come back soon, telling us that the students of Madga still wanted to learn from us, that we should return when the "war" is over and bring our children with us to live with the Manobo, that we would always be welcome.

We thanked Datu and Ricarda for helping us, for teaching us about the Manobo life, for sharing with us, for taking care of us.

We walked to the river with a ragtag gaggle of our kids. I could hardly believe how sad I was. These were *my* kids. We'd been through a lot together. They were laughing, carrying our bags, helping us over the river rocks and into the banka. And as it pulled away from shore and headed downstream, I looked back. There were the faces of my kids, on the shore, still waving.

It was overwhelming to think I'd never see them again, so I figured this would be a little break, that we'd be back in a month, or two, or three, when national politics cooled off. When the rainy season was over. When sweet potatoes were plentiful again. I would help with the school, with the rice planting. This wasn't a final goodbye. It just couldn't be.

⊙⊙⊙

It was our last trip down the river. We took it slow
and stopped several times; the foliage and the birds are
so special and beautiful. The monkey that lives here at
Silco is very friendly. She sits on my lap when I play my
bamboo Manobo flute.

I saw Joe and Flor for lunch today. Janet and I are
thinking about "adopting"—that is, sending some money
for schooling—for Nelson Tawide, who lives with Joe and
Flor now. He is a bright boy from Madga, the best kid
in my class in the early Madga days before he moved
downriver to go to Flor and Joe's school.

I also left my portable typewriter with Joe and Flor
for their school. I'd had it in storage and figured it wasn't
much good because I can't get ribbons for it, and it's too
much to carry around. Flor was incredibly happy to get
this. It was kind of embarrassing, because it seems to me
that a typewriter in a place without access to ribbons is
useless. But Flor says she can teach the kids to type using
carbon paper, and it will help them get jobs.

— Journal, October 11, 1972

⊙⊚⊙

Our time in Davao City has been quite busy. We
haven't even seen one movie yet.

There was mail for me at the Davao Peace Corps
office, so I have letters to answer! None from my family, of course—why do I continue to expect that they will
write me??!!—but several letters from friends. It's so hot
in Davao, perspiration literally runs off me, little rivers down my back, sending a sudden shivery tickle as it
heads for the waistband of my shorts. And I'm not even
in the sun; I'm sitting in the shade, writing. The heat
makes my head pound and my eyes dizzy. It's four o'clock
now, and still too hot to bathe. I could bathe and be cool
for a couple of minutes, but then I'd sweat again. I'll wait

another hour. By then it should be cooler and I can stay cool till the party.

This evening, there's a welcome gathering at Phil and Lynn's house for the new volunteers, and we oldies are invited too. Should be some good food, and it will be fun to talk with the shiny new volunteers—all boys, and all so very naive and uninitiated. It makes me tired, just thinking about what lies ahead for them, the steep learning curve they face. I don't want to tell them the truth of it.

—Journal, October 13-14, 1972

◉◉◉

PART IV

◉

Beyond

...owk...

Home Leave

How important is caring for my "fellow man," who I am coming not to like so much? How important is it to have roots in my home country, which I'm also not sure I like anymore? America just doesn't seem so exceptional to me. And how can any one religion be "right" when there is just as much justification for other religions or world views? How can I decide on one career path when so many are interesting? My family wants answers. I don't have answers.

I have my passport, traveler's checks (₱300, which is about $50), plus $300 US cash, representing my home-leave stipend, plus my recent living allowance, plus some American dollars I'd stashed in the Peace Corps safe in Manila. I'll be traveling with my guitar, my duffle, thirty *pounds of presents for people, and a large carry-on with my camera and purse. I guess I'm ready to go. Peace Corps is giving me home leave—but is Texas my "home" anymore? Do I have a home?*

— Journal, February 10, 1973

◉◉◎

They kept telling me I was entitled to it, and Peace Corps Manila encouraged me to take it. I was, in fact, long overdue. Since I had been granted a series of small extensions, I was already halfway into my third year as a volunteer. Home leave—a free trip, forty-five days in the land of soft beds, clean water, apples, freeways, family, and shopping malls. I'd been entitled for months, but I just didn't want to go back to America. But Peace Corps became insistent; I had to take my home leave.

As I was boarding Northwest Orient Airlines, the stewardess called me aside to ask if I'd like to fly first class. She said they had extra seats up front, and since I was Peace Corps, she singled me out.

There I was, with my long hair, pink polyester skirt—the same one I'd arrived in three years before—and a flimsy blouse purchased in Manila for a New Year's party I never attended. And sandals. It was February, and I was heading to frigid Texas with nothing else to wear. I was seated among well-dressed, affluent Filipina women in three-piece travel suits and furry coats. My across-the-aisle mate didn't even smile when I'd greeted her in Tagalog. I think, to her, I was invisible due to my lack of proper attire. I ate slices of pear garnished with paper-thin sharp cheddar. Then sweet nuts. And chocolate. And a meal with baked chicken breast (an entire breast for one person!) and vegetables and a green salad with fresh, *safe* lettuce. The stewardess stopped to chat, perching on the arm of the empty aisle seat next to me. What was it like, she wanted to know. She said she'd always wanted to join the Peace Corps. I told her some of the easy stories. When I told her how hard it had been to get fresh fruit in the mountains, she excused herself and returned with an entire pear just for me—I'd become a kind of celebrity.

I knew re-entry into America might be a challenge. Once at home, after I scrambled through my college clothes for sweaters, socks, and shoes, I tried settling in. But I had trouble adjusting. I couldn't sleep in my bed, which felt like a suffocating cloud, so I tried sleeping on the carpeted floor between my paired French provincial dresser and bureau, but for days sleep eluded me. I would almost drift off, then jerk awake at the sound of a train whistle or a car door slamming or the noisy sounds of the television where there were just too many words all at once and canned fake laughter on a loop behind the unfunny situation comedies.

My old friends seemed too clean, too happy to see me, and they asked questions about simple things, but not important things. They asked me about bathing, and bathrooms, about Filipino boys, about the weather near the equator, and about flying internationally and managing time-zone changes. They didn't ask about corrupt politics or sexual abuse or infant mortality or malnutrition or war. They didn't ask if it was worth it. Just as well, because I'm not sure how I would have answered. *Was it worth it?* I'd begun as a competent and content college graduate and had become, what?—incompetent and discontented.

My brother took me to a three-story shopping mall, the largest mall in the state—store after store of goods of every sort. "Meet me back here in two hours," he said. "Don't buy the place out." He grinned and left me to my own commercial desires.

I started in the perfume department of a huge department store. Perfume—I'd thought about it many times, a symbol of my vanished femininity. But smelling the samples, fragrances turned cloying along with glamorous marketing that concocted nothing but imitation allure. I turned away. Then I checked the shoes and scoffed at the improbable and impractical styles. Clothing on endless racks was entirely non-utilitarian. Even the luggage seemed impractical, too clean and screaming "tourist!" which would attract unwanted attention in the places I traveled.

I wandered the mall. Jewelry: all flash and glitz and fakery, easily ripped from an arm. Children's toys: ridiculous, a waste of money, give the infant a wad of cloth to suck, give the older child a stick and a rock. Kitchen tools: too clean, those shiny pots would be ludicrous over an open flame and the handles would melt. The chocolate candies looked good, and they'd make great gifts for my friends in the Philippines, but they would surely melt into gooey blobs long before they reached their destination.

I rested on a bench. I liked the mosaic floor of the mega-mall. Beautiful tile work, straight lines, and perfect angles. And I liked the vaulted atrium ceiling, letting natural winter light pour in and bounce across the tiles in shining patches of shadow and light, glittering silver and turquoise beneath my feet.

And at the end of two hours, after I'd checked every level of the mall, wandering past windows or looking through the goods of every store, I rejoined my brother.

"Well, what'd you get?"

"Nothing," I said. "There wasn't anything I needed. But the floor was beautiful."

He looked at me like I was crazy and drove me home.

⊙⊙⊙

Daddy is asking me not to travel home slowly next summer after my three years are up. He thinks I'm gonna turn into a prostitute or a heroin addict if I travel the world. How can I tell my parents that I am and will continue to be a good kid and that traveling on my own won't make me less than that? It's hard to get across. Come home and work, he says. Until you can get enough money to travel in class, the way you're accustomed to, he says. The way I'm accustomed to is through miles of mud, skirting across the tops of steep, killer cliff faces in a speeding logging truck, with a trussed-up pig under my feet. It's hard to explain this to anyone. They don't get it, they can't. I don't think I can reenter this world of Amerika. I'm not sure I want to. I might hate it here.

— Journal, February 17, 1973

⊙⊙⊙

Memphis, Tennessee

Earlier, a raggedy and somewhat smelly man tried to
steal a ride on our bus and the driver had to physically
wrestle him off. The driver called for help to remove
him, and two guys lifted him up and tugged him off
the bus while the man hollered. Nothing like that ever
happened on any of my transportation adventures in
the Philippines—sordid and assorted as they've been.
America is weird in ways I'm not accustomed to.

— Journal, February 18, 1973

☉☺☉

The Memphis Bus Station was cavernous and cold, although warmer inside than it was outside. Big glass doors slid open too frequently, letting in blasts of cold air that circled my legs as I waited out the six-hour layover on my way to D.C. to visit an old Peace Corps friend during my home leave. If my bus could arrive in Washington on time, we were going to hear George McGovern speak.

It was a thirty-eight-hour journey from Dallas to Washington, which was easier than, for example, the forty-eight-hour ride from Butuan City to Davao, when we were stuck in the mud for half a day. But America was scary.

Memphis was a dark and dirty city, and all the downtown businesses were shut down on this dreary Sunday afternoon. I walked around town for a little bit, but there were too many scowling men loitering on the street, smoking, leaning against walls, and they didn't look friendly. The way their eyes followed me gave me the creeps. At least in the Philippines I was bigger than the rude, catcalling men; in Memphis, that wasn't the case. These guys were big.

I slid into the plush, old-style Peabody Hotel and had a sandwich and hot coffee. When I exited, there was a beggar by the door. He said he had $2 toward a $4 room for the night, and he asked for my help. I gave him a quarter, and he said that he appreciated it and grinned a toothless smile. Would he really spend the night on this cold street if he didn't get four dollars?

I returned to the bus terminal and watched the people inside. Sixty of them, I counted. Mostly they were shabbily dressed men, as if they'd just come in off the street to get warm. But there were conservatively dressed women too, with children at their knees or playing tag between benches. There were only three white people in the terminal, one older man, another woman, and me. And two white policemen near the door, watching people come in and go out, big guys with big bellies and guns. Did they make me feel safe? I wasn't sure. Why is this skin color thing such an issue? Why am I even noticing? Is it because there are no in-between browns? Is it because almost all the black men in the terminal seem so unhappy, grumpy, stressed, mean, or otherwise closed off? Why am I so uncomfortable? I'm accustomed to being the only white person in a crowd, to standing out, practically glowing with my whiteness, but this feels different. Am I imagining it?

I read. I wrote. I listened to buses being called. And a little bit before my bus was scheduled to board, I went to the restroom. I was in a stall when I heard another person enter and a stall door slammed. Then I heard moaning, and calling out to Jesus, and more moans and crying as I was washing my hands.

She called out, "Please, you, bring me my suitcase. It's just outside the door,"

"Yes, ma'm. I'll get it for you." It was a small hard leather suitcase, and I scooted it toward her stall. "Here it is. Can I help you?"

The woman opened the stall door just a crack and I could see she was a well-dressed black woman, older than I was, and there was blood everywhere.

"I can get someone. The policeman might help. Do you want me to call one?"

"No!" She was adamant. "I'll be okay. I just need some clean clothes. I thank you, just go on."

But I didn't leave. Not right away. "Are you sure? Maybe you need medical help. I could call."

"No, no, honey. I got what I need right here. You go on now."

"Yes ma'm, but I'm gonna wait here a little bit longer, to help you, if you need it."

"I'm fine, honey." She didn't sound fine.

They were calling my bus. "I gotta leave now," I said.

"You go on," she said again. "I'll be fine."

Should I tell the policeman anyhow? I didn't. I left her there. In the restroom. Alone. And that truly felt awful.

My bus loaded and I never saw her come out of the restroom. I wrote it. I can't stop thinking about her. I think I should have done something, but I didn't. I didn't want to bring in the white policeman any more than she did. It felt terrible, the whole thing. What should I have done? I'm not much help to anyone, not even in my own country let alone in the Philippines. I'm a failure all around.

I think she'd had a miscarriage. But maybe it was just an extra-heavy period. Maybe.

◉◎◉

America: I'm leaving again. I've realized during this home leave that I'm still an American, not an expatriate. I like America. I like being around Americans. I like being in a place where things work, on schedule, without fuss—like roads you can trust to be paved all the way to your destination. In America, you're not likely to come to an abrupt halt due to a washed-out bridge or mudslide or broken axle, where you sit for twelve hours while the driver tries to figure out what to do about it. There are no rifle-toting bandits along the American roads. And the amount of available food is staggering.

I like doing American things and laughing at American humor, but I don't like the plush living style. I don't like modern apartments with all that soft furniture. I don't like the televisions, always on, always stupid—except for the news. I do like hearing news that isn't skewed and full of half lies. I don't like the way groups of people are divided by skin color and the way different groups don't trust each other—based on what, pigmentation? I don't like how they called it "disgusting" when we sat in the restaurant next to two men who were holding hands beneath the table. What was disgusting was the way those men were being treated. It's not like that everywhere in the world, I tried to say. I tried to explain how things like that are easy and acceptable in places I'd been. I might as well have been reasoning with a loco jackrabbit.

I do like American hand lotion, tuna fish, toothpaste, and yogurt. I don't like America's fashion obsession. I do like having fewer pimples. I like the freedom of driving a car, having my own transportation. I don't like the cost of living and how truly poor some people are. Even though the poor in America have more money than their Philippine counterparts, somehow they seem poorer here. My new working hypothesis: In a place where everyone is poor, no one feels poor, they just feel, well, normal. Poverty can only be felt when you can easily compare yourself to others who have so much more and don't share.

I don't like how far Americans live from nature. The closest you get to nature is the backyard barbecue—the cement patio and the mimosa tree. No streams to do laundry in. In fact, in America, travelers can legally camp only in designated campgrounds. How ridiculous!

I do like house shoes, soft and warm, and solid floors that things don't fall through. I like leather, rather than straw, handbags. I like soft new lingerie, and panties without worn-out elastic.

I like music coming at me from all directions, all the time—radio in the car, stereo in the home, and even the live Neil Young concert I went to with my brother last weekend. It was fabulous! By the end, I was dancing in the aisle. The air was thick with marijuana smoke. Maybe I was high just from breathing.

Most of all I like my family and friends. We share many things. Thoughts. They listen. And they converse intelligently. We might not agree, and that seems okay. What seems most important to me now is mearly having the conversations.

Goodbye again, America.

—Journal, February 25, 1973

◉◉◉

Summoned by Imelda

The job will include marketing the handicrafts of ethnic tribes in the gift shop of the Museum of Traditional Culture at Nayong Pilipino, a showcase marketplace center of Filipino culture and crafts, near the airport in Manila. Before martial law, the Museum of Traditional Culture was doing a good business in traditional crafts, but now with the loss of tourism, business has fallen off. So we'll work on marketing and helping put together museum displays and other assignments that Manda wants us to do. He mentioned editing some manuscripts and organizing and cataloging the museum's large collection of artifacts from traditional minorities across the country. The museum has a big collection, but no

inventory or catalog—can you believe it! I'll be the one
creating an inventory system. It's all interesting work.
— Letter home, November 7, 1972

⊚⊚⊚

"Come on, go with me to this thing. There'll be a lot of good food."
I didn't really want to go, because it meant dressing up and spending
an evening being nice and making small talk with people I didn't care
about. But the prospect of free food finally won me over.

What I hadn't counted on was that something interesting would
happen. I met Manuel Elizalde, Manda for short. He was the Tourism
Minister in Ferdinand Marcos's government, and it was First Lady
Imelda Marcos and Manda Elizalde who had established the Philippine
Museum of Traditional Culture—an entire museum dedicated to the
lifestyles of the vanishing, traditional peoples of the Philippines.

With our extended stay among the Manobo of Madga, Janet and I
had already oozed past our original Peace Corps termination date by
nearly seven months, and a job at the Museum of Traditional Culture in
Manila would require a further extension. But the prospect of cataloging
traditional artifacts, documenting tribal stories, and preparing museum
displays was too interesting to pass up.

Janet and I were just back from home leave when word came down
from Manda: "Get ready. We're going to Imelda's house in Leyte. Prepare
for a three-week excursion."

We boarded Manda's yacht, a plush and comfortable cruise ship
with half a dozen staterooms, several open decks, and an outdoor movie
theater. The first night over a chef's spread of fried clams, lobsters, fish,
fruit, vegetables, and desserts, Manda told us more about the mission.

"We have been summoned," he said.

"Summoned?" Janet asked.

"Imelda has called us," he said, "and we go." The wife of President
Ferdinand Marcos, Imelda was all-powerful, and we knew it. "She is
hosting a party at her family home in Leyte. She is asking us to bring the
entertainment."

"What will we do?" I hoped I wouldn't have to sing.

"The museum will provide the dancing. Different dances from different ethnic traditions, different cultures."

"And where do we find these dancers?"

"We are on our way now to collect them. They will accompany us on board. Our first stop is tomorrow. Be ready to go ashore after lunch."

It was early afternoon when the yacht dropped anchor offshore from an unpopulated, white-sand beach encircling a bay whose water was a striking shade of translucent turquoise. The silence of the ocean seemed to hold the entire universe, gentle, calm, and unfathomably deep. Leaning over the side, I could see the sandy bottom—it didn't look far away, but I knew the clear water could be deceptive. It was probably thirty or forty feet deep.

"Can we go swimming?" Janet asked.

"Perhaps, in a while," Manda said.

A little later three sailors from the ship were in the water. "They are checking the water. If it is safe, you may go swimming, Janet. And are you ready to swim?" Manda asked me.

"No thanks, I'll just watch."

Janet changed into her swimsuit and hung on the wooden deck rail, waiting. "Now?"

Manda called down to the crew, still in the water. "Is it safe?"

"Aye," came the reply.

"Okay, Janet, you may swim now." I could hardly believe it, but she walked to the decking's open gate, set her toes on the edge of the ship, and took a flying headlong dive into the calm waters, hardly making a ripple as she broke the surface. She flew deep, then arced and resurfaced, sputtering and grinning.

"It's great! Come on in."

"Not a chance," I hollered down to her. Landlocked Texas girl that I'd been, I couldn't swim much. And I sure couldn't dive. The water was beautiful, but terrifying. Especially after Manda told me confidentially that the sailors would stay in the water as long as Janet did, watching for sharks.

"You mean, you sent them first, to see if there were sharks?"

"Yes, of course."

"What if there were sharks? What would you do?

"Well Janet would not be allowed to swim, of course."

"And the sailors?"

Manda shrugged and smiled, "Life at sea can be dangerous." Was he kidding?

A motorized dinghy was lowered from the port side of the ship to take Manda, Janet, and me ashore. A second dinghy followed, loaded with two sailors and a lot of fifty-pound bags of rice. We were barely ashore when people began to appear. The heads of the women were turbaned, and their dresses embroidered with black and gold thread. Their feet were bare, and they carried head-strap baskets loose and empty against their backs. Somehow—it seemed uncanny how quickly word spread—people heard about us and continued appearing from the tangles of inland vegetation. At first, there were just a few faces on the beach, mostly young people who had spotted our anchored yacht and came to investigate. Then there were more people, older, mostly women. By the time we had the first sacks of rice open on the beach, dozens had materialized. They held out tin cans, baskets, or gourds to hold the rice we scooped.

My job was to open the bags of rice and disperse it to the people. Three scoops of rice—about two pounds— "per family," we said. But actually, everyone got rice. Little children, old men and women, everyone. The more people who appeared, the more rice we scooped. Bend, scoop, and pour. Bend, scoop, and pour. It seemed unending. As the afternoon wore on, I began to feel woozie. My head ached and I was sneezing.

"You take it for a while," I told Janet. "I've got to sit down." With only one of us scooping, the pace slowed.

I sat in the shade that was slating across on a fallen coconut tree, took a few deep breaths, and felt better. I watched Janet scooping and pouring rice. She too was sneezing, demurely turning her head away to cough-sneeze every other scoop.

"It's the talc power in the rice," Ching told me. "You must be allergic."

"Oh, great."

"We'll get someone else to do it. You should rest." While I was resting, two little girls sidled up to me and shyly reached out to rub my arm. They whispered, then giggled. And I smiled back. I knew I was an unusual sight to them. Light skin. Brown, nearly blonde hair. Blue eyes. Long nose. Hairy arms and big feet.

I took a Juicy Fruit chewing-gum stick from my pocket, the last one remaining from my home-leave. "Want to try it? Sweet," I said in Tagalog. I knew it wasn't their main language, but they did seem to understand.

"Only chew. Don't swallow. Try?" I tore the chewing gum into three pieces, keeping one for myself and offering the girls one each. I showed them how to unwrap and chew it. They mimicked me. Chewing, giggling, hugging one another. After a few minutes, I saw them taking the gum from their mouth, examining it, and placing it back in their cheeks, still giggling.

The people with rice smiled gratefully and faded back into the forest.

Then in late afternoon, just at sunset, the dancers appeared. Dancers of the Magindanao people. Two men and two women sat at the shore on the downed coconut tree, talking with Manda. They gestured and talked, and I knew that Manda was telling them that he would take them on the big boat, they would dance in the Magindinao way at the home of Imelda Marcos in Leyte, and then he would return them to this coastline. He convinced them to bring their dancing implements and clothing and accompany us. They agreed, and in a little while a dinghy came to take them and their bundles aboard the yacht.

As the evening darkened, Janet and I boarded the last outboard dinghy for the ride back to the yacht that sat like a magical castle floating between the darkness of the sky and the clear depths of the ocean. The dinghy sliced through the water, sending a satin slip on either side of the bow and I couldn't keep my hand away. I leaned left and trailed my fingers through the water. Then I saw shooting stars—flecks of white lightning trailing out from each of my fingers.

"Look, Ching, stars!" I said.

He laughed. "Little plants of the ocean, food for tiny animals. They glow at night." Like stars scattering in our bow's wake, streaks of luminescence rushed and tumbled; I'd never seen anything so beautiful. I sat suspended between the night sky above—black and clear with infinite specks of stars—and vastness below—translucent silk shot through with streaming points of pure light. Truly, I'd been summoned to paradise.

⊙⊙⊙

So much is happening so quickly, it's hard to keep the threads straight. Just before home leave, we decided we'd had enough of this country, and we went Manila to terminate. But suddenly there was was this job offer, so after our home leaves Janet and I came back to Manila.

I really enjoy the Panamin people associated with the Museum of Traditional Culture. Manda Elizalde, he's the big boss. And there are Ching and Dave, but Amy, Aurora, Janet, and I do most of the actual work in the museum, and we have a great time together.

Ching, Manda's helicopter pilot, has become our personal chauffeur, running us around town, waiting with Manda's jeep while we go to doctor appointments and do shopping and banking. He's attentive and gallant, opening doors, carrying bundles, helping us up stairways, assisting us in and out of the jeep, as if we were fragile creatures. I can feel a problem brewing. It's come to the point that he's kissing our hands and he squeezed my arm, a bit much for me. I've never seen this hand kissing in any other part of Philippine society. He's half-kidding, but I sense a serious undertone. He does it to both Janet and me, while joking and laughing, and it makes me uncomfortable. His attentions are based on my skin and hair color; nothing to do with me, the actual person inside this skin. It feels like reverse discrimination—that is, I receive, on account of my skin color, not negative prejudice, but rather baseless, unwarranted positive perks and prejudice. It feels entirely icky. I think I'd rather get around town on the—exhausting!— bus.

— Journal, March 1973

⊙⊙⊙

Asparagus

I've been having some medical work done. The para-sitologist tells me I have hookworms and maybe round-worms too, lingering gifts from the mountains. He says these parasites along with general malnutrition were probably the reason I felt so bad my last days in Madga. I still feel rundown, depressed, and exhausted most of the time. I take a taxi to work instead of the bus. The taxi is expensive, but when I arrive at the museum after a fifteen-minute ride—instead of the hour-and-a-half bus adventure—I have enough energy to work through the day. I'm taking medicine now; I'll be better soon.

— Journal, November 10, 1972

◉◉◉

We spent days aboard Manda's yacht and only once did I gain a sense of our location among the hundreds of islands of Philippine archipelago. That was the day I asked to see the steering cabin and met the ship's captain. He was brusque, acting as if he didn't want to be bothered, and I stayed just long enough to look over the impressively large navigational chart on his huge oak desk. I'd never seen a map so detailed as this one. Islands, lots of them. Some were tiny specks, mere rock outcrops. Some were large and populated. A red pencil line tracked our route, south and eastward.

Each day, Manda's yacht anchored offshore at one island or another and more dancers and musicians got on board. They were the best dancers of their tribes. Beautiful people, lithe and sleek, with easy, open smiles. At night, they slept on the deck in silence beneath the stars. Manda left me a note, telling me to go into town when we docked at the next city to buy fabric—twelve bolts, any color, to make sleeping sacks.

"What's a sleeping sack," I asked Janet.

"Dunno. Just get the fabric and we'll find out." I got cotton fabric in the brightest colors I could find.

It took Janet and me a day and a half to make sleep sacks for the dancers already on board. Manda had a treadle sewing machine on the yacht, and Janet did the cutting while I did the sewing. Two yards of fabric stitched up the side to make a tube. I called this a *malong*, and I had already learned its practicality from the Moro Muslim culture in Mindanao. Here, we were calling it a sleep sack. At first, I made them hemmed at top and bottom, with a double row of stitching at the stressed side seam. But that took too long. The performers who did not yet have sacks were cold at night. So I started leaving them unhemmed and with a single row of side-stitching.

The performers stood in line, waiting for us to finish one sleep sack at a time. Their thanks were sincere, and we worked late trying to finish as many as possible before my head hurt and my shoulders ached. This must be what it feels like to work in a sweatshop, I thought. I hated how I didn't have time to produce the hemmed and double-stitched quality product I wanted to give them.

"Quit complaining," Janet told me. "Just keep sewing."

By the next afternoon, every performer had a sleep sack, and when

I walked across the deck after dark, I felt definite pride in the colorful cocoons that covered the deck. To me it didn't seem like much, a simple thin cotton bag against the chilly ocean breeze, but to the dancers and musicians, I sensed that it seemed like a lot.

"See. Just do what you can, and it's enough," Janet told me.

"Maybe." I said. But I knew these sleep sacks would have a life in the homes of the dancers long after this voyage, and I wanted them to last. Double stitching would have helped. It's a character flaw of mine, I guess. Unrealistically high expectations.

By the time we'd stopped at half a dozen islands, Manda's yacht was full of colorful dancers and musicians. People were everywhere, sixty or eighty dancers. It felt as though Janet and I had dispersed tons of rice to hungry, coastal villagers and made enough sleep sacks to outfit an army.

At last we docked at the island of Leyte, at a neatly maintained pier near a Western-style plantation home. Imelda's house was sprawling and painted a spotless white, with a grassy lawn rolling from the ocean up to a wide veranda. It was unlike any home I'd ever seen in the Philippines, more like something out of New England.

For three days, the dancers and musicians rehearsed, at first onboard the yacht and later on the broad, grassy lawn. Brass gongs. Bamboo and bone flutes. Hollow gourds. Bamboo jaw harps and brass ankle bracelets. Each group was different, and each was wonderful.

I watched the t'Boli women of southern Mindanao, who wore brass rings on their ankles. When they danced, they stepped together, a synchronized clatter that made music on the wind. "It's a woman's beauty, you know," Ching told me. "Her sound. More important than how she looks is how she sounds." I nodded, hearing the beauty and understanding how it could be so.

At night, Manda showed movies on the big outdoor screen on the ship's deck. Most of dancers and musicians had never seen a movie. And they weren't disappointed, even though it was an old John Wayne western, in English. They hooted and hollered and laughed, as if they understood. And maybe somehow they did.

The day of the performance, the groups rehearsed, and I watched, leaning across the white rail fence near the kitchen.

"What do you think? Will she like it?" It was Manda, and he was looking worried.

"Sure she will." Then I thought again. We were talking about Imelda Marcos, certainly accustomed to the finest of the fine things of life. I liked the rustic dances, the stomping and turning steps, the tuneless music and the rough-cut dancers with betel-stained teeth and calloused hands and broad bare feet. But would Imelda and her Western guests be impressed? "I mean, I guess she'll like it. Probably so," I amended.

Manda looked more worried than ever as he walked away.

The show was to start just after dark, and it was nearly sunset. Janet and I were standing outside Imelda's kitchen when the door opened and a Filipina wearing a frilly white apron stepped toward us with a silver platter in her hand.

"You have been here all afternoon. You must be hungry. Would you like some asparagus?" She held the platter up to us. Janet and I looked at one another. Asparagus?

"Go ahead. It is for you," she said setting the platter on a table.

"Asparagus?" said Janet. "I've never seen asparagus in this country."

"I've never tasted asparagus before, even back home," I admitted.

"You're kidding!"

"Well no. I mean it's not the sort of thing my family would eat. But I've heard of it, of course."

"Well here it is." She took the limp stalk into her mouth. "Canned, Green Giant asparagus. Not the fresh kind. But good. Just the way I remember it. What do you think?"

The shoot hung limp between my fingers and I sucked slightly to get it into my mouth. It was a rich flavor, salty but sweet, and the texture was pudding-like. "Asparagus, huh? Pretty good." And we each took seconds. And thirds.

"It will make your pee smelly and green," Janet warned.

"What are you talking about?"

"You'll find out tomorrow morning."

That night, colored theater lights shone upon the lawn as Imelda's guests gathered. Van Cliburn the American master pianist was there. And a European princess, regal in a long sweeping dress and uplifted blond hair. There was Imelda looking darkly beautiful in the old Spanish style. And me, standing in the night shadows by the kitchen. In the black sky, the stars glittered like fairy lights. The ocean lapped gently, and ocean breezes whispered wizardry.

Magic happened as the music of the earth itself came forth. Rattles, gongs, shell whistles, gourds, bells. The dancers—these rustic island people—became something other than themselves. They floated above the earth, turning on the breeze with gossamer scarves and feathered wings. I forgot to breathe. I was so proud of these simple people, hanging on to traditions at a time when the old ways were vanishing. That night at Imelda's house, the earth sang of herself and the people of the earth danced her heartbeat.

The next day we heard that the First Lady and her guests thought the show was wonderful. I'm glad you liked it, Imelda. And thanks for the asparagus.

◉◉◉

Martial law still impacts us, mostly with the curfew. You have to be off the street between midnight and four a.m. or you'll get arrested. There are a few other martial law restrictions, but for the most part, they don't affect me or my work. But yesterday, I heard that the government announced that no photographic film can leave the country. The government thinks photographs might be subversive. I recently sent you some rolls of slides I took when we went to Imelda's country home for a dance program with traditional dancers from all over the country. I took a lot of pictures. Please write immediately and let me know when/if those rolls of exposed film arrive! If they get there, go ahead and have them processed, and I'll see them someday, I hope.
— Letter home, November 13, 1972

◉◉◉

They Call It Love

*I'm surrounded by loveless "love," this morass of
meaningless male mush, mired in the quicksand of the
Spanish-inspired macho world view. It is such a pervasive world view in this place that I'm beginning to think
I'm the sick one. It's time to leave this country, if for no
other reason than to save my sanity.*

— Journal, December 4, 1972

⊙⊙⊙

Janet popped into a bakery to pick up some bread while Ching and
I waited in the jeep.

"I have something I shouldn't tell you, but I must," he whispered
breathlessly.

"What is it, Ching?" I cringed. I'd felt it coming since he squeezed my arm.

"I know you will be angry, but I love you. I've always loved you. Are you angry?"

Jeez! Here is an over-forty *married* man professing his "love" for me. I knew it was lust, wanting to sleep with a white girl. It depressed me. Ching was a man I'd hoped was a friend and now I had to avoid him.

What would have happened if I'd been the one to hop out of the Jeep and go into the bakery. He probably would have professed his love for Janet. That's how deep I felt his "love" was.

Then Ching said, "Please stay in Manila, for me," as though I would change my life for him. The only change I intended was avoidance.

I tried to explain that I wasn't ready for a relationship, that I wanted to travel. Keep it simple, I told myself. Be nice, he's not a bad guy, just so, so...Filipino. I'd been learning the hard way what that meant.

First there'd been Jun. Jun's friend Charlie was courting Janet, so Jun came to hang around me. He was a small man, slightly older than me and probably fifty pounds lighter. He had a notable mole on his cheek, a black orb with a single very long black hair— three inches at least— growing from it. And he'd stroke that hair as though it were a favorite kitten. He also had fingernails on his thumb, index finger, and pinkie also three-inches long. It must have been impossible for him to use those fingers, and that was the point—a sign of affluence; he didn't work with his hands. I found these oddities gross, but I was trying to keep an open mind about cultural differences. Jun was rich, a crony of Marcos, and when we went dancing with Charlie and Janet, we went to the best clubs in Manila.

Riding in his car, I noticed the dashboard, embossed with photographs of a little boy, and the name Sweetie. "Oh, that's my sister. And my little brother," he told me. I was no longer as naive as I'd once been. I knew it was his wife and child.

Later on, in Manila, I met a nice Filipino fellow named Denny. He was rich, funny, and not pushy. He had a sinus condition that made his eyes tear when he sang. I found him endearing. We dated.

On our first date, he took me to meet his grandmother, an eighty-seven-year-old *lola* in the old Spanish style. She was a beautiful relic of the last century, when Spanish family breeding signaled prosperity and class. Even in her own home, she wore the formal Maria Clara puff-sleeve blouse, a long, embroidered skirt, and handmade embroidered slippers, and she walked with a silver cane. She commanded a host of household servants and had little to say to me, but when I spoke to her in Tagalog, a half-smile cracked her deeply wrinkled face. The rest of her was pure crust. The grandmother I liked. Denny I wasn't sure about.

Denny lived in a Western-style house behind high cement walls. In his workroom were gambling tables with green felt tops, and several slot machines.

"What do you do with these things?" I asked.

"Oh, I fix them."

"Isn't gambling illegal in the Philippines?

"Oh yes. They are for collectors."

On another date some time later, Denny said it was time for me to meet his friends. "It's a special place here in Manila," he told me.

We pulled up alongside a low windowless building with peeling paint. The parking lot was full. Denny guided me down a dim alleyway to a thick mahogany door. He knocked. A peephole slid open, a pair of eyes peering from behind it. Then the door creaked open, a dim streak of smoky light exposing a narrow passageway.

"Denny, welcome," said a butter-smooth female voice. "And I see you have a guest. Come in." In the blue-gray smoke, I saw dozens of people hovering beside green felt-topped tables. In one corner, a roulette wheel rattled. In another was a dice game and a cheering crowd. In the middle was dance floor beside a low stage where a four-piece combo played a smooth Frank Sinatra song.

"Shall we dance?" he asked.

"Um, okay. But Denny, I thought gambling was illegal in the Philippines."

"Oh yes. We do not gamble tonight. We dance."

"But how is it that …"

"Relax. We can enjoy the evening here."

About an hour later, a man tapped Denny on the shoulder and whispered something. Then Denny said, "We should be leaving soon."

"Why?"

He gathered my purse and handed it to me. "We should leave. I have something else to show you this evening."

"You mean now?" I asked as he guided me toward a back entrance.

"Yes, *now*." Others were leaving too. There was a calm exodus as the clientele of elegantly dressed men and women headed for doorways.

We got in his car and drove away. "Denny, I don't understand. What was that place? Why was everyone leaving all at once?"

He sighed and told me. "In a few minutes, the police will arrive. It is better if there is no one in the building. You understand, yes?"

"You know that the police are coming? How?"

"My friend told us. You saw."

"But how did he know?"

Denny looked at me with a sideways grin and shrugged, "It is Manila."

I was beginning to get the picture. "Denny, you do more than repair tables and pinball machines for collectors, don't you?"

"I am a simple repairman. No more," he said with shrug and grin. I knew he wouldn't tell me the truth.

That night he drove me to San Lorenzo Village, a swank residential section of Manila's wealthiest families—mansions behind walled fortresses, swimming pools, security guards, and mastiff dogs. He stopped on the outskirts in front of an open piece of land. It overlooked a sparkling night cityscape.

"My dearest, I am now buying this piece of land. What do you think of it?"

"Here? Will you build a house?"

"Yes. It will be a very nice house. A house you would like to live in, I think. What about you, would you like to live here with me? Would you marry me? I can make you comfortable, I swear."

I could hardly think of anything I would less like. Entrapped in high-society Manila. Kept behind walls. And with a person I barely liked and didn't trust. I tried to respond tactfully.

"That is very kind, Denny, but I want to travel. I want to see the world before I settle down."

"Tell me about what you would like to do," he said. It was practically the first time he'd asked anything about my own dreams and goals.

"I would like to buy a Volkswagen bus and travel all over the United States. Maybe up to Canada and Alaska. Maybe down to Mexico. Maybe drive all the way to the tip of South America. I want to see how people live in different places. I want to explore and think about the world before I settle down."

"I could go with you. We could be together."

"No, Denny." What I couldn't articulate was that I was seeking a relationship in which my partner and I would be equals, where conversations were truthful, where we built our dreams together. No secrets. It would be real love based on mutual trust. I sensed that Denny wouldn't know what I was talking about even if I'd tried to say those things. That kind of love simply didn't exist in this society, where upper-class marriages were made for political or social expedience and where secrecy, extramarital affairs for men, and gilded cages for trophy women were the norm.

Denny and I had one final date at a swank nightclub in the basement of a highrise hotel. A many-faceted mirrored ball circled slowly from the ceiling and streaks of colored lights ricocheted from black walls. A woman in a pewter colored silken evening gown perched on a tall stool before a microphone. As we entered, she said breathily in Tagalog, "Good evening, Denny. I see you have brought a lovely companion."

Naturally, I understood this comment. I responded in Tagalog, loud enough for her to hear. "The singer is also very lovely." The singer smiled and Denny beamed. I knew he was proud of my modest ability to speak the language.

"I will sing your request," she said to me in Tagalog. "What will it be?"

To tell the truth—and I didn't want to let her know—I wasn't all that fluent in Tagalog, the language of Manila, and I could think of only one Tagalog song. It was a love song, probably the most popular Tagalog song in the country, titled "Dahil sa Iyo," Because of You. While she sang, Denny held my hand, looked deeply into my eyes, and whispered the words to me. "Because of you... until I die ... there will be no other..." He's taking this song way too seriously, I thought.

We danced and dined our way through the evening. "Hadn't we better be leaving soon?" I asked. "It's eleven o'clock, and you'll have a long drive home before the midnight curfew."

"It's okay," Denny said. "Don't worry. We have time yet."

At 11:30, I was really worried. "Denny. It's very late. We've both got to get home. Let's go."

"Just a moment more," he said. "Soon."

At a quarter to midnight we walked to the car. "Come on, Denny. We've really got to hurry. You don't want to be on the streets after midnight. Hurry!"

We drove, but Denny seemed to be taking an odd route. It was five minutes until curfew when he said, "We must change our plans. There is not time to take you home."

"What do you mean, change plans?"

He drove another block then pulled the car down a long dark driveway to a dead end with a half dozen open garage doors. He pulled into one and the door rolled shut behind us.

"What? Where are we?"

"It is safe here. You see, it is midnight already. We cannot be out on the streets now."

"Whose garage is this?"

"It's a place we can rest. Come with me."

We walked up a small, dimly lit flight of stairs into a two-room suite painted in shades of dull mustard. In the outer room was a modest wooden table, two upright chairs, and a red plastic-covered love seat. In the room beyond, I saw a bed.

"Denny, this is a hotel?"

"Yes. A place for us to stay for the night. Together." He took my hand, pulled me toward him and kissed me. It was a tender kiss, warm and gentle.

"Denny. I'm not going to sleep with you, if that's what you have in mind."

"But my dearest, I love you. I am in anguish for you. You are so beautiful." He reached for my blouse. It was my favorite blouse, sent by my mom from home, stylish, red polyester with a big brass zipper in front. He yanked at the zipper.

"Denny! No! I won't!" I said.

"Why not? Do you not love me as I love you?" He was cajoling, sweet, a man in pain.

"I like you, Denny. I don't know if I love you. I can't sleep with you, I just can't."

"But why not? You are not a virgin."

He said it as if he knew it for a fact. I looked at him, for he had indeed hit upon my secret. I wasn't proud of it. In 1973, in the era of free love, it was hardly conceivable that a twenty-four-year-old girl would still be a virgin. In fact, I was.

I looked at him and nodded.

"You are not a virgin! You can't be. You are an American!" He was aghast, sure that he must be right.

I looked at him with tears in my eyes, and he saw that I was telling the truth.

Then he laughed loud and long.

I was crushed. Not only did he now know my secret, but he was laughing at me.

He became conciliatory. "I will be very gentle with you. I love you. I know what to do. Believe me, I will not hurt you." He tugged gently at the zipper of my blouse.

"No, Denny!" I said, turning away from him. In that instant I knew that not only did I not want to sleep with him, I was quite sure I did not love him, and I had just decided that I didn't even like him. Not one bit.

I sat in a chair. He sat alone on the plastic love seat.

"Look," he said after a long while, defeated, like a little kid who had been reprimanded. "We must stay here until morning. We may as well sleep. We can share the bed. I promise I won't touch you."

"No."

"We cannot sit here all night."

"You sleep then. I'll sit here." A little while later he went into the bedroom and shut the door. I heard the toilet flush.

He opened the bedroom door again. "Do you want to use the toilet? I promise, I won't touch you."

"No. You stay in there. I'll stay out here." I left no room for negotiation.

He closed the door to the bedroom and a while later I heard him snoring. I lay tucked into a ball on the too-short love seat, the plastic cover sticking to my arms. My bladder was aching. I ignored it. I pulled my blouse up tight to my neck, held on to the brass ring of the zipper with both hands, and cried. For getting myself into this situation. For the anger at Denny, and anger at myself for being so stupid. For knowing nothing about sex. And mostly, for being a virgin.

As curfew lifted at four in the morning, just before the first hints of gray morning streaked the eastern sky, Denny took me home.

For many days, I didn't hear from him. I was relieved. Then one day I saw him again. He told me that his former girlfriend had suddenly showed up in Manila, pregnant, with his baby, or so she'd said. The girl's brother was after Denny with a shotgun. Even though guns were illegal in the entire country, it was, after all, the Philippines. Denny didn't want to marry her, so he'd gone into hiding, which is why he hadn't come to find me, he said.

Now the girlfriend had returned to her family in Iloilo City, and Denny told me he still wanted to marry me. "Because you are so beautiful, so fat," he said with admiration in his voice.

Ah, and he was so … well, not wrong, he was merely being Filipino, a reflection of the way he saw the world of men and women. I told him I wasn't interested, that I had found another special friend. I didn't tell him that the special friend was my very own self, and that was how I liked it. Alone. Forever. And fine with it.

◉◉◉

Janet and I went to visit an American military friend on Clark Air Base. We decorated the Christmas tree in his home and had a party with his friends. We went dancing on base Friday night. I met nice American guys who were bigger than me, and who asked questions about the real me, the inside person, beyond the white skin—white skin was, of course, no big deal to them. I loved the feeling of dancing with a guy who was taller and weighed more than I did. I rode in a big car with air conditioning. I went running and swinging and sliding on a kids' playground at night and no one cared. I got lost in the crowd at a movie and restaurant. I sat in the sun in a backyard, in a lawn chair, and no one came out to tell me

I would get dark and ugly. I ate apples and real chocolate chip cookies and Dr Pepper, a ham sandwich and Fritos! And a gigantic Christmas dinner with an actual turkey and dressing and all the side dishes including exquisite homemade Christmas cookies—stars and bells and elves and Santa hats. I got compliments on the way I looked, without being told I was fat.

— Journal, December 20, 1972

◎◉◎

We went dancing at the fancy club at the Manila Hilton, and we met some US military guys who invited us to come with them the next day, they'd take us on board the USS Coral Sea. It's an American aircraft carrier that has been in Vietnam but is in Manila for rest and repairs. This was an amazing ship! Huge! There are about 3,000 American guys on this ship, and it felt like a city. Our new friends walked us around, and we saw the engines and the sleeping bunks, and most impressive was the cooking and dining rooms—there was an immense mixing and baking kitchen! But most impressive to me, was sitting at a table and drinking milk. Real American milk! Cold, deeply rich, entirely wonderful. I haven't had milk in nearly three years! And, by the way, the American boys who took us around were entirely polite and respectful and funny and interesting.

— Journal, December 1972

◎◉◎

I've been told more than once (generally by shady old men) that I could make a lot of money in the Philippines by selling myself. For a white American virgin, for one night, they say, the price could be in the thousands of American dollars. I have to admit, I gave it a couple of seconds' consideration. For that amount of money, I could travel slowly and comfortably for a long time. But I'm not sure could get past the part where I would puke my guts out on that "special evening." I'm just not cut out for that kind of entrepreneurship.

— Journal, January 1973

◉◉◉

In the Movies

*The story is about sea people—mutants—and their king
and princess. The king is trying to get the princess to
mate to continue the race, but she doesn't want to. Almost
everyone in their clan is killed, and a handsome outsider
triumphs with the beautiful princess. Our eyes kept popping off, so they glued them on with nail polish. There
was only a pin-prick of a hole through which we could
see anything, so we extras were mostly working blind and
kept bumping into each other. The comedy behind the
cameras would probably be a better movie than the hokey
story that will make its way onto the silver screen.*

— Journal, December 4, 1972

◉◉◉

"A fuzzy brown bikini and a pair of bulgy eyeballs? Is that all I'm supposed to wear?" I was dubious. It wasn't like me to be in a movie wearing next to nothing. But there was an incentive.

A chance encounter in an elevator in an upscale Manila apartment got Janet and me into the movie business. Janet had shared the down elevator with a Filipina scout for a local film company. They needed light-skinned extras, so Janet volunteered us.

"How much money do we get?" I asked.

"A hundred pesos a day. Three hundred each if we do all three days. What do you say? It'll be fun. Easy work." My Peace Corps living allowance was ₱450 a month, so the pay for working in the movie seemed extravagant.

"Are you sure it's legal for us to do this? Have you checked it out with the Manila Peace Corps office?"

"Are you crazy? Of course we're not supposed to do this, or at least not take the money for doing it. But who's looking? Come on, it's just one weekend! Nobody's gonna know."

It wasn't that the work was hard, but the costume for this movie was positively ludicrous. The fuzzy brown bikini was bad enough, but the eyes!

"How do you keep these things on?" I asked.

"Squint. Like a monocle."

Squinting didn't work. The big eyes popped out as the camera rolled.

"*Cut.* Fix those eyeballs!" the director hollered. Someone had the idea to glue them on.

"You gotta be kidding. I'm not putting glue near my eyes!"

"Okay, try this," a wardrobe assistant said, brushing nail polish around the lip of the eyeball cup then sticking them around my eyes. They stayed. Peering out through the tiny peephole in the shell eyes, I watched the cameras roll. The eyeballs stayed so well that I had trouble peeling them off and had red raccoon circles around my eyes for a day.

This has got to be the stupidest movie of all time, I thought. *Sea People* was the filming name, but they told me *Beyond Atlantis* would be the release title. Far beyond, I thought, as if any respectable sea person would wear a fuzzy bikini. Utterly impractical for swimming.

"You're too picky," Janet said. "You're getting paid three hundred pesos for this. Relax. It's campy. Funny."

"For you, maybe. I don't look like you do in this fuzzy suit." They didn't have to tell me I was fat. The director told the cameraman, "This one, from the waist up. We'll shoot over her shoulder." Janet got the full body shot. I got the blonde-hair, back-of-the-shoulder shot.

But three hundred pesos was significant. Living in Manila, I didn't have much left over at the end of the month. And if I travelled slowly back to America, taking months as I'd planned, I would certainly be needing a lot more money than I'd been able to save from my monthly Peace Corps stipend.

I made a lot of movies during those months. I learned about how movies are made and how personalities sometimes clash. I saw how some people take the work seriously, and others don't. I learned the art of waiting—waiting for setup, for costumes, for action. I hung with the set photographer who gave me 35mm camera lessons. "Get in close," he told me. "Use a tripod," and he showed me how. "Stop action at a sixtieth of a second or faster. Use the right lens for the shot you want," and he showed me the differences among his lenses.

During shooting for *Beyond Atlantis*, I watched the tryouts for the spear death scene. One of us extras tried out, got the role, and bonus pay. "You've got one take to do this," the director said. "Your blood pack will break and your costume is shot. So make it good."

The spear was on a line attached to the extra's back, and there was a packet of "blood," vegetable dye, in a plastic packet inside the shaft of the spear. The actor ran, the spear was sent whooshing down the line straight to his back where it thudded into his padded suit, the packet ruptured, the blood flowed, making quite a mess, and our guy died with flourish. He arched his back, bucked forward, collapsed over a rail, and fell to the ground. He died with such pizzazz that we applauded him when he rejoined our team of extras.

Sid Haig played a bad guy in this movie. "He's the king of the B's," the photographer told me. "He's made a million of them."

"What's a B?" I asked.

"Filmed on a budget. Not the best writing or acting. But Sid is the best. Just watch him."

Sid Haig was the only character with speaking lines to come over and spend time with us extras. He was tall and thickly built, bald, and had what my mom would call bad skin, pock holes and scars from ancient acne. But he was charming, with open friendliness and a sincere, wide grin. I liked him.

"He's scary looking, but kind of nice," I whispered to my photographer friend.

"Sure thing. He's the king."

And Janet had been correct—working in the movies may have been repetitive, boring, and uncomfortable, but it wasn't hard. So, for a little while during our last weeks in Manila, we took movie jobs on nights and weekends. Once I sat on a tourist bus, Western-style with padded seats, glass windows, and air conditioning. On cue I got up, walked to the front, exited down the steps and— this was my big part—I walked to the right. The starring actress in this scene was at the bus doorway, twirling and peering around, looking expectantly for someone. I was just one face in a crowd. Then the director called for retakes.

"Don't look at the camera," he shouted at us extras. "Keep your eyes down!"

So we kept our eyes down.

"Don't look down so much. Look around, just don't look at the camera." We did it again. "Too slow, move faster." We did it again, trying to get out of the bus in a hurry. "Don't push each other, just walk normally." We did it again. "Normal doesn't mean slow. Hurry up, people!" We did it again. And again. And again.

The next movie was on an airplane. We began shooting at sunset. But nighttime or not, it was unbearably hot aboard that jet on the Manila International Airport tarmac. They wanted an international-looking group of passengers, so I sat on an aisle seat and the camera made one pass along the aisle. I sweated. They passed out water. They took the scene a dozen times. I was about to vomit from the heat when they let us go home.

Each day of shooting I became a hundred pesos richer. I was an inmate in a women's prison camp. I was filmed in the dining hall for a giant food-fight. They gave us a plate of corned beef hash, which we were supposed to throw. I ate some; I couldn't stand the waste after being in Madga, where food was in such short supply, where a can of corned beef was a week's ration of protein. After the food-fight scene, I had a chance to read the script. There was a sex scene involving a shower and a hose nozzle. Even though it wasn't my scene and the camera guy assured me it would be filmed in private, I felt uncomfortable.

"Why do you do movies like this?" I asked one of the two female leads.

"It pays the bills. This movie isn't as bad as some." But it was bad enough for me. I quit that movie.

Eventually I realized I wasn't cut out for the movies. I was self-conscious and hated the long down times when all I could do was wait for the next setup. And there was something ethically troubling about using my white skin to make more money than the Asian extras who were paid only half as much. "Supply and demand," Janet laughed. "Just enjoy it."

By the end of my movie career, I had saved enough pesos to turn into several hundred extra American dollars. I was going to need it. I would be heading back on a freighter ship via Micronesia, spending months visiting Peace Corps volunteers on tiny remote atolls across the Pacific. I didn't know it then, but it would be more than a year before I would finally touch American soil in Honolulu. Those movie dollars underwrote a year's travel.

◉◉◉

1973 has come. I'm still in this crazy country, and I'll be 25 this year. I still have no particular accomplishments to my credit, no revelations, no character. I'm caught by conventions, materialism, shyness, and I'm anchored in this inconveniently overweight body.
— Journal, January 1, 1973

◉◉◉

We've been traveling in Mountain Province, and I've been paying special attention to the women who do weaving on the backstrap looms in this part of the country. In Banaue, where we were visiting friends, there was a lady weaving beside the road, and I went to talk with her. Long story short, I now have my own back-strap loom! The pieces of the loom, the sticks and twine, were easy to purchase in the village. The hard part was finding the strap, and I ended up with one that still has cow hair attached. It's not as soft and supple as older ones that are broken in, but it will work fine for now. My mentor is going to help me warp the loom and get it set up to weave. Even though this project is costing a lot and will be a lot of work, I'm so excited!

— Journal, January 3, 1973

Farewell Philippines

Shortly after home leave, Janet and I moved in with Mimi Davis, an agriculture volunteer in Manila. Her apartment is great—three air-conditioned rooms, two bedrooms and a kitchen/dining room. There's a refrigerator and a sink with cold (no hot, of course) running water, a two-burner stove, and a telephone (though it's not connected). The bath has a working (cold) shower and a flush toilet, and even linoleum flooring. We're on the second floor of a professional building, and this suite used to be a doctor's office. Janet and I share a bedroom. I sleep on top of what was the padded examination table, and Janet sleeps on a mat on the floor. The building has a full-time security guard. And the old, Spanish-style Malate Church (Our Lady of Remedies) is right across

the street. I can see it from the window, and the tower
bells ring every morning at 6 a.m.
— Letter home, March 3, 1973

⊙⊚⊙

There are problems in our apartment. I was coming
in the door and found a building security guard on his
way out of our apartment. He was carrying a tooth-
brush—with a smear of my recognizable (stateside,
from home leave, white with red stripes!) toothpaste on
it. And it was on Mimi's toothbrush! Explain that! Is
he brushing his teeth with our goods, then putting the
toothbrush back?!?! Also, I seem to be missing Tampax,
which I had to bring back from home leave because they
don't have them in this country (because they think
using Tampax makes a girl lose her virginity... geez!)
Does this security guy really need my Tampax? So I've
been locking my valuables and my not-so-valuables
inside my zippered duffle, but it's a hassle. I'm certainly
not going to report the incident—report to who—the
security guards??!! There are constant shenanigans
such as this across the whole culture. So typical and so
entirely irritating. I'm exhausted.
— Journal, April 4, 1973

⊙⊚⊙

It wasn't an easy exit. But I was finally aboard the freighter the
MV Gunners Knot, steaming from Manila Bay southward through the
Philippine archipelago. I stood at the rail on the upper deck, feeling
the clammy salt breeze. This would be the last chapter of my tangled
adventures with Peace Corps Philippines, and I felt as alone as I did the
first day of staging in Philadelphia.

I sat on the deck chair, journal on my lap, remembering and writing
about my last day in Manila. I'd called to see if the ship was in port and if

it would indeed take me as a passenger from Manila to Saipan. Yes, I was told by Mr. Vic Arlee, and that the fare would $90 American.

"Wow. That's a lot." Good thing I'd made extra money in the movies. "Is there any chance I could wash dishes or something, for a reduced fare?"

"Come to the office, and we can discuss it."

So I went. Mr. Arlee said, "Yes, there is a possible discount. Come to lunch with me and I will tell you about it."

It sounded fishy, but I met him at the Bayview Hotel Coffee Shop and we took a table near the window. I watched the traffic on the street while Mr. Arlee laid out his deal.

"We could make arrangements, if you are not in a hurry," he said, staring deeply in my eyes.

"What do you mean?" I thought I might know, but then, didn't want to jump to conclusions based on past experiences.

"Well, I know that you are a wonderful girl. I have been trying three times to marry, but I am still a bachelor."

Sure, I thought. This guy is lying.

"I am thinking that next time the boat comes through, you may have free passage, if you, well, if you will stay with me…" and he tilted his head with a leering glare.

I tried not to guffaw in his face, but really, I was no longer a novice at the Filipino-man stuff. I should have known. I tried not to be too rude, because I would still need that ticket. "No, I am in a hurry."

"You know," he continued, "I understand your impatience. I am planning a trip to the States soon. My business will take me to Baton Rouge. That's near your place, Texas, isn't it?"

"Yes, it's near. But I'm planning to continue my studies when I get back. I will be going to school in"—think quick—"Montreal, Canada."

"Ah. I would like to meet your parents."

"They are retiring. Moving to Maine. So sorry, Mr. Arlee." I wanted to scream, *Leave me alone,* but I also wanted to get a ticket on his freighter.

"Then you seem sure there is no hope for us?"

"Yes, I am sure." I was beyond sure.

"Are you certain?" He got a teary look.

"Yes, I will return to your office later in the day to pay the full ticket price. Goodbye, Mr. Arlee."

When I got to his office at three, Mister Arlee was behind the desk. He was still plying me with, "Stay with me in Manila." I must have made him angry, because he looked at my papers and told me I didn't have the proper clearances. Although I was exempt from needing certain departure documents, he suddenly demanded the application for exemption.

So I complied, catching an expensive taxi and rushing to another office across town. It was late, but I talked my way in using my best Tagalog, got it, and rushed back to get my ticket from Mr. Arlee.

I did a few last-minute errands, and by sunset I was aboard the ship. Who should be waiting for me there but Mr. Arlee.

"I will take you to dinner tonight," he offered. "After all, it is your final night in our country. Please accept."

To tell the truth, I hadn't had a meal all day, I was hungry, and it was dark, and it definitely was not a good time for me to walk out alone along the Manila docks. And since I had just found out that the ship would not feed me until we actually departed, I had no other option.

Mr. Arlee took me to a dark, cavelike night spot where we had another round of, "Are you sure you will not stay the night at my place? I will bring you to the ship in the morning." Finally, just after 8 p.m., he returned me to Pier One, Berth 13 where I spent the evening writing in my journal:

> My little stateroom is quite pleasant. There are two bunks, a fan, and a little bathroom with a shower and toilet. The plumbing seems to work and there is even hot water in the shower. What luxury! I find that I am the only passenger aboard this freighter—and the only woman, of course. Through my porthole, I have a stunning view of piles of lumber and pallets of cement headed for Saipan.

Midmorning the freighter departed Manila Bay, and we headed south and east, across the Pacific toward Micronesia. It would take a week to get to Saipan. I stood on the deck leaning against the cold, iron railing, watching dolphins twirl in the spray off the ship's bow. In the distance

I spotted Mayon Volcano, a steep symmetrical cone rising nearly 8,000 feet. The turquoise ocean, the green peaceful islands beneath a too-blue sky, it seemed picture-postcard perfect. But I knew better.

How I hated this country. I could hardly wait to be in a place where logic is logical, where I could eat lettuce and have ice in my soda, where men didn't pee in the street, where a pet dog wasn't a four-footed feast, where I could be invisible in a crowd and find a pair of shoes that fit. I was sick of ignorance and the acceptance of ignorance. Of politicians and armies that abuse power, and at regular folks who shrug and say, "It's the will of God," and never jump up and holler at social injustice. I was exhausted from unwillingly playing the role of sex goddess. This country was too hot, too heavy, and too deceptive. Had it really taken me three years to discover how much I truly hated this place?

The breeze lifted my hair, and I adjusted the band that held it out of my eyes.

Then I remembered my last look at Manila's dazzling Luneta fountain changing colors in the evening drizzle, and the couples holding hands, and I thought I might miss this country a little. I remembered my last *kalamansi* lemonade drink, my last conversations with local friends, my last walk alongside the vast whispering ocean. The over-sized moon through palm trees. The giggles and good times with my co-teachers. Cold showers on hot afternoons, and sweet rice cakes and roasted corn and warm chicken-rice soup. I remembered all the shy smiles of all the kids, their bright eyes, and how they listen, learn quickly, and laugh with their whole beings. I remembered all the kind acts toward me by total strangers and the respect that had been given me as a young foreign teacher.

No, the Philippines isn't all bad. I looked south, toward the islands far from the city. Somewhere over that horizon were my Manobo kids. And the people who were managing to hang on to their old ways of life. There is something honorable and true about the old river life of Madga. I'd found disease and hunger and death there, but also balance and a calmness of spirit. There is a truth in the mountains, in places like Madga, the lands that time has passed by, with simple people, clean rivers, and deep forests. Those places and those people held my heart.

I whispered into the wind in the language that was once such a challenge, but now came so easily. "Okay, Philippines, I'm leaving now. I wonder if I'll return. Maybe when I'm older and have money and independence and a fresh supply of courage. Maybe someday I'll return to see your green mountains and upland rivers and endless turquoise ocean—and your children. The kids of this place, your Littles, they are the best part of you. The mountain kids. The lowland kids. The ones with bright eyes and curiosity and so much love in their open hearts. Because of them, there may still be hope for you. Maybe."

The ocean breeze lifted a hank of my hair, fluttered open the pages of my journal, and salted my skin. My ballpoint pen fell to the deck and rolled toward the ocean. I stopped it with my foot.

"Enough already," I said. "Farewell, Philippines."

This, for Janet. I'll send a copy to her next time I can send out mail. Maybe in a week or so.

She will know. She will remember these things too.

> Teachers
> Because we knew so little, they took pity on us
> poking fun at the soft soles of our feet,
> and the odd way we scrubbed our teeth,
> while they, at cyclonistic speed, absorbed
> the shapes and sounds of vowels and consonants,
> the slick of paper, the scratch of pencil, the bright of crayons,
> and the worlds that tumbled from pages of *Life* magazines.
>
> We knew less than the babies, they laughed.
> So they began to educate us.
> Chopping wood. Lighting fire.
> Hunting pig. Picking lice.
> Catching fish. Finding fruit.
> Building raft. Pounding rice.
> Dancing. Drumming. Weaving.
> Hungering. Dying. Birthing.
>
> We needed education in the important things of life,
> the survival things, while they begged
> for more books, more stories, more songs,
> and more classes, please mum, even weekends and evenings

under the thatched palm roof on the slat bench
beside the crowing rooster and enormous snoring pig.

They gave so freely, those skinny kids
in the bamboo village beside the silver snaking river.

I hold close these memories of how it was,
in the place where kindly children
instructed their teachers.

⊙⊚⊙

The scenery from the ship is spectacular. We passed the eight-thousand-foot peak of Mayon Volcano on the southern part of the island of Luzon. It was a striking view in the glowing afternoon sun, as if it were planned for me, a goodbye gift from this place where I've spent the past three-plus years. The volcano is a perfect cone shape, now with clouds near the top, like a shawl covering her head in the old Spanish style, framing her beautiful face.

I stayed on the upper deck most of the afternoon, alone, reading and writing. I wrote to Janet, sharing a poem, letting her know I'm truly on my way this time and wishing her well as she stays in-country a while longer. I'm a little scared, but mostly grateful to be traveling independently. Right now, I'm watching the sailors on the cargo deck below cleaning debris, throwing or pushing broken pallets and woven strappings into the ocean. Polluting the ocean. The sailors are mainly Micronesian and a few Filipinos, most about my age. They haven't talked to me much yet, but I can see them watching me, curious-like.

It's starting up again, inside me. I'm heading for a new part of the Pacific. My curiosities are rising. I have a feeling I'm about to learn a lot about Micronesia.

— *Journal, August 10, 1973*

⊙⊚⊙

Afterword

It has been unseasonably hot this summer where I live in the upland rainforest of the island of Hawai`i, and for once, I'm glad to be washing dishes. The task is meditatively repetitive, and the sudsy dishwater is refreshing. I can hear the evening newscast in the next room. Again today, the news of America bleak and troubled. Our national leader is walking a path of personal power and institutional disruption; the rule of law is jeopardized; social injustice is visibly rampant; and the media are at odds over truths versus stretched semi-truths versus outright lies.

I think of this book in process at my desk upstairs. These days of the pandemic virus have given me many extra hours of at-home time to shape this manuscript. I find myself pondering those times fifty years ago when I experienced the downhill slide and ultimate demise of a young democracy beneath the hand of an emerging dictator and his nationwide network of powerful corrupt pals. And with a sigh that no one hears, I think of my own country's current politics and realize I've traveled this path before. I've lived through times like these. I have a personal perspective on what I see happening in America today.

As I look back on this collection of stories, I invite you to use your intuition, your gut sense, the lessons of history, and your somatic intelligence to read beneath the words. Explore the deeper truths of societies and individuals. Examine the complex facets that frame what might be happening in Philippine, American, or in any culture.

This is a memoir of creative nonfiction. I took some liberties with facts. I warped time. I consolidated some characters. I changed some names, squashed some geography, and imagined dialog. I invented spellings for things I could speak but not spell. I trimmed and tucked and stitched together descriptions of environments and events. I delved deeply into my old journals and used not only my own words, but also recollections that those words evoked. And through it all, I held tight to a truthful telling of how things looked, felt, tasted, smelled, and seemed to me.

Reflecting today on those journal entries, I clearly see how high school and college journalism training helped me record events, and separate facts from opinions and conjecture. However, I'm sure misconceptions and errors remain within my stories—things I thought I saw or heard, but because I was young, inexperienced, and living among cultures I didn't fully understand, I might have been wrong. All mistakes are my own and I apologize for any misrepresentations or misinterpretations of the people and events around me.

I recently journeyed from my home on the Big Island of Hawai'i to visit Dr. Janet Bauer in Connecticut, where she has had an acclaimed academic career in International Studies. We laughed. We reminisced. We explored her amazing collection of photos and artifacts from our Madga days. Through our few remaining contacts, we've learned that roads have intruded in the old river places, the forests have been harvested, and that in the mountains there is now war and danger from guerilla fighters and political dissidents. Our Manobo neighbors have dispersed downriver into towns and cities.

To the descendants of our Manobo neighbors, should you ever see these stories, please know that Janet and I have a collection of photographs for you, pictures of your ancestors, the homes, the people, the places—pictures that you might cherish, reminding you of the old ways with an appreciation of the natural world and indigenity, photographs from the days before the entire world changed.

Me ke aloha nui,
Ug daghan salamat

Dina Wood Kageler
Volcano Village, Hawai'i
Summer 2020

An Interpretive Glossary

abaca – also known as Manila hemp, this is a highly valued banana-like plant known for its strong, silky, and fine fiber used for twisting and rolling into ropes and lashings.

adobo – Philippine adaptation of a Spanish marinated dish. It involves meat or seafood, and vegetables, marinated, browned and simmered in a sauce of vinegar, soy sauce, and garlic. Usually served with rice.

baboy – pig, pork, wild boar

banka – small boat used on a river or ocean. An ocean-going banka would have an outrigger attached on one side for stability. A river banka had no outrigger. A banka might be made of plywood or, more rarely, of the burned and scraped-out trunk of a single tree. It might be paddled, poled, or motorized.

bastos – rude, unmannered, crude

barong Tagalog – a lightweight formal shirt for men, traditionally made from translucent fabric such as pineapple fiber, and usually ornately embroidered, worn untucked over a white undershirt. Considered the national formal dress for men of the Philippines.

bayut also ***bayot*** or ***bakla*** – a broad term for a person having sexual attraction to persons of the same sex, also involving transgenders and transvestics.

bolo – machete with a metal blade as long as your forearm, a wooden hilt, and usually housed in a wooden sheath and lashed by rope at the side of a Manobo man. An infinitely useful, ubiquitous tool in the mountains of Mindanao.

cellophane – before plastic bags were common, there was cellophane wrap, transparent, thin and less pliable than plastic wrap.

cotton-picking – an idiom of the American South to declare that which follows is frustrating or irritating.

datu – Manobo word for "chief," the leader of a group of Manobo families.

dimbah – drum, Manobo.

diwata – Manobo. A kind of supernatural being or deity of the river people of Madga. From what I could glean of the Manobo world view, the diwata controlled various parts of the natural world, such as trees, rivers and animals.

dogie – a term in the American West referring to a motherless calf in a cattle herd.

durian – a highly desirable fruit tree endemic to tropical Pacific forests. It is notorious for its odor, which many say is like smelly gym socks, and the fruit is especially odoriferous when very ripe. It is football-sized, and the skin is spiky. The multiple seeds inside are the size of a child's fist, and each is surrounded by glutinous, mucous-like sweet pulp. Appreciation of durian is an acquired taste.

fiesta – or *pista* – a celebration, especially of a religious day. An entire lowland Philippine community would celebrate the day of the community's patron saint with a *barrio fiesta,* with outdoor music, dancing, feasting, and the selection of a young woman and her court to reign for the day. From the Spanish tradition.

gakit – raft. Ours in Madga was about ten long pieces of bamboo lashed together with rattan strips and homemade rope, and it could float approximately 300 pounds of cargo at or just above the surface of the river. The Manobo used bamboo rafts to ferry crops such as watermelons or cucumbers downriver for sale. It took great skill to keep a fully-loaded gakit upright and pole it downriver.

ganta – a unit of measurement of volume, especially for measuring fruit or dry grain such as rice when purchased in an open market. About three quarts.

Ilang-ilang or *ylang-ylang* – a tropical tree known for the pungent sweet fragrance of its greenish-yellow flowers, endemic to Indonesia and known throughout Malaysia, the Philippines and across the Pacific. Scientifically, *Cananga odorata*.

Joe and Flor Habana – Years later, I discovered their names are Jose and Florencia Havana. There are no 'v'-sounds in Visayan; v's are pronounced as 'b's. Never having seen their names written, I only knew what I heard. For the purposes of my stories, I'm keeping the spelling as I heard it and wrote it at the time. For historical reference, their family name is Havana, with a 'v', accent on the first syllable.

jeepney – or *dyipni* – a Jeep-style vehicle used as public transportation, packing in up to 10 or 12 people (or more, if you count the people hanging onto the sides of the vehicle). I heard that jeepneys had come into common use after World War II. When the American army departed, they left behind their military jeeps which were quickly and cleverly modified by the locals to carry passengers. This style vehicle had been developed to become the standard for inner-city public transportation.

kajad – Manobo head-strap basket. Our kajads were about five-gallon-bucket size, made of tightly woven stripped rattan vines and sealed with tree pitch. They were extremely durable and were used as the workhorse carry-all for the women who gathered sweet potatoes, rice, or other foods from the fields and forests. The strap rode high on the forehead so the weight in the basket was carried against the back, centered below the shoulders, and the hiker had both arms available to help her maintain balance on the ups and downs of the mountain trails. Even when heavily packed, the kajad was very comfortable to wear.

kamote – purple sweet potato, deeply purple both inside and out, endemic to South America, which suggests that there had been navigation and trading among Pacific Islanders for centuries. A staple of the Manobo diet, incredibly sweet and tasty when freshly harvested.

kubing – a Manobo musical instrument that is something like a jaw harp, or jew's harp, made from an eight-inch section of bamboo. You play it by changing the resonance in the hollow of your mouth, moving your tongue and cheeks and lips to vary the twanging tone.

kuto – head lice, very common in the lowlands and ubiquitous in the mountain community of Madga. Grooming one another in Madga was a bonding activity.

lansones – a grapelike fruit with a thick skin. The fruit is pearly, nearly translucent, very sweet, and entirely delicious. There is a single large black seed in each fruit, and the seed is very bitter. Don't bite it accidentally. Peel the skin, suck the meat, spit the seed. Buy a *ganta*, because you will want plenty.

lavandera – one who does the laundry. In Butuan City, among our household helpers was one person whose job it was to do the laundry for everyone in the house. There was a cement enclosure behind the house with a big tub and running (cold) water. The flatiron that she used burned charcoal from coconut shells. From Spanish.

lawas nga saging – literally "body of the banana tree." Sections of the banana tree stalk were chopped to make individual lean-to shelters over our young vegetable plants to shield them from the intensity of the tropical sun.

lechon – an entire roasted suckling pig, rotated for hours on an open spit. From Spanish.

lola – grandmother. From Spanish.

lottery number — the US military had a lottery system for drafting young men. Every birthdate was assigned a number, based on a random drawing. The lower your number, the sooner you were required to register and possibly be sent to Vietnam for active duty. Although females were exempt from the draft, it did not go unnoticed by me that my own birth date lottery number would have been 001.

mango – or *mangga* – a delicious seasonal tropical fruit that was found in abundance in markets and from street vendors in the hot summer months from March to June. With its smooth, sweet, succulent golden fruit, the Philippine mango is one of the world's most desirable fruits. I was told that following World War II, the Philippine government was so grateful for American liberation that regular shipments of mango were made to Eisenhower's White House so that he would never be without Philippine mango—eaten fresh, frozen, dried, pickled, or green and sprinkled with rock salt. I was advised to eat only the fruit and not let my mouth touch the skin. Disregarding this warning, Nan and I once purchased a ganta of mangos, ate the fruit, then craving more, we sucked the skins. The result was a painful case of "mango mouth" a red rash around our mouths that lasted for days, a guilty indication of the gluttony of the Americanas.

malong – a long tube of fabric used by men and women, especially in the Muslim areas of Mindanao. I found it useful as a sleep tube, a dress, a bathing shroud, a shawl, a pillow, etc.

may doon ... – "do you have..." or "is there..." in Manobo. It was one of the first things I learned to say in Manobo. Never having seen Manobo as a written language, I had no idea how to spell the words. My journals contain many of my awkward attempts at transcribing Manobo words and phrases that I heard.

merynda – mid-morning snacks, common in the lowland schools, usually soda or coffee with crackers, a fried banana, rice cake, or other sweet treat. From Spanish, merienda, snack.

mestizo – referring to mixed Spanish-Filipino ancestry. Among the lowland culture, it was considered desirable to have mestizo heritage.

mga dako – the bigs. This is what we called the class of bigger kids in our Madga school, from about ages eight to fourteen. These were the kids in my class.

mga gamai – the littles. This is what we called the younger group of students in our Madga school. They ranged from about ages five to seven. Janet taught the mga gamai.

mga gamai kaayo – the very littles. This is what we called the toddler pack and village preschoolers. They would flit through our school or stay long enough to hear a story, but they were not regulars.

modista – seamstress, one who made clothing. From Spanish.

Moro—a catch-all term for several Muslim ethnic groups that lived primarily in the south and western parts of Mindanao. Their populations also stretched through Borneo and other parts of Indonesia. When I traveled through the Moro areas of Mindanao, I especially appreciated their elaborate arts such as brassware and wood carvings. I still have several pieces of Moro art that I purchased in the open markets of Cotabato and Marawi – a big brass gong with high relief embellishments, and a rough-hewn wooden ganta scoop inlaid with mother of pearl. Beautiful!

mosquitero – mosquito net, strung each evening from ceiling or rafters. Tucked in securely under mattress or sleeping mat, it keeps blood-sucking creatures away from the sleeper. Keep your arms and legs away from contact with the mosquitero, because bugs can suck your blood through the mesh. Nets were usually made of nylon or plastic mesh, were flammable, and smelled horrible when ignited. Be careful if you read in bed with a kerosene lamp. I speak from experience.

nipa – a coconut palm frond, used as roofing material for the bamboo houses of Madga and beyond. Half the frond was folded lengthwise along the midrib, doubling the leaves in one direction, and then the fronds were overlapped and lashed onto the frame of a house. They worked well for keeping rain out if the rain came straight down. They didn't work well when the wind blew the fronds open, like the pages of a book. Nipa roofs needed to be replaced from time to time, because they wore out. Beetles, cockroaches, and centipedes lived in aging roofs and the creatures dropped randomly onto unsuspecting victims.

pancit – a noodle dish, usually with bits of vegetables and perhaps slivers of meat.

pandanus – screwpine. An important tree throughout the Pacific for cultural, health, economic, and practical purposes. The leaves are long and supple and can be stripped and woven into useful household items such as bags and sleeping mats. In Madga, Ricarda made a new mat every year for drying the freshly harvested rice in the sun, and through her example, she taught the girls of Madga to weave. Newly woven pandanus mats were desirable for sleep mats, because their fragrance is sweet and restful

pomelo – tropical grapefruit with a thick, pithy rind, generally sweeter than an American grapefruit. It became (and remains) one of my favorite fruits.

rabbit-ear antenna – back in the day when radio and TV waves were transmitted terrestrially from a central source and were captured by individual receiving units, it was sometimes useful for a radio or television to have rabbit-ear antenna. They were usually telescoping metal rods attached to your receiving unit that you could rotate to find the best reception angle. Reception might be further enhanced by attaching aluminum foil or wire to the rabbit ears. The objective was to capture all the TV or radio signals possible, enhancing the clarity of reception.

rattan – a climbing vine-like forest plant which was used for lashing and weaving. The stripped and cleaned fiber was light and strong, flexible and durable.

sala – living room. From Spanish.

sari sari store – a small neighborhood store that sells a variety of common goods, something like a neighborhood convenience store. Frequently a family's front-yard business.

sus- a common expression, something like jeez!, wow! or oh my! I was told that "sus!" was short for Jesus-Mary-Joseph, the holy family of Catholicism. The pronunciation of the entire exclamation would be more like "hay-sus-mar-ee-ho-sep!"

tabi usa – a Visayan phrase roughly meaning "excuse me." You use it when it might be necessary to pass between two people who are conversing, or when passing close around (never over!) a prone person. You should bend at the waist, put your hands together in front indicating the direction of your movement, and pass quickly with head and eyes downcast, demonstrating respect and humility.

tapiz – from the Spanish, for "tapestry." Janet's tapiz was a batik sarong from Bali. In other places in the Pacific, such a garment might be called a *pareo* or *lavalava*.

tendero – a person who tends a store. From Spanish.

tsinelas– rubber slippers, from Spanish, *chinelas*, slippers. In other places of the Pacific, they are called *kalipa*, thongs, zoris or flip-flops. They came in many colors and were the ubiquitous footwear of the lowland Philippines. The mountain people did not use footwear.

tuba – homemade coconut wine.

Visayan – a group of languages of the Southern Philippines that includes Cebuano, the form that I learned during Peace Corps training. On Mindanao, we referred to the language as Binisaya (say Bee-nee-<u>sigh</u>-yah), as it would be pronounced if you are speaking Visayan.

vino kalafu – low-end Chinese wine, perhaps the cheapest store-bought alcohol in the Philippines.

ya-ya – nursemaid. Caretaker for baby or child.

Mahalo Nui

With much gratitude

My family: Tim, Jesse, and Emma Tunison. Special thanks to my botanist husband Tim, for unflagging support of my long writing process and for his fine companionship in our many adventures through the years. And my thanks to Jesse and Emma who have grown up hearing many of these stories as cautionary tales, as humorous asides, and as "old-timey" stories of the world's antiquated ways in pre-technology times.

Dr. Janet Bauer, who was my Madga co-adventurer and who managed to archive hundreds of photographs and artifacts of the Manobo river people. The storage room in her Connecticut home is a treasure trove spawning our reminiscences.

Nan Aruni Futuronsky, co-adventurer in the Butuan days of Peace

Corps, and still a dear friend. We remember how tough it was for female volunteers in those days in the lowlands of the Philippines.

My parents, **Marguerite and Vernon Kageler,** who hardly wrote any letters to me during those years but did keep my letters home and lovingly archived them. Cleaning out my old room after Mother passed away in 2001, I found sixty or so of my letters home, neatly stacked in chronological order. The letters are full of stories.

The Volcano Art Center, Volcano, Hawai'i, for sponsoring many wonderful and encouraging writing workshops through the years.

Molly Giles, author who led a writers' workshop in Volcano twenty-five years ago, heard one of these stories, saw the beads, and instinctively understood that the title for this collection is *Amalya's Beads*. Thanks, Molly.

Garrett Hongo, poet, educator and workshop leader who long ago saw something valuable in the telling of these stories, even before I believed in them. I laughed when he looked at me squarely and said, "Write it!"

Tom Peek, Volcano author and workshop leader, who supported this as a worthy project, checked in from time to time, and encouraged me to keep going.

Lois and Earl Stokes and Lydia Meneses, with Annabelle and Heather Lewis, June Dalde, Elizabeth Ramsey, Ellen O'Dunn, Valdeane Odachi and Pam Barton, Volcano artists and arts educators, for continuing inspiration with our pencils and pens, papers and paints. We are a group of Certified Zentangle® Teachers and tangle aficionados. Also to **Maria Thomas** and **Rick Roberts** who continue to inspire through their generous sharing of the Zentangle method.

My Hawai'i Island writers' groups: **Caroline Garrett, Ma'ata Tukuafu, Bela Johnson, Mililani Hughes, Kanani Aton, Phan Nguyen Barker, Tamara Wong Morrison, Debra Whiteflower, and Linda Merryman** for listening to me read aloud many of these stories, for sharing editorial thoughts, and for a willingness to hear still more.

Dorothy Estes, journalism teacher, and one of the most inspirational educators I ever encountered. Back in high school, it was she who taught me to separate fact from opinion, to avoid passive voice in a lead, and to write from the heart.

Tom Young, a neighbor in Volcano, who formerly published a community electronic newsletter *The Volcano Vent* which carried early versions of my stories *Zoon* and *Typhoon*.

Rosalinda Gozo Cahill, Filipina sister and neighbor in Volcano who speaks Visayan with me, keeping me practiced. When I have one of those "Am I remembering this right?" moments, I go to Rosalinda. She was living in Mindanao when I was there, and the way we figure it, our paths crossed in 1970 at Silliman University where she was a student while I attended a training event and was housed in the home of one of her instructors.

Kahikāhealani Wight, author, Hawaiian language and culture educator, and an appreciator of traditional world views, for her unwavering encouragement and willingness to read these stories in various early drafts. For twenty-five years, she has been encouraging me to publish them.

Arnie Kotler, my Maui-based editor with a keen eye for detail and an ability to unearth the core. Mahalo for his patience and vision as I have slowly manifested this document.

Lisa Carta for her thoughtful and beautiful design of this book.

Ken Charon and **Jesse Tunison**, Volcano community artists, for helping scan my sketches.

Eastman Kodak Company of Rochester, New York, and especially a manager named Bill who was a professional associate of my Dad's, for developing all those rolls of color slides, for free, back in the early '70s. When I returned from Asia/Pacific adventures to visit my family 1975, I finally got to see my complete collections of photographic images. I wish I'd taken more photographs, but considering how scarce and expensive film was at the time, I'm grateful to have this collection.

The People of the Republic of the Philippines. As I have approached the end of this storytelling, I look back through the writings and recognize a glaring omission. I have failed to adequately convey the kindness, hospitality, and acceptance that came to me from most of the people of this remarkable island nation. Innumerable times in my travels I was watched over, taken in, supported, guided, and helped along my way through the kindness of strangers. *Daghan salamat sa inyong tanan.*

The **United States Peace Corps**, which offered me a new window to the world and changed…well, everything.

About the Art

The sketches in this work are my own. I base them on the renderings in my journals 1970-73, and also on my photographs from the era.

Dina Wood Kageler

Dina Wood Kageler is a storyteller and adventurer who grew up in Texas and journeyed through islands of the Pacific in the early 1970s. Settling in Hawai`i, she has for many years been a respected visual, vocal and performing artist and arts educator. Today she lives on several acres of treefern and `ōhi`a forest in the uplands of the Island of Hawai`i with her botanist husband and two entrepreneurial adult children. Finding inspiration in true-life stories and from the rainforest around her, Dina writes, works with clay, mosaics, pen and ink, and creates hand-dyed textiles and quilts. She dances Hawaiian hula and plays the ukulele and slack key guitar in the Hawaiian style alongside some talented musician friends. She walks on Kīlauea volcano, inspired to catch songs, find harmonies or chant into the wind.

Made in the USA
Middletown, DE
22 October 2023

41206948R00288